BX
9423
.S63
R33
2021

D0221996

Reformed Public Theology

A Global Vision for Life in the World

Edited by

Matthew Kaemingk

Baker Academic
a division of Baker Publishing Group
Grand Rapids, Michigan

Nyack College
Eastman Library

© 2021 by Matthew Kaemingk

Published by Baker Academic
a division of Baker Publishing Group
PO Box 6287, Grand Rapids, MI 49516-6287
www.bakeracademic.com

Printed in the United States of America

All rights reserved. No part of this publication may be reproduced, stored in a retrieval system, or transmitted in any form or by any means—for example, electronic, photocopy, recording—without the prior written permission of the publisher. The only exception is brief quotations in printed reviews.

Library of Congress Cataloging-in-Publication Data
Names: Kaemingk, Matthew, 1981– editor.
Title: Reformed public theology : a global vision for life in the world / edited by Matthew Kaemingk.
Description: Grand Rapids, Michigan : Baker Academic, a division of Baker Publishing Group, [2021] | Includes bibliographical references and index.
Identifiers: LCCN 2020058685 | ISBN 9781540964281 (casebound) | ISBN 9781540961976 (paperback)
Subjects: LCSH: Christian sociology—Reformed Church. | Public theology. | Reformed Church—Doctrines.
Classification: LCC BX9423.S63 R33 2021 | DDC 261.088/2842—dc23
LC record available at https://lccn.loc.gov/2020058685

Unless otherwise indicated, Scripture quotations are from THE HOLY BIBLE, NEW INTERNATIONAL VERSION®, NIV® Copyright © 1973, 1978, 1984, 2011 by Biblica, Inc.® Used by permission. All rights reserved worldwide.

Scripture quotations labeled ESV are from The Holy Bible, English Standard Version® (ESV®), copyright © 2001 by Crossway, a publishing ministry of Good News Publishers. Used by permission. All rights reserved. ESV Text Edition: 2016

Scripture quotations labeled NRSV are from the New Revised Standard Version of the Bible, copyright © 1989 National Council of the Churches of Christ in the United States of America. Used by permission. All rights reserved.

21 22 23 24 25 26 27   7 6 5 4 3 2 1

In keeping with biblical principles of creation stewardship, Baker Publishing Group advocates the responsible use of our natural resources. As a member of the Green Press Initiative, our company uses recycled paper when possible. The text paper of this book is composed in part of post-consumer waste.

Contents

Baptism

Confession

Piety

Dedication

The gospel in its fullness must be directed to all dimensions of human life. Christ's atoning work offers liberation for people in their cultural endeavors, in their family lives, in their educational pursuits, in their quests for sexual fulfillment, in their desire for physical well-being. It also offers liberation in the building of political institutions and the making of public policy.

—Richard Mouw, *Political Evangelism*

The Holy Worldliness of Richard Mouw

This book was composed in honor of Richard Mouw (1940–), one of the world's leading voices in Reformed philosophy, ethics, and public theology. With an academic career spanning more than fifty years, Mouw has published more than twenty books, hundreds of articles, and has traveled the world over, speaking on a wide range of public issues including politics, race, science, globalization, interfaith dialogue, nuclear disarmament, poverty, marketplace ethics, and Christian education.

Addressing these complex global issues, Richard Mouw has consistently drawn insight and inspiration from the Reformed tradition. Its hymns and catechisms, devotionals and prayers; its historic works of philosophy and theology; all these inform the way Mouw engages public life. For over fifty years Mouw has made a career of harvesting these theological resources and articulating, in creative and generative ways, how they might inform Christian engagement in public life.

Even though Richard Mouw loves Reformed theology, he does so with critical appreciation, not blind adoration. Calvinistic chauvinism makes him bristle. Mouw readily names the tradition's weaknesses and blind spots. He repeatedly calls upon his fellow Calvinists to humble themselves, listen to their critics, and learn from other traditions, other faiths, and other cultures. After listening with genuine curiosity and vulnerability, Mouw calls upon the tradition to publicly confess, get up, and reform yet again.[1]

For Mouw, Reformed public theology can never be an abstract intellectual exercise. Instead, it must carefully deal with the deep complexity, beauty, and brokenness that is *life in this world*. Thus Mouw's work should be understood as a constant search for a "holy worldliness," as he calls it, a righteous way of being in the world. Longing to faithfully navigate the complex avenues and arteries of public life, Mouw's writings are shot through with this search for a holy worldliness.[2]

The Search for Holy Worldliness

Richard Mouw came of age in the 1960s, and his public theology developed amid the tempest that was American public life in the age of revolution. As a doctoral student in philosophy at the University of Chicago and also both an evangelical Christian and a passionate activist, Mouw was particularly engaged with the issues of poverty, racism, and civil rights. He was an active member of the anti-war movement and the SNCC (the Student Nonviolent Coordinating Committee). In all this, Mouw was fueled by a deep and pious love for Christ and a burning desire to see Christ's justice made manifest in public life. He would study the political philosophy of Kant, Locke, and Rousseau during the week; then the weekends would be split between organizing in the streets and worship in the sanctuary. From an early age, Mouw was convinced that he could, in fact that *he should*, sing songs of praise and songs of protest. The reign of God had to be proclaimed, not simply in the church but in the

---

1. Mouw's threefold pattern of appreciation, critique, and aggiornamento within the Reformed tradition can be found throughout his work. A sampling includes *Talking with Mormons: An Invitation to Evangelicals* (Grand Rapids: Eerdmans, 2012); "Reflections on My Encounter with the Anabaptist-Methodist Tradition," *Mennonite Quarterly Review* 74, no. 4 (2000): 571–76; "Calvinists and Catholic Renewal," *Reformed Journal* 25, no. 2 (1975): 6–7; "State Theology," in *The Kairos Covenant: Standing with South African Christians*, ed. Willis W. Logan (New York: Friendship Press, 1988), 50–58; "A Kinder, Gentler Calvinism," *Reformed Journal* 40 (October 1990): 11–13; "It's Time for Charismatic Calvinism," *The Banner* 133, no. 11 (May 25, 1998): 18–19; *The Challenges of Cultural Discipleship: Essays in the Line of Abraham Kuyper* (Grand Rapids: Eerdmans, 2011); and *Abraham Kuyper: A Short and Personal Introduction* (Grand Rapids: Eerdmans, 2011).

2. Mouw's search is best captured in the titles he chose for three books written for the laity: *Called to Holy Worldliness* (Philadelphia: Fortress, 1980); *Calvinism in the Las Vegas Airport: Making Connections in Today's World* (Grand Rapids: Zondervan, 2004); and *Praying at Burger King* (Grand Rapids: Eerdmans, 2007).

city as well. From an early age, these three callings to philosophical reflection, political action, and spiritual devotion were constantly churning in Mouw's mind and heart in uncomfortable but profoundly generative ways.[3] Later, on the first page of his first book, Mouw writes: "My training within the environs of 'conservative-evangelical' Christianity did not provide me with a theological framework adequate to deal with the concerns over social justice, racism, and militarism that were so much a part of the years I spent doing graduate study at secular universities. Yet it seemed to me then . . . that such concerns must be integrated into a larger concern for sound theology and faithful witness."[4]

Dissatisfied with the public imaginations of the Christian right and the Christian left, the young Mouw ultimately found a home in Reformed public theology. Therein Mouw has spent a career developing and embodying what we might call a "third way" for American Christians to engage in public life. This third way comes to the fore in Mouw's somewhat playful use of para-doxical phrases like "holy worldliness," "political evangelism," "convicted civility," "principled pluralism," "baptismal politics," and "common grace." In each of these phrases, Mouw invites his readers to question their more narrow or ideologically bound paradigms for thinking about the connections between faith and public life. What if "evangelism" is both spiritual and ma-terial? What if baptism is both personal and political? What if Christians are called to be a public force of conviction *and* civility, principles *and* pluralism? What if God's grace is uniquely manifest in the cross of Jesus Christ and yet we also see God's goodness mysteriously manifesting itself in our Muslim neighbors? Writing for an American audience gripped by myopic ideologies bereft of humility, creativity, or imagination, Mouw's playful questioning and vulnerable curiosity consistently model a public-theological imagination that invites a creative dialogue rather than a didactic monologue. The conversation is not closed down: it is opened up.

Following his doctoral studies at the University of Chicago, Richard Mouw moved to Michigan in the summer of 1968 to serve Calvin College as a pro-fessor of Christian philosophy. While there, he and his wife, Phyllis, helped to establish an intentional Christian community in the heart of one of the poorest neighborhoods in Grand Rapids. At the time, Worden Street was a largely Black neighborhood that had been hit hard by economic and racial-ized forces within the city. White residents (many of them Reformed) had fled the neighborhood for the comfort and security of the suburbs. Richard

---

3. For a window into his wrestling with the intersection between Christian worship and public life, see Richard J. Mouw, "Baptismal Politics," *Reformed Journal* 28, no. 7 (1978): 2–3.
4. Richard J. Mouw, *Political Evangelism* (Grand Rapids: Eerdmans, 1973).

and Phyllis, along with their young son, Dirk, joined several other Christian families to reinvest in the neighborhood. The families purchased some homes on Worden Street and founded what they called "the Community." The fourfold purpose of "the Community" came to embody much of the public theology that Richard Mouw wrote about for the next fifty years. First, they would regularly gather for meals, prayer, worship, and Scripture study. Second, they would house and mentor young Calvin students. Third, they would live alongside, learn from, serve, and invest in the neighbors and the surrounding neighborhood. Fourth, they would support the neighborhood's local Christian school and its efforts to serve the neighborhood children with high-quality Christian education. Here in "the Community," we see the unique combination of education and action, piety and community, friendship and mentoring, as shown in the life and career of Richard Mouw.[5]

In 1985, after seventeen years at Calvin College (now Calvin University), Mouw and his family left Worden Street and moved to California, where Richard served as a professor of Christian ethics and philosophy at Fuller Theological Seminary. Here Mouw's potential for institutional leadership quickly developed as he was appointed to the position of provost in 1989 and president in 1993. During his tenure as president, Mouw became a nationally recognized leader in theological education and administration. For many years he served as a critically important voice within the Association of Theological Schools in the United States and Canada. Eventually he was named the association's vice president.

As the leader of one of the largest seminaries within American evangelicalism, Mouw regularly served as a public voice for the movement and a critically important dialogue partner with the Catholic, Jewish, Mormon, and Muslim communities in the United States. Traveling, speaking, and preaching around the world on behalf of Fuller, Mouw invested a significant amount of time in building institutional relationships with Christian communities in China, South Korea, North Korea, Japan, and the Netherlands. These international experiences and interfaith dialogues shaped and informed his later writings in a wide variety of ways.

Following his retirement from the presidency in 2013, Mouw invested much of his time mentoring doctoral students. Their research placed Reformed theology into creative dialogue with a wide range of public issues, such as politics and literature, immigration and labor, racism and Islam, fashion and

---

5. See Jeff Bouman, Don DeGraaf, Mark Mulder, et al., "Connecting the Mind, Heart, and Hands through Intentional Community at Calvin College," *Journal of College and Character* 6 (2005): 5.

video games.[6] Several of these researchers contributed important essays to this volume.

Who is Richard Mouw the teacher? As one of his doctoral students, I have three brief comments. First, Mouw approaches personal meetings with students with a sense of eager anticipation—as if these discussions are his own personal opportunity to learn something from *us*. He responds to our work, not with monologues or preordained solutions, but with new questions and new tensions with which he himself has been wrestling for years. Meetings are his opportunity to invite us into his wrestling. Second, Mouw is a champion of his students. He is always looking to create spaces, opportunities, and connections for his students to develop and grow. It is not uncommon to hear a secondhand report from some distant conference that Richard Mouw is singing the praises of one of his students. In his own selflessness, Mouw managed to cultivate an academic community in which doctoral students serve, support, and encourage one another (imagine that). Third and finally, the reason so many doctoral students came to study with Richard Mouw is rather simple. We suspected that he might be contagious. We wondered to ourselves, "If we hang around him long enough, might some of his character become our own?"

6. Mouw either directly oversaw or contributed to the following dissertations in 2013–2020: Justin Ariel Bailey, "The Apologetics of Hope: Imagination and Witness in the Age of Authenticity with Special Consideration of the Work of George MacDonald and Marilynne Robinson" (Fuller Seminary, 2017); Kyle David Bennett, "Involved Withdrawal: A Phenomenology of Fasting" (Fuller Seminary, 2013); Agnes Chiu, "Common Grace and Common Good for China: An Exposition of Abraham Kuyper and Leo XIII on Labor Struggles in Twenty-First Century China" (Fuller Seminary, 2017); Clay Cooke, "World-Formative Rest: Cultural Discipleship in a Secular Age" (Vrije Universiteit and Fuller Seminary, 2015); Robert Covolo, "What Has Paris to Do with Jerusalem? New Horizons in Theology and Fashion" (Fuller Seminary, 2016); Bradley Hickey, "A Neo-Calvinist Theology of Video Games" (Fuller Seminary, forthcoming); Brant M. Himes, "For a Better Worldliness: The Theological Discipleship of Abraham Kuyper and Dietrich Bonhoeffer" (Fuller Seminary and Vrije Universiteit, 2015); Eric Jacobsen, "The Role of Ecclesial Thresholds and Practices in Enacting, Engaging, and Transforming the Public Realm" (Fuller Seminary, 2007); Marinus de Jong, "The Church Is the Means, the World Is the End: The Development of Klaas Schilder's Thought on the Relationship between the Church and the World" (Theologische Universiteit Kampen, 2019); Jessica R. Joustra, "Following the Way of Jesus: Herman Bavinck and John Howard Yoder in Dialogue on the Imitation of Christ" (Fuller Seminary, 2019); Matthew Kaemingk, "Mecca and Amsterdam: Christian Ethics between Islam and Liberalism" (Vrije Universiteit and Fuller Seminary, 2013); Alexander E. Massad, "Witnessing God: Missiology through Neo-Calvinism, Reformism, and Comparative Theology" (Fuller Seminary, 2020); Louise Prideaux, "Approaching the Complex, Cultural Other: Towards a Renewal of Christian Cultural Engagement in the Reformed Tradition" (University of Exeter, 2020); Cory B. Willson, "Shaping the Lenses on Everyday Work: A Neo-Calvinist Understanding of the Poetics of Work and Human Flourishing" (Vrije Universiteit and Fuller Seminary, 2015 and 2016).

In 2020, after thirty-five years at Fuller Seminary, Mouw retired and returned to Calvin University to serve as a senior research fellow at the Paul B. Henry Institute for the Study of Christianity and Politics. As a research fellow there, Mouw returns to his first love: the intersection between political philosophy and Reformed theology. At this moment in American public life, the political forces of populism and nationalism are swirling. Ever responsive, Mouw is developing a Reformed theology of patriotism. We wait, with great anticipation, for his third way.

The Search Continues

The topics covered in this book honor the life and legacy of Richard Mouw, not by repeating his work but by pressing forward in that search for a holy worldliness. The contributors come from diverse cultures, backgrounds, and disciplines. We step through the doors that Richard Mouw and countless other Reformed voices have opened for us. We are in debt to him and these others. We honor their voices, not by idolizing them, but by continuing their legacy of exploring the contours of holy worldliness for a new day.

> We serve a God who cares about the depths—and the breadths and the heights—of the reality that he has created: "The earth is the Lord's and the fullness thereof, the world and all who dwell therein" (Psalm 24:1). We scholars study various aspects of that world, but we must do it in the awareness that what we focus on is indeed part of the fullness of a created reality that we are also called to love. . . . The world desperately needs lovers of created reality.[7]

---

7. Richard J. Mouw, *Called to the Life of the Mind: Some Advice for Evangelical Scholars* (Grand Rapids: Eerdmans, 2014), 56.

Introduction

Toward a Reformed Public Theology

MATTHEW KAEMINGK

Christians face a complex array of public issues in the world today. As they navigate the dynamic arenas of politics and health care, media and the marketplace, race and culture, these Christians often reach for biblical texts and theological themes to make sense of their lives in the public square. Swimming amid the undulating waters of globalization, Christians look to the church and the Scriptures for some form of public direction, answer, or hope.

What, if anything, does Reformed theology have to say to the complex public issues that Christians around the world face every day? When coal miners are killed while laboring in unsafe Chinese mines. When a church in Jakarta wrestles with how to remain faithful in a Muslim-majority nation. When college students debate critical race theory on a university campus in Los Angeles. When a chaplain sits with a dying woman in a Dutch hospital and wrestles with the question of euthanasia. When a community of Gaelic speakers in Scotland begins to die out under the public pressure of an English-speaking majority. When a Black child is baptized into a racially diverse church in apartheid South Africa. When a drug war rages in the Philippines.

These issues are not theoretical. They represent just a few of the concrete public moments discussed in the essays that follow. What does Reformed theology *have to say* in these moments? What does Reformed theology *have to learn* by engaging them?

1

This book explores the intersection between Reformed theology and public life. Here some leading Reformed voices from around the world discuss complex public issues and arenas through the interpretive lens of the Reformed faith. They are philosophers and theologians, artists and lawyers, business leaders and activists, chaplains and ethicists. They engage these issues from a variety of contexts and disciplines in Asia and Europe, Africa and the Americas.

Despite their differences, these authors share a common Reformed desire to glorify God, not simply in the privacy of their own home or church but also in the public square. Within the Reformed tradition they have each found an interpretive theological resource that equips them to navigate complex worlds like medicine and the marketplace, art and fashion, politics and poetry. These authors occasionally point out the Reformed tradition's flaws, blind spots, and areas in which it stands in need of judgment and confession, amendment and growth. Yet within the tradition they have found a deep theological well from which they continue to draw.

In this introduction I focus on three things. First, I briefly introduce "public theology" as an emerging global and ecumenical discipline. Second, I propose some marks of a distinctly *Reformed* approach to engaging in public theology. And third, I close with a few editorial notes on how to read this book.

Public Theology: A Global and Ecumenical Discipline

> We need, in short, not merely to defend the public character of theology but to develop it.
>
> —Linell Cady, "A Model for Public Theology"

While the international and ecumenical discipline formally known as "public theology" did not emerge until the late twentieth century, debates about faith and public life are as old as Christianity itself. We can witness seeds of public theology in early Christian debates over the violence, sexuality, and politics of the Roman Empire. We can see it in the ancient Christian responses to orphans, the sick and the poor, taxes and persecution, pagan philosophy and magic. We can see public theology dripping from Christ's beatitudes and his interactions with tax collectors, soldiers, merchants, governors, and women. We can see it in the prophets' jeremiads against the injustices of Israel's markets, fields, and courts. We can trace its development in the lives of Esther, Daniel, and Joseph as they navigate the foreign palaces of Persia, Babylon, and Egypt.

Yahweh is first introduced to the people of Israel as the one who saves, not in spiritual abstraction but in the concrete public reality of the Egyptian slave economy. Thus Yahweh is revealed to Israel as a peculiar deity who is dedicated to their complete liberation—political and economic, cultural and spiritual. Under Yahweh's public reign, Israel is commanded to "walk in the ways of the LORD" in every area of their lives (cf. Deut. 30:16 NRSV). In farming and trade, sexuality and health, politics and prayer, every aspect of Israel's public life is to exhibit holy integrity.

Today the contemporary academic discipline known as "public theology" is still young, developing, and contested. Its precise definition and methodology are a matter of considerable debate. Founded in 2007, the Global Network for Public Theology is composed of scholars from a wide variety of cultural, political, and theological backgrounds.[1] The *International Journal for Public Theology* regularly publishes a broad array of European Lutherans, African Anglicans, North American Baptists, Latin American Liberationists, Congregationalists from Oceania, and many more. Emerging from such diverse contexts, these scholars harbor a wide variety of public concerns and points of theological emphasis, as expected. Given the profound contestation within the field, it might even be best to speak of public theologies, in the plural.

While the global diversity of the field is profound, some common patterns are beginning to emerge within the literature. Below I've summarized nine "marks" of public theology. Each of these is a matter of considerable debate and contestation. That said, their prevalence within the field is undeniable. I am drawing heavily on the foundational work of several leading public theologians, including Elaine Graham, Nico Koopman, Heinrich Bedford-Strom, Dirk Smit, Katie Day, and Sebastian Kim.[2] Readers looking

---

1. Elaine Graham, *Between a Rock and a Hard Place: Public Theology in a Post-Secular Age* (London: SCM, 2013), 75.

2. For a background on the historical and methodological development of public theology, see Sebastian Kim and Katie Day, eds., *A Companion to Public Theology* (Leiden: Brill, 2017); Sebastian Kim, *Theology in the Public Sphere: Public Theology as a Catalyst for Open Debate* (London: SCM, 2011); Dirk J. Smit, "The Paradigm of Public Theology: Origins and Development," in *Contextuality and Intercontextuality in Public Theology*, ed. Heinrich Bedford-Strohm, Florian Höhne, and Tobias Reitmeier (Berlin: Lit, 2013), 11–23; William F. Storrar and Andrew R. Morton, eds., *Public Theology for the 21st Century* (London: T&T Clark, 2004); Deirdre King Hainsworth and Scott R. Paeth, eds., *Public Theology for a Global Society: Essays in Honor of Max L. Stackhouse* (Grand Rapids: Eerdmans, 2010); Heinrich Bedford-Strohm, *Position beziehen: Perspektiven einer öffentliche Theologie* (Munich: Claudius, 2012); Graham, *Between a Rock and a Hard Place*.

Some of the earliest developments of the term "public theology" can be found in Martin Marty, "Reinhold Niebuhr: Public Theology and the American Experience," *Journal of Religion* 54, no. 4 (October 1974): 332–59; Marty, *Public Church: Mainline–Evangelical–Catholic* (New York: Crossroad, 1981); David Tracy, "Defending the Public Character of Theology," *Christian*

for a more comprehensive analysis of the field's development should consult their work.[3]

1. *Scripture and Theology as Public.* Public theologians hold that both Scripture and theology carry with them public value, authority, and consequence. Hence the field explores the implications and purchase of biblical commands and narratives, theological themes, and metaphors for public life. While the precise methods used for textual interpretation and application are matters of significant debate, the public nature of Scripture and theology are not. Here public theology directly challenges the modern Western push to relegate faith to a privatized sphere of personal values and spirituality.[4] In this, true public theology must emerge from a deep and transformative encounter with scriptural and theological sources. If public theologians at any time untether themselves from these sources, their work ceases to be public theology proper and becomes something else.

Finally, the interpretive flow in public theology does not run in one direction, from scriptural reflection to public application. The field is also deeply interested in the ways in which our public lives inform our readings of Scripture and theology. Readers do not engage these texts in a private or spiritual vacuum. Their readings of God (and of God's mission in the world) are impacted by the ways in which they inhabit public life. Here public theologians are careful to remind Christians that the perceived boundaries between the text and the context, the church and the world, are all profoundly porous.

Century (April 1, 1981), 352; Tracy, *The Analogical Imagination: Christian Theology and the Culture of Pluralism* (New York: Crossroads, 1981); Max Stackhouse, "An Ecumenist's Plea for a Public Theology," *This World* 8 (1984): 47–79; Robert N. Bellah, "Public Philosophy and Public Theology in America Today," in *Civil Religion and Political Theology*, ed. Leroy S. Rouner (Notre Dame, IN: Notre Dame University Press, 1986), 79–97; Linell E. Cady, "A Model for a Public Theology," *Harvard Theological Review* 80, no. 2 (1987): 193–212.

Some of the earliest book-length works on public theology are Max L. Stackhouse, *Public Theology and Political Economy: Christian Stewardship in Modern Society* (Grand Rapids: Eerdmans, 1991); and Ronald F. Thiemann, *Constructing a Public Theology: The Church in a Pluralistic Culture* (Louisville: Westminster John Knox, 1991).

3. "As the project of public theology has developed there is no single, identifiable corpus of orthodoxy that has been produced, but rather some 'marks' have generally recognized as essential to the process of constructive public theology. While scholars might vary in the weight given to these, there is emerging consensus on the indicators which distinguish . . . public theology as such." Katie Day and Sebastian Kim, "Introduction," in Kim and Day, *Companion to Public Theology*, 10.

4. Kathryn Tanner, "Public Theology and the Character of Public Debate," *Annual of the Society of Christian Ethics* 16 (1996): 79.

2. *Public Listening.* Public theology assumes that it can and *must* listen
   to the world around it. As a result, it assumes a posture of curiosity
   and openness toward the world and its many voices. This posture can
   be witnessed in the field's profoundly interdisciplinary character. Here
   public theologians immerse themselves in other fields of study, including political and social theory, economics, literature, cultural studies,
   and so on. Public theologians also seek to learn from different cultures,
   religions, industries, and political dispositions. A Muslim scientist in
   Cairo, an atheist artist in Berlin, an agnostic entrepreneur in New York,
   and a socialist activist in Mumbai—each of them has important insights
   to share. A good public theologian will be ready and willing to listen.

   Finally, many public theologians place specific theological value on
   listening to the voices of those on the underside of global power. Much
   can be learned about the true nature of social systems and structures by
   listening to those who view those structures from the underside. Listening to their voices and walking at their side, public theologians hope to
   gain deeper insights into the true nature of the world's principalities
   and powers.

3. *Public Speech.* Having listened carefully, public theologians begin to
   develop their own unique forms of public speech. Over time they become
   increasingly bilingual or even multilingual. Here they slowly develop
   the competence to speak *both* theologically and publicly with diverse
   interlocutors in the church and the world, in the academy and on the
   street.

   Public theologians attempt to speak—however haltingly—across
   the boundaries of diverse cultures and disciplines, religions and ideologies. While their multilingual abilities are always partial, imperfect,
   and incomplete, public theologians endeavor to serve as translators and
   bridge builders across worlds long divided. When they do speak, public
   theologians tend to engage in two primary forms of discourse: public
   persuasion and public critique.

4. *Public Persuasion.* Public theologians believe that it is possible for Christians to engage in persuasive dialogues across deep cultural and religious
   differences. Although they differ as to exactly *how* these discursive connections are possible, they believe that, by the power of God, they can
   make their theologically informed arguments understood and persuasive
   even within a religiously diverse public square.

   Some public theologians appeal to a universal natural law, reason,
   or moral consciousness; others appeal to a divine work of universal

providence, general revelation, common grace, or simply the power of the Holy Spirit. Whatever their foundation, public theologians harbor some level of confidence that theologically informed public speech can actually connect with and persuade their neighbors.

In summation, though their precise methods and levels of optimism differ, public theologians believe that Christians have a responsibility for trying to be persuasive within public life.

5. *Public Critique.* Some public theologians go beyond the bounds of persuasion and engage in forceful acts of public critique. They see themselves as having a prophetic calling from God to tell the truth about public injustice, ugliness, and evil. For them, it is not sufficient merely to theologically reflect on the principalities and powers, they must publicly expose and confront them as well.[5]

Some public theologians even criticize the very construction of the "public square" and the rules of "public discourse" themselves. They point out that marginalized populations are being actively excluded from public life: what is called a "public consensus" is really just the consensus of the dominant. Herein the social construction of who counts as a "public voice" and what counts as a "public issue" is placed under their prophetic scrutiny.[6]

While their prophetic critique is often aimed at "the world," public theologians can also be found criticizing the destructive ways in which the church shows up in public life. Here public theologians point out the manifold ways in which Christian communities and theologies have visited manifold forms of destruction onto public life.

6. *Praxis and Reflection.* The best public theology is developed in the streets. It is performed, embodied, and lived. Public theologians emphasize the

---

5. "Forrester contrasts two approaches to public theology, the 'magisterial' and the 'liberationist,' the first being more 'top-down' and the second being more 'bottom-up.' The first tends to reflect the perspective of theologians who are used to talking to the powers that be, whereas the second tends to reflect that of theologians close to the least powerful." Andrew R. Morton, "Duncan Forrester: A Public Theologian," in Storrar and Morton, *Public Theology for the 21st Century*, 34.

6. See Stephen Burns and Anita Monroe, eds., *Public Theology and the Challenge of Feminism* (New York: Routledge, 2014). Also see Nancy Fraser, "Rethinking the Public Sphere: A Contribution to the Critique of Actually Existing Democracy," *Social Text* 25/26 (1990): 56–80. Here Fraser critiques modern European constructions of public space, civil society, and public discourse that fail to include marginalized voices: "This network of clubs and associations—philanthropic, civic, professional, and cultural—was anything but accessible to everyone. On the contrary, it was the arena, the training ground, and eventually the power base of a stratum of bourgeois men, who were coming to see themselves as a 'universal class' and preparing to assert their fitness to govern" (60).

importance of concrete and practice-based theological reflection. As an academic discipline, public theology endeavors to avoid losing itself in theoretical abstraction.[7] As such, public theology is at its best when it is developed *in and through* Christian community and public action in specific times, spaces, and issues.

This is critically important. Being a disciple of Jesus is a *way of walking* in and through the world. The faith is active, embodied, and lived. The way of Jesus cannot be reduced to a set of disembodied ideas or dogmas. Christian theology—like Christian people—cannot remain above the fray. Christians must actually walk with Christ amid the highways and byways of Tokyo and Kinshasa, Seattle and São Paulo. *Public theology is an active reflection on the walking.*

7. *The Diversity of Publics and Theologies.* There is not one "public square" that all global Christians are called to engage. There are, instead, a multiplicity of public squares, each with their own unique challenges and opportunities. There is a public square of New York art, of Parisian fashion, of Pakistani farming, of Mexican telecommunications, of Vietnamese housing, and of Egyptian health care. These are obviously diverse publics, which invite diverse forms of Christian engagement.

Just as there are many public spaces, there are also many different public times. Consider the city of Berlin in the years 1940, 1980, and 2020. Consider the diverse ways in which Christians might be called to inhabit Berlin within those distinct eras. This is why it is not at all helpful to speak of "the public square" as if it were a single or stable thing that all Christians are called to engage.[8] Instead, public theologians try to grapple with the ways in which distinct times and places have called for distinct Christian responses.

To further complicate matters, there are also a variety of theological traditions by which Christians can interpret and engage public life. Globally speaking, there are a multiplicity of Lutheran and Catholic,

7. Within public theology "there is not a one-way movement from theological reflection that is then 'applied' to a social context; rather the two are interactive. Theology is being produced even as it is being performed or expressed in the public sphere. Action challenges and informs theological understandings, even as theology interrogates the methods of activism." Day and Kim, "Introduction," 18.

8. "The dichotomy of 'public' and 'private' is not helpful in defining public theology. Public theology should not be understood as interested only in public issues in contrast to domestic or private matters. 'Public' does not refer to the place of doing theology but to the openness of theology for any party to engage in debate; it [has] to do with universal access and open debate for all members of the society." Kim, *Theology in the Public Sphere*, 10.

Pentecostal and postcolonial, fundamentalist and feminist forms of public theological engagement.

Acknowledging this somewhat overwhelming diversity, public theologians often seek to do two things at once. First, they seek to focus on and develop their own specific theological tradition in conversation with their own public context. Second, they seek to "look over the fence" and learn from other theological traditions engaging other contexts.[9]

One final note: when public theologians pay close attention to their own contexts and theological traditions, their specificity and particularity does not necessarily disconnect them from the larger global public. In fact, their specificity can actually *enable* their connections with other traditions and other public discourses. Benjamin Valentin's work within Latino public theology is representative of this phenomenon. In his work he demonstrates how his very particular identity, context, and theological tradition help him to better connect with broader global issues and communities.[10] In this way, diverse forms of public theology might be understood as having undergone a form of "glocalization."[11] Accordingly, public theologians aim to be *both* deeply embedded in their local communities while also being conversant with other settings. This phenomenon is born out as the local and global repeatedly intersect in fascinating, unexpected, and "glocal" ways.

8. *Reformation over Revolution.* Through public persuasion, confrontation, and active participation, public theologians aim to bend and reform the powers, principalities, and institutions of the world in more just and life-giving directions. This method distinguishes public theology from other forms of theological discourse that call for a more "revolutionary" posture and practice. Revolutionary discourses in theology tend to see the dominant structures and institutions of public life as, on the whole, irreparable and unredeemable. Attempts at public compromise, deliberation, and negotiation are foolhardy. A belief in reformation is folly. There is nothing to do but deconstruct what is and build what could be. While public theologians differ in their

9. "To face several publics is not to be at home in any of them, but to be always away from the place where one really belongs. This experience of displacement is theology-generating discomfort, part of the grinding in this crucible of the simultaneity of publics." Morton, "Duncan Forrester," 33.

10. See Benjamin Valentin, *Mapping Public Theology: Beyond Culture, Identity, and Difference* (New York: Bloomsbury, 2002).

11. For insight into glocalization's early development, see Roland Robertson, "Glocalization: Time-Space and Homogeneity-Heterogeneity," in *Global Modernities*, ed. Michael Featherstone, Scott Lash, and Roland Robertson (London: Sage, 1995), 25–44.

methods and levels of optimism, they tend more toward public reform than public revolution.

9. *Complex Flourishing.* The final mark of public theology is its concern for the multifaceted flourishing of creation and culture, individuals and institutions, and a wide variety of global publics. Here "flourishing" cannot be narrowly measured by any single metric. Flourishing cannot be reduced to a marked increase in economic wealth, political justice, aesthetic beauty, intellectual discovery, leisurely play, or religious worship.[12] Human beings are complex and multifaceted creatures; their flourishing involves a complex array of public goods. The flourishing of one individual requires the flourishing of schools and families, courts and businesses, artist guilds and sports teams, newspapers and unions, churches and sewer systems. Public theologians therefore refuse to narrow their theological conception of flourishing to just the political, the economic, the spiritual, or the aesthetic. Instead, they aim to further the manifold flourishing of public life.

Elaine Graham, a leading public theologian in the United Kingdom, offers a definition of public theology that, while not comprehensive, connects well with the essays found in this book. She defines public theology as an "academic discipline and ecclesial discourse" that "seeks to comment and critically reflect from a theological perspective on aspects of public life such as economics, politics, culture and media. Traditionally, public theology sees itself as rooted in religious traditions, but strongly in conversation with secular discourse and public institutions."[13] Nico Koopman, a South African public theologian, offers a welcome Christocentric framing for the field, arguing that public theology "reflects upon the implication of the confession of the Lordship of Christ for life and for life together in all public spheres, from the most intimate to the most social, global and cosmic."[14]

Although the essays in this book do not cohere around any single definition of public theology, these nine marks surface again and again. Now, having surveyed the international and ecumenical field of public theology, the next

12. "Yet in contrast to political theology, public theology is not exclusively or primarily concerned with politics and political institutions; . . . [public theologians often] propose a more expanded notion of the areas of life to which public theology should attend." E. Harold Breitenberg, "To Tell the Truth: Will the Real Public Theology Please Stand Up?," *Journal of the Society of Christian Ethics* 23, no. 2 (2003): 59.

13. Graham, *Between a Rock and a Hard Place*, xix.

14. Nico Koopman, "Public Theology in the Context of Nationalist Ideologies: A South African Example," in Kim and Day, *Companion to Public Theology*, 161.

section will briefly drill down and consider the unique marks of a *Reformed* approach to public theology.

Toward a *Reformed* Public Theology

Even the most cursory reading of Reformation history reveals that the Reformed tradition has been a profoundly public enterprise from its very beginning. John Calvin and the early Reformers were constantly grappling with issues of language and culture, art and clothing, immigration and poverty, debt and interest, sex and politics.[15] These early Reformed leaders were navigating profound public challenges and developing a theological tradition at one and the same time.

What we today call "Reformed theology" was not formulated on a remote university campus; it was worked out in the marketplaces and street.[16] We can see the development of a Reformed public theology in the early Reformers' letters to princes and kings. We can see it in their public appeals to local city councils. We can read it in their proposed civic laws on trade and clothing, sanitation and cursing, farming and foreigners. We can see Reformed public theology take on institutional flesh in their newly founded hospitals, universities, and businesses. It is embodied in their earliest charity organizations dedicated to serving refugees, widows, and the poor.

These early leaders sought a reformation, not simply of the church but also of the public structures, institutions, patterns, and morals that shaped their

15. For historical examinations of the intersection between faith and public life in the early Reformation, see John Witte Jr. and Amy Wheeler, eds., *The Protestant Reformation of the Church and the World* (Louisville: Westminster John Knox, 2018); William A. Dyrness, *The Origins of Protestant Aesthetics in Early Modern Europe: Calvin's Reformation Poetics* (Cambridge: Cambridge University Press, 2019); John Witte Jr., *The Reformation of Rights: Law, Religion and Human Rights in Early Modern Calvinism* (Cambridge: Cambridge University Press, 2015); Kirsi Stjerna, *Women and the Reformation* (Oxford: Wiley-Blackwell, 2008); David P. Henreckson, *The Immortal Commonwealth: Covenant, Community, and Political Resistance in Early Reformed Thought* (Cambridge: Cambridge University Press, 2019); Timothy J. Demy, Mark J. Larson, and J. Daryl Charles, *The Reformers on War, Peace, and Justice* (Eugene, OR: Pickwick Publications, 2019); W. Fred Graham, *The Constructive Revolutionary: John Calvin and His Socio-Economic Impact* (Richmond: John Knox, 1971); Harro M. Höpfl, *The Christian Polity of John Calvin* (Cambridge: Cambridge University Press, 1982); R. Po-Chia Hsia and Henk van Nierop, *Calvinism and Religious Toleration in the Dutch Golden Age* (Cambridge: Cambridge University Press, 2002); John Bowlin, ed., *The Kuyper Center Review*, vol. 4, *Calvinism and Democracy* (Grand Rapids: Eerdmans, 2014).

16. For an examination of Reformed theology's impact on the intellectual and public life of Europe, see Gijsbert van den Brink and Harro M. Höpfl, *Calvinism and the Making of the European Mind* (Leiden: Brill, 2014). For an examination of the formative influence of Calvin's early public-theological conflicts, see Gary Jenkins, *Calvin's Tormentors: Understanding the Conflicts That Shaped the Reformer* (Grand Rapids: Baker Academic, 2018).

common life.[17] Although medieval Roman Catholics tended to see themselves as part of a natural social order that was established, given, and settled, the early Reformers tended to see themselves as moral agents who were fundamentally responsible for the political, economic, and ecclesial patterns of public life. Nicholas Wolterstorff explains that, as the Reformation continued to develop, its leaders began to see themselves as morally and publicly "responsible for the structure of the social world in which they find themselves. That structure is not simply part of the order of nature; to the contrary, it is the result of human decision, and by concerted effort it can be altered. Indeed it *should* be altered, for its fallen structure is in need of reform."[18] In 1641, a Puritan pastor offered a revealing sermon to the English House of Commons charging the nation's leaders with this holy and public task: "Reformation must be universal. . . . Reform all places, all persons and callings; reform the benches of judgment, the inferior magistrates. . . . Reform the universities, reform the cities, reform the countries, reform interior schools of learning, reform the Sabbath, reform the ordinances, the worship of God. . . . You have more work to do than I can speak. . . . Every plant which my heavenly father hath not planted shall be rooted up."[19] The zeal for the reformation of both church and public life was obviously intense, sometimes rather self-righteous and even unbearable. And yet, their constant call for public reform came from a core Reformed conviction: God alone, not the king, was sovereign over the public order, and the Holy Scriptures were a trustworthy guide for its renewal and reformation.

For the Reformers, the world was not a damned pit from which souls of humanity would be rescued. Instead, the world was a performative space in which God's glory would be made manifest in and through creation. Within the global vision of John Calvin, Susan Schreiner argues, the whole of creation becomes the grand "theatre of God's glory."[20] Here is the key point: God's glory would shine, not simply through God's work of creation, but

17. "For Calvin the real world was to be taken seriously, and for him the real world involved shoemakers, printers, and clockmakers, as well as farmers, scholars, knights, and clergymen. . . . Calvin grimly assumes that all human enterprise is tainted with evil—a safe assumption—and sets about to make the gospel relevant to the city of commerce in which he lived and labored. . . . In other words, true religion not only visits the sick and takes care of the widows and orphans, but also tries to see the relevance of the gospel in the rest of the world that is." Graham, *Constructive Revolutionary*, 79.

18. Nicholas Wolterstorff, *Until Justice and Peace Embrace* (Grand Rapids: Eerdmans, 1983), 3.

19. Quoted in Michael Walzer, *Revolution of the Saints: A Study in the Origins of Radical Politics* (Cambridge, MA: Harvard University Press, 1990), 10–11.

20. Susan Elizabeth Schreiner, *Theater of His Glory: Nature and the Natural Order in the Thought of John Calvin* (Grand Rapids: Baker, 1995).

also through humanity's holy work, worship, and service in the world. Here the world becomes a performative stage upon which people can serve and glorify their God through tilling fields and raising families, saying prayers and cleaning streets, cooking meals and housing refugees. Every vocation is a public calling to holy work and worship. For, as Calvin writes, "the faithful, to whom [God] has given eyes, see sparks of his glory, as it were, glittering in every created thing. The world was no doubt made that it might be the theatre of divine glory."[21]

In view of this theological understanding of public life, it is no accident that the paintings of Rembrandt, Vermeer, and Van Gogh positively glory in the vocations of farmers and housewives, sailors and cooks. It is no accident that their paint brushes illuminate the creational glory of the fields, skies, and seas. Raised in the soil of the Dutch reformation, their theological and aesthetic imagination saw the inbreaking of divine glory in both creation and culture. As the South African public theologian John de Gruchy writes, "For artists imbued with the spirit of the Reformation, true piety was not to be found in the monastery but in the marketplace and the home, amidst the ordinary things and events of life."[22] A theological aesthetic that is informed by the tradition of Calvin "does not encourage flight from the world but assumes Christian participation in God's mission to transform the world."[23] De Gruchy argues that "no one expressed this better than Vincent van Gogh, the son of a Dutch Reformed pastor who turned to art only when he failed to become a theologian himself. In rejecting [Catholic] paintings of the *Annunciation, Christ in the Garden of Olives*, and the *Adoration of the Magi* by his friend Emil Bernard, Van Gogh declared: 'I bow down before that study, powerful enough to make a Millet tremble—of peasants carrying home to the farm a calf which has been born in the fields.'"[24] Rather than painting the Virgin Mary, artists like Van Gogh painted the holy work and worship of common workers laboring in God's fields and kitchens. Rembrandt, Vermeer, and Van Gogh portray in paint what Calvin depicts in his commentary on the Psalms: "The whole world is a theatre for the display of divine goodness, wisdom, justice, and power."[25]

21. Calvin's *Commentary on Hebrews*, on Heb. 11:4; quoted in W. David O. Taylor, *The Theater of God's Glory: Calvin, Creation, and the Liturgical Arts* (Grand Rapids: Eerdmans, 2017), 36, punctuation adjusted.

22. John W. de Gruchy, *Christianity, Art, and Transformation* (Cambridge: Cambridge University Press, 2001), 46.

23. De Gruchy, *Christianity, Art, and Transformation*, 129.

24. De Gruchy, *Christianity, Art, and Transformation*, 46.

25. John Calvin is commenting on Ps. 135:13 in his *Commentary on the Psalms*, vol. 5, trans. James Anderson (repr., Grand Rapids: Baker Books, 2003), 126.

The Marks of Reformed Public Theology

In many ways, the search for a definitively *Reformed* approach to public theology is a doomed project from the start. Neither John Calvin nor his progeny ever created a single Reformed denomination or confession into which all others would fall into line. The Reformed tradition, in its theological method and its public expression, has always been deeply contested.[26]

Unlike the Lutheran tradition, whose early public theological identity was built around the cultural identity of the German people, the Reformed identity was stretched across the kingdoms of Switzerland and Scotland, Hungary and the Netherlands, France and later New England. Rather early, the tradition was forced to make space for a diversity of nations, cultures, languages, ethnicities, and political arrangements. As a multinational phenomenon, Reformed leaders had to wrestle with the public consequences of their theology in diverse contexts.

Today the contested global conversation between Reformed theology and public life goes on. Reformed communities around the world continue to grapple with the texts they treasure and contexts to which they have been called. We can watch in real time as Reformed communities in Jakarta and Cape Town, São Paulo and New York, Amsterdam and Hong Kong—each wrestle with the age-old questions of Reformed theology and public life.[27] Every year new voices join what surely must become a more diverse multidisciplinary and multinational Reformed conversation.

In many ways Reformed public theology shares much in common with the larger ecumenical project of global public theology. As we will see in the essays that follow, Reformed public theologians also seek to examine the public nature of Scripture and theology. They listen and learn from diverse disciplines, cultures, contexts, and from those on the underside of power. They dive into the unique disciplinary languages like economics, urban design, and critical race theory. They find ways to speak within diverse publics and contexts in ways that are appropriate and understandable. At times they attempt public dialogue and persuasion; on other occasions they assume the posture of prophetic critique and forceful rebuttal. Many of the authors in this volume are practitioners first and theorists second. Public theology's prescription for a combination of praxis and reflection is a way of life for them. Finally,

---

26. Wallace M. Alston Jr. and Michael Welker, *Reformed Theology: Identity and Ecumenicity* (Grand Rapids: Eerdmans, 2003).

27. For a Kenyan sociopolitical conversation with the theology of John Calvin, see David Kirwa Tarus, *A Different Way of Being: Towards a Reformed Theology of Ethnopolitical Cohesion for the Kenyan Context* (Cumbria, UK: Langham, 2019).

these authors engage a diversity of publics, including law in China, sexism in Africa, urban design in Brazil, racism in America, language in Scotland, business in New York, and Islam in Indonesia.

Although Reformed public theology shares much in common with the ecumenical project we have described as "public theology," a few points of emphasis appear to set the tradition apart. While not exclusively owned by the Reformed tradition, these marks appear repeatedly within tradition's public imagination. To be clear, these marks are not universally held by all Reformed Christians around the world. However, in the diverse essays contained within this book these points of emphasis will surface again and again. In a way, we might consider them "the public habits of the Reformed heart."

1. *Listening to the Laity.* Reformed public theology does not belong to any specific guild of academic theologians or ordained clergy. The tradition's emphasis on the priesthood of all believers demands that the laity be active participants in any public theological project that the tradition produces.

    Though these essays are works of public theology, many of the authors do not consider themselves to be "public theologians." They are Reformed activists and artists, painters and philosophers, lawyers and business leaders, chaplains and community organizers—all of whom are seeking to engage public life in a theologically conversant way. While many hold degrees in theology, philosophy, and ethics, I have been careful to include several voices whose theology has grown primarily through embodied public action in the boardroom, the courtroom, the studio, the campus, and the street protest. As Richard Mouw writes, "We would all think it odd if a lifelong resident of Paris wrote a book about how to live a life of discipleship in Latin America. . . . Similarly there something odd about an attempt by clergy and professional theologians to speak with authority about the situations faced by mechanics, insurance agents, and farmers."[28]

2. *Dispersing Power.* Reformed public theologians appear to be particularly concerned with pushing power *both down and out* throughout society. In pushing power *down*, they show a particular theological allergy to hierarchical consolidations of social power. In politics, the marketplace, the church, and beyond, dominating leaders and cabals are out of bounds. In pushing power *out*, Reformed public theologians also demonstrate a public allergy to the singular dominance of either the

28. Richard J. Mouw, *Called to Holy Worldliness* (Philadelphia: Fortress, 1980), 25.

state, the marketplace, or the church. No single institution or sphere of public life should dominate the others. Instead, public power should be pushed *out*; it should be extended generously to the arts and sciences, markets and courts, universities and nonprofits.

In this volume and beyond, Reformed public theologians heartily disagree on the specifics of power dispersal; yet in general, this theological desire to push public power both down and out throughout society comes up again and again in their work.

Much can be said about the origins of this Reformed allergy toward the collection and consolidation of public power. For now, I will briefly mention the public consequences of a Reformed theology of creation and fall. First, in creation, Reformed theologians see the Creator gifting the whole of humanity with a diverse array of gifts, callings, and responsibilities. These gifts are not exclusively given to a specific class of elites or a particular institution or sphere of life (like the state, the market, or the church). Instead, these divine gifts and responsibilities are distributed widely throughout human society. Therefore, any consolidation of power in the hands of a single leader, community, or institution is interpreted by Reformed theologians as a form of creational theft. It robs diverse individuals and institutions of their own *God-given* gifts, callings, and responsibilities.

Second, in the rebellious fall of human society into sin, every single public leader, institution, and discourse struggles to access, interpret, and do the will of God. No public force has a perfect knowledge of God's public will. In the light of society's collective blindness and depravity, Reformed public theologians argue that it is wise and prudent to disperse public power widely, pushing it further down and further out.

Finally, when discussing complex public evils like racism, colonialism, and economic oppression, the Reformed voices in this volume do not simply reach for a spiritual analysis of the issue; they reach for a structural analysis as well. Within the Reformed tradition, they find theological resources for thinking about the systemic, institutional, and structural nature of power. Within these complex social systems of power, they see the potential for both divine flourishing and human destruction.

3. *Temporal Awareness*. Again and again these essays seem profoundly concerned that Christians in public life recognize "what time it is." They insist that Christians become more aware of the divine epoch in which they live. According to their theological "watches," Christians

live, work, and play within the time of God's "already" and "not yet." The kingdom of God has already broken into the world in the person and work of Jesus Christ. The Holy Spirit is already alive and active within its social structures and systems. That said, the fulfillment of the Lord's mission and work is not yet fully manifest. The creation is still groaning. The principalities and powers still wield their swords. Every tear has not yet been wiped away.

As Christians move in and through public life, these Reformed voices emphasize the need for them to grapple with their temporal place *between* the divine epochs. These theologians are particularly concerned with the public consequences of Christians who harbor either an over-realized or underrealized understanding of the kingdom's arrival in the public square today.

4. *Historical Humility.* The authors in this volume will quote, in one and the same breath, a sixteenth-century voice on theology and a twenty-first-century voice on critical race theory, fashion theory, or urban design. While the authors fully recognize the vast historical chasms that exist between these worlds, they are convinced that historical voices within the Reformed tradition have something important to offer Christians in public life today. The authors' peculiar willingness to learn from the historical wisdom of the tradition might be a contribution to a broader public theology movement, which could stand to grow in its willingness to engage historical sources.

5. *Aesthetic Neighborliness.* While the ecumenical movement for public theology tends to focus the bulk of its energy on the issues of politics, economics, and culture, the questions of art and public aesthetics are somewhat less prominent. This volume—with essays exploring the public importance of poetry and painting, pottery and fashion, urban design and architecture—highlights a Reformed interest in the importance of aesthetics for public life.

Here Reformed public theology is pointing to aesthetics as a medium through which Christians are called to love and serve their neighbors. Here Christians can inhabit and engage public life through artistic and architectural creativity, decoration and dress, poetic rhyme and musical rhythm.

6. *Culture Making.* Although much of contemporary public theology tends to focus on verbal and intellectual forms of public discourse and exchange, in these essays we can see a broader Reformed concern for the nonverbal and more common ways in which the laity engage

the public square every day. We notice the creation of a business plan or a new institution, the teaching of a class or the raising of a child, the writing of a novel or a new investment strategy: all of these are profound and embodied ways in which Christians impact public life every day. Through the *making* of culture, as opposed to simply criticizing it, Christian architects, entrepreneurs, farmers, and city planners offer their neighbors new ways of living and being in the public square.

Although the guild of public theology has historically been concerned with the public exchange of words, ideas, and beliefs, Reformed public theology thus emphasizes that the cultural creations we *make* constitute a critical aspect of Christian public exchange and global discourse.[29]

7. *Public Delight.* As noted earlier, a universal mark of public theology is a desire to listen to and learn from the wisdom of diverse cultures, disciplines, and religions. In this sense, the Reformed tradition offers nothing unique in its belief that God has something to teach the church in and through the world.

That said, something somewhat distinct appears to happen in these essays when the authors examine the theological value of the world's words and work. Here we detect a rather unique display of joy, gratitude, and delight as these authors theologically reflect upon the beauty and insight they find in the world outside.

By way of their essays, we begin to suspect that *God* actually takes joy in the cultural wisdom, insight, virtue, and creativity of those outside the church. The essays repeatedly argue that Christians should not simply learn from their non-Christian neighbors; they should also be *grateful* for and take *delight* in their contributions to the global public square. Whether these essays are surveying well-designed neighborhoods, new fashion trends, Japanese tea ceremonies, Brazilian coffee shops, or African American poetry, one detects within them a call to Christian gratitude and delight in the world. Here the authors reflect John Calvin's words: "It is no small honor that God for our sake has so magnificently adorned the world, in order that we may not only be spectators of this beauteous theater, but also enjoy the multiplied abundance and variety of good things which are presented to us in it."[30]

---

29. For a discussion of this form of public engagement, see Andy Crouch, *Culture Making: Recovering Our Creative Calling* (Downers Grove, IL: InterVarsity, 2013).

30. Calvin's *Commentary on the Psalms*, on Ps. 104:31, quoted in Taylor, *Theater of God's Glory*, 37.

8. *A Liturgical Life.* In a sexist and misogynistic society, a woman is baptized and declared a full member of the priesthood of all believers. Caught in a state of legal limbo between Peru and the USA, an undocumented immigrant finds a home at the Lord's Table. Flooded by distressing economic news about the COVID-19 pandemic, a congregation learns to offer their petitions and intercessions before God in public prayer. A nation demands that a lying politician publicly confess his sins and seek absolution. These are just a few of the many intersections between Christian worship and public life that are discussed in this book.

The best public theology emerges from a robust public liturgy. Within this volume an entire section of essays is dedicated to the Reformed desire to form a deeper connection between its worship and its public life. This section argues repeatedly that the walls between the sanctuary and the street should be made increasingly porous. The patterns of grace sung in the sanctuary should be reflected in the patterns of life lived in the world. Likewise, the public burdens carried by the people in the world should be carried directly into the sanctuary and laid upon the altar. The integrity of both worship and public life depend on it.

9. *A Liberated Solidarity.* Finally, these essays wrestle continuously with a twofold desire to liberate individuals from oppressive institutions and communities while, at the same time, conceiving of institutions and communities in which individuals might flourish. Here the Reformed public imagination is particularly concerned with avoiding the Scylla and Charybdis of *both* rootless individualism *and* oppressive collectivism.

These essays exhibit a profound yearning within the Reformed tradition to articulate a nuanced vision of individual freedom that can be found *within* communities, institutions, and civic structures. The Reformed imagination retains a strong refusal to accept the modern notion that individual liberty and communal solidarity are mutually exclusive. Articulating a relationship of mutuality between individuals and institutions is an ongoing Reformed concern.

How (Not) to Read this Book

How might Reformed theology engage Chinese labor laws, New York fashion trends, African colonialism, or the Philippine drug war? This book is specifically designed to serve as a "taste and see" introduction to a variety of select ways in which Reformed theology and public life intersect.

In no way is this book comprehensive. Because of strict space restrictions, authors were not permitted to offer an exhaustive account of their contexts or theological categories. Rather than clearing their throats with pages of theological methodology or cultural analysis, the authors were instructed to dive in, get to work, and actually do public theology. They were asked to show rather than tell. Readers looking for more intricate and nuanced discussions of the authors' contexts and theological categories are urged to consult the footnotes. Many of the authors have written on these subjects at great length, in their own books, dissertations, and articles.

By and large, the authors were instructed to explore the ways in which Reformed theology *positively* informs their engagement with public life. Although they occasionally challenge and criticize the failures, missteps, and outright injustices of the Reformed tradition, their primary interest is in constructively building on the generative resources that they have found within the tradition.

Designing the book in this way presents several dangers to the reader. First, it might give the impression that the authors view the Reformed tradition through a set of rose-colored glasses—as if the tradition has no public sins or theological blind spots for which it must account. Furthermore, it might even give the impression that we believe there is no public question to which Reformed theology does not already have the answer. This is clearly false. Given sufficient space, these authors could have expanded on a variety of ways in which they differ from the Reformed tradition. They recognize the clay-footed fallenness of Reformed heroes like Calvin and Edwards, Barth and Kuyper. The authors know, as do we all, that the Reformed tradition is complicit in any number of public sins, whether political or cultural, racial or colonial.

Second, such a book might inspire in its readers an ugly sort of theological chauvinism, in which Reformed theology is depicted as superior to all other theological traditions. Once again, given the requisite space and time, many of these authors would have listed their deep ecumenical indebtedness to the wisdom of Catholic, Lutheran, postcolonial, evangelical, and Pentecostal voices. These essays do not exist on the isolated island of "pure" Reformed theology. They exist as part of a deeper catholic archipelago. As Reformed catholics, we are connected to an ecumenical lineage of diverse theological traditions deeply linked beneath the sea. Calvinistic jingoism has no place here.

In selecting the authors for this book, the hope was to demonstrate a four-fold diversity of disciplines, denominations, issues, and contexts. While we have managed to include an impressive diversity of denominations and issues, it is important to briefly name the volume's shortcomings. We do not cover important issues like the environment, gender, and technology.[31] We have no authors representing the critically important regions of the Middle East or the Indian subcontinent. We have no authors representing the disciplines of science, psychology, or literature. The author list remains heavily American, mostly male, and primarily centered within the guild of the theological academy. These shortcomings signal that, despite the tradition's laudable progress, much more needs to be done.

With these notes and cautions made, we proceed with our task. The reigning purpose of this book is to explore a variety of ways in which Reformed theology and public life are intersecting in the world today. In and through this project, our hope is to demonstrate the tradition's continued ability to learn and grow, explore and serve, all within the complex public spaces to which it has been called.

31. For contemporary Reformed engagements with these issues see, for example, Derek Schuurman, *Shaping a Digital World: Faith, Culture, and Computer Technology* (Downers Grove, IL: IVP Academic, 2013); Steven Bouma Prediger, *For the Beauty of the Earth: A Christian Vision for Creation Care*, 2nd ed. (Grand Rapids: Baker Academic, 2010); Amy Plantinga Pauw and Serene Jones, eds., *Feminist and Womanist Essays in Reformed Dogmatics* (Louisville: Westminster John Knox, 2011).

Part One

Public Culture

1

Immigrants, Refugees, and Asylum Seekers

The Migratory Beginnings of Reformed Public Theology

RUBÉN ROSARIO RODRÍGUEZ

Immigration was a defining characteristic of the early Reformation.[1] Whether fleeing political persecution, seeking religious freedom, sending missionaries, or welcoming refugees into their midst, the sixteenth-century Reformers were a people on the move. They were constantly interacting with different languages and cultures, crossing borders, planting churches in new soil, and wrestling with biblical demands to provide justice and hospitality for foreigners.

John Calvin's Geneva offers a fascinating case study of a community of faith struggling to make space for newcomers, all the while resisting the temptations of xenophobia and nativist protectionism. As a community, Geneva was intimately aware of both ends of the immigrant experience. The city not only gathered thousands of dislocated refugees from cultures and kingdoms all over Europe, it also scattered settlers, missionaries, and pastors to different nations all over the continent and beyond. As historian Carter Lindberg observes,

---

1. See Mack P. Holt, "International Calvinism," in *John Calvin in Context*, ed. R. Ward Holder (Cambridge: Cambridge University Press, 2020), 375–82.

"Geneva not only welcomed refugees, it created them."[2] The migratory experiences of the early Reformers had a profound impact on the movement's self-understanding. Their spiritual and political responses to these profound experiences of dislocation have a lot to offer to twenty-first-century Christians as they wrestle with the contemporary (and enduring) issue of immigration.

John Calvin, himself a French political exile, had fled to Strasbourg and later settled in Geneva, where he established a church order that specifically allowed the city to become a haven for Protestant refugees fleeing persecution from all over Europe. Throughout his life, Calvin worked tirelessly on behalf of persecuted Protestants, especially those from his native France (the Huguenots). The persecution in France sent a massive wave of refugees to Geneva between 1545 and 1555. During this time, the city's cramped geographic borders and limited resources prevented its citizens from permanently welcoming all refugees. The lack of space combined with a passion for global mission eventually inspired several Protestant resettlement missions throughout Europe and beyond. Through it all, John Calvin and his fellow Reformers fostered a diverse and complex international movement that was both migratory and hospitable, transnational and ecumenical. An enduring message within sixteenth-century Geneva was, quite simply, to offer hospitality when you are in a position of privilege; soon enough, you may find that you yourself are the migrant in need of hospitality.[3]

Today in the United States, ironically, many self-identified Calvinists willingly support anti-immigrant (and borderline racist) leaders and cruel immigration policies. These Calvinists will sometimes even attempt to use their faith as a tool by which they can calmly turn refugees away and ignore the moral horrors being perpetrated on the US southern border. Their moral and political quietism will sometimes be fostered through politically passive readings of Romans 13 and a vague emphasis on submissive acceptance of the laws and leaders whom God has placed in authority.

In 2020 the US government's zero-tolerance border enforcement policies created holding facilities that act as de facto concentration camps. These camps viciously squander innocent lives,[4] separate children from their parents, and subject the most vulnerable detainees (women and children) to physical

2. Carter Lindberg, *The European Reformations*, 2nd ed. (Malden, MA: Wiley-Blackwell, 2010), 249.

3. See Kaarin Maag, *Seminary or University? The Genevan Academy and Reformed Higher Education, 1560–1620* (Aldershot, UK: Scolar, 1995). Under Calvin, Geneva was heavily involved in mission work, mostly in France, with many of the French pastors trained in Geneva and then serving repatriated Huguenot churches.

4. Cynthia Pompa, "Immigrant Kids Keep Dying in CBP Detention Centers, and DHS Won't Take Accountability," in *ACLU: 100 Years* (June 24, 2019), https://www.aclu.org/blog/immigrants-rights/immigrants-rights-and-detention/immigrant-kids-keep-dying-cbp-detention.

and sexual abuse at the hands of their jailers.[5] Calvinist silence and submission in the face of such cruelty is at best tacit approval of these policies; at worst it is complicity in a new wave of nativist anti-immigrant violence currently plaguing the nation.[6]

This chapter demonstrates that Calvinists' moral and political quietism is a tragic betrayal of a long Calvinist legacy of welcoming strangers, resisting tyrants, establishing justice, and stepping across borders and cultures in vulnerability and faith. It will also discredit the common misconception that John Calvin was a cold and pharisaic stickler for the rule of law. Instead, it will offer a more accurate representation of John Calvin as a humanistic reformer whose ecclesiastical and civil polities sought that "every resident of Geneva [be] integrated into a caring community." Unlike our modern social welfare networks, these church-led ministries were designed to be "real networks of caring."[7] As Scottish Reformer John Knox commented after his sojourn in Geneva, the city "is the most perfect school of Christ that ever was in the earth since the days of the apostles."[8] John Bale, a fellow refugee fleeing Mary Tudor's persecution, added: "Geneva seems to me to be the wonderful miracle of the whole world. . . . Is it not wonderful that Spaniards, Italians, Scots, Englishmen, Frenchmen, Germans, disagreeing on manners, speech, and apparel, . . . [yet] coupled with only the yoke of Christ, should live so . . . like a spiritual and Christian congregation?"[9] When balancing the biblical demand for the rule of law (Rom. 13) with Peter's exhortation that "We must obey God rather than any human authority" (Acts 5:29 NRSV), Calvin erred on the side of compassion for the immigrant.[10] He was firmly

5. See Richard Gonzales, "Sexual Assault of Detained Migrant Children Reported in the Thousands Since 2015," in *National Public Radio* (February 26, 2019), https://www.npr.org/2019/02/26/698397631/sexual-assault-of-detained-migrant-children-reported-in-the-thousands-since-2015; also see "Sexual Abuse in Immigration Detention—Raquel's Story," American Civil Liberties Union, https://www.aclu.org/other/sexual-abuse-immigration-detention-raquels-story.

6. Tyler Anbinder, "Trump Has Spread More Hatred of Immigrants Than Any American in History," *Washington Post*, November 7, 2019, https://www.washingtonpost.com/outlook/trump-has-spread-more-hatred-of-immigrants-than-any-american-in-history/2019/11/07/7e253236-ff54-11e9-8bab-0fc209e065a8_story.html.

7. Robert M. Kingdon, "Calvinist Discipline in the Old World and the New," in *The Reformation in Germany and Europe: Interpretations and Issues*, special volume, *Archive for Reformation History / Archiv für Reformationsgeschichte* 84, ed. Hans R. Guggisberg and Gottfried Krodel (Gütersloh: Gütersloher Verlagshaus, 1993), 665–79.

8. John Knox, *The Works of John Knox*, ed. David Laing (Edinburgh: Bannatyne Society, 1848), 4:240.

9. Cited in John T. McNeill, *The History and Character of Calvinism* (New York: Oxford University Press, 1967), 178.

10. See David M. Whitford, "Robbing Paul to Pay Peter: The Reception of Paul in Sixteenth Century Political Theology," in *A Companion to Paul in the Reformation*, ed. R. Ward Holder

convinced that, as citizens and as Christians, we are called to "take as strong a stand against evil as we can."[11]

Refugees Gathered in Geneva

During Calvin's pastoral tenure in Geneva (1538–64), the Reformation was fighting for its very life. The movement was encountering Catholic persecution across the whole of Europe. In 1555, a flood of French refugees fleeing persecution overwhelmed Geneva. Historians estimate that, in the space of a single decade, the population of Geneva grew from 13,100 to as high as 21,400.[12]

Needless to say, this crushing influx of refugees exacerbated the city's already strained social welfare infrastructure. In a normal year, about 5 percent of Geneva's native population depended on regular assistance from the general hospital (more than 500 people). Add to that the massive flow of refugees, and the social welfare agencies would likely have had to serve up to an additional ten thousand strangers during any one-year period.[13] Thankfully, not all these refugees would settle permanently in the small city of Geneva. Many would merely pass through to other Reformed settlements and sanctuaries. This pressing need to resettle refugees directly impacted (and informed) Geneva's later missionary efforts.

One of the constant causes of friction between Calvin and the native Genevans was his spiritual and political insistence on providing hospitality to exiles. This was no inconsequential matter, for what had been a trickle in 1523 became a flood thirty years later.[14] By 1555 there were more immigrants than native citizens in the city. Not surprisingly, the natives had some grievances. They complained that refugees were taking jobs and straining resources, that wealthy exiled French nobles were taking over the city, that the culture of the city would be destroyed, and that Geneva itself would decline.

(Leiden: Brill, 2009): 573–606. The author argues that Calvin prioritized Peter's Acts (5:29) statement over Paul's in Rom. 13.

11. John Calvin, *Sermons on 2 Samuel: Chapters 1–13*, trans. Douglas Kelly (Carlisle, PA: Banner of Truth Trust, 1992), 419.

12. Cited in Robert M. Kingdon, "Calvinism and Social Welfare," *Calvin Theological Journal* 17 (1982): 223.

13. William Naphy, "Calvin's Church in Geneva: Constructed or Gathered? Local or Foreign? French or Swiss?," in *Calvin and His Influence, 1509–2009*, ed. Irena Backus and Philip Benedict (Oxford: Oxford University Press, 2011), 114–15.

14. During Calvin's tenure, Protestant refugees were attracted to Geneva due to the popularity of his preaching and the success of his church. They were also attracted to the hospitable civil reforms that he had helped to foster. While many of Geneva's charitable institutions predated Calvin's arrival in Geneva, their long-term success and impact benefited from Calvin's astute reorganization of church and civil governance.

Still, one can appreciate the concerns of the native Genevans. One can even understand their resentment. By mid-century, every single one of their local pastors was foreign born. In claiming their city's independence years earlier, the Genevans had liberated themselves from the local nobility. Now they had to watch as nobles fleeing from France and Italy entered their gates and wielded a disproportionate amount of influence in their economic matters.[15]

Anti-immigrant sentiment reached its peak in 1555 under the leadership of Ami Perrin, who called himself a Genevan patriot. Perrin goaded a street mob to threaten foreign-owned businesses in the city. The mob gathered outside the city council to intimidate the magistrates. John Calvin himself stepped into the fray. He stood amid the angry crowd that was chanting, "Kill the French," and proclaimed: "If you must shed blood, let mine be first."[16] Perrin later sought to oust Calvin by force but was defeated and exiled from the city. Calvin's public victory allowed him to consolidate his authority as pastor and direct his political support to better care for the needs of refugees.

The French Fund (*Bourse française*) was established in Geneva to provide diaconal care for French Protestants fleeing Catholic persecution. John Calvin himself quietly supported the work of the French Fund for many years from his own modest income. Apart from emergency relief and medical services, the deacons used this fund to obtain housing for refugee families and to help refugees secure employment in the city. The fund provided tools for the refugees so they could work for themselves. It even paid for vocational training to ensure that the refugees did not depend on charity for their long-term subsistence. Early on, any refugee from any nation who was in genuine need received assistance from the French Fund. However, as persecution spread across Europe, similar funds were established in Geneva by and for the various ethnic communities seeking refuge (Italian, Spanish, Polish, etc.).

The multinational character of the Reformation underlaid Calvin's commitment to the social and economic practices of the diaconal ministry in Geneva. A similar cosmopolitan character was also embodied in the founding of the Genevan Academy. This international school was designed to educate clergy and doctors to serve in nascent Protestant communities throughout the diverse nations and cultures of Europe and later of the world.

It is no surprise, therefore, that within this international and migratory reformation, Calvin's vision for church order and ecclesial communion across borders evinced a certain level of what we might today call "localism" or

---

15. See William C. Innes, *Social Concern in Calvin's Geneva* (Eugene, OR: Wipf & Stock, 1983), 205–36.

16. Lindberg, *European Reformations*, 251.

"multicultural tolerance." Rather than the top-down universalism of Rome, Calvin took steps to bring diverse congregations into a "network of churches, geographically separate, each possessing its own confession."[17] This international and multicultural "network was intended to be both mutually supportive and mutually correcting, a family in which there was room for some diversity in common communion."[18] The catechisms were one way for diverse churches across political and cultural boundaries to mutually recognize one another and form unified and yet diverse community.

A Spiritual and Temporal Theology of Compassion

In his *Institutes*, Calvin argues that God established governments so "that humanity may be maintained among men";[19] he views magistrates as the divinely appointed protectors and guardians of public well-being, "a calling, not only lawful before God, but also the most sacred and by far the most honorable of all callings, in the whole life of mortal men."[20] By this view, temporal governments exist "to cherish and protect the outward worship of God, to defend sound doctrine of piety, and the position of the church, to adjust our life to the society of men, to form our social behavior to civil righteousness, to reconcile us with one another, and to promote general peace and tranquility."[21]

It follows that there are preferable forms of government for Calvin. Despite believing in a division of labor between *spiritual* (church) and *temporal* (state) governments, Calvin argues that the temporal "establishment of civil justice and outward morality" is grounded in and springs from "that spiritual and inward Kingdom of Christ, so we must know that they are not at variance. For spiritual government, indeed, is already initiating in us upon earth certain beginnings of the Heavenly Kingdom, and in this mortal and fleeting life affords a certain forecast of an immortal and incorruptible blessedness."[22] By this understanding, neither the church nor the state represents perfect and holy communities, but both are mixed societies of saints and sinners, elect

17. Elsie Anne McKee, "The Character and Significance of John Calvin's Teaching on Social and Economic Issues," in *John Calvin Rediscovered: The Impact of His Social and Economic Thought*, ed. Edward Dommen and James D. Bratt (Louisville: Westminster John Knox, 2007), 19.

18. McKee, "Calvin's Teaching," 19.

19. John Calvin, *Institutes of the Christian Religion*, ed. John T. McNeill, trans. Ford Lewis Battles, 2 vols. (Philadelphia: Westminster, 1960), 4.20.3.

20. Calvin, *Institutes* 4.20.6.

21. Calvin, *Institutes* 4.20.1–2.

22. Calvin, *Institutes* 4.20.2.

and reprobate, making it necessary to acknowledge certain ambiguities and tensions within both spiritual and temporal governance.

Even when advocating some separation of church and state as Calvin did, he did not separate theology from politics. One reason theology needed to engage public life was to ensure that the fundamental Christian obligation of compassion toward those in need was carried out properly. For Calvin and for those traditions influenced by Calvin, the establishment of a just social order is part and parcel of the Christian life. The call to minister to the poor, the sick, the widow, the orphan, the refugee, and the prisoner (Matt. 25:34–40) is a matter of concern for both the church and the state because it is first and foremost a spiritual concern for all Christians. As Calvin preached, "Take as strong a stand against evil as we can. This command is given to everyone, not only to princes, magistrates, and officers of justice, but to all private persons as well."[23]

Genevan resistance to immigration continued throughout and beyond Calvin's public ministry. It was not until 1559 that the first son of an immigrant was allowed to sit in the Council of Two Hundred, and it was thirty-five years later, in 1594—long after Calvin's death—that the first son of an immigrant sat in the Small Council, which was the real seat of political power.

Calvin disagreed with the anti-immigration party theologically and politically on the basis of simple Christian duty. Commenting on the passage in Hebrews (13:2) about those who entertained angels unawares, he writes:

> He is not only speaking about the right of hospitality which used to be practised among the rich, but rather he is giving orders that the poor and the needy are to be received since at that time many were refugees from their homes for the Name of Christ. To add additional commendation for this kind of duty, he says that angels have sometimes been entertained by those who thought they were receiving men. I have no doubt that he is thinking of Abraham and Lot. . . . If anyone objects that this was an unusual occurrence, I have a ready answer in the fact that we receive not only angels but Christ himself when we receive the poor in His Name.[24]

Refugees Scattered to Brazil

In telling the story of the European conquest and colonization of the New World, certain narratives continue to dominate. Examples are the claims that

23. Calvin, *Sermons on 2 Samuel: Chapters 1–13*, 419.
24. John Calvin, *Calvin's New Testament Commentaries*, vol. 12, *The Epistle of Paul the Apostle to the Hebrews and the First and Second Epistles of St. Peter*, ed. T. F. Torrance (Grand Rapids: Eerdmans, 1994), 204–5.

Protestantism first settled in New England or that Latin America was settled exclusively by the Roman Catholic Church. The brief history of Fort Coligny, a Protestant settlement just outside present-day Rio de Janeiro, challenges these prevailing assumptions. For our purposes, Fort Coligny provides a brief but illuminating glimpse into the migratory nature, vision, and character of the early Reformation.

In 1555 the Reformed churches of Geneva decided to establish their first Protestant mission in the Americas. More than sixty years before English-speaking Protestants would establish Plymouth in New England, French-speaking Huguenot refugees embarked for a new colony in what was then called "Antarctic France," in modern-day Brazil.

Geneva, bursting at the seams with Huguenot refugees, blessed and sent settlers and two pastors who were trained and funded by the consistory in Geneva. The immigrants from Geneva experienced a sense of profound dislocation, which came from being uninvited and politically disenfranchised guests in a strange land.

These Reformed settlers elected to go to Latin America, even though it was under Spanish and Portuguese domination and was viewed as the exclusive mission field of the Roman Catholic Church by the papal bull *Inter caetera* (1493).[25] Consequently, the fragile fate of Protestants in Latin America was often that "they were promptly detected, captured and tried by the Inquisition. Under the ordeal, a majority recanted, mainly in order to avoid punishment, but some, who remained loyal to the end, were burnt at the stake."[26] The migratory experience of these early Calvinists was one of danger, fragility, and dislocation.

In 1555 the Catholic French crown gave permission for the construction of an island fortress sheltering six hundred French citizens as part of an exploratory venture in the New World. It was named Fort Coligny, after Gaspard de Coligny, who was both a Huguenot and a French admiral.[27] The fort was under the command of Vice Admiral Nicolas Durand de Villegagnon,

25. This papal bull granted the Catholic sovereigns Ferdinand and Isabella of Spain all lands to the "west and south" of a pole-to-pole line one hundred leagues west and south of any of the islands of the Azores or the Cape Verde Islands.

26. G. Baez-Camargo, "The Earliest Protestant Missionary Venture in Latin America," *Church History* 21, no. 2 (June 1952): 135.

27. Admiral Coligny is remembered as one of the leaders of the Huguenots during the French Wars of Religion (1562–98); he had a close relationship with King Charles IX of France, a friendship greatly opposed by his mother, Catherine de Medici, who conspired to assassinate Coligny on August 22, 1572. This triggered the St. Bartholomew's Day massacre (Aug. 24, 1572), which resulted in the deaths of over ten thousand Huguenots in Paris and the outlying provinces. See R. J. Knecht, *The French Civil Wars, 1562–1598* (London: Routledge, 2014), 157–70.

a recent convert to Protestantism himself. Villegagnon convinced Admiral Coligny to staff the fortress with Huguenot refugees.[28] Very little is known about this colonial effort since the only two eyewitness accounts were written by Huguenots who were soon killed when the fort was overrun by the Portuguese in 1560.[29] The Catholic king ultimately supported this Protestant venture because of the political and economic advantages he could gain by establishing a colony in the New World.[30]

The settlers of Coligny had to overcome many difficulties in their new home. A letter from Villegagnon narrates that his soldiers and the Huguenot refugees alike faced severe shortages of food and struggled to survive in the new climate. Amid this struggle, he describes the Huguenot immigrants as "a race, fearing God, patient and kind," who performed the bulk of the labor and became his "best workmen [and] would exert a good influence on the others."[31] Villegagnon was so impressed by the settlers that he wrote to both King Henry II and the magistrates of Geneva, requesting that more Reformed artisans, as well as ministers, be sent to Fort Coligny from Geneva. Those letters are not extant. According to the consistory minutes, the Genevan Church sent two more ministers, Peter Richier and William Chartier, bearing letters from John Calvin to Villegagnon in Brazil. The letters arrived on March 7, 1557.

So, with the backing of a French Catholic crown, Fort Coligny became a Protestant refuge for Reformed migrants seeking religious freedom and desiring to evangelize the indigenous population. That is how, in 1557, the very first Reformed worship and Communion service (following the Genevan Church Order) was celebrated in the New World—not in New England, but in Brazil.[32]

A letter from Villegagnon and letters from the two ministers were sent to Calvin and the Geneva Consistory on the returning ship in April 1557. In his letter Villegagnon expresses joy at the arrival of the Protestant ministers. He also mentions a variety of concerns about threats from the indigenous

28. Coligny was able to gain the support of the crown to establish a colony in Brazil that would serve as a refuge for French Huguenots; even with this incentive, they still had to scour the Parisian prisons in order "to get enough men . . . to add to his Huguenot contingent." See James I. Good, "Calvin and the New World," *Journal of the Presbyterian Historical Society* 5, no. 4 (December 1909): 179.

29. See John McGrath, "Polemic and History in French Brazil, 1555–1560," *Sixteenth Century Journal* 27, no. 2 (Summer 1996): 385–97. These memoirs were published in the Protestant *Foxe's Book of Martyrs* (1563), were used by Protestants in their arguments with Catholics during the French Wars of Religion, and so are largely discredited as reliable sources by historians.

30. Good, "Calvin and the New World," 179.

31. Cited in Good, "Calvin and the New World," 180.

32. See R. Pierce Beaver, "The Geneva Mission to Brazil," *Reformed Journal* 17 (July–August 1967): 14–20.

population, the physical hardships of surviving in the region, and lamentations that some settlers "had gone back to France on account of the hardships they had endured, and he himself had been somewhat discouraged at the difficulties. But when he remembered that the object of the voyage was to promote Christ's kingdom, he felt he would dishonor His [Christ's] name if he should be deterred by the perils."[33] Villegagnon's letter demonstrates tolerance for the Huguenot settlers and closes with language supportive of Calvin's missionary effort: "Our Lord Jesus Christ preserve you and your colleagues from all evil, strengthen you with His Spirit and prolong your life for the Church's Work."[34]

Unfortunately, Villegagnon's support for Calvin—rooted in pragmatism and lukewarm at best—eroded when the Lutheran Jean Cointat raised objections to the local Genevan celebration of the Lord's Supper and baptism. Villegagnon sided with Cointat and eventually forbade the Genevan order of worship despite his promise and assurances to Calvin that they would adhere to the Genevan Church Order.[35] Whatever Admiral Coligny's original intentions, Villegagnon's Protestant profession of faith proved insincere: he eventually imposed Roman Catholic doctrine over all of Fort Coligny, forbade Reformed worship (though it continued in secret), and eventually drove the Huguenots off the island. They were refugees yet again.

Ironically, it was during this exile on the Brazilian mainland that the Huguenots began their true missionary efforts, evangelizing the Topinambu (Tupinamba) tribe who had welcomed them in their vulnerable state.[36] Sadly, their missionary efforts were short-lived: Villegagnon charged them as heretics and had them arrested as spies and sentenced to death. One recanted, but three were executed—Peter Bourdon, John Bortel, and Matthew Vernuil—becoming the first martyrs to die for sake of Protestant doctrine and mission in the New World. A fifth, John Boles, settled south of Fort Coligny and became such a successful preacher among the indigenous tribes that the Jesuits had

33. Cited in Good, "Calvin and the New World," 181.
34. Good, "Calvin and the New World," 181.
35. In their April 1557 letter to John Calvin, Richier and Chartier assured Calvin that they had presided over the proper celebration of the Lord's Supper and even reported that Vice Admiral Villegagnon had made a public profession of faith. A few months later (in June), Villegagnon placed Chartier on a ship to Geneva to consult with Calvin on how to resolve the matter, while Richier was allowed to continue preaching and leading worship so long as he did not celebrate the sacraments. See Charles E. Nowell, "The French in Sixteenth-Century Brazil," *The Americas* 5, no. 4 (April 1949): 388–91.
36. During this time Jean De Léry, one of the colonists, even developed a dictionary of the Tupinamba language for the benefit of future missionaries. For a translation of De Léry's brief account of his missionary adventure, see Francis Parkman, *Pioneers of France in the New World* (Boston: Little, Brown, 1865), 16–27.

him arrested and imprisoned for eight years before burning him at the stake in 1567, "the first Protestant auto-da-fé in America."[37]

Conclusion

In the *Institutes*, Calvin connects hospitality and care for the poor, refugees, and foreigners directly to the theological doctrines of grace and the divine image in humankind. In one instance, Calvin appears to be speaking specifically about religious refugees when he argues that, within them, the divine image "is most carefully to be noted." On this basis, Calvin instructs:

> Therefore, we have no reason to refuse any who come before us needing our help. If we say that he is a stranger, the Lord has stamped on him a sign that we know [the image of God]. . . . If we allege that he is contemptible and worthless, the Lord responds by showing us that he has honored him by making his own image to shine in him. If we say that we owe him nothing, the Lord tells us that he has brought him before us so that in him we may see the many benefits that we owe to him. If we say that he is unworthy that we take even a step in his behalf, the image of God which we are to see in him is quite worthy that we give for it all that we are and have. Even when it is someone who not only is worthless, but also has insulted and injured us, this is not reason enough for us to cease loving, pleasing, and serving him.[38]

It is not enough to say that Calvin, himself an exile, defended others who were also exiles. There is a direct line from Calvin's ministries of hospitality and social equity to migrants in Geneva to Calvin's missionary efforts in Brazil. The two narratives reflect a larger truth about the migratory and multinational character of the early Reformation movement. Multicultural Geneva was "part of a broader international (or perhaps better put, universal) struggle for truth in a battle that went beyond the confines of any civic jurisdiction."[39]

The Genevan and Coligny narratives challenge contemporary Christians to address the underlying (and haunting) question of the day: *What does God demand of Christ's followers concerning the least of our brothers and sisters* (Matt. 25)? The hospitality of Reformed hosts in Geneva and the fragility, danger, and suffering of Reformed migrants in Coligny ought to inform our present-day experiences and struggles around the issue of global immigration.

37. Good, "Calvin and the New World," 185.
38. Calvin, *Institutes* 3.7.6.
39. Jesse Spohnholz, "Refugees," in *John Calvin in Context*, ed. R. Ward Holder (Cambridge: Cambridge University Press, 2020), 147.

Following Christ faithfully in the world involves movement; it is a journey, a pilgrimage. For Calvin, bearing one's cross always involves suffering. Our faithful movement, he argues, is possible when we "learn that this life, judged in itself, is troubled, turbulent, unhappy in countless ways, and in no respect clearly happy; that all those things which are judged to be its goods are uncertain, fleeting, vain, and vitiated by many intermingled evils. From this, at the same time, we conclude that in this life we are to seek and hope for nothing but struggle."[40]

But there is hope. Because of Christ's cross, because of his sacrifice for us, Christ's followers can bear a cross for others as they move and migrate through this world. Christ's gracious gift to us demands a public and even political response. For John Calvin, standing by while the poor, the immigrant, and political refugee are suffering and exploited—that is a sinful act, a violation of "the image of God."[41] It is our Christian duty not only to alleviate such suffering through ministries of compassion, but also to order our political life in faithfulness to God so as to eliminate such suffering.

Idolatry and Calvinism are antithetical to one another, absolutely inimical. For the Calvinist, God alone is sovereign. *Nothing* can be allowed to compete with or diminish God's image, God's law, or God's sovereign power. When Reformed Christians in the United States ignore the suffering of refugees (the image of God in their midst), when they quietly hide behind an unjust rule of law (placing the nation's laws above God's laws), when they passively submit to an unjust leader (placing the leader's sovereignty above God's sovereignty)— such Reformed Christians are in danger not simply of injustice against their neighbor but also idolatry against God.

The twenty-first century is already marked by massive global migration. Religious persecution, economic distress, racial hatred, and political conflict are all driving enormous movements of souls and bodies created in the image of God. As Reformed Christians around the world wrestle with how to respond to such unprecedented dislocation, they would do well to learn from their own migratory past.

40. Calvin, *Institutes* 3.9.1.
41. Calvin, *Institutes* 3.7.6.

LANGUAGE

2

Let Every Tongue Confess

Language Diversity and Reformed Public Theology

JAMES EGLINTON

Language can unite and divide, liberate and oppress—a fact of life well-known to my people group, the Gàidhlig-speaking Celts of the Scottish Highlands and Outer Hebrides. The Gàidhlig[1] word *dàimheil* describes the feeling of being at home in the company of a fellow Gàidhlig speaker, even if you were otherwise perfect strangers. For all its warm beauty, however, this sense of kinship stems from a long-standing experience of linguistic exclusion and oppression. From the seventeenth century onward, our language suffered as a result of enforced anglicization. Even into the mid-twentieth century, it was normal for Gàidhlig children to be beaten by their English-speaking schoolteachers for using their mother tongue. These children were required to adopt English names. Even as recently as 2003, a Scottish family had to go through the court system to be allowed to register their daughter's full name in Gàidhlig rather than in English.[2]

---

1. For clarity: the Celtic language spoken in Scotland, Gàidhlig, and the closely related language spoken in Ireland, Gaeilge, are both commonly—and often confusingly—referred to in English simply as "Gaelic."

2. Shirley English, "Father Registers a Protest after Daughter's Gaelic Name Is Barred," *The [UK]Times*, May 31, 2003.

Although the language is now given explicit (but limited) state support, Gàidhlig continues to be looked down on by many in the United Kingdom and even in Scotland itself. In 2014, when registering my twin sons' births at the Edinburgh City Chambers, I gave their Gàidhlig names to the clerk, who then asked me, "Are you sure you want to do this?" before rolling her eyes in disdain. In the present day, the number of fluent Gàidhlig speakers has dwindled to just over 1 percent of the Scottish population. Little wonder, then, that we feel *dàimheil* when we meet a stranger who speaks our own language.

Our quickly globalizing world now contains more than seven thousand living languages. Linguists estimate that by the end of the century nearly half of those languages may be extinct. How should Christians theologically assess and respond to linguistic diversity and the political and cultural forces that would endanger it? What ethical obligations do they owe to linguistic minority groups? Finally, what, if anything, does Christian *theology* have to say to a world of diverse and often vulnerable minority tongues?

Christianity and Multilingualism

In 2021 Christians speak, worship, pray, and study Scripture in more languages than at any previous point in the church's history. The translation of the Bible into more and more languages continues apace. In recent years peoples as diverse as the Ifè of Togo and Benin, as well as my own people group, have received the New Testament in their own languages.[3] This readiness to undergo translation is deeply rooted in Christianity, which has been a multilingual faith from the outset.

In the aftermath of Pentecost, the earliest Christians—Parthians, Medes, Libyans, Jews, Egyptians, Arabians—were well aware of their differences in mother tongue (Acts 2:7–11), just as they revered Scriptures that were themselves written in Hebrew, Aramaic, and Greek. Theirs was a community within which God's Word was translatable across human languages; no single linguistic group held a position of distinct privilege simply because it used one particular language.

In this, Christianity was somewhat of an anomaly in the Roman Empire, where Greek and Latin fought for imperial dominance.[4] Local languages were

3. The previous Gàidhlig translation of the Bible was published in 1801 in a dialect that has long since died out and that is not easily comprehensible to the dialects of many modern-day speakers.

4. For the early spread of Christianity outside the Roman world and into Africa and Asia, see Vince Bantu, *A Multitude of All Peoples: Engaging Ancient Christianity's Global Identity* (Downers Grove, IL: IVP Academic, 2020).

tolerated dimly, and the speech of non-Romans (so-called barbarians) was reduced to a subhuman caricature: *bar bar bar*. Pagan Romans viewed linguistic diversity as a problem to be solved rather than something to be praised. Cicero, for example, claimed that a people could only be united when they shared a common ethnicity, nationality, and language.[5] In their day, the readiness with which early Christians were willing to embrace one another regardless of linguistic differences was striking.

In contrast to the typical Roman trait of looking down on minority languages,[6] the patristic father Augustine of Hippo (354–430) described how "the Heavenly City calls out to citizens from every nation, and thereby collects a society of aliens, speaking every language."[7] Within the pagan political imagination of Rome, the idea of a kingdom whose unifying factors needed no common language would have been strange indeed.

A surprising (and rather disappointing) development in the history of Christianity concerns how the early church's readiness to hear the beauty in each barbarian tongue was flattened out under the weight of a newly Christianized Latin. In the centuries following Augustine, Latin came to be seen as the single and sacred language of the church. All other languages were deemed secular in comparison.[8]

At various points across Christianity's long history, however, the church's historic receptivity to linguistic diversity has come roaring back. Think, for example, of Martin Luther's efforts to translate Scripture into a new kind of German comprehensible to prince and farmer alike; or Calvin's choice to write the *Institutes* in both Latin and French; or more recently, the explosion of Christianity in the majority world through Pentecostalism, a branch of Protestantism with its own idiosyncratic approach to linguistic diversity.

In the twenty-first century, most Christians take the translatability of Scripture and the linguistic diversity of the Christian community for granted. As it was for pre-Christian Romans, they regard it simply as a fact of life, as a thing

5. Cicero, *De officiis* 1.53, "Eiusdem gentis, nationis, linguae, qua maxime homines coniunguntur."

6. Frédérique Briville has argued that pre-Christian Romans shunned the concept of multilingualism (a notion capacious enough to hold the languages of humanity together ad infinitum) and instead favored a distinctly Roman alternative: trilingualism (*trilinguis*). Rather than considering all languages together, their preferred notion dealt only with Latin, Greek, and (in an act of condescension) whatever local language was spoken in one's own part of the empire. Briville, "Multilingualism in the Roman World," *Oxford Handbooks Online*, September 10, 2018, https://www.oxfordhandbooks.com/view/10.1093/oxfordhb/9780199935390.001.0001/oxfordhb-9780199935390-e-101.

7. Augustine, *City of God* 19.17.

8. See Christine Mohrmann, "How Latin Came to Be the Language of Early Christendom," *Studies: An Irish Quarterly Review* 40, no. 159 (September 1951): 277–88.

that can unite and divide. While Catholicism initially resisted the Reformation's return to the vernacular, by the mid-twentieth century the Second Vatican Council (1962–65) promoted the use of diverse languages in the celebration of the Mass. In the present day, the church is a thoroughly global, multiethnic, and multilingual community—as it was in the beginning. When this picture is looked at more closely, however, a twofold paradox becomes apparent.

Babel's Shadow

First, it is striking that despite Christianity's multilingual past and present, many Christians (across history and into the current day) take a dim view of linguistic diversity. They regard it as a curse rather than a blessing.[9] Even Luther and Calvin, who championed the practice of theologizing in the language of the people, regarded the existence of multiple languages in stark and negative ways. For Luther, this "seedbed of all evils and discords" was a cause of linguistic division and confusion across the human race.[10] Although Calvin saw the emergence of languages in a more positive light, he nonetheless held that humanity's rapid departure from its monolingual origins was evidence of a terrible divine judgment for sin.[11]

In Christian tradition (broadly construed), Luther's and Calvin's views are fairly standard. They demonstrate the strange and paradoxical reality of a religion that simultaneously embraces and despises its own multilingual nature. Discrete Christian traditions certainly have their own ways of approaching multilingualism. Pentecostals, Calvinists, and Roman Catholics, for example, are each shaped by particular traditions that bequeath quite distinct imaginations vis-à-vis languages. For the most part, however, the Christian imagination toward the existence of multiple languages, across traditions, has been shaped profoundly by a cultural icon: the story of the tower of Babel (Gen. 11). Here, readers conclude, God humbled proud monolinguals by confusing their language. No longer able to understand each other, they abandoned their tower to incompletion.

In tracing the history of the reception of the Babel narrative, Theodore Hiebert notes that even "outside of Biblical scholarship, this reading of the

9. Theodore Hiebert, "Babel: Babble or Blueprint? Calvin, Cultural Diversity, and the Interpretation of Gen. 11:1–9," in *Reformed Theology: Identity and Ecumenicity*, ed. Wallace Alston and Michael Welker (Grand Rapids: Eerdmans, 2007), 2:127–45.

10. Martin Luther, *Luther's Works*, vol. 2, *Lectures on Genesis: Chapters 6–14*, ed. Jaroslav Pelikan (St Louis: Concordia, 1960), 226.

11. John Calvin, *Commentary on the First Book of Moses, Called Genesis*, trans. John King (Edinburgh: Calvin Translation Society, 1848), 331.

Babel story has been given broad cultural legitimacy in classics such as Milton's *Paradise Lost*, in many works of art such as Pieter Brueghel's masterpiece, and in all children's story Bibles."[12] Babel informs the most widely held Christian sensibilities toward multilingualism. Grounded in sin, disobedience, and divine judgment, the Babel narrative has inclined generations of Christians to frame linguistic diversity in negative ways.

Little wonder, then, that Christianity has often struggled to tell its own plurilingual history in positive terms. How could it be otherwise? Why, for example, should the church celebrate the translation of Scripture into Gàidhlig or Ifè? Clearly, having access to Scripture is an obvious good. But, if the Gàidhlig and Ifè languages only exist because of human sin, are there compelling theological reasons to invest considerable resources in strengthening those minority languages through new Bible translations? Why not simply encourage these people to read Scripture in a surrounding majority language (English for the Gaels, French for the Ifè)?

After Babel, what inherent good, if any, might Christians attribute to these minority languages? Is there anything beyond the bare pragmatism of evangelistic opportunity and strategy? The longer one looks at these questions, the more they appear to be a gnarled knot of theological tensions.

From Tower to Garden: Toward a Creational Account of Linguistic Diversity

The second paradox we must discuss is that relatively little theological work has been done to help Christians think constructively about linguistic diversity. For the most part, Christian theologians have done little to help the church move beyond its strange and paradoxical combination of multilingual self-acceptance and self-despair.[13]

In both Judaism and Christianity, deviations from the sin-based and Babel-centric account of linguistic diversity are surprisingly rare.[14] Yet one minority

12. Theodore Hiebert, "The Tower of Babel and the Origin of the World's Cultures," *Journal of Biblical Literature* 126, no. 1 (2007): 29.

13. For an overview of works engaging with this topic, see James Eglinton, "From Babel to Pentecost via Paris and Amsterdam: Multilingualism in neo-Calvinist and Revolutionary Thought," in *Neo-Calvinism and the French Revolution*, ed. James Eglinton and George Harinck (London: Bloomsbury T&T Clark, 2014), 31–60.

14. Hiebert, "Babel: Babble or Blueprint?," 129–30. For an account of attitudes toward the existence of multiple languages in Hasidic Judaism, see Simeon D. Baumel, *Sacred Speakers: Language and Culture among the Haredim in Israel* (New York: Berghahn Books, 2006). Also see Nahum M. Sarna, *Genesis: The Traditional Hebrew Text with New JPS Translation*, The JPS Torah Commentary (New York: Jewish Publication Society, 1989), 80–81.

account has made some progress in that direction: the thought of Calvin and then a branch of the tradition that later bore his name, neo-Calvinism.

Like Luther, Calvin believed that human language became divided at Babel.[15] Unlike Luther, however, Calvin was able to see something good, even godly, moving amid the linguistic diversity of the world. God, Calvin argued, was actively and providentially responding to this plurilingual world with a loving combination of both special and common grace.

By an act of special grace, Calvin thought, the Holy Spirit had enabled the church to communicate and connect across vast linguistic differences. By grace, God "has proclaimed one gospel, in all languages, through the whole world, . . . that they who before were miserably divided, have coalesced in the unity of faith."[16]

By an act of common grace, God continues to give humans the capacity to learn more than one language. In this common and gracious gift, the Holy Spirit empowers people in diverse cultures around the world with the ability to overcome potential hostilities exacerbated by linguistic differences. Through this divine providence the "nations hold mutual communication among themselves, although in different languages."[17]

Moreover, Calvin's interpretation allowed for the possibility that language diversity and development were already taking place organically *before* Babel (Gen. 10, e.g., already records the existence of different languages in vv. 5, 20, and 31). In this, linguistic diversity need not be the exclusive result of sin and judgment.[18] Calvin argued that a good and godly dispersion of humans across the face of the earth—a migration of "those whom the Lord had before

---

15. Calvin, *On the First Book of Moses*, 326.
16. Calvin, *On the First Book of Moses*, 331.
17. Calvin, *On the First Book of Moses*, 331.
18. The significance of Calvin's particular exegesis of Gen. 10–11 is that chap. 10 indicates the presence of divergent human groups that were already spread out in different locations (and that spoke different languages), whereas Gen. 11 deals with one (monolingual) people group in a particular location that is then dispersed (spatially and linguistically) by God's judgment. Exegetes who assert that human diversity, including diversity of languages, was instigated by God's judgment at Babel (in Gen. 11) have historically argued that the respective contents of these chapters should not be understood as chronologically sequential (in the terms memorably described by Sherman as "Dischronology and Flashback"), whereby the events in Gen. 11 occurred first in history but are located after Gen. 10's picture of a dispersed, multilingual humanity as a subsequent explanation of how they came to be so. See Phillip Michael Sherman, *Babel's Tower Translated: Genesis 11 and Ancient Jewish Interpretation* (Leiden: Brill, 2014), 48. Calvin diverged from this interpretation to argue that the chapters were indeed written in chronological sequence and that God was already orchestrating the spread of humanity across the earth—a divine purpose resisted by the proud Babelites. As such, the process of increasing diversity of language appears to have been set in motion regardless of the events surrounding God's wrath at the tower of Babel.

distributed in honour in various abodes"[19]—was already underway before Nimrod and his monolingual band had laid a single brick on the plain of Shinar. As such, while Calvin had committed himself to the view that God had flooded the world with words at Babel in an effort to restrain the progress of sin, Calvin also left the door open to another possibility: *Without Babel, without a fall into sin, a harmonious and holy diversity of languages still would have arisen.*[20]

At this point, the similarities between Luther and Calvin become superficial. Rather than seeing a "seedbed of all evil," Calvin's account of linguistic diversity pointed—albeit very subtly—to the seedbed of Eden's garden. Rather than grounding linguistic diversity in the doctrine of sin (hamartiology), a way is made to ground our many tongues in the doctrine of creation (protology).

Planted in Eden's soil, linguistic diversity could now grow and develop out of God's creational command to the first humans to "be fruitful and multiply." In seed form, Calvin hinted at a theological expectation that God would be glorified by humanity's slowly unfolding diversity and development. Linguistic diversity could be a part of humanity's spread and fruitful multiplication throughout God's creation. Calvin's approach, underdeveloped as it was,[21] signaled an important shift in theological linguistics. Here we see the beginnings of theological praise for linguistic diversity as a phenomenon that pleases and even glorifies God.

Developing a Reformed Theology of Linguistic Diversity

Unfortunately, in the three centuries that followed Calvin, the subtlety of Calvin's exegesis of Genesis 10–11 was scarcely noticed by his Reformed descendants. They, like their Lutheran cousins, carried on with little thought

19. Calvin, *On the First Book of Moses*, 332.

20. As such, the theological starting point of Calvin's account of language diversity becomes less exclusively attached to Babel and the doctrine of sin and judgment. For him, divine judgment explained an unnaturally rapid acceleration in the onset of linguistic change at Babel. Ordinarily, Calvin thought, language changed at a glacial pace. In the absence of divine intervention, one language would not become hundreds of new languages overnight. Rather, its normal pattern of change was gentler, preserving familiarity and a sense of kinship among people groups over centuries, despite their gradually changing ways of speech. Babel was different. There, in an instant, God enforced drastic language change to replace the Babelites' close kinship with utter foreignness. This was a distinct and terrible judgment.

21. Famously, Calvin's extensive production of biblical commentaries did not include a commentary on the book of Revelation, an exegetical task that would have required him to account for the apparent presence of linguistic and ethnic diversity in the eschaton (Rev. 7:9).

toward the aforementioned hamartiological or protological distinctions. In the sixteenth, seventeenth, and eighteenth centuries, the common Christian consensus was that language was created by God to be static in nature and that whatever change had beset it was evidence of God's displeasure in days of yore.[22]

In the nineteenth century, this sleepy Christian accord was shaken violently by a new scientific discipline: evolutionary linguistics. Led by August Schleicher (1821–68), its proponents argued that language existed in a constant process of dynamic change and was best understood in Darwinian evolutionary terms. Language was neither static nor monolithic, Schleicher argued. Rather, it was like a range of living organisms demonstrating development, maturity, and finally, decline.[23] To Schleicher and his supporters, the notion of a normatively monolingual humanity, made multilingual only through divine intervention, flew in the face of their new science. After all, they could point confidently to connections between languages across India and Europe and posit plausible accounts of their shared linguistic ancestry (and predictable patterns of linguistic development).

Some Protestants responded to this new science dismissively and continued to insist on their old static view of language.[24] Yet in the Netherlands a resurgent and modern form of Calvinism was in full swing; there the seeds sown by Calvin's delicate exegesis of Genesis 10–11 finally began to germinate.[25]

The neo-Calvinist Herman Bavinck (1854–1921) offers a prime example of this development in Reformed theological linguistics in his four-volume *Reformed Dogmatics*. Bavinck's protology and his eschatology both address the issue of language and linguistic diversity in ways that are marked by a Calvinesque handling of Babel. Writing within the doctrine of creation, Bavinck argues:

> In Genesis 11, Scripture accordingly traces the origination of languages and of peoples to a single act of God, by which he intervened in the development of humanity. . . . The more savage and rough humanity becomes, the more languages,

22. Eglinton, "From Babel to Pentecost," 33.
23. August Schleicher, "The Darwinian Theory and the Science of Language (1863)," trans. Alexander V. W. Blikkers, in *Linguistics and Evolutionary Theory: Three Essays by August Schleicher, Ernst Haeckel, and Wilhelm Bleek*, ed. Konrad Koerner, vol. 6 of Amsterdam Classics in Linguistics, and in Series 1 of Amsterdam Studies in the Theory and History of Linguistic Science, 1800–1925 (Amsterdam: John Benjamins, 1983), 1–72.
24. For example, Henry Morris, *The Biblical Basis for Modern Science* (Green Forest, AR: Master Books, 2002), 385–406.
25. Elsewhere I have written at length on Abraham Kuyper's interactions with the new ideas presented by nineteenth-century evolutionary linguistics. I have argued that his contributions are best viewed as a complex mix of scientific concern and political expedience. See Eglinton, "From Babel to Pentecost," 45–56.

ideas, and so forth, will take different tracks. The more people live in isolation, the more language differences increase. The confusion of languages is the result of confusion in ideas, in the mind, and in life. Still, in all that division and brokenness unity has been preserved. The science of linguistics has discovered kinship and unity of origin even where in the past it was not even remotely suspected.[26]

On this point, Calvin's influence is palpable. Bavinck thought the development of multiple languages was occasioned by sin and divine judgment. However, Babel is not the whole story of God's dealings with human linguistics. Building on Calvin, Bavinck argues that God continues to intervene graciously in the world's languages, developing, connecting, and bridging linguistic divides. Interestingly, while Bavinck's Calvinist heritage had given him the exegetical resources to affirm the existence of multiple languages pre-Babel (drawing on Calvin's reading of Gen. 10), Bavinck does not seem to have done so here. Regardless of this, Bavinck was no Luddite: he praised Schleicher's new science of linguistics and thought his own exegesis of Genesis was compatible with it.

One of Bavinck's critical contributions to a Reformed theology of language is in placing Calvin's earlier Genesis-based reflections on linguistics into conversation with eschatology and the book of Revelation. In the fourth volume of his *Dogmatics*, Bavinck reflects on Revelation 7 and the many diverse nations of the earth being gathered into the new Jerusalem:

> Undoubtedly the divisions of the church of Christ are caused by sin; in heaven there will no longer be any room for them. But this is far from being the whole story. In unity God loves the diversity. Among all creatures there was diversity even when as yet there was no sin. As a result of sin that diversity has been perverted and corrupted, but diversity as such is good and important also for the church. Difference in sex and age, in character and disposition, in mind and heart, in gifts and goods, in time and place is to the advantage also of the truth that is in Christ. He takes all these differences into his service and adorns the church with them. Indeed, *though the division of humanity into peoples and languages was occasioned by sin, it has something good in it, which is brought into the church and thus preserved for eternity.* From many races and languages and peoples and nations[,] Christ gathers his church on earth.[27]

Bavinck has made an utterly Calvinistic move here. By hook or by crook, God will make something good out of creation and the people of Babel.

26. Herman Bavinck, *Reformed Dogmatics*, vol. 2, *God and Creation*, ed. John Bolt, trans. John Vriend (Grand Rapids: Baker Academic, 2004), 525.

27. Herman Bavinck, *Reformed Dogmatics*, vol. 4, *Holy Spirit, Church, and New Creation*, ed. John Bolt, trans. John Vriend (Grand Rapids: Baker Academic, 2008), 318, emphasis added.

God will encourage a fallen humanity to take part in the creation mandate (Gen. 1:28)—to disperse throughout creation, to multiply, explore, name the creatures, and fill the earth with diverse manifestations of culture and language.

Once a person makes this theological move, a strong stream of ideas necessarily begins to flow. Since God is not the author of sin, his providential introduction of linguistic diversity was not the creation of something sinful. God is not a Father who feeds his children stones or scorpions. Rather, Babel was a divine act, a gracious gift, one that brought a proud people back to God's creational command to multiply, fill, and develop. In dispersing the people of Babel, God sent humanity out into the diverse regions of creation to explore and diversify according to God's creational will. The diversity of human language, Bavinck believed, would have occurred without the fall into sin. In the new creation, furthermore, linguistic diversity will continue to proliferate for all eternity. Here the biblical story of linguistic diversity rests, not simply in Babel, but also in both creation and the eschaton.

Standing on Calvin's shoulders, Bavinck was able to trace out a clear arc across Scripture's story of redemption as it depicts the multilingual *imago Dei*. This biblical arc points not only to a future reality of a harmonious linguistic diversity in the new heaven and new earth but also to a present reality in which God takes great delight in the diversity of human languages in the here and now. Richard Mouw, a Christian philosopher and theologian who stands in Calvin's and Bavinck's line, captures it well:

> God's decision at Babel to scatter the peoples was a regrettable one. It was a necessary response to human rebellion, which meant that historical development moved along very different lines than it would have if sin had not entered human affairs. This does not mean, however, that the sinful development of humankind has produced no good. Indeed, linguistic, racial, and national boundaries have provided the framework for a variety of cultural and social experiments involving the human spirit. When the end of history arrives, then, there is something to be gathered in. Diverse cultural riches will be brought into the Heavenly City. That which has been parceled out in human history must now be collected for the glory of the Creator.[28]

According to this Reformed reading, the Ifè and Gàidhlig languages will be welcomed into the new Jerusalem, to the glory and delight of their creator. In light of this eschatological truth, the present inclusion of Ifè and Gàidhlig in

---

28. Richard J. Mouw, *When the Kings Come Marching In: Isaiah and the New Jerusalem*, rev. ed. (Grand Rapids: Eerdmans, 2002), 86.

the global church today is one concrete way for Christians to anticipate and participate in the multilingual kingdom that is already and not yet.

A Public Theology for Linguistic Minorities

Beyond the church, this approach has considerable consequences for a public theology of language in a globalizing world. How should Christians respond to the public issue of linguistic diversity in general and vulnerable linguistic minorities in particular?

Here I propose the Christian understanding of "creational stewardship" as one way of theologically framing a Christian response. Humanity is called to care for and protect the complexity of God's good creation as it unfolds in all that surrounds us: in its flora and fauna, in the birds of the air and fish of the seas, and in the languages spoken by the sons and daughters of Adam and Eve. Good stewardship of this complex creation is a theological imperative.

Today a large part of humanity has taught itself to grasp, monetize, and devour both creation and human culture for its own economic purposes. The existence of diverse trees, animals, landscapes, peoples, and *languages* is justified in brute economic terms. As a case in point, generations of Scottish children were historically told that their own Gàidhlig language was not "worth" speaking because it was not an economically "useful" language. After all, why learn a language spoken only by "peasants" when one could learn the language of merchants.

In trying to defend the future of the Gàidhlig language, some advocates adopt this language of finance and attempt to play the game of economics. They argue that the Scottish tourist industry could promote the use of Gàidhlig labels for food and drink in an effort to provide tourists with a more "authentic" Scottish experience. Gàidhlig labels, they argue, could be worth many millions of pounds to the Scottish food and drink industry. (Of course, these faux-Gàidhlig branded whiskey and kilt shops—where not a word of Gàidhlig is actually spoken—are more or less irrelevant to the tiny minority of us for whom Gàidhlig remains a living language.)

The doctrine of creational stewardship provides an altogether different approach to vulnerable minority languages, holding that they are to be protected, cultivated, and grown like the diverse flowers of Eden.

To illustrate the point one might ask, If the Great Barrier Reef were to die, should such a death matter to Christians? It should, but not primarily for reasons of finance. Rather, the death of the reef should matter because, above all else, its complex ecology exists for the flourishing of the earth and the glory of God. Its beauty and complexity have no price. The same is true of minority languages—even those labeled "financially unviable."

The roots of this idea are much older than John Calvin. In the fifth century, Augustine, a Christian keenly aware of the linguistic power dynamics of the Roman Empire, publicly defended the Punic language—a minority tongue spoken in the rural areas surrounding Carthage.[29] Although Punic had formerly been an economically important language within the once-great Phoenician Empire, by Augustine's time its rural use was dwindling under the urban and imperial pressure of Latin.

Well aware of this, Augustine defended and furthered this beleaguered language. He approvingly quoted Punic proverbs (and translated them into Latin for non-Punic speakers). Augustine campaigned for theological translations into Punic. He even petitioned Pope Celestine for the appointment of a Punic-speaking bishop in the Punic-speaking region around Fussala.[30] In response to the pagan grammarian Maximus's insults toward the apparent backwardness of parents giving their children Punic names in a Latin world, Augustine wrote, "If the Punic language is rejected by you, you virtually deny what has been admitted by most learned men, that many things have been wisely preserved from oblivion in books written in the Punic tongue. Nay, you even ought to be ashamed of having been born in the country in which the cradle of this language is still warm, *i.e.* in which this language was originally, and until very recently, the language of the people."[31]

Augustine's public defense of an endangered minority language was made in a context where the linguistic heavyweights of Latin and Greek were jostling for dominance in the empire, and Punic's rural existence was gravely under threat.[32] Indeed, the last historical reference to Punic as a living language comes from Augustine's writings on it: within a century of his lifetime, it had all but died out. The theological rationale for his public defense of an ailing minority language was not fleshed out in detail. That lacuna, however, might be filled in by the reflections on multilingualism found in the Augustinian writings of Calvin and Bavinck. It is perhaps no great surprise that those who stand on their shoulders—Mouw being a prime example—find themselves to be public advocates of linguistic diversity for distinctly Christian reasons.

29. On the history of Punic, see Charles R. Krahmalkov, *A Phoenician-Punic Grammar* (Leiden: Brill, 2001), 10–14.

30. M'hamed-Hassine Fantar, "Death and Transfiguration: Punic Culture after 146," in *A Companion to the Punic Wars*, ed. Dexter Hoyos (Hoboken, NJ: Wiley-Blackwell, 2015), 462.

31. Cited in Mark Ellingsen, *The Richness of Augustine: His Contextual and Pastoral Theology* (Louisville: Westminster John Knox, 2005), 9.

32. Hugh Elton, *Frontiers of the Roman Empire* (Bloomington: Indiana University Press, 1996), 25.

3

African Decolonization and Reformed Theology

NICO VORSTER

John Calvin famously described sin as "blindness."[1] Here in South Africa, my own vision was recently challenged by a group of young and mostly Black students protesting about exclusionary practices in our universities. Through raised voices, the students sought to open the eyes of their fellow students and professors to the frustrations and challenges they experience. This, of course, is standard fare for any student protest. But there was a deeper reality that my own blinded eyes needed to behold and consider. I can try to examine and understand oppressive structures from above. But I can never visualize those structures with the same clarity as those who see them from the underside. If Calvin is right, if sin is "blindness," someone else needs to help me see.

African decolonization discourse claims that patterns and practices of power, solidified during the colonial period, continue to determine the continent's image of itself as well as its practices, experiences, and social structures. The discourse identifies this state of being as "coloniality."[2] Conversely,

1. John Calvin, *Ioannis Calvini Opera quae supersunt omnia: Ad fidem editionum principium et authenticarum ex parte*, ed. J. Guilielmus Baum, A. Eduardus Cunitz, and Eduardus W. E. Reuss, Corpus Reformatorum (Berlin: C. A. Scwetschke & Son, 1863–1900), 2:49.
2. Coloniality depicts "long-standing patterns of power that emerged as a result of colonialism, but that define culture, labour, intersubjective relation and knowledge production well

African *decolonization* signifies a wide-ranging interdisciplinary effort to overhaul, liberate, and transform previously colonized societies. The ultimate goal is to reorganize the global matrixes of power and rid African societies of all forms of "coloniality."

In this chapter I put a variety of decolonial discourses into a dialogue with the Reformed theological tradition. Appropriately, the dialogue runs in two directions. I hope to explore not only how the Reformed tradition might contribute to these decolonial discourses but also how the Reformed tradition might learn from these important discourses.

From my introductory anecdote, it is clear that my reflections do not come from a place of cultural, racial, or theological neutrality. I have inevitably been influenced by my own background, which is Reformed, white, and South African, but I aspire to present a fair perspective on the topic. Decolonialism is an urgent question in South Africa and around the world. Christian communities are wrestling with how they should respond to it. As more and more cultures wrestle with these questions, the Reformed tradition has no choice but to engage with decolonial discourse.

Two Strands of Thought

As in most academic discourses, decolonial theory comes in all shapes, sizes, and nuances. They range from the moderate to the radical and extreme. Up to the present time, two major traditions of decolonial thought have taken shape in the African academy. These two traditions have gathered around the groundbreaking work of two figures: Frantz Fanon and Ngũgĩ wa Thiong'o. The Fanonian rendering largely concerns itself with the psychological, political, and socioeconomic liberation of Africa. Ngũgĩ's rendering largely focuses on the epistemological and linguistic impact of (de)colonialism in Africa. The two strands of thought do not exclude one another: they share basic premises and commitments. That said, their agendas differ to some degree.

The Algerian psychiatrist and political philosopher Frantz Fanon (1925–61) was concerned with the ways in which the "perverse logic" of colonialism created pathologies among Africans.[3] He contended that colonialism caused

---

beyond the strict limitations of colonial administrations." Nelson Maldonado-Torres, "On the Coloniality of Being: Contributions to the Development of a Concept," *Cultural Studies* 21, nos. 2–3 (2007): 243.

3. See Walter D. Mignolo, "Delinking," *Cultural Studies* 21, no. 2 (2007): 450.

Africans to internalize inferiority complexes.[4] For, he argues, if outsiders project a certain image on a people consistently enough, those persons will likely adopt that image and make it their own. In the case of Africans, the image projected was one of being colonized and living in a space of servitude.[5]

Fanon suggests that Africans need to consciously liberate themselves from these colonial pathologies. He criticizes the nationalist liberation movements that gained power in the postcolonial period of the 1950s and 1960s. Fanon argues that they merely mimicked the chauvinistic and racist conduct of colonialism.[6] For true liberation, every colonial structure and system needed to be completely destroyed—through violence if need be. Nothing could remain. Only then could radically new structures be erected that serve the interests and reflect the perspectives of the wretched (French: *damnés*).[7]

True decolonization, he argues, could materialize only if a "certain species of men" are replaced by "another species of men."[8] In other words, Africa needs a new mode of human existence.[9] For Fanon, decolonization begins with "self-ownership," with taking power back from others and protecting that power, by force if necessary.[10]

Since the 1970s many African intellectuals and activists[11] have elaborated on the basic tenets of Fanon. Persistent themes include the radical and comprehensive overthrow of colonial structures, critiques of postcolonial governments that mimic the racist and oppressive conduct of colonial regimes, efforts to develop a Black consciousness liberated from negative colonial stereotypes, the importance of reforming the iconography of public spaces, resistance to

4. See Frantz Fanon, *Black Skin, White Masks*, trans. C. L. Markmann (New York: Grove, 1967); Fanon, *The Wretched of the Earth*, trans. Constance Farrington (New York: Grove, 1968).

5. To be "acceptable" in a colonized society, Africans were inclined to adopt "a white mask" by assimilating into European colonial values. Fanon identifies the Western Christianity exported to Africa as integrally complicit in colonizing the Black psyche. Fanon, *Wretched of the Earth*, 42.

6. See Achille Mbembe, "Decolonising Knowledge and the Question of the Archive," lecture series delivered at the Wits Institute for Social and Economic Research in 2015, https://africa isacountry.atavist.com/decolonizing-knowledge-and-the-question-of-the-archive.

7. Frantz Fanon, *Towards the African Revolution*, trans. Haakon Chevalier (New York: Grove, 1967), 36. Also see Mignolo, "Delinking," 458.

8. Fanon, *Black Skin, White Masks*, 35.

9. According to Mbembe, Fanon understands by "a new species of men" a new category of human not "limited or predetermined" by appearance, respected for who they truly are. Mbembe, "Decolonising Knowledge."

10. Mbembe, "Decolonising Knowledge."

11. Most notably Steve Biko, Barney Pityana, Achille Mbembe, Nigel C. Gibson, and Sabelo J. Ndlovu-Gatsheni.

global capitalism, and the development of a grassroots form of democracy that gives a voice to the poor.

Decolonizing Language

The work and witness of the Kenyan novelist and academic Ngũgĩ wa Thiong'o (1938–) focuses on the need for decolonization in the areas of epistemology, linguistics, and education. According to him, the European colonial powers did more than divide, arrange, and dominate Africa through the hard power of politics; they also used the soft power of language and education.

Ngũgĩ argues that language and education are carriers of cultural, political, and psychological power. Consider, for example, that the complex tongues, tribes, and cultures of Africa came to be seen (and see themselves) as either English-speaking, French-speaking, or Portuguese-speaking.[12] The colonial imposition of European languages and education on the African people allowed imperial powers to control the "mental universe of the colonised."[13] Through language and education, Ngũgĩ argues, colonialism alienated African children from their own cultural and natural environments. These pedagogical and linguistic systems portrayed Europe as the center of the cultural universe and further aggravated Africa's sense of alienation.[14] Thus "the child was now being exposed exclusively to a culture that was a product of a world external to himself. He was being made to stand outside himself to look at himself."[15]

In response to this, Ngũgĩ calls for the decolonization of knowledge, which he describes as "the search for a liberating perspective within which to see ourselves clearly in relation to ourselves and to other selves in the universe."[16] He advocates an African cultural renaissance in which teaching, studying, and writing in African languages take center stage. The self-image of Africans would be repaired through the cultural power of linguistics and education. It would open up "new avenues for our creative imagination."[17] Ngũgĩ's foundational insights on decolonial epistemology have inspired the works of many other intellectuals and activists in Africa and beyond.[18]

12. Ngũgĩ wa Thiong'o, *Decolonising the Mind: The Politics of Language in African Culture* (Nairobi: Heinemann, 1986), 5.
13. Ngũgĩ wa Thiong'o, *Decolonising the Mind*, 16.
14. Ngũgĩ wa Thiong'o, *Decolonising the Mind*, 17.
15. Ngũgĩ wa Thiong'o, *Decolonising the Mind*, 17.
16. Ngũgĩ wa Thiong'o, *Decolonising the Mind*, 87.
17. Ngũgĩ wa Thiong'o, *Decolonising the Mind*, 73.
18. Examples are Kwasi Wiredu and Vuyisile Msila, as well as South American decolonization philosophers such as Walter D. Mignolo, Rámon Grosfoguel, and Aníbal Quijano. Prevalent themes here are the quest for connecting knowledge to transformative practices, utilizing

African Decolonization Theology

As the winds of political revolution and liberation swept through the continent in the 1960s, African theology needed to respond. Christian theologians developed contextual African theologies that not only addressed the needs and longings of Africans but also creatively engaged Africa's religious and cultural heritage. Various theologians made attempts to theologically connect, translate, and bridge the divide between traditional African religions and key Christian concepts.

Other theologians considered these bridging efforts to be too moderate. Strongly influenced by Frantz Fanon, theologians like Steve Biko and Dibinga wa Said agitated for a more radical and authentically African theology. They sought a new theological method that would not simply repeat Western doctrines in African guises but also would offer difference in both substance and form. Thus they questioned African Christianity's allegiance to Western missionaries, who imposed a "white Jesus" and "white God" on Africans. They criticized the African church's uncritical appropriation of a "white theology."

Dibinga wa Said depicts colonialism as a project of enslavement. According to Said, Jesus of Nazareth was on a mission of decolonization of sorts: in Luke 4:18–19 Jesus states that he came to the earth to set free those in bondage.[19] Citing Fanon, Said claims that Christians need to enact a decolonial "programme of disorder." Violence in the name of decolonization, he argues, may very well constitute an appropriate form of Christian action.[20]

The South African political activist Steve Biko argues that Christian theology should never be practiced in abstract, universal terms; it must always be contextual and situational in nature. The task of Black theology is to relate God to the daily experiences and sufferings of Black people.[21] God deliberately created Black people black. Black people therefore need to free themselves from the sense of inferiority that colonialism imposed on them and ascertain God's unique will for Black humanity.[22]

---

precolonial sources of knowledge, delinking intellectual thought from universalist metanarratives, striving after a pluriversality that recognizes the legitimacy of a variety of epistemologies, and promoting learning through lived experience, that is, gaining knowledge from the experiences and choices that a person makes. Some of these topics are also eminent in African decolonization theology.

19. Dibinga wa Said, "An African Theology of Decolonization," *Harvard Theological Review* 64, no. 4 (1971): 503.

20. Said, "An African Theology of Decolonization," 503.

21. Steve Biko, *I Write What I Like: Selected Writings*, ed. Aelred Stubbs (Chicago: Chicago University Press, 2002), 59.

22. See Graham Duncan, "Steve Biko's Religious Consciousness and Thought and Its Influence on Theological Education, with Special Reference to the Federal Theological Seminary of

Writing in apartheid South Africa, Biko is highly critical of the institutional church and its complicity in maintaining white power and privilege.[23] Biko accuses the church of being obsessed with individual sins yet meanwhile ignoring evil's perpetual transmission through unjust structures.[24] Biko is critical of denominations that have a largely Black membership and yet are mostly controlled by white clergy. He agitates for the decolonization of denominational structures and encourages Black people to take control.[25]

Various theologians followed Biko and Said in their efforts to address the self-image of Black people, to relate Christ to Black experiences, to liberate Black people from oppressive colonial structures, and to change ecclesiastical leadership and structures.[26] Though they do not necessarily typify their theologies as "decolonial," the basic premises of Fanon are part and parcel of their theological method.

A new chapter in decolonial theology, influenced by Ngũgĩ's strand of epistemological decolonization, was introduced with the 2015 rise of the Fallist movements for the transformation of higher education.[27] Theologians followed suit: the work of earlier decolonization philosophers and theologians gained new traction, and novel theological questions emerged for discussion.

Renewed criticism was leveled at Western distinctions between the spiritual and physical, private and public, the natural and supranatural.[28] African theologians generally find these binary categories unintelligible and problematic. They perceive them as separating subject from object, the knower from the known, as if we can "know the world without being part of that world."[29] To know something requires engagement; we cannot observe something (or someone) objectively from a distance. God's world cannot be compartmentalized into categories; creation is interconnected, dynamic, intrinsically spiritual, and reciprocal.[30]

South Africa," in *The Legacy of Stephen Bantu Biko: Theological Challenges*, ed. Cornel W. du Toit (Pretoria: UNISA Research Institute for Theology and Religion, 2008), 3.

23. Biko, *I Write What I Like*, 56.

24. Biko, *I Write What I Like*, 56–57.

25. Biko, *I Write What I Like*, 59.

26. Here we could mention Alan Boesak, Gwinyai Muzorewa, Manas Buthelezi, and Kwesi Dickson.

27. Teddy Chalwe Sakupapa, "The Decolonizing Content of African Theology and the Decolonization of African Theology: Reflections on a Decolonial Future for African Theology," *Missionalia* 46, no. 3 (2018): 406–7, 417.

28. See Kwasi Wiredu, "Toward Decolonizing African Philosophy and Religion," *African Studies Quarterly* 1, no. 4 (1998): 19.

29. Mbembe, "Decolonising Knowledge."

30. See Pascah Mungwini, "The Question of Recentering Africa: Thoughts and Issues from the Global South," *South African Journal of Philosophy* 35, no. 4 (2016): 531.

Decolonial theologians are deeply suspicious of grand metanarratives that make totalizing claims and espouse "absolute truths." They accuse these discourses of engaging in "epistemological colonialization" by forcing human thought into fixed systems while marginalizing other narratives.[31] In response, they propose that Africans *de-link* their epistemologies from Western metanarratives. Rejecting universality, theology must strive for *pluriversality*.

For some, "de-linking" demands a total abandonment of dialogue with Western theology and an exclusive reliance on the wisdom of precolonial indigenous societies. For others, it does not negate dialogue, but it does denote an active exploration of the resources that indigenous knowledge systems offer and a critical examination of the ways in which African Christians uncritically adopt Western frameworks.[32]

A third theme in African decolonial theology is "epistemic justice." This relates to a number of related efforts, including the desire to read Scripture through an African lens, the desire to rewrite African church history from the perspective of the colonized, and the desire to transform theological education to reflect the decolonial mission.

When it comes to biblical hermeneutics, decolonization theologians follow liberation theologians in supporting a reader-oriented approach to Scripture, utilizing social location, specifically the colonial setting, as a heuristic device. Hulisani Ramantswana, for instance, holds that Scripture needs to be read from the perspective of the *damnés*.[33] This, he argues, is a liberating act of "dethroning whiteness."[34]

In theological education, epistemic justice attempts to counter the curricular hegemony of Western theology and epistemology. Decolonial theologians argue that the curricula should be rooted in African realities and that Eurocentric theology should be shifted to the periphery.[35] They also propose a bottom-up learning process that is grounded in transformative praxis that involves grassroots communities as active participants in the process of knowledge creation.

---

31. Mungwini, "Question of Recentering Africa," 528.

32. See Wiredu, "Toward Decolonizing African Philosophy," 22; Mungwini, "Question of Recentering Africa," 530.

33. The social location of "whiteness" in postcolonial societies is, according to Ramantswana, one of privilege and "structural advantage," while the position of blackness is governed by oppression, discrimination, and inequality. See Hulisani Ramantswana, "Decolonising Biblical Hermeneutics in the (South) African Context," *Acta Theologica* 24 (2016): 182–84.

34. Ramantswana, "Decolonising Biblical Hermeneutics," 184.

35. See Nontando M. Hadebe, "Commodification, Decolonization and Theological Education in Africa: Renewed Challenges for African Theologians," *HTS Teologiese Studies* 73, no. 3 (2017): 6.

Reformed Theological Affirmation

Decolonization theology offers several insights that Reformed theologians can and *must* affirm. Its critique of dualist categories of Western thought is critical. The Enlightenment's view of the world as a "thing" outside of us that we can objectively observe, know, and control has cultivated an instrumentalist ethos in which moderns seek to master and control both nature and society. These categories make us prone not simply to epistemological blindness but also to ecological, cultural, and political violence.

Reformed theology, rightly understood, should encourage a humble epistemology and a chastened form of human reason. The noetic effects of sin on the fallen human mind are real. Outside the gates of Eden, Reformed epistemologies, rightly conceived, emphasize the not-yet reality of human knowing. The tradition's emphasis on the epistemological and noetic effects of sin should support decolonial efforts to unmask idolatrous "mastering" narratives that impose hegemonic utopian ideals on societies.

Calvin's powerful critiques of human reason are as relevant today as they were in the sixteenth century. For Calvin, knowledge is always related to the predicament of the sinful self. Sin affects our reasoning faculties and exposes us to "misunderstanding." Detached from God, reason tends to idolize itself and to create "all kinds of spectres in the place of God."[36] Calvin's basic insight serves as a reminder that social scientists and theologians alike need to guard against bold epistemological attempts to explain or "control" natural and political environments through the use of human reason.[37] Reformed theologians can and must wholeheartedly support decolonial investigations into the ways in which sinful patterns of thinking contribute to injustice.

A second important feature of decolonization theology is its commitment to defending and restoring the dignity of the oppressed. This theme is prominent in the Christian canon, specifically in the Gospels and prophetic literature, and—rightly understood—should occupy a central place in Reformed theological reflection. Calvin himself insisted that civil authorities have a duty to protect the freedoms of citizens and to treat all persons, including the poor, as equal before the law.[38] He considered love of the poor and the refugee to be an integral part of the Christian life. Calvin grounded the universal reach of Christian love in the fact of humanity sharing one flesh, being universally

36. Calvin, *Opera*, 2:9.
37. See Nico Vorster, *The Brightest Mirror of God's Works: John Calvin's Theological Anthropology* (Eugene, OR: Pickwick Publications, 2019).
38. Calvin, *Opera*, 5:354.

created in God's image.[39] In a sermon on Deuteronomy 24:14–18, Calvin specifically addresses the connection between poverty and injustice. He argues that poverty is, in part, due to the rights of the poor being violated. Calvin cautions the rich and well-fed, "The cries of the poor rise up to heaven, and we must not think to be found without guilt before God."[40]

Reformed theologians can also learn much from decolonization theorists about the psychological and social pathologies at work within systems of oppression.[41] Doing justice to the poor, as Calvin taught, requires that we explore the psychological and political pathologies of colonial oppression.

The value that decolonization theologians place on indigenous and vernacular cultures and languages is a position that the Reformed tradition can and should support. From the very beginning, Calvinism has been a multinational and multicultural tradition. In its first decades the tradition moved through France, Switzerland, the Netherlands, Scotland, and England. Linguistic translation, cultural adaptation, and locally specific governance was a central concern from the very beginning. The Reformed tradition allowed for cultural, theological, and ecclesiastical diversity across those nations and especially emphasized the importance of translating the Bible into vernacular languages and preaching and proclaiming the Word in the native languages. This Reformed sensitivity to and interest in cultural pluriformity urgently needs to be revived.

African languages contain a wealth of idioms, wisdom sayings, and proverbs that offer profound philosophical and theological insight to the global church.[42] Reformed theology can enrich itself by engaging with and learning from these indigenous systems. Unfortunately, Reformed preaching in Africa has not always succeeded in engaging indigenous worldviews and knowledge systems properly. Too often, African congregants were expected to employ Eurocentric-styled liturgies during worship services and typical Western-style meeting procedures at synods and church-assembly gatherings.

Decolonization theology rightly calls the Reformed tradition to self-critique about its own complex complicity in the colonial project. Although the tradition made important political contributions to the development of

39. Calvin, *Opera*, 37:330. See Vorster, *Brightest Mirror of God's Works*, 86.
40. John Calvin, *Sermons on Deuteronomy: Facsimile of the 1583 Edition*, trans. Arthur Golding (London: Banner of Truth Trust, 1987), 1716; Calvin, *Opera*, 28:188.
41. This is specifically relevant when it comes to the harm that oppressors can do to others by projecting a negative image on them, the dangers involved in mission work that conflates religious values with cultural customs, the ways in which social structures can dehumanize human beings, and the pathologies created by excessive sin doctrines.
42. Since these African offerings cannot always be directly translated into European languages, a new theological effort to revive and engage African languages and narratives is needed.

fair and just political orders in Europe, the same cannot be said for the Reformed faith that was exported to the colonies. In South Africa, Calvinist doctrines around predestination, covenant, and sphere sovereignty were all distorted by proponents of apartheid to justify racial segregation and injustice.[43] Doctrines of sin positing the total destruction of the *imago Dei* after the fall were used to counter efforts to extol human rights.[44] Reformed denominations of 1600–1900 showed little interest in countering the slave trade: many Reformed congregants participated in and perpetuated the monstrous evil. No theological system is immune to the temptations of social oppression. *A discipline of listening to those from the underside of power is absolutely critical for the global future of Reformed theology.*

A Reformed Theological Critique

Reformed and decolonial methods of theology are not natural bedfellows. For starters, they begin with different hermeneutical premises. Classical Reformed theology begins with the divine authority and inspiration of Scripture. Decolonial theologians generally approach Scripture with a measure of suspicion. They consider it to be a potential source of reflection and a model for experience, rather than an infallible or divinely inspired text. Decolonial hermeneutics is a strongly reader-oriented process. Social location is used as an authoritative hermeneutical tool to generate new horizons of divine revelation. These new horizons may surpass the original intent of the biblical text.[45]

Reformed hermeneutics, on the other hand, emphasizes a wrestling with the original message of the text, the intent of the biblical authors, the historical context, and the structural-textual considerations of the passage such as its genre, literary devices, and so on. Reformed scholars may very well employ reader-oriented methods, but they view the imposition of excessive meaning on the text as a hermeneutical danger that needs to be cautiously avoided.

This is where Reformed hermeneutics offers a word of warning to their decolonial brothers and sisters. First, radically reader-oriented approaches

43. See John de Gruchy, *Apartheid Is a Heresy* (Grand Rapids: Eerdmans, 1983); Robert R. Vosloo, "The Bible and the Justification of Apartheid in the 1940's in South Africa: Some Historical, Hermeneutical and Theological Remarks," *Stellenbosch Theological Journal* 1, no. 2 (2015): 195–215; Nico Vorster, "Christian Theology and Racist Ideology: A Case Study of Nazi Theology and Apartheid Theology," *Journal for the Study of Religions and Ideologies* 7, no. 19 (2008): 144–61.

44. See Vorster, "Christian Theology and Racist Ideology," 149.

45. Decolonizing readers might also wish to subvert biblical passages that are undergirded by ancient power interests.

to Scripture can easily lead to abuse of texts and eventually even to an abuse of other people. When the original intent of biblical authors is no longer regarded as a checking mechanism, new forms of violence can emerge. Second, a deliberately subjective interpretation of Scripture makes constructive dialogues and debates with other Christians impossible. Subjective interpretations cannot be challenged on objective textual grounds. When I selectively use biblical passages that suit my decolonizing agenda and reject those that do not share my claims from the outset, I risk becoming so elusive that others cannot engage me as an interlocutor.

From a Reformed point of view, Fanon's decolonial justification of violence as a means to subvert oppressive structures is potentially problematic. To be sure, the Reformed tradition is not pacifist in orientation. Historically, it has supported the just-war tradition by arguing that, under certain extreme conditions, violence can be justified for the sake of justice, order, and peace. The Catholic massacre of Protestants following Bartholomew's Day in 1572 inspired Reformed theologians and jurists such as Theodore Beza (1519–1605) and Johannes Althusius (1557–1638) to develop a theological defense of resistance.[46] A decade or two after the massacre, Althusius argued that God, the prince, and the people stand in a covenantal relationship with one another. He believed that both the prince and people are obligated to "render justice to each other."[47] If a prince transgresses the terms of God's covenant, he becomes a tyrant. Once a tyrant, he can be forcefully removed by lower magistrates. For the Reformers, this potentially violent process of removal should go through a legal governmental process and should seek restoration of social order.[48]

Despite being open to violent political resistance under extreme circumstances, the Reformed tradition does not allow space for the more anarchic and expansive revolutionary violence permitted by Frantz Fanon. Fanon's notion of social resistance is concerned with the total subversion of an existing social order and the creation of a revolutionary new one from the ground up. Having a more chastened view of human nature, Reformed political theology argues that political revolutions (even ones with great ideals), when combined with unchecked anarchic violence, will fail to establish a new heaven and a new earth. More than likely, these revolutions will only further the forces of injustice, violence, and instability.

Serious questions also need to be asked of the highly racialized nature of decolonization discourse and the theology it produces. Decolonialism

---

46. David P. Henreckson, "Resisting the Devil's Instruments: Early Modern Resistance Theory for Late Modern Times," *Journal of the Society of Christian Ethics* 38, no. 1 (2018): 43–57.
47. Henreckson, "Resisting the Devil's Instruments," 47.
48. Henreckson, "Resisting the Devil's Instruments," 47–48.

rejects nonracialized language, considering it to be a neutral discourse that conspires to deny the realities of racial oppression and uphold the status quo. In contrast, it affirms race as a, if not *the*, determining factor in African society, discourse, and analysis,[49] in which "blackness" is associated with being oppressed and disadvantaged, and "whiteness" is identified with racial oppression and privilege.

But is there not something "essentialist" in the way decolonization theorists go about defining their opponents through the lenses of "whiteness" and "blackness"? Does their essentializing social analysis really accord with contemporary reality? Historically, white Africans have indeed benefited from colonialism, but do they all really wield the overbearing kind of social power as alleged by decolonization theorists? Factually speaking, they constitute a small minority in sub-Saharan Africa, they have lost substantial political power, and their upward social mobility has been significantly curbed by postcolonial affirmative-action legislation, land reforms (especially in Zimbabwe), and Black empowerment programs.[50] The vast complexity of cultural and political dynamics in Africa makes it increasingly problematic to simplistically use race as representing advantage and disadvantage.

The same kind of question arises when it comes to decolonial theology's simplistic dismissal of all Western intellectual discourse. Can we typify all Western thought as an overbearing and oppressive metanarrative that does not tolerate alternative epistemologies? Surely Western discourse entered the postmodern and globalized era long ago. What we call "Western discourse" is increasingly becoming plural, diverse, fluid, and permeable as a result of postmodern deconstruction and globalization. In the same way, Western theological discourse is not the monolithic oppressive Other as often depicted by the decolonial theologians.

A final critique pertains to the plausibility of decolonization theology's aim to purify its sources of knowledge, to return to a precolonial indigenous theology. Graham Ward summarizes this "reversal project" as "peeling away the colonial layers to get at the precolonial kernel of the kerygma, often in terms of the original language of the people." But he describes the project as "highly naïve" because reality does not consist of simple layers of super-

---

49. Nico Vorster, "Reformed Theology and Decolonised Identity," *HTS Teologiese Studies* 74, no. 4 (2018): 5.

50. See Theuns Eloff, "The Historical and Recent Sociopolitical Context for Considering Racism and Related Concepts in South Africa," in *Togetherness in South Africa: Religious Perspectives on Racism, Xenophobia, and Economic Inequality*, ed. Jan Du Rand, Koos Vorster, and Nico Vorster (Pretoria: Aosis, 2017), 1–28; Ferial Haffajee, *What If There Were No Whites in South Africa?* (Johannesburg: Picador Africa, 2015).

structures and substructures. Knowledge functions more like an ecosystem, with "ever shifting sets of intricate relations."[51] We never can make "clean" decolonized breaks between the "past and present."[52] On the contrary, once we start the "peeling away," at the end of the process we risk being left with nothing.[53]

Reformed theologians would agree with Ward. While Reformed theology emphasizes the importance of *semper reformanda*, it also recognizes the work and wisdom of the Holy Spirit in past generations. Throwing the past away is not an option. Yes, we must rearticulate our faith in every new context, but we cannot simply discard the wisdom that the Christian tradition has developed throughout the ages. Like it or not, we stand on the shoulders of past generations. Yes, they were sinfully blind, but so are we.[54]

Conclusion

Decolonization theology poses critically important challenges to the Reformed faith, questions worthy of consideration and needing to be answered: What public role did Reformed doctrines play in oppressive colonial structures? What role does it need to play in the reformation of those structures today? What does it mean to be Reformed in non-Western contexts? How should Reformed hermeneutics deal with reader contexts?

Dialogue with non-Reformed traditions, narratives, and experiences is absolutely critical for the vitality and faithfulness of the Reformed theological imagination. When a tradition insulates itself from outside critique, unhealthy patterns of thought and unjust patterns of public behavior set in.

John Calvin was right: our sins blind us. We struggle to see our power and privilege; we struggle to see the unjust structures that prop us up and push others down. In our sinful blindness, we dare not ignore the reports of those on the underside: Christ may well be using them to open our sinful eyes. The critique of outsiders can sting. It can feel like mud and spit shoved in our eyes. But, as we see in the Gospels, Christ will use these things to make the blind see.

---

51. Graham Ward, "Decolonizing Theology," *Stellenbosch Theological Journal*, 3, no. 2 (2017): 561–84, here 577.

52. Ward, "Decolonizing Theology," 574–75.

53. Ward continues to argue that the "reversal project" is itself a deeply "colonial project that simply replicates, albeit in a different fashion, colonial mentality." For him it is akin to the demythologization project of Rudolf Bultmann and other Enlightenment rationalists who wanted to put the Dark Ages aside to get to an unadulterated kerygma. Ward, "Decolonizing Theology," 576–78.

54. See Cornelis van der Kooi and Gijsbert van den Brink, *Christian Dogmatics: An Introduction* (Grand Rapids: Eerdmans, 2017), 65–66.

4

The Dutch and Death

Pastoral Observations and Theological Reflections

MARGRIET VAN DER KOOI AND CORNELIS VAN DER KOOI

Who commands the levers of life and death? Who decides when a life has been "fully lived"? Euthanasia is a topic of heated debate in many countries and cultures around the world. This chapter focuses on the Netherlands, a country that is famous (or notorious) for its progressive and experimental approach to the end of life. The cultural context of the Netherlands merits theological reflection on this matter because, in many ways, it represents the cultural vanguard of secular and modernist medical ethics. The Dutch, after all, were the first people in the world to legalize euthanasia in 2001. In a globalizing world, the questions currently being asked in the Netherlands will, no doubt, be asked elsewhere.

We hope to outline a few of the central questions arising in the Dutch context regarding end-of-life questions and the medicalization of modern society. Throughout the chapter we place those questions into a creative conversation with Reformed theology.

As coauthors, we are both native Dutch citizens and pastors within the local Reformed community. We offer these theological reflections from two different pastoral vantage points. Margriet has worked as a hospital chaplain for forty years. She has sat and prayed with countless patients and their families as they have made difficult decisions regarding the end of life. Kees (Cornelis) has worked as a pastor for eight years and taught systematic theology for twenty-seven years. Since we are a married couple, questions about death and its relationship to Reformed theology have been a household topic of conversation for many years.

We begin with a brief story that illustrates an attitude about death prominent in some Dutch circles today. Margriet will offer other stories from her experience as a chaplain as well. Her narratives stand alongside Kees's theological exposition, yet not as mere ornamental decorations: these people and their profound experiences are theologically informative in and of themselves.[1]

I (Margriet) was invited to speak at a local church on death and the "completed" life. I usually begin these presentations by asking the audience a simple question: "What made you put on your coat and come here tonight?" On this evening a friendly looking older woman put up her finger. "I'll start," she said. "Our grandson recently asked me something that probably summarizes why I am here. His other grandmother is suffering from Alzheimer's. She has put it in writing that, when her family feels her life is 'completed,' it will be time to end it. My grandson then turned to me and asked, 'Will you ask for a shot when you feel like you're too old?' I did not know how to respond to my grandson. Can the complex questions and struggles of life and death be resolved with a simple injection?"

Death in the Netherlands

When children are raised to believe that an injection is the way to solve the "problem" of old age, sickness, and suffering, what can we say about the surrounding cultural milieu? This brief story reveals two important aspects of discourse surrounding euthanasia in the Netherlands. First, the Dutch are relatively open and candid in their discussions about life and death. Second, many of them tend to view these discussions through the hermeneutical lenses of secular modernism, autonomous choice, and individual control. I decide when my life is "complete." I decide when I have nothing left to offer. I decide when and how it will end.

1. In this presentation we attempt to honor the narrative approach of Richard Mouw. In his addresses, articles, and books, stories are frequently used, not as an ornament or example, but as a critical aspect of a wider theological discourse. The narratives function as a generous way of reaching out and building bridges over cultural and ideological divides. Mouw's narrative approach is grounded in theological soil: the doctrine of common grace. God's benevolence and goodness does not stop at the boundaries of the Christian church. The world and its fullness are the Lord's. His light and grace may surface everywhere, and Christian theology should be ready to notice and value it.

Dutch culture is obviously far more complex than simply being blunt or individualistic, modern or secular. We are a nation containing many minority cultures and faiths. International news stories about euthanasia in the Netherlands regularly exaggerate its scale and cultural meaning. Simplistic portrayals of the Dutch will not do. Therefore, before we reflect theologically on the euthanasia, we need to attend more carefully to the complex culture that has brought the issue to the global fore.

Medicalization

Modern medicine's ability to alter and extend human life has grown exponentially over the past century. Previously fatal diseases and chronic forms of illness and pain have been overcome through advances in medical science and technology. While medicine played a relatively limited role in nineteenth-century Dutch life, today it feels almost omnipresent. The healthcare industry is enormous. As medicine's power and reach expand, investment in medical technology, reliance on medical treatment, and trust in medical professionals continue to grow. Many Dutch citizens now expect their every illness or injury to be overcome through the power of medical technique. As the scope and power of medicine expand, our lives are becoming increasingly *medicalized*.[2]

The increase in our technological ability to extend life, though truly welcome, only increases the ethical question of how and when a life *ought* to be extended.[3] Here medicalization runs into a moral and spiritual dead end. Medicine is incapable of defining the "completed" life. An X-ray machine cannot tell us when it is time to die. A radiologist cannot train us to die well. With each passing year, the medicalization of our modern society raises more and more questions—questions it cannot answer.

Secularization

Dutch society has secularized rapidly since the 1960s. The center of national discourse surrounding medical ethics has shifted from Christianity to modern

2. See James Kennedy, *Een weloverwogen dood: Euthanasie in Nederland* (Amsterdam: Bert Bakker, 2002).

3. During the nineteenth century, major illnesses and injuries would normally take one's life rather quickly. Medicine was relatively powerless to resist the force of death. Today, medicine has the ability to keep bodies breathing and hearts pumping despite tremendous amounts of physical trauma. Dutch families now face difficult end-of-life decisions that their nineteenth-century ancestors never could have imagined.

individualism. Today *the* sacred value is an individual's sovereign control over their body, life, and (for our inquiry) death. Individuals should have the right and the ability to define and control a good life, and even a good death.

Before secularization, the "good life" in the Netherlands was largely circumscribed by one's community and church. An individual's life (and death) was defined and bounded by certain religious norms—norms that were larger than individual preferences. With the 1960s the national understanding of the "good life" began to shift dramatically. Increasingly the "good life" was defined as an *individual* life that was long, healthy, happy, free, and authentically one's own. Dutch society reorganized itself to protect and produce this sort of authentic and autonomous life. Individuals now enjoy generous access to medical care, welfare, social security, and education for all. These systems were designed to protect and empower individuals to make their own choices and live their own lives.

By the end of the twentieth century, the secular belief that the "good life" is one that you freely choose for yourself led to a second conclusion: the "good death" is one that you freely choose for yourself. The 1960s generation, the young people who waved the revolutionary flags of individual freedom, were growing older. As they aged, they carried their dogmas about personal empowerment into the hospital and began to demand power over their death. The 1960s generation and its secularizing narrative looms large within the political, moral, and cultural imagination of the Dutch. This all played an influential role in the legislation that followed.

The Law on Euthanasia

In 2001, after a long national debate, the Netherlands passed the *Wet op levensbeëindiging* (The law regarding the termination of life).[4] Throughout the 1980s and 1990s, doctors were increasingly being asked and pressured to end lives. The public closely followed and debated several lawsuits on the matter. These court cases confronted the public with the daunting reality of age, sickness, suffering, and death. Public debates and conflicts increased. In the end, the public decided that, rather than having euthanasia exist secretly in the shadows, they needed a law to ensure that people engaged in the practice with transparency and care, in the light of day.

As a general rule, euthanasia remains illegal in the Netherlands. The 2001 law makes *exceptions* to the general rule for situations of "unbearable and

---

4. Before 2001, doctors in the Netherlands were forbidden from participating in assisted suicide, though some small medical exceptions existed.

futureless suffering."[5] It should be no surprise that this rather vague language has left the law open to both subjective interpretation and public uncertainty. Some doctors are afraid that a judge will convict them of misinterpreting this ruling or abusing the exception. Some patients misunderstand the law as a carte blanche allowance for euthanasia at any time.[6]

Theological Reflections

How should Dutch Christians respond to all of this? What theological resources can chaplains and pastors reach for as they sit with families in hospital rooms? There is not enough space to say everything that needs to be said. However, in what follows is a number of key theological resources available within the Reformed tradition. These resources have been invaluable for us as we have served among the living and dying here in the Netherlands.

Putting Medicine in Its Place

Christians cannot forever ignore the inevitable reality of sickness, age, and death. People are finite. Medical technology can function as a convenient and tempting way for Christians to avoid difficult but important discussions about their own mortality. While Christians are young, strong, and healthy, they can largely avoid wrestling with their own finitude and God's sovereignty over it. But, as the writer of Ecclesiastes reminds us, we must "remember our Creator" in the days of our youth, "before the days of trouble come and the years approach when you will say, 'I find no pleasure in them'" (12:1).

My father was dying. The worst part was that, even at the very end, my parents and I still could not talk openly about what was happening. It still exhausts me. We could not

5. The doctor may only act on the request of the patient and must take into consideration several carefully outlined requirements.

6. In recent years some political liberals have advocated making euthanasia completely legal. They argue that individuals should have the unmitigated freedom to choose when they want to end their lives. At the moment there is not enough support for complete legalization. A recent government study, however, questions the "freedom" under which some individuals make these choices. They found evidence that these choices are sometimes made rashly, during momentary experiences of anxiety and disappointment. See E. van Wijngaarden, G. van Thiel, I. Hartog, et al., *Perspectieven op de doodswens van ouderen die niet ernstig ziek zijn: De mensen en de cijfers* [Perspectives on the death wish in older people who are not severely ill: The people and the numbers] (Den Haag: ZonMw, 2020).

talk about anything important. When my father got ill, my parents were distraught. They spent all of their time on their computers, looking for new treatments and alternative therapies. They focused on the search for a cure. It was their everything. They spent a fortune. They were always traveling and searching. They never stopped. They never wanted to ask, "Is this wise?" We could never just talk about it. The regular doctors did not advise this endless searching, but my parents said it was their only hope. Their only hope! I had hoped to talk with my father about his life, about us, about me, about leaving this life, the things he was proud of, what he regretted, and so on. But no, nothing of this. Nothing of the comfort that the Heidelberg Catechism teaches us, that "I am not my own, but belong—in life and death, body and soul—to my faithful Savior Jesus Christ." That was not what they were dealing with now. It was totally gone. It was all about drugs, vitamins, and therapy. I was and am deeply disappointed.

Instead of hiding from the bitter reality of death, Reformed theology can help Christians face their finitude and place their mortality within the light of Christ's resurrection. This resurrection light does not deny or soften the sting of death, nor does it cover it up or ignore it. Instead, resurrection reframes death within Christ's larger light and life. Here we offer three brief examples from three Reformed voices: John Calvin, Karl Barth, and Abraham Kuyper.

Life during the sixteenth century was, as Thomas Hobbes later quipped, "nasty, brutish, and short." John Calvin, like all pastors at this time, was very frank about people's mortality; the pastors had to be so. Neither Calvin's theology nor his ministry attempted to hide from the grim omnipresence of sickness, suffering, and death. As we read Calvin from the relative comfort of modernity, his candid theological reflections on suffering and death strike our ears as rather rough and rude.

In the face of medieval pain and suffering, Calvin did not adopt a stoic apathy or a resigned detachment. Instead, he asked what Christians might learn from these inevitable realities of life. More importantly, he explored how, in suffering, a heart might be redirected toward the true fountain of eternal life.[7] For Calvin, sickness and suffering, rightly conceived, could direct a disciple's desires and longings toward their true home. Herein the believer

---

7. This ongoing communion with Christ was Calvin's deepest motive for his vehement defense of the immortality of the soul in his *Psychopannuchia*, a work that he already wrote in 1534, before his breach with the Roman Catholic Church, and was published in 1542 as *Vivere apud Christum non dormire animis sanctos* (Strasbourg: Rihel). See also John Calvin, *Institutes of the Christian Religion*, ed. John T. McNeill, trans. Ford Lewis Battles, 2 vols. (Philadelphia: Westminster, 1960), 3.9; Heiko A. Oberman, "Calvin's Legacy: Its Greatness and Limitations," in *The Two Reformations: The Journey from the Last Days to the New World*, ed. Donald Weinstein (New Haven: Yale University Press, 2003), 116–68, especially 126–27.

learns that, even amid great loss, they gain something that can never be taken away: immediate and unending communion with Christ.[8]

For Karl Barth, human beings are created as finite creatures, meant to live in a loving and trusting covenant with God. Their finitude is not evil: it is a created good. Through sin, the covenant is broken and humanity's finitude suddenly becomes a threatening reality, a curse. Because of sin, death is now a haunting and unwelcome reminder of the judgment of God and our estrangement from him.

But Barth also argues that the universal human experiences of sickness and death have a second side. In itself, death is an aspect of our chaotic rebellion against God, a sign of divine wrath, "from which there is no deliverance apart from the mercy of God in Jesus Christ."[9] And yet, in this last phrase the other side of death is revealed. Within the experience of death, we encounter divine deliverance in our absolute dependence on the gracious initiative of God. Through reliance on Jesus Christ as the face of God and his final word of mercy, a disciple can face sickness and death while laying their finite lives in God's gracious hands.

This absolute dependence does not mean that Barth propagates a stoic or spiritual quietism toward sickness and death. Divine initiative should not produce human resignation. Barth saw the active pursuit of science and medicine as an important aspect of God's creation, a gift of God in Jesus Christ. Precisely *because* they are divine gifts, medical sciences and technology should be developed as a part of human culture and activity.

This point about the divine goodness of medicine, science, and technology was made with great clarity and force by Abraham Kuyper and later twentieth-century neo-Calvinists.[10] For them, if God wills the health and flourishing of human bodies he created, Christians should follow that divine lead and take steps to improve health and bodily flourishing. Advances in medical science; hidden medicines in plants; the care, creativity, and wisdom of doctors—all these are evidences of God's mercy and common grace for a creation that is groaning with sickness and death.

This positive attitude toward medicine did not compete with Kuyper's strong emphasis on a person's absolute dependency and reliance on the

8. See John Calvin, *Calvini Opera quae supersunt omnia: Ad fidem editionum principium et authenticarum ex parte*, ed. J. Guilielmus Baum, A. Eduardus Cunitz, and Eduardus W. E. Reuss, Corpus Reformatorum (Berlin: C. A. Scwetschke & Son, 1863–1900), 5:177–232.

9. Karl Barth, *Church Dogmatics*, III/4, *The Doctrine of Creation*, ed. G. W. Bromiley and T. F. Torrance, trans. A. T. Mackay et al. (Edinburgh: T&T Clark, 1961), 366–67.

10. See particularly Abraham Kuyper, *Common Grace: God's Gifts for a Fallen World*, ed. Jordan J. Ballor and Stephen J. Grabill, trans. Nelson D. Kloosterman and Ed M. van der Maas, 3 vols., Collected Writings in Public Theology (Bellingham, WA: Lexham, 2015–20), vol. 2, especially chap. 68, on the means to combat suffering and illness.

sovereignty of God. Kuyper's mutual regard for both these elements can be seen in his own life. Kuyper strongly advocated for the training of Christian doctors and the development of science and medical technology. He and many others established a medical school at their Reformed university precisely for this purpose. Kuyper also wrote passionately about his ultimate longing to "be near unto God" in his daily devotionals.[11] Drawing from the spirituality of the Psalms, Kuyper argued that the ultimate end of life was to abide in the shelter of God's wings. To be *with God*, even in the shadow of death.

While Barth and Kuyper elevated the goodness of modern medicine, neither of them deified it. Medical technology was not God: it was a gift of God. Health and youth are good things; they are not the only thing. Here Reformed theology demands that we make a careful distinction between the creation and the Creator. Looking to modern medicine as our savior is an example of that confusion.[12]

A tension is clearly developing between the Reformed desire to rest in the sovereign will of God and the modern desire to rest in the power of medical technology and the medicalization of human frailty. Calvin, Barth, and Kuyper want to put the dying Christian into direct relationship with the living God in Christ. They want to invite the dying Christian to seek a deeper and prayerful refuge in Christ, the only place where the human heart and body can find ultimate rest.

Those holding to this Reformed vision do not wish to discard modern medicine: they want to put medical care in its rightful place. Positioned within the larger economy and mission of God, medicine can be cherished as a gift from God. Doctors and nurses can alleviate sickness, pain, loneliness, and fear. In many ways, they echo Christ's gentle and healing nature.

Medical professionals do not, however, replace Christ or the healing and life that only he can give. Indeed, medical professionals of all faiths do not appreciate it when patients impose salvific expectations on their work. These professionals do not flourish in medicalized cultures that attribute godlike qualities to them. Putting medicine in its proper place is not only honoring to the Great Physician; it also enables human physicians, patients, families, and chaplains to collaborate effectively and graciously as they journey together through human experiences of sickness and death.

11. Abraham Kuyper, *To Be Near unto God*, trans. J. H. deVries (Grand Rapids: Eerdmans-Sevensma, 1918); Kuyper, *In the Shadow of Death: Meditations for the Sick-Room and at the Sick-Bed* (Audubon, NJ: Old Path, 1994). These are only two of the several titles under which some of Kuyper's meditations were published.
12. Barth, *Church Dogmatics*, III/4:367–68.

Life and Death in the "Not Yet"

Not understanding "what time it is" within God's story can be dangerous when it comes to our experiences of aging, sickness, and death. Unending youth, complete health, and eternal life are not yet. Those things will not come until God's final consummation of creation. Not understanding that we presently live in the not-yet portion of God's story cultivates human anxiety and disappointment.

Without this critically important qualifier, our experiences of aging become shot through with added pressure and intensity. Happiness and success must be achieved right now, in this present life. Sickness, old age, and death must be kept at bay—at any cost. Christians in Western countries like the Netherlands often fall into this modern trap. Resisting their own finitude, they make high-pressure "bucket lists" of the things they must do in this present life. Failing to rely on God's timing, they frantically resist aging. Placing our lives within God's not yet releases the pressure on the present.

Without this qualifier, youth and health become an idol and a slave driver. The natural experiences of aging, suffering, and sickness are no longer opportunities to grow deeper in union with Christ; they are ultimate battles that must be waged and won. In this way, Reformed theology challenges this idolatry of the present. It tells us "what time it is" within God's larger story. It positions our present suffering within God's past, present, and future work. Herein God's temporal work of creation, redemption, sanctification, and consummation frames our present experiences of sickness and death.

Unfortunately, some Christians struggle to see the larger story. They fixate on one moment within the story. Some expect immediate healing because they are living in the age of the resurrection or the age of the Holy Spirit. But the resurrection of Jesus Christ was not the final victory, nor was his exaltation, nor was the outpouring of his Spirit. God's story is larger than all these. More has happened and more will happen.

In this, Reformed theology helps us make these important temporal distinctions in the story of our lives and the story of our God. It helps us know the difference between the already and the not yet. In short, it helps us "tell time." In doing so, we are better prepared to place our present suffering and death within the larger story of God's grace. Knowing that the final battle against death will be God's, not ours, puts medicine in its proper place. It allows us to rest and be grateful for what medicine can, at present, do.

Finally, within this present not yet, the church has a mission with those who are dying. In praying for the sick and anointing the suffering, the church carries frail human bodies before the face of the life-giving God.[13] Healing might occur, by God's grace and mercy, but the essence of the church's mission at the end of life is prayer. Through prayer, the church offers its finitude, frailty, and fear to God, the source of life and hope. This is the task of the church.[14]

Make no mistake: in a medicalized society such a mission is profoundly countercultural. This ministry refuses to surrender the final moments of sickness and death to the complete sovereignty of the medical practice. The church has its own practice. Its practices of prayer, anointing, and worship remind patients, families, and doctors alike of the greater sovereignty and mercy of Jesus Christ. These practices put medicine and suffering in their proper place—and time.

Moral Ambiguity

Living and dying in the not yet means that the answers are not always clear. End-of-life decisions often involve experiences of moral ambiguity.[15] People of all faiths—and no faith—often have no idea how they should proceed. Feelings of ambiguity and confusion are always difficult, but they are particularly challenging when a loved one is sick and dying. We want to do the right thing, and yet no clear path has presented itself. No clear voice has spoken. The doctors are asking questions, but there is no clear answer.

Waiting and listening is hard. We want to decide. We want to act. But sometimes the human preference for action over contemplation needs to be resisted.

An eighty-six-year-old woman was brought into the hospital with a broken hip. She can no longer speak clearly. Sitting at her bedside, her daughter explains that her mother had gotten lost again. Her daughter suggests that a psalm and prayer would be a comfort. As her chaplain, I happily oblige. Soon a young female surgeon comes to the room. The question on the table is whether this woman should undergo hip surgery. Grabbing a stool and taking a seat, the surgeon makes it clear that she is in no hurry to make a decision. The surgeon's whole body communicates patience and calm. There is no rush. In my heart I applaud her. The surgeon gently explains to the daughter that hip surgery will be a dramatic, invasive, and risky experience for her mother. The anesthesia alone may heighten her current levels of confusion. She counsels the daughter that there is

13. The metaphor of anointing is the unused wiring in the house of Reformed theology. See Cornelis van der Kooi, *This Incredibly Benevolent Force: The Holy Spirit in Reformed Theology and Spirituality* (Grand Rapids: Eerdmans, 2018), 99–101.

14. Cf. Allen Verhey, *Remembering Jesus: Christian Community, Scripture, and the Moral Life* (Grand Rapids: Eerdmans, 2002), 114–15.

15. Verhey, *Remembering Jesus*, 115.

absolutely no rush for a decision, and she recommends that the family wait for a few days to see how her mother responds. The daughter leans over and tells her mother that she will stay with her in the hospital. I give her mother a blessing and pray for both daughter and mother.

When I returned the following morning, the old lady had just passed away. I'm grateful for that young doctor. She responded to the ambiguity with patience rather than action. She knew her craft: always comfort patients, often alleviate their pain, and sometimes cure them. The family was grateful that their mother was spared a painful and dramatic surgery: she did not die on a cold operating table; she died being caressed and blessed, held and surrounded by those she loved. That is good care.

In the face of ambiguity, we sometimes need to resist the temptation for action and accept the ambiguity as a divine invitation to wait, listen, and contemplate.

Conclusion

Although we have been critical of Dutch medical culture, we should close with a point of praise and hope. More and more doctors and families in the Netherlands are opting for less intervention and medicine at the end of life. Instead of filling their final months with desperate and dramatic surgeries, medicines, and treatments, patients are increasingly choosing to have quality time with their loved ones. The cultural preference for quality over quantity is steadily increasing.

The Christian practices of faithful listening, contemplation, and reliance are never easy—especially in times of suffering and death. At the end, when we don't know how to proceed, we may be helped by a prominent metaphor in Calvin's life and theology: pilgrimage.[16] According to Calvin, believers are pilgrims, exiled travelers in the middle of a journey home. The pilgrimage is uncertain, and it is finite. When we are young, strong, and healthy, caught up in the questions of life, career, family, and friendships, we tend to forget its finitude. We do not have the patience to think of it. But sometimes our lives are interrupted; the future of our journey becomes uncertain. We find ourselves cresting a hill, approaching an unknown horizon. In times like these, the liturgy of the old Dutch Reformed worship service offers assurance for the journey ahead: "He will not forsake the works of his hands."

16. Cf. Oberman, "Calvin's Legacy," 156–65.

5

Religious Pluralism in Indonesia

Reformed Reflections

N. GRAY SUTANTO

Indonesia: the largest Islamic country in the world. This is perhaps the most common way of describing the country of Indonesia in global media. While it is true that Indonesia is the most populous Muslim-majority nation in the world, the country institutionally recognizes and protects the freedoms of six of the world's major religions: Islam, Catholicism, Protestantism, Buddhism, Hinduism, and Confucianism. Moreover, because the many islands and regions that comprise Indonesia are separated by seas and difficult terrain, each indigenous culture has developed distinct religious trajectories. Although the major parts of Java, Aceh, and Lombok, for example, adhere to Islam, Bali remains a largely Hindu island; and the Manadonese, Bataks, and Ambonese have largely adopted Christian values and beliefs. There is also diversity within each island. For one example, Northern Bali—the area closest to Menjangan Island—is more economically and socially in touch with the population of East Java and thus hosts a Muslim-majority population, separated as they are from the rest of the Hindu-majority island by a large mountainous area. Professing Christians, both Catholic and Protestant, make up about 10 percent of the country's population, a not insubstantial number

71

of about twenty-five million people.[1] This picture thus makes Indonesia one of the most religiously diverse nations in the world, so much so that in 2016 *The Atlantic* published an extensive article attributing the lack of ISIS recruits from Indonesia—in contrast to the number of ISIS recruits from Western Europe and the Middle East—in part to the nation's emphasis on the "freedom of expression," fostering the sense that violence is unnecessary to propel the preferred worldviews of the local communities.[2]

Indeed, my own person is reflective of this diversity. I was born of Chinese-Indonesian descent. My father is an agnostic Confucianist, and my mother is a professing Roman Catholic. I'm a Reformed Protestant, and my wife and her family were Muslims before they converted to Christianity. I grew up with secularist friends who fasted with their Muslim neighbors merely out of friendly solidarity, and we all took holidays in Bali and visited Hindu temples for recreation. I visited my ancestors' temples during Chinese New Year and paid my respects to my wife's Muslim grandparents at Eid al-Fitr. Weddings, too, were ceremonially interreligious. Partners with Catholics and Protestants in their families would celebrate dual weddings to appease both parties: one Roman Catholic-styled wedding and the other Protestant, and in different churches. Clearly, pluralism is part and parcel of the Indonesian imagination.

The development of this diversity is made possible by the "five principles," called *Pancasila*, that make up the foundations of Indonesia's constitutional and public philosophy. The brainchild of President Sukarno, the first president of the Republic of Indonesia, the principles were generated for the purposes of satisfying Islamic, Christian, and secular nationalists. The five principles are these: (1) the belief in a supreme deity, (2) the dignity of all humanity, (3) the unity of Indonesia as a nation, (4) the implementation of wise democracy, and (5) the prioritization of social justice. The first principle concerning the worship of the supreme deity further entails that religion is a matter between the individual and God and that expressions of worship specific to each religion are all publicly recognized ways of relating to this God.

These five pillars are enforced by law to be proliferated in schools and read aloud monthly in flag ceremonies around the country. Together these principles inculcate a kind of civil religion that prioritizes the diversity of religious expression in order to promote the welfare and unity of the nation. The national motto, "Bhinneka Tunggal Ika" (Unity in Diversity), enshrines these

1. For an extensive survey of the history of Christianity in Indonesia, see Jan Sihar Aritonang and Karel Steenbrink, eds., *A History of Christianity in Indonesia* (Leiden: Brill, 2008).

2. Edward Delman, "ISIS in the World's Largest Muslim Country: Why Are So Few Indonesians Joining the Islamic State?," *The Atlantic*, January 3, 2016, https://www.theatlantic.com/international/archive/2016/01/isis-indonesia-foreign-fighters/422403/.

values; the people groups should collaborate for national unity in a manner that preserves their respective ethnic, cultural, and religious identities. While the coexistence of such explicitly pluralist public ideals with the aspirations of the majority Muslim population and other exclusivist religions—including orthodox Christianity—has often created tensions and social unrest, they have decisively "positioned Indonesia as neither a secular nor an Islamic State, but a religious or Godly state."[3]

These public ideological conditions are ripe for fruitful reflection on the part of the Reformed theologian. What follows here are reflections suggesting that (1) Christians globally can learn from the inherently *limiting* function of Pancasila for the Christian faith, and that (2) these public principles require specifically *Christian* theological grounds if they are to be carried out practically and articulated coherently. While a Christian citizen might be tempted to respond to these pluralistic realities in Indonesia with a triumphalist outlook, in order to "take back" the country for Christ, I argue for a measured, positive, yet theological stance toward them. Indeed, I suggest that Christianity offers Indonesia's constitutional pluralism a firm basis from which it could be implemented and that Pancasila as a civil framework reminds Christians of the exilic themes of Scripture that are often muted in the attempts to grasp or maintain a cultural stronghold for Christianity in the West. Hence, I suggest that Reformed theology allows Indonesian Christians to respond to Pancasila with both appreciative theological gratitude and yet offer a useful Christ-centered critique.

This chapter thus moves in three steps. First, it sketches the limitations that Pancasila has placed upon Christians and the common triumphalist reactions that arise in reaction to those limitations. Second, it canvasses a Reformed alternative in response to Pancasila and in contrast to triumphalism. Finally, the chapter closes with some reflections on the specific theological identity of the divine deity that Pancasila seems to require for it to empower citizens to live peacefully in religious diversity.

3. Chang-Yau Hoon, "Religious Aspirations among Urban Christians in Contemporary Indonesia," *International Sociology* 31 (2016): 416. On the complexity of the coexistence of Pancasila, secularism, Christianity, and Islam, see also Hoon, "Between Evangelism and Multiculturalism: The Dynamics of Protestant Christianity in Indonesia," *Social Compass* 60 (2013): 457–70; Karel Steenbrink, "Muslim-Christian Religions in the *Pancasila* State of Indonesia," *Muslim World* 88 (1998): 320–52; Steenbrink, "Towards a *Pancasila* Society: The Indonesian Debate on Secularization, Liberation and Development, 1969–1989," *Exchange* 54 (1989): 1–28. In an attempt to ward off communism, "The New Order Administration actively promoted religious affiliation. . . . Every Indonesian was required to register a religion to which they adhered." Chang-Yau Hoon, "Mapping 'Chinese' Christian Schools in Indonesia: Ethnicity, Class, and Religion," *Asia Pacific Education Review* 12 (2011): 405.

Pancasila's Limits and Christian Triumphalism

Christians in Indonesia have the state-sanctioned right to gather, worship, and propel their doctrinal convictions in coexistence with the believers of other faiths. However, we need to keep in mind that Pancasila has an inherently *limiting* and pluralist aim. That is, while Indonesia's civil philosophy protects the freedom of Christians to worship, it also ensures that Christianity remains only one among many public religious expressions in the country. A few public policies manifest this limiting aim. The first is the Joint Decree No. 1 in 1969, a law issued by the Minister of Religion and Home affairs, who controls and monitors the ability of churches to construct buildings for worship spaces. The 1974 Marriage Law effectively disallows religious intermarriages: partners now need to prove that they both adhere to the same faith by, say, producing baptismal certificates for proof of conversions (these certificates would be issued by the church in which one was baptized) or by showing an identical religion on their ID cards. Laws have also restricted the entrance of foreign workers for religious and educational institutions to avoid the advancement of one religion over another and to ensure that the development of religions is locally motivated.

In other words, Pancasila and the decrees of the Indonesian Ministry of Religion ensure that Christianity would not be an all-dominating cultural force that it often aims to be in some global contexts. It is easy to approach these conditions with a cynical mindset that these laws are merely established to ensure that the majority religion remains in control; yet on paper they are meant to communicate the right of each religion to coexist and to preserve its vitality within the country. Again, Indonesia's democratic model and public-theological philosophy is inherently limiting: it protects all the major religions and seeks to preserve their distinct expressions within the country, thus curbing the ambitions of any one religion from monopolizing, even as it ensures their continued existence. Islam might be the nation's majority religion, and hence its powerful presence will remain a major influence in Indonesian public discourse and policy making, but at least on paper, Islam will not be an enforced state religion.[4]

---

4. The influence of the Islamic majority is especially seen in the passing of laws that delimit non-Islamic religious influences. As Hoon summarizes, the state, driven by worries concerning Christianity's seemingly rapid growth, "issues various legislations to curb Christian activities, including religious propagation, receiving foreign aid, inter-religious marriage, and building places of worship." "Religious Aspirations," 417. This means that converted Christians need to provide evidence to the state that they have indeed converted, in the form of formal baptismal certificates, in order to marry another Christian, since the identification cards of both partners need to indicate a homogenous religion. Western missionaries also often enter the country by registering themselves as English teachers rather than religious workers.

Perhaps unsurprisingly, these conditions form a source of anxiety among Christians, such that some Christians may desire to find ways of strategically resisting these limiting boundaries. The most common way of manifesting this is by a triumphalism that seeks to take over the city for Christ's name by way of capitalist shrewdness and strategic pragmatism. In Indonesia the National Prayer Network and Transform World Connection have propelled a particular theology of the kingdom of God that is often referred to as the "Seven Spheres Movement." It has a formal resemblance to a Reformed understanding of the public space as comprising the life-spheres of the arts, science, and state. Yet according to this movement, Christians have the duty to take over the different spheres of life now and to keep these spheres under their authority in preparation for Christ's return. Having its roots in the thought of American evangelical theologians like Bill Bright (1921–2003) and Loren Cunningham (1935–), this movement targets the business class of Indonesian urban societies for their own strategic purposes. As Hoon aptly summarizes:

> The Seven Mountains Theology maintains that Christians are biblically mandated to control all earthly institutions until the second coming of Christ. The seven mountains of culture are adapted and abbreviated in alphabetical order from A to G: Arts, media, and entertainment; Business and marketplace; Church; Development of the poor; Education; Family; and Governance. These seven spheres foreground a new type of Christian movement in Indonesia that attempts to transcend denominational divides and penetrate Christian values into *all* sectors of society. This movement is ambitious, combative, well-organized, and resourceful. Its urban focus endeavors to capture the aspirations and imaginations of the nation's emerging urban middle class. It also claims to offer a counterbalance to the social, familial, and moral degradations and polarizations experienced in a city amid forces of rising intolerance and Islamic conservatism in Indonesia. . . . The discussion will also reveal the Pentecostal character of the movement, raising the question of whether being "transdenominational" is an aspiration rather than a reality.[5]

The movement emphasizes that God's favor upon one's life consists in the gain of health and wealth. Proliferated by healing rallies, capitalist expansion, and even by TV soap operas, the Seven Sphere movement is quickly becoming a major influence within the business class and finds an ally in the prosperity gospel that is proliferating throughout the world. The Full Gospel Business Men's Fellowship International is one manifestation of this movement and has utilized their wide business networks to propel this kingdom-oriented

5. Hoon, "Religious Aspirations," 421.

theology. While this theology might formally adhere to the principle of the lordship of Christ in order to motivate its project, a Reformed account provides a stark alternative on precisely christological grounds.

A Reformed Alternative to Triumphalism

What alternative does a Reformed perspective provide within the backdrop of Indonesia's civil religion? The triumphalist public-theological movement outlined above has only a formal resemblance to a properly Reformed account of public engagement. Instead of this civil religion, which believes that all the world religions ought to be preserved and coexist with their particularities intact, causing anxiety in the minds of Christians, I suggest that it approximates the kind of vision that Kuyper and Bavinck imagined.

Indeed, the Reformed vision is subtle yet powerful. We proclaim that Christ is sovereign, *not* Christians, and that it is *his* timing and *his* prerogative to bring about the unity of every life sphere in the last days. A few key concepts within the Reformed tradition flow from this basic christological insight: common grace, the stages of God's plan within history, and the character of the new heaven and the new earth.

In a post-fall world prior to the second coming of Christ, Christians live in an era of common grace, where Christ rules the world by forbearance and patience, willing for none to perish and for all to hear the gospel. Until he returns, Christians live in an exilic outpost, seeking the good of their earthly cities while being citizens of another kingdom. To seek to be the cultural and political monopoly or to bring about the kingdom now is a misunderstanding of the Christians' mission and place in God's redemptive-historical plan. The state, then, has its own "sovereignty," a "sphere sovereignty" that understands its nonredemptive purpose while realizing that it exists precisely to "permit the Kingdom of God to affect and to penetrate its people and nation."[6] In Kuyper's understanding, Christ alone has the sovereignty and right to judge the value and worth of the differing religious directions of the diverse communities in the nations. The state, then, cannot be an "octopus, which stifles the whole of life"; instead, its honor is precisely in the maintaining of "every form of life which grows independently in its own sacred autonomy."[7]

The kingdom of God, in other words, is witnessed to not by any one specific nation embodying it but by the exiled citizens of heaven in the dispersion of

6. Herman Bavinck, "The Kingdom of God, the Highest Good," trans. Nelson D. Kloosterman, *The Bavinck Review* 2 (2011): 160.

7. Abraham Kuyper, *Lectures on Calvinism* (Grand Rapids: Eerdmans, 1953), 96–97.

every tribe, nation, and tongue. A Christian understanding of the state realizes that the state's goal is that of creating space and of *permitting* the various life spheres to coexist, while realizing that the perfect unity-in-diversity of the life spheres can only be achieved in the new heaven and new earth. Only Jesus's return can establish a global theocracy. The new city is a kingdom not progressively brought about by Christian political effort but by God himself in a decisive epochal shift that recreates the world and brings about the eschatological new creational order.

In that sense, Pancasila and "Bhinneka Tunggal Ika" convey, perhaps unintentionally, a view of public philosophy attuned to where we are in God's plan in history. This challenges Christian attempts to secure their public privileges or remain victors of some cultural war. Western Christianity, as expressed in some of the political efforts of the Christian Right in the USA, might be missing this vision of a Reformed neo-Calvinistic public theology that understands its present existence as that of an exile witnessing to a better city rather than a redemptive agent bringing about that city down here on earth. This redemptive-historical understanding of seeing this present age as an "evil" age (Gal. 1:4), in labor pains and waiting for the fullness of God's redemption (Rom. 8), curbs Christian ambitions that might resort to ethical compromise in order to "win" some public or cultural war for Christ. In other words, this age is not the time of God's fully realized eschatological kingdom, but of his patience. The attempt to secure God's kingdom now by way of capitalist strategy or by resorting to ethical compromise, then, shows misunderstanding of the present era within God's plan for history.

Moreover, contrary to the wholly transformationalist endeavors of the Seven Sphere movement, Herman Bavinck emphasizes that the future eschatological order is brought about by divine power alone. Indeed, the new Jerusalem's "architect and builder is God himself"[8]: mistaking the material gain of the present world as the glories of the kingdom of God greatly underestimates the fullness of eschatological glory. Instead of mandating Indonesian Christians to take over the different spheres of society and to rule them in anticipation of Christ's return, Jesus desires that Christians engaged in the different spheres of society seek the neighbor's good and proclaim the gospel by means of Word and Spirit, not by political sword or by shrewd capitalist expansion. The utilization of ruthlessly pragmatic business practices and political maneuvering, then, runs counter to the command to lay our lives down for our neighbor and to suffer virtuously, with Christ as our example.

---

8. Herman Bavinck, *Reformed Dogmatics*, vol. 4, *Holy Spirit, Church, and New Creation*, ed. John Bolt, trans. John Vriend (Grand Rapids: Baker Academic, 2008), 720; cf. Heb. 11:10.

Christianity thus offers fruitful resources for an outward-looking faith. Notice that particularly *Christian theological ground* aids the coherent implementation of the pluralist ideals of Pancasila. This is the second reflection. A theologically attuned public theology informs an account of the state. The state's sovereignty is to protect the freedoms of the people and thus enable the development of the *structural diversity* of society. Although it is the state's role to preserve justice and ensure that citizens can enjoy the structures of schools, marketplaces, and the arts, the state would be overstepping its bounds if it tried to determine the *directional* trajectories of these structures. A state's proper functioning thus allows a healthy directionally pluralistic society to develop. This understanding of the state thus cuts across attempts at enforced ideological uniformity from any specific worldview, whether Christian or secularist. Christians who expect a theocratic unity now certainly misunderstand their role in society and project an overrealized eschatology into the present order. Secularists who enforce their nontheistic worldviews through the state unduly bind the freedom of conscience and systematically suppress the sense of divinity within all humanity.[9] For Kuyper, Calvinism therefore is a "Source and Stronghold of Our Constitutional Liberties."[10] Perhaps counterintuitively, then, an emphasis on *specific* Christian revelation as an epistemological principle actually results not in a constraining force of uniformity but rather in a theologically anchored support for principled pluralism.[11] This account sits comfortably with the ideals of Pancasila and gives it a firm grounding.[12]

9. J. H. Bavinck's analysis of the relationship between general revelation and religious diversity remains one of the most incisive. See especially J. H. Bavinck, "Religious Consciousness and Christian Faith," in *The J. H. Bavinck Reader*, ed. John Bolt, James Bratt, and Paul Vissers (Grand Rapids: Eerdmans, 2013), 277–301. I draw out the continuities between Herman Bavinck (1854–1921) and his nephew Johan Herman Bavinck (1895–1964) on general revelation: Nathaniel Gray Sutanto, "Neo-Calvinism on General Revelation: A Dogmatic Sketch," *International Journal of Systematic Theology* 20 (2018): 495–516.

10. Abraham Kuyper, "Calvinism: Source and Stronghold of Our Constitutional Liberties [1874]," in *Abraham Kuyper: A Centennial Reader*, ed. James Bratt (Grand Rapids: Eerdmans, 1998), 277–322.

11. Harry Van Dyke calls this ideal an "institutionalized worldview pluralism" in his "Translator's Introduction" to Guillaume Groen van Prinsterer, *Unbelief and Revolution*, trans. Harry Van Dyke (Bellingham, WA: Lexham, 2018), xxvi. For a contemporary exposition of the Kuyperian ideal of pluralism applied to some contemporary issues in religious dialogue and immigration, see Matthew Kaemingk, *Christian Hospitality and Muslim Immigration in an Age of Fear* (Grand Rapids: Eerdmans, 2018), especially chaps. 4 and 5. See also Nathaniel Gray Sutanto, "The Limits of Christian Pluralism, and the Relevance of Neo-Calvinism for Indonesia," *ABC Religion*, March 8, 2018, https://www.abc.net.au/religion/the-limits-of-christian-pluralism-and-the-relevance-of-neo-calvi/10094918.

12. Regarding the neo-Calvinist emphasis on the epistemological consequences of Christian revelation, see Nathaniel Gray Sutanto, *God and Knowledge: Herman Bavinck's Theological Epistemology* (London: Bloomsbury T&T Clark, 2020).

The Divine Identity of the Supreme Deity of Pancasila

Let us now turn directly to the claims of Pancasila itself, rather than looking at the ways in which Christians could respond to it. Indeed, though Pancasila establishes neither an Islamic nor secular state, but rather a "godly" state, it is worth inquiring into what kind of god or supreme deity would be presupposed by its principles, which contain claims about human dignity and welcome religious diversity and social equality. Here we need to remember that the supreme deity of the Christian Scriptures is not just the transcendent King ruling the universe. He is also the Christ, the Word enfleshed, who came down to become our substitute, and who condescended to the level of his creatures. Christ, the God-man, showed us that the Lord of the universe did not come to reign over his enemies in immediate judgment, but to die for them, to welcome those who are most needy, and even to love those who reject him. This king is thus also a loving priest, and it is this priest who rules today. If this is the truth that Christians proclaim, it creates a faith in a supreme deity that beckons them truly to tolerate and embrace those who are religiously different and to welcome those who are strangers in hospitality and embrace. This gives us unique resources to respond patiently to those who disagree with us religiously.

Pancasila has a public theology of its own. It tells us that there is one sovereign God and that several world religions worship this God in good standing. But what kind of God would actually welcome the religious diversity that Pancasila envisions? Why would this God be patient with their worship? And what moral resources can this undefined deity provide for us who are living daily in common with those who disagree with us? All that an undefined deity could ground is an authoritarian filler that tells us to live in peace with our neighbor without providing for us the reasons, example, or grounds to do so. At worst, this undefined deity would welcome the natural-theological projections of the citizens to fill in the deity's identity, construing it any way they see fit, and thus motivating us to welcome our neighbor by way of our own culturally conditioned and manufactured reflections, untethered to divine revelation.

Hence, I suggest that Pancasila could only empower—and not just mandate—its citizens to live alongside the religious Other in peace and hospitality if it presupposes not a religiously amorphous theistic belief but a particular person who has been revealed. It requires the kind of God that the Christian faith has revealed him to be: Jesus of Nazareth, the risen and exalted crucified Savior.

Precisely this specific Christian gospel also gives us the kind of power that citizens need to become the welcoming and virtuous people Pancasila envisions.[13] Claims of possessing an absolute truth, indeed, can create a kind of exclusivity that inculcates a prideful haughtiness in us: "I have the truth and you don't." But Christianity proclaims that those "in" the truth are in the truth by sheer grace. If such is the case, it is a truth that, when properly held, creates a humble and repentant person who sees oneself as no greater than the neighbor. As Tim Keller articulates well, here is an identity that welcomes rather than excludes:

> If you believe in Jesus's message, you believe in a truth, but not a truth that leads to exclusion. Many voices argue that it is exclusionary to claim that you have the truth, but as we have seen, that view itself sets up a dichotomy with you as the heroically tolerant and others as villainously or pathetically bigoted. You cannot avoid truth claims and binaries. The real issue is, then, which kind of truth—and which kind of identity that the truth produces— leads you to embrace people who are deeply different from you? Which truth claims lead you to scorn people who oppose you as fools? Which truth claims lead to community? Which truth claims both humble and affirm you so that you're not afraid of people who are different than you are, nor can you despise them? If I build my identity on what Jesus Christ did for me and the fact [that] I have an everlasting name in him by grace, I can't, on the one hand, feel superior to anybody, nor do I have to fear anybody else. . . . My identity is based on somebody who was excluded for me, who was cast out for me, who loved his enemies, and that is going to turn me into someone who embraces the Different.[14]

Indonesia's public-theological principles guarantee that Christians remain a minority amid a religiously diverse nation. It thus requires citizens who will remain content to *be* a minority and to love their neighbors. Christianity thus offers resources that not only ground Pancasila epistemologically but also provide the moral resources that create the citizens needed for Pancasila to be a lived reality rather than a mere constitutional ideal. This communicates, once again, that Reformed theology enables us to appreciate Pancasila in gratitude and yet to offer constructive criticism of it in order to better fulfill its ends. Reformed theology emphasizes the specific claims of God's sovereignty, common grace, redemptive history, and the need of sinners for the good news of the gospel; it thus remains highly relevant for this unique

13. For an exploration of how specifically Christian grounds can create wise citizens, see James K. A. Smith, *Awaiting the King: Reforming Public Theology* (Grand Rapids: Baker Academic, 2017).

14. Tim Keller, *Making Sense of God: An Invitation to the Skeptical* (New York: Viking, 2016), 151.

and global context. Instead of encouraging a triumphalism that distances Christians from the religious other, it motivates Christians toward humble public engagement while being content with their own position as a minority faith. Christians thus seek to be active in order to be a gracious leaven for all Indonesians of all faiths.

Part Two

Public Markets

6

A Reformed Theology of Work in New York

KATHERINE LEARY ALSDORF

Over the past thirty years, New York City became a popular destination for college graduates, aspiring professionals, and rising stars in arts and entertainment, finance, law, health care, business, and technology. Richard Florida coined the term "creative class" in 2002 to describe this new generation of workers flocking to global urban centers like New York.[1] As of 2018 nearly 40 percent of Manhattan's workforce—just over one million—were deemed members of the creative class.[2]

This concentration of youth, ambition, creativity, and talent has been an economic and cultural boon for a city that was on the brink of bankruptcy in 1975. Aided by television series like *Sex and the City* in the late 1990s, chronicling the dating scene of beautiful, affluent, single New Yorkers, New York City became *the* place to live. Young people moved to the city for jobs,

1. This chapter was written in early 2020, before the COVID-19 pandemic and the migration of significant numbers of young professionals out of New York City. It is too early to tell the long-term effects of the pandemic on the city dynamics discussed here. See Richard Florida, *The Rise of the Creative Class: And How It's Transforming Work, Leisure, Community, and Everyday Life* (New York: Basic Books, 2002).

2. NYUSPS Urban Lab, "Manhattan: Powered by the Creative Class," *Medium*, March 6, 2018, https://medium.com/@NYUurbanlab/manhattan-powered-by-the-creative-class-6b622af11eac.

status, lifestyle freedoms, romantic ideas of excitement and adventure, and simply the opportunity to be part of something big.

Nonetheless, New York City can be tough. Competition is ruthless. Every sector of life and labor evidences a fierce Darwinian struggle to survive and succeed. Wall Street firms hire only the top business school grads. Teach for America accepts only 15 percent of its qualified applicants. Even low-budget, indie theater productions cast one in fifty of the talented actors who audition.[3] These are the challenges just to get in the door; as workers move up the ladder, competition only increases. Life in the "city that never sleeps" is physically and emotionally demanding as well. Wall Street bankers typically work seventy-three hours a week, with younger associates clocking hours over ninety. The promise of bonuses, promotions, or just keeping the job incentivizes an all-consuming culture of work. Add to that the ubiquitous opportunities to consume entertainment and culture in the city. If you ask a New Yorker, "How are you?" the most common response is "Busy."

This busyness is central to a New Yorker's identity; it's a status symbol.[4] When busyness, work, and career make up the core of one's identity, a whole range of emotional and spiritual issues tend to emerge. That identity is reinforced by an entire cultural milieu tied to career achievements and influence. As one's professional identity is threatened by economic downturns, layoffs, or younger competition, the results can be existentially devastating. Workers each seek to forge their own identity, write their own story, and make their own meaning; when work itself becomes the means of self-actualization, the existential weight placed on a worker's career becomes a crushing burden.[5]

The Creative Class and the Church

Established in 1989, Redeemer Presbyterian Church grew in large part by connecting with the spiritual and vocational longings of New York's emerging creative class. In 2002 the church launched the Center for Faith & Work (CFW)

3. Anthony J. Piccione, "10 Pieces of Advice for Theatre People Moving to NYC," *OnStage Blog*, March 22, 2018, https://www.onstageblog.com/columns/2018/3/22/10-pieces-of-advice-for-theatre-people-moving-to-nyc.

4. Researchers argue that "busyness and overwork, rather than a leisurely life, have become a status symbol." Silvia Bellezza, Neeru Paharia, and Anat Keinan, "Conspicuous Consumption of Time: When Busyness and Lack of Leisure Time Become a Status Symbol," *Journal of Consumer Research* 44, no. 1 (June 2017): 119.

5. Robert N. Bellah, *Habits of the Heart: Individualism and Commitment in American Life* (Berkeley: University of California Press, 1985), 287–88.

to specifically equip, connect, and mobilize the congregation for faithfully living out the gospel through their vocations, in hopes of contributing to the peace and prosperity of the city (Jer. 29:7).

Soon CFW was responding to pent-up demand within the church and the city for deeper conversations around faith, work, and calling. The center cultivated these conversations through a wide range of programs: classes, retreats, vocation groups, arts programs, job-search support, business-plan competitions, and coaching.

Programs are one thing, changed lives are another. How would CFW help these workers surrender their vocational idols, find vocational purpose, and be transformed by the gospel of Jesus Christ? How would CFW help them find peace, not in their work, but in God's work? To do this, the center needed *a theology of work* to undergird and direct our mission.

Reformed Resources

When I was hired in 2002 to envision and lead the Center for Faith & Work, I'd been working in the high-tech industry for thirty years. I was familiar with many of the vocational challenges, questions, and crises facing Christian workers in the marketplace. And yet, though I knew their questions intimately, I was unschooled in the theological answers and resources available to them within the history and theology of the Christian faith.[6]

Before I arrived at CFW, I had attended several Christian workshops on faith and work in both Silicon Valley and New York City, but generally found them disappointing. Many of these trainings were filled with simplistic and individualistic lists of "do's and don'ts" for Christians in the office: don't work on Sunday, do keep a Bible on your desk, don't engage in office gossip. The gospel was reduced to moralism. Be a "good person," put God first, family second, and work third. The deeper and more complex questions in the global marketplace were never discussed: How does our work matter to God? What do fair and just work policies look like? How can workers "walk humbly with God" (Mic. 6:8)? If I was going to lead CFW well, I would need a deeper theological well to draw from. I would need theological resources that could connect with the vocational and existential questions haunting New York's creative class.

6. I had taken several courses on theology, faith, and work at Regent College in Vancouver, a seminary committed to helping people integrate their faith with their work. Regent has recently launched a master of arts program in Leadership, Theology, and Society specifically for Christian professionals working in all sectors.

Over time, I found those theological resources in the Reformed tradition. Puritans like Jonathan Edwards and John Owen, Scottish Presbyterians like Thomas Chalmers, Dutch neo-Calvinists like Abraham Kuyper and Richard Mouw, and our own Presbyterian pastor, Tim Keller, gave us the theological grounding and imagination we so desperately needed. The Reformed belief that the gospel of Jesus Christ informs and transforms all of life became the central and organizing conviction for everything that we did at the center.

Inspired by this theological vision, CFW developed a threefold approach to vocational transformation. In everything we did, we sought to explore how the gospel impacts the heart, relationships, and world of a worker. In transforming *hearts*, Christ frees workers from their professional idolatry and gives them a new orientation for work. A gospel-transformed heart will long to work, not for self-actualization but for one's neighbor, one's city, and God. In transforming *relationships*, the gospel impacts the way workers interact with their colleagues and clients, their employees and employers. In Christ, these professional relationships become spaces of self-sacrifice, opportunities for service, justice, and grace. Finally, the gospel transforms a worker's *world*. Here the worker learns that God is already at work in their working world, in their industries and institutions. Christ is inviting workers into his ministry of reconciliation and transformation in the world. In this threefold vision of vocational heart, relationships, and world, workers can witness the depth and breadth of the Reformed conviction that Christ's redemption is never partial but is pervasive. It is both spiritual and material, personal and professional, relational and structural. As Christ promised, "I have come that they may have life, and have it to the full" (John 10:10).

The Reformed tradition's more holistic understanding of work is grounded in the biblical narrative. Scripture affirms the goodness of diverse capacities for human work embedded by God in creation. Scripture acknowledges the pain and frustration of work after the fall. And finally, Scripture points to a holistic hope for our daily work's renewed participation in Christ's present work of restoration and reconciliation in creation. Our day-to-day work in the city is not ancillary to God's mission and work in the world but integral to it all.[7]

This holistic theology of work was a radical and disruptive departure for many evangelicals arriving at Redeemer Presbyterian Church for the first time. Many of them came from a church background that either ignored or undervalued their work in the world. They carried an underlying guilt for working outside of "professional ministry." Entering into this new vision and

---

7. See Steven Garber, *Visions of Vocation: Common Grace for the Common Good* (Downers Grove, IL: InterVarsity, 2014).

community, they found a new motivation for work. Suddenly they were able to connect their daily work to the cosmic work of God.

Dorothy Sayers's theology of work has been foundational reading for many of us at the center. She's inspired us to approach our work "as a creative activity undertaken for the love of the work itself."[8] Her definition of Christian work as, quite simply, "good work, well done" frees many evangelicals from the misguided guilt they feel for not working as a pastor or missionary. The sparks of delight they feel while working in science, finance, the arts, medicine, and marketing are a reflection of the God who delights in his own complex works of creation. This God, they discover, still works with delight today, right at their sides.

Heart: The Idols of Vocation

When a career constitutes the core of one's identity—the ultimate hope for self-actualization—that career is, quite simply, an idol. God intended for work to be a secondary gift, marked by joy, creativity, freedom, and service. When work becomes a primary object of worship and identity (an idol), it enslaves, controls, and ultimately exhausts the worker/worshiper.

Martin Luther defined idolatry as expecting some created thing to offer what only God can give.[9] Work in New York City is a veritable Pandora's box of potential idols or false gods. Workers are tempted to place their trust in their own career and its promises to provide power, pleasure, money, recognition, education, savvy, or beauty.

In our ministry with the creative class, we sought to help workers expose and reckon with their own vocational idols. Although writing in 1656, John Owen's theological work on idolatry and sin is not only relevant, it is also convicting for twenty-first-century workers in New York. Owen's writings walk them through a rather uncomfortable process of exposing the widespread effects of evil and idolatry in their own lives and labor. He calls them to "mortify" their sin in Christ. These workers can change; through God's grace, they can mortify—curtail or even put to death—the vocational idols that have captured their hearts.

Calvinists like John Owen discuss terms like "sin," "depravity," "evil," and "idolatry" with uncomfortable regularity. Of course, in a postmodern

---

8. Dorothy L. Sayers, "Why Work?," in *Creed or Chaos?* (New York: Harcourt, Brace, 1949), 53.
9. See Martin Luther, "The Large Catechism," in *The Book of Concord: The Confessions of the Evangelical Lutheran Church*, ed. Robert Kolb and Timothy Wengert, trans. Charles Arand et al. (Minneapolis: Fortress, 2000), 386.

and post-Christian work environment, terms like these are not popular. All the same, Owen directly and effectively confronts readers with their own sinful and rebellious hearts. He invites them to consider the ways in which their vocational patterns of idolatry are destructive: personally and publicly, emotionally and economically. Covetous desires, the lust for recognition, and the failure to forgive will all "harden man's heart to his ruin." In this, the worker's "soul becomes indifferent to the seed of sin as it continues to grow."[10]

At first Owen's words cut deep. They sound legalistic, overwhelming, and— dare we say—puritanical. However, for workers "seeking to gain victory over disquieting lusts,"[11] Owen's words are ultimately found to be profoundly help-ful and even hopeful. Year after year at the Center for Faith and Work, young professionals have, through the power of the Holy Spirit, taken hold of Owen's basic principles and practices for the mortification of sin,[12] thus to weaken their vocational idolatries.

The process of spiritual mortification and regeneration is, of course, life-long. Professional idolatries and vices cannot be managed; they need to be named, confessed, and killed. No amount of willpower, meditation, or exer-cise can free the fallen heart. Christ's cross alone can break a worker's heart free from the bondage of marketplace idols. As Owen says, a person "may beat down the bitter fruit from an evil tree until he is weary, but while the root of the tree continues to abide in strength and vigour, the beating down of the present fruit will not hinder it from bearing more fruit."[13]

The affections of a worker's heart are powerful. The heart is always look-ing for something to worship. The pastoral challenge is to redirect the work-er's affections toward the only one who is worthy of our work and worship. Thomas Chalmers, a nineteenth-century Reformed theologian, argues that deep heart change results from "the expulsive power of a greater affection." He asserts that "the way to disengage the heart from the positive love of one great and ascendant object is to fasten it in positive love to another." The heart is secured from idolatry "not by exposing the worthlessness" of

---

10. John Owen, *The Mortification of Sin* (Edinburgh: Banner of Truth Trust, 2004), 8.

11. Owen, *Mortification of Sin*, 54. Owen uses the word *lust* to encompass all indwelling sin, as in "the flesh lusteth against the Spirit, so that we cannot do the things that we would" (cf. Gal. 5:17 KJV).

12. Others have followed in his wake and provide helpful resources: James K. A. Smith, *You Are What You Love: The Spiritual Power of Habit* (Grand Rapids: Brazos, 2016); Timothy S. Lane and Paul David Tripp, *How People Change* (Greensboro, NC: New Growth, 2006); Tim Keller, *Counterfeit Gods: The Empty Promises of Money, Sex, and Power, and the Only Hope That Matters* (New York: Penguin, 2016).

13. Owen, *Mortification of Sin*, 35.

our "love of the world," but by orienting the heart toward "the worth and excellence" of God.[14] It is impossible for a man "to shut out the world from his heart" if he "has nothing to replace it." However, it is "not impossible with him who has found in God a sure and satisfying portion, . . . to him whose view has been opened up to the loveliness and glory of the things that are above."[15]

Briefly put, the task is not to stifle the vocational affections of the worker but to reorient those vocational desires toward the one deserving of that ultimate affection. To elaborate on C. S. Lewis's famous metaphor, you cannot persuade children to desire a trip to the sea by denigrating the muddy puddle in which they play. Instead you need to place before them the beauty and wonder that is the true sea—allow their eyes, heart, imagination, and affections the opportunity to envision a new horizon.[16]

At the center we have found again and again that the vocational transformation must begin with a painful but liberating reorientation of the worker's heart. Here the worker finds vocational rest, purpose, and identity, not simply in their own work, but indeed in God's work.

Gospel-Changed Relationships

Chris wanted his colleague to be transferred or fired. He was annoying and frustrating. Chris was a rising star in a national consulting firm, and he had no time and, frankly, no respect for this particular colleague at all.

As a worker's heart is reoriented toward God, their workplace relationships experience a reorientation as well. Chris shared his vocational issues with his small group in the church and asked for prayer. His initial request was for God to get this colleague out of his way. As Chris read the work of John Owen, he was increasingly convicted about his own self-centeredness and lack of respect for this colleague. He saw how his own desires for recognition and advancement fed his workplace behaviors of hyperproductivity and control. Chris was humbled. He desired to change the way he was responding to his colleague, in hopes that God would change his heart along the way. One year later, the colleague is still there and continues to be annoying at times. However, there is now an underlying relationship of respect and grace between

---

14. Thomas Chalmers, "The Expulsive Power of a New Affection," in *Select Works of Thomas Chalmers*, ed. William Hanna, vol. 3 (Edinburgh: Thomas Constable, 1855), 253–54.

15. Chalmers, "Power of a New Affection," 259.

16. C. S. Lewis, "The Weight of Glory," in *The Weight of Glory and Other Addresses* (New York: Harper Collins, 2001), 25–46; cf. http://www.wheelersburg.net/Downloads/Lewis%20Glory.pdf.

the two men. Chris reports that rather than dissolving the relationship, God used it to refine Chris and draw him closer.

Time and again we see that the move from self-centered to God-centered work bears relational fruit in the workplace. Workers begin to openly practice humility and vulnerability: speaking the truth in love (we call this "redemptive feedback"), they begin resolving conflicts, using Matthew 18 as their model; they begin extending grace to colleagues who are bothersome and annoying.

Western workplaces have a well-documented history of monetizing working relationships. In industries where relationships are constantly being leveraged for power, money, and status, a worker who deeply values professional relationships as ends in and of themselves can be both disruptive and transformative.

Gospel-Changed World

In New York City, creative-class workers are often "short-termers." They come to the city seeking a quick path to success and adventure before leaving for some other part of the country. Short-termers want to enjoy and *take* everything they can from the city—money, culture, education, entertainment, and career advancement—and ultimately settle down elsewhere.

Redeemer's pastor, Tim Keller, uses Jeremiah 29 to challenge this consumptive posture toward the city. In Jeremiah's letter to the Jewish exiles (who thought they were "short-termers" in Babylon), the prophet exhorts them to settle down, build houses, plant gardens, and "seek the peace and prosperity of the city to which I [God] have carried you into exile. Pray to the LORD for it, because if it prospers, you too will prosper" (29:7). Using this text, Keller argues that the gospel reorients more than workers' hearts and relationships; it also reorients their posture toward their city. The gospel shifts the workers' mindset away from exploiting the city to that of praying, serving, and working for its shalom. Investing in the flourishing of the city can take many forms, such as charitable giving, volunteering, and political action. However, at Redeemer's CFW we focus on how Christians can love and serve their city *through their daily work.*

But how exactly does this happen? How should committed Christian workers actually engage the brokenness and beauty of this complex and pluralistic city? In closing, I highlight two Reformed concepts that have been pivotal in helping our workers serve their neighbors and glorify God in the New York marketplace: common grace and vocation.

Common Grace: Loving and Working in Babylon

Working faithfully and sustainably in "Babylon" raises lots of questions and challenges for Christian workers. One is loneliness: many of them feel isolated and alone, lamenting that they don't know of any other Christians at their workplace. That raises a second question: How can committed Christians work alongside, learn from, and collaborate with colleagues who are very different from them in terms of their faith and values?

It is here that the Reformed doctrine of common grace has proved to be especially helpful. In the power and pervasive presence of the Holy Spirit, these workers are never alone. They are connected to a great cloud of witnesses, and their God is present and active, working before and beside them. Moreover, through the common-grace workings of the Holy Spirit, their non-Christian coworkers are the graced recipients of many blessings from God. These non-Christian workers have received the gifts of creativity, education, virtue, generosity, wisdom, and insight from the Holy Spirit.

Therefore, Christian workers not only can but also *must* collaborate with, learn from, and celebrate the good work done by their non-Christian colleagues. God has blessed all humanity with gifts of morality, aesthetics, and craftsmanship. Christian workers can appeal to their coworkers' kindness, ethics, and excellence because—by the grace of God—these good gifts are within them as well.

On multiple occasions Tim Keller has said that because of common grace, the works—the thoughts, contributions, cultural creations, science—of non-believers are never as bad as their wrong beliefs should make them. Likewise, because of total depravity, the works—the thoughts, contributions, cultural creations, science—of believers are never as good as their right beliefs should make them.

Understanding that the work of *all people* can participate in the work of God enables the Christian worker to place a high value on the good work being done in "Babylon." Despite the ever-apparent presence of sin and brokenness, God is always at work in the city and the world, holding it together, beautifying it, providing for its renewal. Our task is to observe and discern where and how God is at work—even through our coworkers—and to join our labors to God's working.

Vocation: Your Distinct Sphere of Responsibility

Early in our ministry we discovered a pent-up demand for Christians in specific industries to gather and discuss the unique struggles and questions arising within their industry. Christians in the diverse fields of finance, theater, medi-cine, and media encounter spiritual, economic, and cultural challenges unique to their field. Workers in various lines of work desire time and space to gather, pray, encourage, and support one another.

"Work," we realized, is not a uniform human experience: it is a profoundly diverse and complex activity. Yes, all Christian workers are universally called to love their neighbors and glorify their God, but this universal love command takes on distinct forms in diverse fields and industries.

John Calvin and his fellow reformers understood God's desire "that human beings should live in a society bound together by common needs and mutual service, . . . [with] each member contributing according to his specific talents and receiving according to his need."[17] According to Calvin, the diversity of vocations is, in one sense, extremely practical. In order to survive, Calvin's Geneva needed butchers and bakers, teachers and builders, soldiers and mer-chants. Martin Luther wrote that these diverse vocations were the diverse "masks" that God wears to bless cities with the food, shelter, and beauty they need to flourish.

Moreover, this vocational diversity not only serves humanity, it also actu-ally delights God. Just as God delights in the diversity of flowers and fish, God delights in diverse workers with a complex and pluriform array of gifts, talents, and insights. When workers develop these diverse talents into the unique vocations of architecture and fashion, cooking and policing, singing and preaching, the Creator takes delight in that complexity.

Reformed theology conceives of creation as a seed that is filled with growth potential or as a flower whose petals are slowly unfolding. God embedded in creation diverse patterns and potencies that human beings are always dis-covering, exploring, and developing. At the Center for Faith and Work, in our many different vocational groups, workers seek to explore the diverse unfolding goodness that God might be revealing for their specific industry.

Two Reformed doctrines have proved to be extremely helpful in these ef-forts: "the priesthood of all believers" and "sphere sovereignty." According to the priesthood of all believers, Christian workers are holy priests, each one offering life and labor as sacrifices of holy worship to God. These priests have direct access to God, to God's Word, and to God's world. In Christ's priesthood, they are priests. No mediator is needed. Worker priests are called to discern the direction of God's calling in their career, in free submission to the Word of God and Christian community.

17. Lee Hardy, *The Fabric of This World: Inquiries into Calling, Career Choice, and the Design of Human Work* (Grand Rapids: Eerdmans, 1990), 60.

According to the Reformed doctrine of sphere sovereignty, God has a unique and diverse set of purposes and designs for human work. Art, law, commerce, science, education, and government are unique spaces of Christian service, with their own unique patterns and practices. These unique spheres of human work and responsibility all engage each other in society, like cogwheels, to enable a rich, multifaceted, flourishing of human life. In the light of sphere sovereignty, diverse workers are called to investigate their specific spheres and their callings within them.

In light of these two doctrines, each vocational group at CFW looks carefully at their own industry or sphere and asks three questions:

- How are things in this sphere supposed to be (as created by God)?
- How are things in this sphere going wrong (because of systemic evil)?[18]
- How might God be calling me/us to join him in the redemption and renewal of this particular sphere?

Lawyers need to wrestle with God's purposes for law, what God's justice is calling them to do in this specific time and place, and how they should pursue it. Artists, doctors, and pastors cannot answer these questions for lawyers. They are priests. They need to wrestle together with the unique purposes and responsibilities God has for them.

As the global financial industry collapsed all around them in 2008, our finance fellowship group could see quite clearly the unique importance of their work and their unique responsibility for the welfare of their neighbors. Together in community, this priesthood of believers began examining what was broken in their industry. As a body of believers, they began to reenvision how finance is supposed to function within the economy of God. Quite a few of them discerned that God was calling them to engage in redemptive and transformative action deep within the heart of their industries.

Conclusion

Over the past eighteen years, the theological and spiritual resources found within the Reformed tradition have made deep and profound differences in the vocational lives of our workers. A transformed heart and career, placed within

18. Al Wolters, *Creation Regained: Biblical Basics for a Reformational Worldview* (Grand Rapids: Eerdmans, 2005), 53. The effects of sin touch all of creation; no created things (such as societal structures, cultural pursuits, or bodily functions) are "in principle untouched by the corrosive effects of the fall."

the story of Scripture and the economy of God, not only releases workers from the burden of forging their own identity through professional accomplishments, it also gives their careers a deeper and more fulfilling purpose. Understanding their own sin, these workers are more humble, gracious, and forgiving contributors to their teams. Understanding God's common grace, these workers are freed to learn from and collaborate with their non-Christian colleagues in selfless joy and gratitude. And finally, recognizing that they labor in the "already and not yet" encourages their present work for restoration and helps them recognize and accept that some aspects of vocational restoration (including their own hearts) will not be fully accomplished until Christ comes again.

7

Political Economy in Brazil

A Reformed Response

LUCAS G. FREIRE

"If you want to open a business, you first need an address. But in order to register an address, you first need a business." When Marco Kerkmeester decided to start a coffee company in Brazil, this was only the beginning of the legal and bureaucratic morass he would encounter. Originally from New Zealand, Kerkmeester sat down with me for an interview in his São Paulo office. The entrepreneur certainly did not want to start his first day of business in Brazil in a state of legal limbo. But what was he to do? Kerkmeester's friend, who was a lawyer, said simply, "Don't worry, Marco. The law is wrong. Go ahead."[1]

Kerkmeester's experience with Brazilian bureaucracy is not unique. The miles of red tape needed to start and run a business are choking Brazil's

I would like to thank Matthew Kaemingk for all his hard work providing editorial support for this chapter.

1. Marcos Antonio Franklin, Lucas Freire, and Allan Augusto Gallo Antonio, "O que acontece quando um neozelandês empreende no Brasil?," *Centro Mackenzie de Liberdade Econômica*, April 30, 2019, https://www.mackenzie.br/es/noticias/artigo/n/a/i/o-que-acontece-quando-um -neozelandes-empreende-no-brasil.

economy. The legal quagmire adds to the cost of pursuing a business opportunity and doing just about anything.

The conversation with Kerkmeester illustrates a small corner of the voluminous legal contradictions, bureaucratic inefficiencies, and poorly conceived regulations that paralyze economic innovation and growth in Brazil. Labor regulations discourage Kerkmeester from taking chances on young or unproven employees. The laws make it difficult for him to hire employees for a trial period. Businesses must pay a special fee to register new employees, and they are required to have at least a three-month contract. If you hire the wrong person, the business is obligated to pay the entire contract regardless. You do not need to be an economist to understand that laws and fees like these discourage businesses from hiring workers.

Even when they are not hiring workers, businesses do need to hire a *despachante*. This is a person whose entire job is to represent a business in government buildings. They stand in long lines and sign piles of legal paperwork. Businesses hire *despachantes* in part because all their documents require a special government stamp that can be received only in a *cartório*. A *cartório* is a kind of private notary business with special government privileges to authenticate signatures, contracts, and documents with official seals and stamps. Contrasting this with the business environment in New Zealand, Kerkmeester reports, "It takes me about 15 minutes to open a business. To shut it down, online, 15 seconds. *Despachante? Cartório?* No way. Do you know how much that would cost?"[2]

The overwhelming cost of doing business greatly discourages Brazilian entrepreneurship. The average person on the street simply does not have the time, money, political connections, or bureaucratic know-how to start a business. As a result, many poor Brazilians with entrepreneurial gifts, dreams, and ambitions give up and join the bureaucracy themselves.[3] Every day the entrepreneurial energy of the Brazilian people is being squandered and suppressed under the weight of government interference and bureaucratic morass. Small-business owners in Brazil need to be released to create, innovate, collaborate, and produce goods and services for the common good. They need a public voice to speak up for them and the socioeconomic potential they represent.

2. Franklin, Freire, and Antonio, "O que acontece quando um neozelandês empreende no Brasil?"

3. A survey showed that in 2016 there were around 11.5 million government jobs in Brazil. At the time, the workforce was around 101 million people. Carlos Eduardo M. Feliciano, "O funcionalismo público no Brasil," *Migalhas*, January 18, 2019, https://www.migalhas.com.br /depeso/294367/o-funcionalismo-publico-no-brasil.

Reformed Political Economy

Listening to the coffee entrepreneur and hearing his frustration reminded me of Abraham Kuyper's public fight for the political and economic rights of the *kleine luyden* (little people) in the Netherlands.[4] As a Reformed theologian and politician, Kuyper spoke out on their behalf. He publicly argued that these workers had dignity and potential. Although the elites ignored them, Kuyper insisted that they were, in fact, the backbone of the nation's economic, political, and spiritual flourishing. Rather than ignoring the *kleine luyden*, Kuyper argued that the Dutch state should empower and release them to work and flourish for the good of the whole nation.

In this chapter my goal is to explore Brazil's economic challenges in light of Abraham Kuyper's view that issues of poverty, labor, and political economy need to be dealt with through an "architectonic critique of human society itself."[5] In essence, the solution to Brazil's economic ills is not simply less government regulation, though that certainly would be a step in the right direction. Instead, Brazil needs to have a larger discussion about the nature of the relationship between the state, the marketplace, and workers. What does freedom and flourishing between these different spheres of life look like? How should they interact with one another? What is a marketplace for? What is a state for? Politicians could cut a few regulations here and there, and that would be helpful. But without a larger discussion about the structural relationship between politics, economics, and society, the choking power of political bureaucracy will always come creeping back in.

The Burden of Regulation

In September 2019 a congressional representative visited Mackenzie Presbyterian University in São Paulo, where I serve as a professor of economics and political science. He had called our Center for Economic Freedom to request a meeting. I attended the session along with our other research fellows. This man, a left-of-center politician, was concerned that his party had lost votes in a recent election to a party that favored a more free-market approach. He wanted to learn more about how the market works and what sorts of policies would enable, rather than hinder, economic flourishing in Brazil.

4. Enne Kopps, "Abraham Kuyper: 'Klokkenist der kleine luyden,'" *Historiek*, March 14, 2018, https://historiek.net/abraham-kuyper-klokkenist-der-kleine-luyden/57653/.

5. Abraham Kuyper, *Christianity and the Class Struggle*, trans. Dirk Jellema (Grand Rapids: Piet Hein, 1950), 40.

Nyack College
Freeman Library

This was by no means an isolated case. Jair Bolsonaro, the current president (2019–), and many other political insiders have recently signaled a change in the Brazilian perspective on economics. Politicians are realizing that voters are increasingly concerned about economic stagnation, unemployment, and corruption. Voters are beginning to recognize the burden that bureaucracy and corruption place on the marketplace. They perceive it as a constraint, not simply on some distant corporation, but on their own immediate lives. For the first time in their history, some Brazilian voters are coming to see the marketplace as more of a solution than a root problem. Recognizing this shift in the people's economic vision, opportunistic politicians are increasingly happy to cater to it.

For some time, international observers have been reporting that Brazilian markets are being suffocated by heavy regulations, an overwhelming bureaucracy, and a labyrinthine tax code. A recent World Bank study shows that, in terms of ease of doing business, Brazil ranks 109th out of 190 countries around the world, way behind other emerging economies such as India and South Africa. In specific aspects of regulation, Brazil performs even more poorly. Only fifteen countries are worse when it comes to dealing with construction permits, and only six countries are worse when we consider taxes and the administrative burden of paying them for an average-sized company.[6] Another international study offers a composite ranking of economic freedom and reports that, out of 162 countries, Brazil occupies the 120th position. Whether you look at Brazil's legal system, property rights, regulation, or the size of its government, our country is more akin to Zimbabwe or Venezuela than to any developed political economy.[7] According to the World Bank, if Brazil would like to combat its many social problems, it is going to need to focus on its comparatively low levels of productivity. It argues that low productivity is, to a large extent, a consequence of the "important regulatory challenges" inhibiting Brazil's markets from functioning more dynamically.[8]

Historically speaking, Brazil's government has "sought to protect entrenched companies from . . . competition." While sometimes well intentioned, this pattern of economic intervention and favoritism has led to "harm-

---

6. World Bank Group, *Doing Business 2019: Training for Reform*, 16th ed. (Washington, DC: World Bank, 2019), 131–35, 159. These figures also take into account that since 2017 Brazil has been improving on some of the assessed criteria.

7. James Gwartney et al., *Economic Freedom of the World: 2019 Annual Report* (Vancouver: Fraser Institute, 2019), 9, 46.

8. World Bank Group, *Retaking the Path to Inclusion, Growth, and Sustainability: Brazil Systematic Country Diagnostic* (Washington, DC: World Bank, 2016), 121.

ful side effects."[9] Smaller entrepreneurs and businesses are discouraged from entering the marketplace and challenging politically protected businesses. Without this competition, market creativity and innovation stagnate, and the economy sputters and falls further and further behind.

Within such a dysfunctional, unfair, and complex regulatory architecture, only a small Brazilian elite can possibly participate—let alone benefit.[10] The economic consequences could not be clearer. Only 39 percent of the country's economically active population is engaged in some form of formal or informal entrepreneurship, whether by choice or necessity. All this combines to destroy the key things that Brazil so desperately needs to flourish in a global economy: innovation, creativity, and productivity.[11] Without that, the gears of social life grind to a halt.

Brazilian Responses

What should be done? Several voices currently dominate public discourse in Brazil. We will focus on three: incremental pragmatism, religious populism, and leftist radicalism. As we will see, these three voices ignore the comprehensive and architectonic need for structural reformation within the political economy of Brazil.

The first voice we examine is that of incremental pragmatism. Brazilian pragmatists argue that nothing is fundamentally wrong with the political economy of Brazil. The country is simply suffering from several isolated cases of corruption and abuse. To combat these isolated problems, Brazil's marketplace needs more and better laws, intervention, and bureaucracy. With some pragmatic adjustments here and there, the Brazilian machine should be up and running in no time.

Incremental and pragmatic discourse tends to focus very narrowly on isolated corruption scandals and their isolated and pragmatic resolution. What, for example, is to be done with the former president Lula da Silva, who is accused of corruption? Or how might Brazil improve its poor public services? How might it update its infrastructure? These pragmatic and technocratic voices ignore the deeper architectonic problems facing Brazil's political

9. Armando Castelar Pinheiro and Paulo de Carvalho Lins, "Current Constraints on Growth," in *Brazil: Boom, Bust, and the Road to Recovery*, ed. Antonio Spilimbergo and Krishna Srinvasan (Washington, DC: International Monetary Fund, 2018), 47.

10. "Brazil Digital Report, 1st ed.," McKinsey & Company, April 8, 2019, https://www.mckinsey.com/br/our-insights/blog-made-in-brazil/brazil-digital-report.

11. Klaus Schwab, *The Global Competitiveness Report 2019* (Geneva: World Economic Forum, 2019), 14, 110–13.

economy. Instead, they focus on what is immediately in front of them: isolated cases of corruption and poor technocratic management.

The second voice is religious populism. Evangelical Christianity is a growing religious and political force within Brazilian public life. Lacking a comprehensive theology of public life or a structural approach to politics and economics, Brazilian evangelicals largely follow the incremental and pragmatic voices. But they take it a step further, blending it with a demand for strong moral leadership.

These evangelicals believe that if a strong anticorruption candidate were given power, that popular leader would be able to root out the moral evils of corruption once and for all. This moral renewal of the nation would give Brazil a new political and economic start. As a bonus, a culturally conservative leader could shift the nation's culture away from secularism and deal with the nation's moral problems at a deeper level. According to these evangelicals, what we need is a powerful and confrontational leader who can root out the bad apples with moral strength and conviction.

Many Brazilian evangelicals believed that they had found their moral and political savior in the populist Jair Bolsonaro. A pro-family and anticorruption candidate, he would be the strong leader who would save the nation. Sadly, less than two years into Bolsonaro's first term, evangelical support increasingly turned into blind following. These evangelicals frame Bolsonaro as a leader appointed by God to do God's holy will. To go against Bolsonaro is to go against God.[12]

This uncritical adulation for Bolsonaro among evangelicals is alarming and has puzzled several public theologians in Brazil. Some who were initially part of his government soon quit. Perhaps the most emblematic case is that of the reformational theologian, pastor, and L'Abri worker Guilherme de Carvalho. He had served Bolsonaro's administration but ultimately felt compelled to resign.[13] In a long essay following his resignation, Carvalho offers a theological critique of the political idolatry inherent within the administration's messianic tone. He criticizes the government's bellicose language and the divisive "anti-institutional, populist, and nationalist way" in which the executive branch was dealing with both the press and the rest of the government. "Politics,"

---

12. These followers sometimes call him *O Mito* (The Myth/Legend). What began for evangelicals as moral and economic pragmatism has become a near religious form of populism and nationalism. The man himself is now their mythical hero. See Aldo Fornazieri, "Jair Messias Bolsonaro: 'O Eleito de Deus,'" *Brasil 247*, May 20, 2019, https://www.brasil247.com/blog/jair-messias-bolsonaro-o-eleito-de-deus.

13. Carvalho served as the Director for Promoting Education in Human Rights at the Ministry of Women, Family and Human Rights.

Carvalho argues, should be "a means of loving and caring" for our Brazilian neighbors. Unfortunately, Bolsonaro's government was turning political life "into an extension of war, an instrument to crush, destroy and extirpate."[14] The third voice in Brazilian politics is the leftist radicals. For them, a nuanced critique is not enough. They support da Silva's leftist legacy and his progressive Workers' Party (PT, *Partido dos Trabalhadores*). These leftists defend the party's achievements on behalf of the poor during its previous thirteen years in power (2003–16). In their view, there was nothing fundamentally wrong with the ever-increasing government regulation and intervention in the market economy. If anything, leftist radicals believe that Brazil should radically *increase* the size and scope of government intervention into markets. Intervention, they believe, is the only way to promote economic flourishing and equality.

A Christian example of this leftist radicalism can be found in the activism of Ronilso Pacheco. He is a Baptist pastor, a vocal journalist, and a leading proponent of Black and liberation theology in Brazil. In a strongly worded essay, Pacheco outlines an extremely critical case against Guilherme de Carvalho and other "evangelicals who silently advance in Bolsonaro's administration." He argues that these evangelicals have failed to defend poor, marginalized, and vulnerable social groups who are being threatened and oppressed by Bolsonaro and his administration.[15]

In the end, when Brazilian Christians discuss politics and poverty (be they on the political right or the political left), they tend to avoid the deeper structural and architectonic questions facing Brazil's economy. Instead, Christian political discourse largely focuses on the momentary pros and cons of different leaders, culture wars over family values and morality, the latest corruption scandal, and possible threats that uncivil politicians might pose to the political culture of Brazil.

What is the proper structural relationship between the state, the market, and society? For the most part, Brazilian evangelicals follow the secular rhetoric advanced by their favorite political and cultural leaders on the right or the left. *In short, they lack a theology of political economy. They lack an architectonic Christian vision for the flourishing of markets, states, and*

---

14. While Carvalho was careful to note that this indictment is not applicable to every official in Bolsonaro's government, the populist virus, he argues, is widespread. Guilherme de Carvalho, "O nome de Deus no governo Bolsonaro: Uma crítica teológico-política," March 20, 2020, https://guilhermedecarvalho.com.br/2020/03/20/o-nome-de-deus-no-governo-bolsonaro-uma-critica-teologico-politica/.

15. Ronilso Pacheco, "Quem São os evangélicos calvinistas que avançam silenciosamente no governo Bolsonaro," *The Intercept Brasil*, February 4, 2020, https://theintercept.com/2020/02/04/evangelicos-calvinistas-bolsonaro/.

society. Without this grounding, they are distracted by the personalities and ideologies of the day.

These three voices offer simplistic solutions to a complex problem. Brazil's corrupt, inefficient, and exclusionary political economy is not simple, nor did it appear overnight. It emerged from a complex cultural history of economic exclusion, inequality, and hierarchy.[16] The virus is deep, pervasive, and pathological. Adding or subtracting some technocratic regulation here and there will not solve the issue. Neither will elevating politicians who are louder, more disruptive, or moralistic. There is no quick fix. There is no incremental fix. The problem is too deep and too vast.

A Reformed Approach

Christians in Brazil need a robust theology of political economy that is both deeper and more architectonic. The Reformed tradition is by no means a cure-all for everything that ails Brazil. However, it does offer some resources for developing a more comprehensive Christian response to political economy.

Interestingly enough, the current situation in Brazil intersects rather closely with some of the points raised by Abraham Kuyper more than a century ago, when he offered a Reformed response to Europe's growing economic inequality and injustice in the wake of the Industrial Revolution. At the time, a major debate was brewing in Europe concerning the burgeoning issues of poverty, worker's rights, and the role of the government in industrial affairs.

Pope Leo XIII addressed these economic issues in his now-famous encyclical *Rerum Novarum* (1891). He championed the values of economic solidarity, cooperation, and charity as counterpoints to the emerging class-conflict model proposed by socialists. The pope's encyclical avoided the two growing voices in Europe at the time: the vast expansion of the state on one side, and the crude industrial individualism of the Victorian era on the other. As a third way beyond collectivism and individualism, Pope Leo XIII proposed a political economy directed by the Catholic principle of subsidiarity.

A few months after *Rerum Novarum*, Kuyper delivered his own address at the Christian Social Congress in Amsterdam. There he specifically discussed the pope's economic proposal and offered his own "third way" in a manner that was consistent with his Reformed public theology, something he had been developing for a few decades. Although the economic theologies of Leo XIII and Abraham Kuyper were distinct, Jordan Ballor observes that both were

---

16. Raymundo Faoro, *Os Donos do Poder* (Porto Alegre, Brazil: Globo, 1958).

inspired by a shared concern for the poor and a shared theological critique of the secular foundations of both socialist collectivism and atomistic individualism.[17] Kuyper, in particular, pointed out that while collectivism and individualism appear to be at political loggerheads on the surface, the two share a common root in secular modernity.

Kuyper opposed secularism and defended a form of limited government and a free economy that was grounded in Christian anthropology and Reformed public theology. He denounced mechanistic socialism as incompatible with a Christian view of the organic relationship between the state, the market, and the people. Kuyper also denounced radical individualism and economic anarchism, arguing that the government had a legitimate and God-given ordinance to pursue public justice.

On questions of poverty and charity, Kuyper was critical of an overly expansive state apparatus, which gave little room for diverse churches, schools, organizations, and organic communities to respond to the poor around them. Kuyper was also critical of individualistic industrialism, which oppressed the poor, isolated citizens, and pulverized communities through self-absorbed greed. Finally, Kuyper was critical of governmental interventions in the economy that played favorites and benefited the few. As in Brazil today, these forms of intervention contributed to the suffering of the poor.[18]

What was Kuyper's alternative to secular forms of collectivism and individualism? To be brief, the organizing concept for Kuyper's architectonic vision was the doctrine of sphere sovereignty.[19] In short, if God alone is sovereign, then the sovereignty of *both* the state *and* the market is limited and bounded by God's sovereignty. In essence, *neither* the state *nor* the market should be allowed to dominate social life. Instead, the cultural, economic, religious, and political spheres of national life should exist *alongside* one another, working in freedom, flourishing, and mutual regard. In this way Kuyper rejected social hierarchies that would place either the state or corporations on top of society. They must exist *alongside* the rest of social and communal life *because God alone is sovereign over the social architecture.*

According to Kuyper, the state has a public and God-given responsibility to do three things with regard to the other spheres of public life. It must protect

17. See Jordan J. Ballor, ed., *Makers of Modern Christian Social Thought: Leo XIII and Abraham Kuyper on the Social Question* (Grand Rapids: Acton Institute, 2016).

18. For more on Kuyper's view of political liberalism, see Lucas G. Freire, "Abraham Kuyper and Guillaume Groen van Prinsterer as Anti-Rationalist Liberals," *Journal of Church and State*, April 26, 2020, https://doi.org/10.1093/jcs/csaa029.

19. Abraham Kuyper, *Our Program: A Christian Political Manifesto*, trans. Harry Van Dyke (Bellingham, WA: Lexham, 2015), 16–18.

and police the boundaries of the spheres so that they do not dominate one another. It must protect the "weak ones" from internal domination within the specific spheres. And finally, it must encourage commerce between the different spheres of social life. Kuyper argued that the state's three responsibilities should be carefully limited in their scope by both a *legal* constitution and a *spiritual* commitment to public virtue, human dignity, and freedom of human life.

What does this mean for the marketplace? It means that God alone—*not the state*—is ultimately sovereign over the marketplace. The state may protect the other spheres of life from the overly dominant power of the marketplace. It may intervene in the marketplace to execute public justice on behalf of the weak. That said, the state may not redesign, redirect, or manage the marketplace to serve its own political ends or that of its cronies. In all its regulatory activity, the state must demonstrate a profound deference, restraint, and respect for the market's dignity and unique calling before God.

Kuyper specifically denounced political overreach and the overregulation of markets. He contrasted "the regulatory mania of the meddlesome state" with a government that exists to "provide legal protection."[20] In his view, overregulation is always in danger of "tipping the scales in favor of one sector of society at the expense of another."[21] He discusses how overregulation unintentionally creates social hierarchies, divides the classes, and tears at the social fabric of nations.[22] Kuyper offers several examples from the Netherlands. Its conscription laws, he warned, excuse the rich and take poor workers "from their jobs, their homes and families, and expose . . . [them] to moral poisoning."[23] Laws to register property "take away . . . from the little man."[24] The poor laws "discourage private philanthropy" and fail to solve the problem of poverty.[25] Criminal laws favor the "person of status" against the "common person."

Here Kuyper's principle is simple. The wealthy and the well-connected can navigate and manipulate a market and a state that are deeply intertwined with heaps of laws and regulations. Those without money, privilege, and connections cannot do so.[26]

20. Kuyper, *Our Program*, 339.
21. Kuyper, *Our Program*, 337.
22. Kuyper, *Christianity and the Class Struggle*, 21–22.
23. Kuyper, *Christianity and the Class Struggle*, 341.
24. Kuyper, *Our Program*, 340.
25. Kuyper, *Our Program*, 340.
26. "There has never been a government in any land of the world which did not in various ways dominate both the course of social life and its relations with material wealth. . . . It cannot for a moment be doubted that this intervention, in many ways proceeding from untrue principles, has through all ages made unsound a state of affairs which could have been sound;

Kuyper discussed the consequences of aggressive intervention in shipping and industry. The intervention generated a temporary bubble of economic euphoria in the Netherlands, "only to produce the bitter fruit after a while of seeing most trade languish, shipping go downhill, and shipyards lie idle. The consequence was a considerable loss of jobs for . . . shipwrights, riggers, dockhands, and warehousers, as well as jobs in the supply industries."[27]

Likewise, Kuyper discussed how the overregulation of capital movements served to encourage the concentration of capital in the hands of the few. Such well-meaning regulations "rendered smaller businesses unable to compete and caused smaller financial assets to be wiped out during financial crises."[28]

All of this serves to illustrate Kuyper's general principle. Left to its own devices, an interventionist political economy will slowly come to favor those who are wealthy and connected enough to capture the state and to drive its bureaucratic machinery in their own favor: "The stronger, almost without exception, have always known how to bend every usage and magisterial ordinance so that the profit is theirs and the loss belongs to the weaker. . . . And whenever the magistrate came forward as a servant of God to protect the weak, the more powerful class of society soon knew how to exercise such an overpowering influence on the government that the governmental power, which should have protected the weak, became an instrument against them."[29]

This salient economic point made by Kuyper (and not many others in the nineteenth century) is now widely accepted by economists as an important warning against excessive regulation. Contrary to popular belief, powerful businesses do not always want a free and fair market. Instead, they prefer a strong state that is willing to secure their position of economic dominance—as we see in present-day Brazil.

"New Zealand is a poor country full of wealthy people. Brazil is a rich country full of poor people. It doesn't have to be this way." In a few short sentences, Marco Kerkmeester captured the critical link between a country's socioeconomic architecture and its socioeconomic consequences. The structural relationship between the state, the market, and society can either encourage economic flourishing or crush it.

---

has in many senses poisoned our mutual relationships; and has brought about nameless misery, whereas the goal of all statesmanship should be the happiness and honor of a nation." Kuyper, *Christianity and the Class Struggle*, 21–22.

27. Kuyper, *Our Program*, 342.
28. Kuyper, *Our Program*, 342.
29. Kuyper, *Christianity and the Class Struggle*, 22–23.

Kuyper's prophetic words from the nineteenth century have, in many ways, been corroborated by contemporary economists.[30] These scholars criticize interventionist and conflictual economic structures and propose a more respectful relationship of mutuality between the state, the market, and society.[31] Limiting the role of government through constitutional mechanisms (such as the rule of law) is now a commonly prescribed way to reduce the problem of "regulatory capture" by the strong against the weak.[32]

Conclusion

This is a brief chapter. There is much more that needs to be said. My hope has been to demonstrate that Brazilian Christians have, in the Reformed tradition, a number of theological resources for thinking comprehensively and theologically about political economy. With these theological resources in hand, they no longer need to follow the secular voices of incrementalism or populism, collectivism or individualism.

As I write these lines, the Brazilian government is struggling to implement a series of reforms to modify the structure of its political economy, aiming at results that will have an impact long after the global economic downturn of 2020. Any attempt, large or small, to cultivate a more fruitful and just relationship between the market and the state is, in my view, to be welcomed.

However, a Reformed public theology will always insist that the reformation of Brazil's political economy will need more than improved public policy. It will require an institutional, cultural, and ultimately *spiritual* reformation of Brazil itself. A nation's political economy consists of more than simply a mechanistic system of laws, capital, and industry. A political economy is a complex organic, spiritual, and communal network of human beings made

30. See the watershed analysis of George J. Stigler, "The Theory of Economic Regulation," *Bell Journal of Economics and Management Science* 2 (1971): 3–21.

31. Economic historians today note that the "architectonics" of a nation (its legal, political, cultural, and economic institutions) have a considerable influence on the nation's economic output. Economies dominated by "extractive" governments (i.e., webs of rules, regulations, courts, and taxes that ignore the rule of law) have a particularly poor record of economic development. High levels of corruption are a mere side effect, a symptom of a much deeper architectonic disease.

32. A particularly insightful recent diagnosis of the situation with a prescriptive focus on limiting the size of government can be found in Randall G. Holcombe, *Political Capitalism: How Economic and Political Power Is Made and Maintained* (Cambridge: Cambridge University Press, 2018). See also Daren Acemoglu and James A. Robinson, *Why Nations Fail: The Origins of Power, Prosperity, and Poverty* (New York: Crown, 2012).

in the image of God. As such, they have been endowed by their creator and thus have a wide variety of complex vocations within which they are called to serve, care, and create. Our task is to cultivate a political economy in which workers and entrepreneurs can serve their neighbors and honor their creator through economic activity that is free, innovative, just, and generous.

8

Workers' Rights in China

A Reformed Case for Labor Unions

AGNES CHIU

Either put an end to the tension that undeniably exists between the bosses of the industrial enterprises and the manual laborers—not by putting them off with empty promises but by truly eliminating the abuses and creating the climate for well-organized cooperation. Or, if you don't want this, then things will stay on a war footing, and the struggle already begun by the manual laborers against the machine, against capital, and the social order becomes unavoidable.

—Abraham Kuyper, "Manual Labor," in
Abraham Kuyper: A Centennial Reader

China is a global leader in coal mining production. Unfortunately, China is also a global leader in coal mining accidents, injuries, and deaths. Coal mine explosions, floodings, and mine collapses are common. From 2001 to 2008, the records show that 24,239 people died in mining-related accidents—4,899 in 2003 alone.[1] Young Chinese workers, unaware of the significant workplace

---

1. Wang Ming-Xiao, Zhang Tao, Xie Miao-Rong, et al., "Analysis of National Coal-mining Accident Data in China, 2001–2008," *Public Health Reports* 126, no. 2 (March–April 2011): 270–75, https://www.ncbi.nlm.nih.gov/pmc/articles/PMC3056041/.

dangers, are consistently drawn to the higher wages offered by mining companies. Without the proper protective gear, exposure to chemicals and poisonous gases leave workers with chronic lung diseases, including pneumoconiosis, silicosis, and fibrosis.[2] These incurable illnesses can leave them permanently disabled in just a few short years. Despite the promise of legal recourse, many miners are left to fight for their lives on their own, often losing the battle and leaving their families devastated.

I grew up in Hong Kong under British colonial rule, feeling both a distance and yet a strong connection with Communist China, my "motherland." In 1984 I came to the United States for college and later law school. After graduation I joined a large law firm, defending large corporations against workers' employment claims. Early on I realized the inherent unfairness in the system and the limitations of the legal system, regardless of localities. In 2006 I became aware of the unusually high frequency of coal mining accidents in China and the horrible conditions being pressed upon its coal miners. As an employment lawyer and someone with a deep love for my motherland, I felt a call to respond. I understood that meaningful reform for Chinese workers would take both a legal *and* a spiritual reckoning. This was the beginning of my quest to make an impact.

The Challenge

One of the most effective tools to quickly and sustainably improve labor laws and conditions is the modern labor union. The creation and protection of effective unions in mainland China faces several cultural, legal, and economic challenges.

Culturally speaking, the idea of a labor union is "foreign" to Chinese culture and history. In traditional Chinese culture, "work" has historically been considered one aspect of a larger family ecosystem. During the early years of Communist China, government-run factories continued to style themselves as large Chinese families. Workers were part of the industrial "family," and they looked up to their employers or government as the heads of their families. There was no need for workers to "advocate" for themselves within the ecosystem. Their economic "parents" would take care of them. When the time came to retire, your "family" would take care of you.

But this familial vision was shattered during a period of Chinese modernization and economic reform that began in the late 1970s. Rather than family members, workers were increasingly treated like cogs in an economic machine

---

2. A. Scott Laney and David N. Weissman, "Respiratory Diseases Caused by Coal Mine Dust," *Journal of Occupational and Environmental Medicine* 56 (October 2014): S18–S22.

designed for one thing: economic production. To attract international investment, China needed a favorable labor-management environment. It therefore systematically discouraged and undermined any effort to establish strong labor laws and unions. The underlying assumption was that international corporations would invest in China only if they could be promised loose labor regulations and a union-free environment.

On the surface, China has a strong national trade union—the All-China Federation of Trade Unions (ACFTU). It also has a set of labor laws titled Trade Union Law (TUL).[3] However, this union and these laws are both profoundly ineffective; in fact, they often make labor conditions worse. The ACFTU is the only legally recognized union in China, and it governs all local union branches. The goal of the ACFTU is to "ensure the status of the country's political, economic, and social living" and the "overall interests of the country." In short, the country's economic growth takes priority over workers' rights and safety.[4] The union's loyalty lies with the country, not the workers.

A primary role of the union is to "support" the company in executing its management decisions.[5] Even when changes are needed to protect the workers' safety, the union can only "recommend" the needed changes.[6] When management refuses, the role of the union is only to "support" the workers, not to represent them. Under these conditions, there are only five serious labor scenarios where employers can be sued.[7] Yet, even in these scenarios, the exact language for the union is only suggestive rather than obligatory.

The right to strike is absolutely foundational to the creation and protection of workers' rights. This right was specifically removed from the Chinese constitution in 1982 as a part of the "modernizing" reforms of then-leader Deng Xiaoping.[8] The Chinese government not only discourages and suppresses strikes, it also actively dismantles advocacy groups when strikes occur. In 2019 five workers were detained for simply organizing a strike.[9] Since strikes are technically not illegal, organizers are usually charged with "gathering a

---

3. The TUL was enacted in 1992 and amended in 2001. Standing Committee of the National People's Congress, The Trade Union Law 1992, as amended in 2001. 全國人民代表大會常務委員會, 中華人民共和國工會法 (2001 修正). Labor Law Website (勞動法寶網), October 27, 2001. See http://law.51labour.com/lawshow-68038.html.

4. Articles 1, 2, and 6, TUL.

5. Article 36, TUL.

6. Article 24, TUL.

7. Articles 21 and 22, TUL.

8. *China Labour Bulletin*, updated to June 2020, https://clb.org.hk/content/labour-relations-china-some-frequently-asked-questions.

9. Javier C. Hernandez, "Workers' Activism Rises as China's Economy Slows: Xi Aims to Rein Them In," *New York Times*, February 6, 2019, https://www.nytimes.com/2019/02/06/world/asia/china-workers-protests.html.

crowd to disturb public order."[10] Without a meaningful right to strike, the national union can only communicate the workers' needs, but it can never fight for them.

Economics wins. The constant demand to increase economic power, production, and progress is the sovereign driver of labor conditions in China. Qinglian He (何清漣) is an economist and a critic of the Chinese labor conditions. She thoroughly outlines how China's misguided focus on continuous economic growth quickly leads to a deterioration of working conditions.[11] Labor disputes cannot be allowed to interrupt economic growth. The union must partner with management to "continue with the operation," "resume production," and "restore work order."[12]

Within mainland China these economic, cultural, and legal challenges collectively inhibit the cultivation of effective labor unions and meaningful labor laws. The economic logic of power and profit, the cultural pressure to submit to one's "family," and the legal loopholes and loose regulations all combine to leave workers profoundly vulnerable. Without effective labor laws or unions, workers will continue to suffer—and suffer greatly.

A Reformed Case for Workers in China

China clearly needs a legal framework for developing meaningful labor laws and autonomous labor unions. That much is clear. What is less clear—and what I intend to argue—is that China also needs a *spiritual* framework for reckoning with the inherent dignity of work and the sovereignty of workers. Without a deep understanding of the sacred dignity and inalienable rights of workers, the economic logic of the marketplace will continue to bend labor laws and unions to its single-minded will. China needs an underlying spiritual worldview that refuses to subordinate workers to economic production. It needs a spiritual vision that will place these two good things—workers and production—alongside one another as equally valuable and equally sovereign.

Within Christianity and specifically within the Reformed tradition, I believe that I have found a wealth of spiritual resources for valuing both work and workers. In this chapter I hope not only to explore those theological resources but also to apply them to the current challenges facing workers in China.

10. Hernandez, "Workers' Activism."
11. Qinglian He, "世界工廠中的勞工現狀 [The Current Labor Status in the World Factory]," *Modern China Studies* 當代中國研究 2 (July 31, 2008): https://www.modernchinastudies.org/us/issues/past-issues/100-mcs-2008-issue-2/1044-2012-01-05-15-35-31.html.
12. Article 27, TUL.

The Reformed tradition has a long history of theological reflection on the meaning and dignity of both work and workers. Numerous times, John Calvin mentioned work and workers. He argued that even the most mundane work in a village could be understood as a divine vocation, a holy calling from God. Farmers, parents, and blacksmiths are all members of and participants in Christ's holy priesthood. Calvin regarded these as holy vocations, callings from God: "The Lord commands every one of us, in all the actions of life, to regard [one's work as a] vocation. . . . [God] has appointed to all their particular duties in different spheres of life. And that no one might rashly transgress the limits prescribed, he has styled such spheres of life *vocations*, or *callings*. Every individual's line of life, therefore, is, as it was, a post assigned him by the Lord."[13] These vocations all have a godly purpose and design. One dare not look down on workers whom God loves. Calvin esteemed the value of work: "There will be no employment so mean and sordid (provided we follow our vocation) as not to appear truly respectable, and be deemed highly important in the sight of God."[14] Rather, workers and their work carry a prestigious purpose from God. All vocations and works are to glorify God.

After Calvin established the founding Reformed principles for valuing work and workers within the tradition, Abraham Kuyper developed the economic and political implications of those principles. As a Calvinist theologian and politician of his era, Kuyper (1837–1920) developed a theopolitical case for the establishment and protection of labor laws and unions. If Calvin was right, if workers are beloved by God, if their work is holy, then it follows—politically speaking—that those workers deserve economic, legal, and political protection and recognition. Moreover, if workers have been called by God himself, they ultimately answer not merely to an economic manager or political leader. Workers ultimately answer to God, who alone is sovereign over all workers. Companies and governments cannot claim God's throne of absolute sovereignty over workers.

In Kuyper's time, manual workers were without long-term contracts and were at the disposal of companies. He recognized the problems inherent within the laissez-faire system. According to Kuyper, government has the God-given responsibility to create a fair balance of power between labor and the marketplace. If the government allows the market to dominate, Kuyper warns, workers could react destructively. A careful and ethical political balance requires legislative and structural reforms that ensure a meaningful representation of

13. John Calvin, *Institutes of the Christian Religion*, trans. Henry Beveridge (Grand Rapids: Eerdmans, 1997), 3.10.6.
14. Calvin, *Institutes* 3.10.6, on p. 650.

workers. Without proper representation, labor would begin "fighting without restraint to defend its right of existence," striking with "anger," resisting "the tyranny of capital," perhaps even intending to "overturn . . . the entire social order."[15] Thus Kuyper urges the freedom for workers to form their unions and gain true representation in labor contract negotiation. The current system in China is not only immoral; it is also politically destabilizing.

Early in his political career, Kuyper was known as an advocate for the "little people" (de kleine luyden), his favorite phrase for the common Dutch workers; he believed that they made up the backbone of Dutch society. Kuyper was concerned about high levels of economic and political inequality between the rich and the poor. He led a political movement to fight for universal suffrage, abolishing the old system that conditioned the right to vote on tax payments. In 1887 he helped to pass the Labor Act, which barred child labor and limited the workday to no more than eleven hours. Kuyper outlined foundational rights for organized labor, including the right to associate, the ability to negotiate, and the right to strike. During the nineteenth-century rush for European industrialization, these were significant measures in the fight for workers' rights.[16]

In two major essays, "Sphere Sovereignty" and "Manual Labor," Kuyper presents the theological groundwork for a Reformed approach to labor policy. "Sphere Sovereignty" lays the philosophical framework for labor as an autonomous "sphere" of human activity within the life of a nation and the sovereign reign of God.[17] "Manual Labor," on the other hand, speaks of the moral and spiritual fiber needed for the flourishing of workers. In the next section I contend that Kuyper's Reformed vision for work and workers offers some important insights for the future of labor in China.

Sovereignty and Labor

Power matters. Any meaningful discussion of labor laws and labor unions must include an honest discussion about power and sovereignty. Who is sovereign over working conditions? Who gets the final say? If all power over labor is collected and concentrated solely in the hands of either the Chinese state or international corporations, Chinese workers are without meaningful

15. Abraham Kuyper, "Manual Labor [1889]," in Abraham Kuyper: A Centennial Reader, ed. James D. Bratt (Grand Rapids: Eerdmans, 1998), 231–54, here 245.

16. James D. Bratt, Abraham Kuyper: Modern Calvinist, Christian Democrat (Grand Rapids: Eerdmans, 2013), 218.

17. Abraham Kuyper, "Sphere Sovereignty [1880]," in Bratt, Abraham Kuyper: A Centennial Reader, 463–90.

protection. The issue of sovereignty is absolutely central to solving the challenges facing workers in China today. The power of the market and the state needs to be checked by the power of organized labor.

Abraham Kuyper articulated and advocated a vision of societal flourishing in which different "spheres" of life (education, the arts, the marketplace, science, politics, religion, etc.) were all recognized as independent, valuable, and sovereign. He called his vision "sphere sovereignty." Under this societal outlook, no area of life should be given complete power. No sphere of life could be allowed to completely dominate or direct the other spheres of life. Sphere sovereignty challenged *theocrats*, who willed that the church should dominate. It challenged *statists*, who willed that the government should dominate. It challenged industrialists, who willed that the market should dominate.

According to Kuyper, God wills that power should be distributed, that sovereignty be pushed down and out throughout society into families, towns, schools, companies, churches, and—yes—labor unions. Power should not be concentrated but distributed for the good of all. What made sphere sovereignty *theological* was its grounding in the belief that Christ alone held the reins of total societal power. No social force could justifiably claim Christ's sovereignty for itself. The total societal dominance of the state, the market, or the church was not only unwise and unjust; it also was an affront to Christ's kingship.

Within Kuyper's theopolitical vision, the government is, in many ways, one sphere among many. The government is not absolutely sovereign over the other spheres of life. The state cannot dictate what scientists study, what artists paint, what companies sell, or what religions worship. The state cannot direct these spheres. It cannot show favoritism. It cannot help one sphere dominate another. It is not empowered nor competent to do these things.

Instead, Kuyper argues, the state is a humble steward of a *portion* of God's sovereign power. The state is given the sovereign power to do three things. First, the state is to protect the boundaries between spheres through enacting and enforcing laws. It must protect the spheres from the domination of others. Second, it must protect "weak ones" from abuse within the spheres. If smaller and weaker members within specific universities, families, religions, corporations, and other entities are being mistreated, the state has the responsibility to step in and protect them. Third, the state has a responsibility to enable dynamic exchange and commerce between the spheres. A healthy and just state will allow the diverse spheres of human life to freely interact like "cogwheels," giving rise to a "rich, multifaceted multiformity of human life."[18]

18. Richard J. Mouw, *The Challenges of Cultural Discipleship: Essays in the Line of Abraham Kuyper* (Grand Rapids: Eerdmans, 2012), 467–68.

Kuyper's vision of sphere sovereignty intersects with the Chinese labor crisis in several ways. First, neither the Chinese state nor international corporations can justifiably claim total sovereignty of work and workers. They do not "own" labor. Chinese workers are ultimately owned by God alone. No political or economic authority should claim total sovereignty over them. Second, God wants power and sovereignty of work to be distributed, not collected. Sovereignty over work should be shared between companies and workers. Companies and workers should cooperate and share power when it comes to making decisions about labor conditions, pay, and production. The role of the state is not to help labor or management to "win." The role of the state is to ensure that the sovereignty of both are respected and honored. The role of the state is to protect both sides from the inordinate dominance of the other.

A Spiritual and Moral Force for Labor

While most modern labor discourse focuses on external labor conditions— wages, benefits, laws, and protections—Kuyper's analysis is more penetrating. He is interested in the moral and spiritual flourishing of workers as well. Kuyper's concern is not simply for their economic and political rights but also for their spiritual dignity and honor as beloved human beings, made in the image of God. Within an economic culture, Kuyper argues, it is not enough for workers to be paid; they also need to be recognized and affirmed for their value. The flourishing of workers goes beyond mere monetary compensation; it also concerns the spiritual and cultural respect and honor that is due to them under God.

In his essay "Manual Labor," Kuyper identifies a spiritual desire for justice and compassion as a critical cultural ingredient in the improvement of labor conditions within the nation. The improvement of manual labor in the Netherlands depended on a spiritual awakening to the inherent dignity of human beings generally and manual laborers specifically. Kuyper tied the oppression of workers in industrial societies directly to a "spiritual exhaustion" or "spiritual miasma" that precedes the cultural and political deterioration of all forms of life.[19]

According to Kuyper, economic and political justice require something the states and markets cannot provide: spiritual life and vitality. A flourishing and protected labor force requires a spiritual power that affirms their value and

19. Kuyper, "Manual Labor," 233.

their contribution. The Reformed doctrine of vocation, the priesthood of all workers, provides the spiritual purpose, the "moral fiber" that the labor movement needs. Work, even lowly manual labor, is a sacred fulfillment of God's calling. When governments honor and acknowledge the spiritual and moral aspects of labor, true contentment in work can be sought. Here the Reformed contribution to labor reform is to allow freely public faiths to freely develop the spiritual and moral fiber of workers and national life. The flourishing of labor depends not simply on some combination of political reform or economic production; it also requires the free flourishing of spiritual and moral life in a national culture. Kuyper's biographer James Bratt explains: "For Kuyper the antidote to unitary power was . . . a resolute citizenry whose moral strength animates the spheres with vitality enough to resist encroachment (from other spheres). . . . People need a vision contrary to that offered by the hegemonic threat. . . . In other words, the core of political resistance lay in *culture*."[20]

Christian Labor in a Non-Christian Country?

In many ways, the proposal of a Christian labor policy for a non-Christian nation like China feels foolhardy. The Chinese Communist Party is atheistic, and its record of antagonism toward Christianity, Islam, Buddhism, and a variety of other faiths is well documented. How can a labor policy founded on a belief in the sovereignty of God and the *imago Dei* possibly flourish under a state that actively privileges atheism?

While our hopes for immediate change within China must be chastened, the Reformed doctrine of common grace gives us a theological reason and resource for hope. According to the doctrine, non-Christian individuals, cultures, and nations are constantly being blessed by God with the gifts of moral insight, virtue, and wisdom. The Holy Spirit is active and moving in Chinese workers, markets, courts, and government buildings. While official policies appear to be purely materialistic and profit-driven, there is a haunting spiritual sense among the Chinese people that there is *something more* to life and work. They sense and intuitively know that economic and political power should not be concentrated, that workers have rights, that profit is not the only good to pursue. The Holy Spirit is living and active in the Chinese conscience and its culture. This is the assurance that a doctrine like common grace can bring.

We can see the wisdom and beauty of God's common grace at work even in the ancient Confucian roots of our Chinese culture. Confucius valued family,

20. Bratt, *Abraham Kuyper: Modern Calvinist, Christian Democrat*, 135.

virtue, responsibility, generosity, harmony, and a concern for one's neighbor and the common good. He recognized that different members of society had different responsibilities. Confucius realized that different members needed to be allowed to contribute to social harmony. He also recognized that no human power should be unrestrained. The moral imagination of Confucian culture is also shot through with the concept of "honor." This spiritual value could be critical in the future of China as it learns to honor the value and dignity of workers and their contribution to social harmony and flourishing. Within Confucianism, the pursuit of wealth is not independent; it is under the spiritual guidance of "heaven."

Likewise, the Communist revolution of Mao Tse Tung in the 1940s, though ultimately devastating, was founded on several laudable values: the beliefs that work and workers matter, that labor justice matters, that power should be given to workers. Although the Communist revolution took many violent and horrific turns, even there observant Christians can affirm the Communist thirst for worker justice, dignity, and power.

There are, of course, quite important differences between the Confucian, Communist, and Christian worldviews. However, these disagreements should not obstruct a Christian's recognition of and appreciation for the ways in which the Holy Spirit is active in China.

A Christian labor policy in China need not be an alien Western imposition. Because of God's common grace working amid the traditional values and moral vision of Confucianism and Communism, improved labor conditions can be developed in a spiritual, moral, and political *dialogue* between Confucianism, Communism, and Christianity. Abraham Kuyper's nineteenth-century analysis of the Dutch labor laws should not be dropped onto twenty-first-century China. Rather, they should inform Chinese Christians in the church, the marketplace, and the state as they work alongside their non-Christian neighbors.

Conclusion

Workers account for almost 50 percent of China's population, nearly eight hundred million people.[21] The welfare of these workers matters, not only to them but also to the economic, political, and cultural flourishing of China as a whole. The growing levels of labor unrest, discontent, injustice, injury, and instability are unsustainable. Something must be done.

21. "Number of Employed People in China from 2008 to 2018 (in Millions)," Statista, https://www.statista.com/statistics/251380/number-of-employed-persons-in-china/.

Abraham Kuyper understood that the welfare of workers is critical to social harmony. "Harmony" (和諧) is a central aspect of the Chinese social imagination. For Kuyper, the welfare of workers largely depends on whether or not their divinely given sovereignty is recognized in the workplace. If workers are not given the power to negotiate and participate in economic decision making, Kuyper warns of social unrest.[22]

While China has passed several new labor laws in recent years, the actual implementation and local enforcement of these regulations have largely failed for a variety of political, moral, and cultural reasons. The overpowering desire for the economic increase of wealth and power continues to overrun labor laws, restrictions, and regulations.

Chinese culture needs what Kuyper calls a strong moral and spiritual "fiber." A sense of spiritual power that can resist the might of economic and political greed. It needs to develop a cultural set of bulwarks that can protect workers against the dominance of both the Communist Party and international corporations. The commodification of human labor and the moral vacuum of Chinese markets needs to be met and filled by a spiritual awakening. Religious freedom and flourishing in China are therefore critical ingredients in the renewal of labor policy and labor conditions.

If changes are not made quickly, China will face greater unrest in the coming years. In the late nineteenth century, Kuyper warned the industrialists of the impending danger. If the needs of the lower class were not addressed, "bitter misery that divides the lower and higher classes of society in hatred, resentment, and passionate anger" would inevitably follow.[23]

If only for their own self-interest, the Communist Party in China should listen to Kuyper's warning. Suppression of labor's economic, political, and spiritual life will not eliminate the labor tension. In a country where one party is dominant, the contentment of workers is more critical than ever. If workers feel cared for and heard, they may accept Communist dominance. If they are not treated fairly, the situation will grow increasingly unstable.

22. Kuyper, "Sphere Sovereignty," 473.
23. Kuyper, "Manual Labor," 245.

Part Three

Public Justice

9

Modern Political Ideologies

A Reformed Alternative

BRUCE RILEY ASHFORD AND DENNIS GREESON

The Western political landscape is currently contending with a variety of powerful political ideologies. Since the American and French revolutions, classical liberalism has been a powerful and defining ideological force within the Western political imagination. For the past half century, both progressivism and conservativism, each iterations of classical liberalism, have been the predominant options in America. In recent years, populist nationalism and socialism have also witnessed a resurgence, after being pushed from the mainstream since the Second World War. Even libertarianism of a more anarchic persuasion and Catholic integralism have attracted cult followings in recent years. The ideological options are abundant.

On the ground, however, this ideological diversity hardly seems like the flowering of the best of the Western political life and culture. Instead, it appears that we are witnessing a political devolution into hardened political ideologies at war with one another and often imploding from within their own echo chambers. There is a widespread sense that something is profoundly wrong with Western political life and culture. The political salvation, long promised, has yet to be seen.

Our framing of these various political orientations as "ideologies" is intentional. Each of these ideologies exhibit certain totalizing aspirations that go far beyond mere public policy. They brook no compromise with other models of political life, elevating their cause to one of moral superiority while seeing others as degeneracies to be stamped out. Taking the form of religious zealots, ideologues tend to view issues of public policy in black-and-white terms of moral certitude. Those who disagree with them are at best simply mistaken; at worst, they are political infidels to be either converted or defeated at all costs. Put in theological terms, such ideological arrangements are inherently idolatrous. As David Koyzis argues, ideologues imbue certain tenets of belief with ultimate or salvific status, worshiping elements of the creation rather than the Creator.[1] In this chapter we propose a particular strand of Reformed political theology as a *nonideological* alternative to modernity's regnant political ideologies.

Reformed political theory is neither foreign nor new to the Western political landscape. Early modern political thought in both Europe and America was influenced by Reformed political theology in a wide variety of important ways. The political imaginations of Scotland, Switzerland, the Netherlands, England, and New England were all deeply informed by the Presbyterian or Reformed lines of political imagination. Their early modern experiments with religious liberty, federalism, human rights, constitutional constraints, democracy, and free markets all took place in political soil deeply influenced by the Reformed tradition. While these early Reformed contributions to the history and development of modern political thought are largely taken for granted today, historians are increasingly rediscovering the considerable fruit of Reformed influence in the West.[2]

Rather than providing a broad introduction to the complex and diverse world of Reformed political thought, we focus more deeply on one of the most promising and developed strands of the tradition known as the "Reformational" tradition of political thought.[3] Drawing on an older line of Christian

1. David Koyzis, *Political Visions and Illusions: A Survey and Christian Critique of Contemporary Ideologies*, 2nd ed. (Downers Grove, IL: IVP Academic, 2019), 3.

2. Concerns about religious freedom, free markets, and the like are hardly exclusive to the Reformed tradition. However, the tradition supplied many important contributions to these various pillars of Western political thought, giving them their specific shape in modernity. See Robert Louis Wilken, *Liberty in the Things of God: The Christian Origins of Religious Freedom* (New Haven: Yale University Press, 2019), 63–117; Johan J. Graafland, "Weber Revisited: Critical Perspectives from Calvinism on Capitalism in Economic Crisis," in *Calvinism and the Making of the European Mind*, ed. Gijsbert van den Brink and Harro Höpfl, Studies in Reformed Theology 27 (Leiden: Brill, 2014), 177–98.

3. In this chapter we follow theologians and philosophers such as Al (Albert) Wolters, Craig Bartholomew, and Gordon Spykman in employing the term "Reformational" instead of the more commonly used term "Reformed." Though there is much ambiguity regarding the term

political theology that includes Augustine, John Calvin, and Johannes Althusius, a group of nineteenth-century Calvinists in the Netherlands developed their own Christian response to the modern ideologies of liberalism, socialism, nationalism, and conservatism that were emerging all around them. Although Guillaume Groen van Prinsterer and Abraham Kuyper were the initiating voices in this effort, many more have since followed in their line, taking the tradition in new and exciting directions.

In this chapter we offer these Reformational voices as a critical resource for contemporary Christians seeking a faithful way beyond the idolatrous and divided postures that dominate our collective political life. What we highlight is that more than a mere shift in political thinking is required: what is urgently needed is a transfer of allegiance, involving both knowledge and affections. Understanding the present in light of the future consummated rule of Christ over his creation imposes certain political habits of the heart, which are the fruit of the Reformational tradition.

What (or Who) Is Ultimate? The Fundamental Problem with Modern Political Ideologies

When exploring the manifold dysfunctions of Western politics, Reformational political thinkers tend to dive deeper than the particular "issue of the day." For them, the most deeply ingrained problems in modern politics are not related principally to specific political personalities, parties, disputes, or policy issues. The problem, they argue, is deeper than that.

Instead, at its core the real political problem is that of *misdirected worship*. As the apostle Paul argued in his Letter to the Romans, all human beings are worshipers. They worship the Creator or created things, God or idols (Rom. 1:25). In short, we are a species who bow. Scripture indicates that human worship is matter of the heart, with "heart" signifying the central organizer and director of a person's life. The chosen object of the heart's worship sits at the center of persons' lives, commanding their allegiance, ordering their

---

"Reformed," we hold it to properly denote the confessional ecclesiastical traditions that hold to the Reformed confessions (Heidelberg Catechism, Belgic Confession, Canons of Dort, Westminster Standards, etc.). The Reformational approach for which we advocate is unquestionably indebted to these confessional traditions, and we therefore seek to locate ourselves in relation to them. From one angle, our aim is to broaden the theological tent, so to speak, in order that those who may not share in Reformed confessional unity may benefit from and claim the political and theological legacies of such thinkers as Calvin, Groen van Prinsterer, and Kuyper, yet without necessitating agreement on every doctrinal point. From another angle, our aim is to narrow the tent, to recognize that there are other Reformed approaches to political thought that are in some ways opposed to the approach advocated in this chapter.

affections, and shaping their thought and life. Thus Scripture reminds us, "Keep your heart with all vigilance, for from it flow the springs of life" (Prov. 4:23 ESV).

Informed by this pervasive biblical warning against misdirected worship, the Reformed tradition is keen to reject political ideologies that elevate some earthly political good to the level of ultimacy reserved for God alone. This is Augustine's point in *The City of God* as he argues that a political arrangement can be just only to the extent that its citizens corporately embrace the worship of God rather than false gods.[4] Expanding on Augustine's insight, the Reformational philosopher Bob Goudzwaard argues that individuals are often transformed into the image of the god that they worship. Moreover, these individual idolatries can quickly coalesce into societal and political idolatries, transforming and misdirecting every sector of cultural and political life.[5]

Such was the pivotal observation of John Calvin, the fountainhead of Reformational political theology. As he famously remarked, the human heart "is a perpetual factory of idols." Informed by this view of humanity, Calvin's approach to political life was rather cautious and sober minded.[6] Against the backdrop of human idolatry and depravity, Calvin held that political authority ought to be anchored within a strict system of checks and balances and with well-defined boundaries.[7] Further, the state's proper aim should be to cooperate with the church, albeit indirectly, for developing the best social conditions for citizens to freely worship God.[8] Thus the state ought to only be viewed as a penultimate good, a means to allow for the ultimate good of worshiping God.

At this point, Calvin's more chastened approach to politics as a penultimate good stands in stark contrast to the more grand and optimistic political projects of Western modernity. Steven D. Smith characterizes post-Enlightenment visions of social order as resurgent pagan spiritualities, whereby social goods and eschatological hopes can only be defined by immanence.[9] Within the modern political imagination, what is of ultimate meaning or value can be found only within the creation itself. This, once again, is idolatrous.

4. Augustine, *The City of God*, trans. Marcus Dods (New York: Modern Library, 1950), 19.21–27; Robert Dodaro, *Christ and the Just Society in the Thought of Augustine* (Cambridge: Cambridge University Press, 2004), 72–114.

5. Bob Goudzwaard, *Aid for the Overdeveloped West* (Toronto: Wedge, 1975), 14–15.

6. John Calvin, *Institutes of the Christian Religion*, ed. John T. McNeill, trans. Ford Lewis Battles, 2 vols. (1960; repr., Louisville: Westminster John Knox, 2006), 1.11.8.

7. Calvin, *Institutes* 4.20.1–8. Cf. John Witte, "Moderate Religious Liberty in the Theology of John Calvin," *Calvin Theological Journal* 31, no. 2 (1996): 359–403.

8. Witte, "Moderate Religious Liberty," 385.

9. Steven D. Smith, *Pagans and Christians in the City: Culture Wars from the Tiber to the Potomac* (Grand Rapids: Eerdmans, 2016), 217–57.

In a similar vein, David Koyzis, a Reformational political philosopher, argues that all modern political ideologies follow a familiar twofold pattern: (1) they ascribe ultimacy to some political ideal, thereby making it an idol, and (2) they offer to "save" society by eradicating the "evils" that threaten their idol.[10] Koyzis criticizes four modern ideologies—liberalism, conservatism, nationalism, and socialism—but also makes clear that even a procedural arrangement such as democracy can become an idolatrous ideology when the voice of the people is equated with the voice of God.

But this is rather abstract: we need to illustrate the point in more concrete terms. In the next sections we illustrate the contours of political idolatry and the ways in which it has manifested itself in both liberalism and socialism. The same, of course, could be done with nationalism, conservatism, and idolatrous forms of democracy.

The Idolatry of Liberalism and Socialism

Classical liberalism, the most foundational ideology of the modern Western political order, is the ideology from which other ideologies developed or against which they rose as a reaction. In its earliest iterations, classical liberalism was not necessarily idolatrous. It simply represented an early modern commitment to a constitutional and representative government emphasizing liberty, justice, and equality for all. Yet, with the advent of the French Revolution, modern liberalism quickly took on more radical and ideological dimensions. This began by absolutizing the political ideal of individual autonomy. The name itself, "liberalism," hints at this emphasis on personal liberty and freedom. Absent any form of constraint, liberalism became a banner for pursuing absolute and unfettered individualism.

For years, modern and secular forms of liberalism have maintained a tight grip on the Western political imagination. The ideology still retains an almost instinctive power among many. But precisely because of its overly myopic focus on personal freedom, modern liberalism soon began to unravel. Early liberalism conceived of society as little more than a collection of autonomous individuals. Government was a "necessary evil," meant to do nothing but protect individual life and liberty. However, as time went on, the narrow liberal focus on government as "protecting individuals" unintentionally and radically expanded the role and size of government to protect individuals from a wide range of ill-defined threats such as a "lack of resources." Ironically,

10. Koyzis, *Political Visions and Illusions*, 1–26.

an ideology designed to constrain the state ultimately served its profound expansion.

As time went on, liberals came to demand that governments actively affirm their individuality by accommodating and even empowering their individual choices. Thus, when individuals made unwise choices that reaped negative consequences, a liberal citizenry came to expect that the government would ameliorate those consequences.[11] In this and other ways, Koyzis argues, liberalism has proved to be self-defeating. It was born out of a good desire to protect individual freedom and limit the role of government. But its myopic view of society and public justice forced liberalism to expand government's role and scope dramatically in an effort to alleviate its own negative effects.

Alternately, consider modern socialism and its most prominent secular iteration: Marxism. This modern ideology is manifestly idolatrous and antithetical to Christianity. Within this ideology, Karl Marx plays the role of a secular prophet, pointing the way toward a wholly immanent form of social salvation. "Communism," writes Marx, "is the *genuine* resolution of the antagonism between man and nature and between man and man. . . . It is the riddle of history solved and knows itself as this solution." Furthermore, Communism provides for "the complete and conscious restoration of man to himself, . . . the restoration of man as a *social*, that is, human being."[12] Indeed, Marxism fulfills many of the functions that sociologists normally ascribe to religion.[13]

Although liberalism ascribes ultimacy to individual autonomy, Marxism absolutizes material equality for persons and reckons that their immanent salvation is achieved through social revolution. Unsurprisingly, Marx and his progeny reconceived ethics, with "good" and "evil" corresponding, respectively, to whatever advances or opposes the revolution. Marx was resolute in believing that his system would usher in an "end times" in which revolutionaries would abolish capitalism, achieve material equality, and therefore rid the world of evil. This is the gospel message of Marxist socialism.

Empowered by an unrestrained modern optimism about their own human nature, Marxist states have historically been authoritarian and often totalitarian. Instead of liberating society, Marxist states suppress it, stripping citizens of basic human rights and relentlessly opposing free and diverse social

11. For example, if a man fathers five children out of wedlock, with five different mothers, he might expect the government to take care of the problem—perhaps by taxing other citizens to pay for those children's well-being, or by taking those children's lives in the womb beforehand. And he may expect the government to do this without casting any judgment on his exercise of liberty.

12. Karl Marx, "Economic and Philosophic Manuscripts," in *Karl Marx: Selected Writings*, ed. Lawrence H. Simon (Indianapolis: Hackett, 1994), 71.

13. Raymond Aron, *The Opium of the Intellectuals* (New York: Routledge, 2017), 265–94.

communities and institutions, including churches. Instead of ushering in material equality, Marxists have exacerbated disparities, leaving the working class in destitution while party leaders live in opulence.

Ironically, therefore, Marxism's failure as an ideology was revealed by its own benchmark: the course of history and the distribution of material wealth. The abolition of private property led to oppression, not liberation; it led to rampant need, not abundance.

Socialism tried to bear the weight of humanity's eschatological hopes and dreams, a task no political ideology can accomplish. The same goes for liberalism, for no amount of government expansion can ever arrive at the complete freedom and shalom that is to come under Christ's future rule. This is precisely why Reformational writers emphasize the temporal limits of political goods on earth. Humanity's ultimate political salvation will only be achieved when something greater comes, when Someone greater is on the throne. Complete justice and peace are reserved for the new heaven and the new earth. In this, Christian citizens must understand the already and the not yet of God's time.

Understanding the Present in Light of the Future

Reformational political thought offers a nonideological alternative rooted in the temporal and spatial sovereignty of God. God alone can sovereignly bring political history to its fulfillment. God alone can sovereignly judge and direct individuals and communities within society. No human state should try to seize the temporal or spatial sovereignty of God for itself. Jesus is Lord, Caesar is not. Here the basic Christian confession forms a political bulwark against idolatrous ideologies and totalizing political arrangements.

This confession raises an important question: If Christ alone is Lord, how should we relate to earthly states in this intermediate age? We could, for example, wait for Christ's future reign to come and abstain from contemporary political life. Or alternatively, we could try to anticipate or even hasten Christ's coming kingdom through using political force. We could attempt to marry the church and the state and try to establish Christ's kingdom on earth in the here and now.

Reformational theology argues against both of these eschatological distortions of political theology. Rather, the tradition holds that the present age is a *saeculum*, a time of divine patience in which sacred and secular history are necessarily intermingled. In this present age, human beings are not able to cleanly separate or distinguish God's actions in history from fallen humanity's deeds. We cannot make infallible political pronouncements about which exact policies and forms of government are endowed with God's blessings.

During the saeculum, we cannot crown mortal leaders and laws with the divine mantle of Christ's heavenly rule on earth.

If Christ alone will establish political consensus, Reformational theology can resist the ever-present temptation to secure a premature consensus by means of political coercion, whether secular or theocratic. On the other side, Reformational eschatology enables it to resist the temptation to completely retreat from political life. Here it pushes back against Christian forms of political quietism and anarchy that would frame the present government as an illegitimate authority usurping Christ's future dominion. Instead, Reformational theology seeks to understand present politics in the light of Christ's future. Here two extremely helpful theological dialectics come into play.

The Origin and End of Politics

The first theological dialectic we must consider is the relationship between God's work within both *creation* and *re-creation*. This temporal distinction between the two is critically important for the political life of a Christian.

In creation, God has planted a variety of purposes, patterns, and potencies for the life of humanity and all creation. God intends these creational potencies to develop and flourish throughout the course of history. In the new creation, their fulfillment will be realized. As Kuyper is fond of saying, the seeds sown in this creation will ripen into buds through God's direction in history; they will not fully bloom until the eschaton.[14]

In the eschaton, or *re-creation*, God will not start over. He will not scrap what he created in the beginning through fire and destruction. Rather, the new creation will emerge as a purified form of the original, demonstrating that what comes about in the present, while distinct from the future, nevertheless bears an organic relation to the coming kingdom.

For a properly Christian understanding of government and politics, Christians need to understand this dialectical relationship between creation and re-creation. Human beings are social creatures. God created and intended them to form political communities of justice, freedom, and flourishing. The institution of government is a natural and good outgrowth of creation's potential. In this sense, government is a profoundly good, natural, and wonderful thing. Likewise, participation in communal political life is as natural as being human. To be sure, specific iterations of political action may be imprudent,

---

14. Abraham Kuyper, *Common Grace*, ed. Jordan J. Ballor and Stephen J. Grabill, trans. Nelson D. Kloosterman and Ed M. Van der Maas, vol. 1, *God's Gifts for a Fallen World*, Collected Works in Public Theology (Bellingham, WA: Lexham, 2016), 536.

unjust, violent, and profoundly evil. But political life, at its ontological core, should never be viewed as fundamentally evil or inherently worthless. God made human beings to live in political community with one another.

In light of this dialectic, Christians can—indeed, should—be politically active, for the good of their neighbors and the glory of God. In seeking public justice, Christian citizens can explore and develop God's good designs and the hidden potential in human community. Yet they need to do everything with humility and prudence.

Far from undermining political engagement, this temporal framing of political life inspires it. As we know, every political action that honors God will somehow, whether literally or metaphorically, be redeemed and renewed in the Holy City that is to come.[15] Of course, we may not be able to clearly see God's future city or its government any more than we could clearly see an oak tree by pondering an acorn. But in Scripture we have this promise: Christ has come, and he will come again. Christ is coming, not to burn, destroy, and replace, but to restore and renew every aspect of this world, including its politics. For behold, Christ is making all things new (cf. Rev. 21:5), reconciling all things to the Father through his blood on the cross (cf. Col. 1:20).

Church and State

The second dialectic concerns the *church's* relation to the *state*. As we stand between the first and second comings of our Lord, we live in an age in which the church serves a unique role in the Christian life. The church fulfills a societal purpose altogether different from the state. It cannot, therefore, take its place. At the same time, because the gospel of Jesus Christ is a profoundly public truth that bears importance for all of life, the church is not unrelated to the state, nor is it to be cordoned off from public and political life.

Here Reformational theology attempts to avoid two simplistic mistakes in political theology: first, the unjust dominance of the church over the state (or vice versa); and second, the simplistic belief that a separation of church and state implies an inconceivable separation of faith and politics.

Reformational theology avoids these mistakes by positing a distinction between the church as an organism and the church as an institution.[16] As a

15. Richard J. Mouw, *When the Kings Come Marching In: Isaiah and the New Jerusalem*, rev. ed. (Grand Rapids: Eerdmans, 2002), 34–42.

16. Abraham Kuyper, "Rooted and Grounded: The Church as Organism and Institution," in *On the Church*, ed. John Halsey Wood Jr. and Andrew M. McGinnis, trans. Harry Van Dyke et al., Collected Works in Public Theology (Bellingham, WA: Lexham, 2016), 49–51.

people bound together in Christ, the church exists as an organism, an organic body of believers. They are the hands and feet of Christ, scattered into every area of society.

However, the scattered church is also instructed to gather in Christ's name to worship him and to be nourished by the Word. These gatherings, like all institutions, are organized with purpose according to certain institutional principles. Thus the church as organism also composes an institution: local churches set themselves apart from society through gathering under the direct or immediate rule of Christ through obedience to his Word.

Both the organism and the institution have public significance, though in different ways. As institution, the church forms an organization that exists alongside other societal institutions—such as families, schools, and businesses—all of which are ordained and governed by God.[17] As an institution, the church bears a particular purpose to nourish Christians and to proclaim publicly the Word of God. This unique mission sets the institution apart from all other associations. The institution leverages no coercive power over those not under its purview. This does not mean it bears no public influence, for the proclamation of the law, justice, and Word of God is a profoundly public act.

The church as an organic body of believers extends its influence into social and political life in a wide variety of ways. Through shaping Christians to fill society with new habits of the heart, the church as institution informs the organism as its spreads into every sphere of culture.

A Present and Political Calling

These two dialectics provide a unique vision for Christian engagement with political life in general and with political ideologies in particular. First, they make clear that a proper understanding of political life allows for a certain level of ideological diversity and freedom.[18] This is not a wholesale affirmation of absolute relativism. Instead, it is a pragmatic and principled political determination to allow individuals—in this present saeculum—to seek their own goods freely, openly, and without fear. In this present age, indeed, true

17. This is not to say that the church is merely an association like other social institutions. It alone is unique in that it alone produces something new for society. As a spiritual mother, it gives birth to a new people, bringing the spiritually dead to life in its ministry. Cf. Kuyper, "Rooted and Grounded," 56.

18. The common good may occasionally require the law to establish civic norms and curtail certain behaviors. See Richard J. Mouw and Sander Griffioen, *Pluralisms and Horizons: An Essay in Christian Public Philosophy* (Grand Rapids: Eerdmans, 1993), 13–18.

worship cannot be coerced. Thus Christians must protect religious freedom and ideological pluralism for all citizens.

This does not mean that Christian political action in this present age stops with religious freedom. As second principle, a right reading of the times means that Christian citizens should use their religious freedom to publicly advocate ways for a public order that is more just, life-giving, and God-honoring.

What does a just and life-giving public order look like? Drawing on Calvin and Althusius, Abraham Kuyper and his Reformational progeny hold that God created human beings to form diverse forms of social life (families, schools, businesses, laboratories, arts collectives, etc.). These diverse social spheres cannot be reduced to one another. Each sphere has its own unique purpose and calling given to it by God.[19] These spheres glorify God and serve the common good in their own unique ways. On the spatial analogy, each social sphere has a circumference (certain limits to its jurisdiction) and its own center (its unique reason for being). Art exists to achieve aesthetic excellence. Science exists to gain knowledge about the natural world. The church exists to orient the human heart toward God. Thus, each sphere of culture plays a unique and vital role in achieving the public good.

What is the role of the state in this public order? According to Kuyper, the state exists to (1) protect the spheres from dominating one another, (2) protect the weak within the spheres from domination, and (3) ensure commerce and communication between the spheres. The state does not have the authority to define or direct these spheres in the way they should go. The state guards the circumference of a sphere; it does not determine its center. This is the responsibility of the sphere itself. The family, university board, the baker's union, and the members of the soccer club—all these determine their own ends and means. According to the ultimate conviction of sphere sovereignty, it is best for public order when the state understands that it did not create social life but instead stands under God to humbly steward and protect social life within the limits of its God-given responsibility.

Active Patience: The Habits of a Reformed Heart

Reformational political theology emerged out of the conviction that God alone is sovereign and that God's Word speaks with public truth for every area of human life. Upon this foundation comes the political "habits of the heart" that we have outlined: creation is good but not ultimate, and our hope

---

19. Abraham Kuyper, "Sphere Sovereignty [1880]," in *Abraham Kuyper: A Centennial Reader*, ed. James D. Bratt (Grand Rapids: Eerdmans, 1998), 463–90.

of Christ's coming earthly reign motivates our life in the public square toward specific ends. These habits of the heart remind us that working toward the public good is a matter of faithfulness, not victory. Political victories will come, as will political defeats. But the end is not yet. In this "time between the times," God has called us neither to victory nor to defeat, but to obedience. In the end, Christ will sit on the throne. His political vision will win the day. We may be encouraged to see just how many of our political efforts he resurrects to become something glorious and enduring in the new kingdom. But for today, we labor in faithfulness, working toward the good of today and with an eye toward the hope of tomorrow.

10

Power Politics in the Philippines

A Reformed Response to the Populism and Violence of Duterte

ROMEL REGALADO BAGARES

Fired at close range, the bullet went straight into his chest. Efren Morillo, a wiry twenty-nine-year-old, pulled up his shirt and showed me the scar. Breathing, he reports, is still difficult. As a human rights attorney, I interviewed Morillo inside a safe house belonging to the Philippine Commission on Human Rights.[1] There he told me the story of how he had survived a summary

---

I am grateful to James W. Skillen and Daniel Stoddard for their comments on an earlier version of this essay. I also thank Roy A. Clouser for suggesting the reference to Deut. 29:29 during an email exchange on a related issue, which provided much of this work's inspiration. Matthew Kaemingk deserves special recognition for patiently shepherding this chapter through several drafts and for suggesting the work of John Witte Jr. on Johannes Althusius as an additional resource. I am deeply honored to contribute to this Festschrift for the philosopher-theologian Richard J. Mouw, who with Sander Griffioen coauthored *Pluralisms and Horizons: An Essay in Christian Public Philosophy* (Grand Rapids: Eerdmans, 1993); Griffioen taught me this approach and has helped to shape my own vision of faith and public life.

1. This account is based on an English translation of an interview originally done in Filipino, the Philippine national language, in October of 2016. The interview served as a basis for

execution, which had killed four of his friends. Who were the executioners? Their own government, the Philippine National Police (PNP).

According to police reports, Efren and his friends were drug dealers who had engaged the officers in a firefight. The police's claims, however, were thoroughly undermined by forensic evidence at the scene, testimony from the victims' families, contradictions in the PNP's report, and the simple fact that the four men who died made their living working as *basureros* (garbage pickers) in a nearby dump.

The young men had been playing pool in the slums of Payatas in Quezon City. Police suddenly charged into the compound where they were playing, sealed it off, and shot the victims one by one in execution style. Morillo later testified, "I fell to the ground and felt a burning sensation in my chest but I didn't lose consciousness."[2] Efren managed to survive the attack by playing dead. But his friends Marcelo Daa Jr., Raffy Gabo, Anthony Comendo, and Jessie Cule all died instantly. Sadly, this story is not unique.

Manufactured Crisis

These young men were the victims of a widespread and deadly drug war launched by a tough-talking populist president, Rodrigo Roa Duterte. Before his presidency (2016–), Duterte ruled the city of Davao in Southern Philippines with an iron fist for nearly three decades. As mayor, he gained national notoriety as the alleged brains behind the Davao Death Squad (DDS). The DDS was a shadowy vigilante group allegedly responsible for killing hundreds of petty criminals and street children in an effort to lower crime rates.[3]

Early on, Duterte made a habit of exploiting the people's discontent with drugs, crime, and the failures of liberal democratic government for his own

---

the sworn statement mentioned in note 2. A relative of Efren Morillo had sought help from an evangelical urban-poor mission work in the slums, which in turn referred the matter to me. At that time, I was executive director of the Center for International Law–Philippines, a nonprofit engaged in advocacy, training, and strategic litigation for the rule of law.

2. Sworn statement made on May 5, 2017, submitted to the bi-partisan Tom Lantos Human Rights Commission of the United States Congress. The author helped prepare the statement, based on the first interview with Morillo at the Philippine Commission on Human Rights in October 2016. Details of the Tom Lantos Commission hearings on the consequences of the Duterte drug war, as well as copies of the statement in Filipino and English, may be accessed at https://humanrightscommission.house.gov/sites/humanrightscommission.house.gov/files /documents/Statement%20of%20Efren%20Morillo%20-%20US%20Congress.pdf.

3. "You Can Die Anytime: Death Squad Killings in Mindanao," *Human Rights Watch Report*, April 6, 2009, https://www.hrw.org/report/2009/04/06/you-can-die-any-time/death-squad -killings-mindanao.

political gain. Through fierce populism and nationalism, he projected the strong political image of a man with a decisive political will.[4] His presidential campaign cultivated this image through the sophisticated manipulation of Filipino voters through Facebook and the controversial political consulting firm Cambridge Analytica.[5]

Duterte's platform had a simple and singular focus: the drug trade is killing the Philippines, and he alone could resurrect it. Using the tough anti-crime tactics that he had employed as a mayor, Duterte promised to destroy the national drug trade in six months. His 2016 campaign was a watershed moment in Philippine political history. Duterte won the election with a level of rhetorical vulgarity and violence heretofore unseen. Filipinos wanted salvation, and Duterte's rhetoric of fierce nationalist strength promised to give it to them. Filipinos longed for law and order. And, as they say in English, Duterte was to be the judge, jury, and executioner.

A Reformed Response to Populism and Power Politics

Reformed political philosophy is founded on the belief that all creation and all human culture, including politics and all statecraft, is *normed* by God alone. God is the author of creation's laws and norms of justice—not the state and not any single leader. *Normative politics*, therefore, seeks to discern, acknowledge, submit to, disclose, develop, and respect the laws and limits of God. Normative statecraft is marked by leaders' submissive and respectful desire to conduct their political leadership humbly, under the ultimate law, sovereignty, and justice of God.

In this chapter, I hope to serve Christians in the Philippines (and around the world) who are wrestling with the growing global influence of populism and power politics. I hope to demonstrate how Reformed political theory not only can resist the allure of power politics but can also point a new way forward for Christian statecraft. My task, therefore, is both critical and constructive. Here I outline a Reformed critique of Duterte's populism and power politics.

4. See Walden Bello, "Duterte's Revolt against Liberal Democracy," *Global Dialogue* 7, no. 2 (May 2017), https://globaldialogue.isa-sociology.org/dutertes-revolt-against-liberal-democracy; Bonn Juego, "The Philippines 2017: Duterte-Led Authoritarian Populism and Its Liberal-Democratic Roots," *Journal of the Italian Think Tank on Asia* 28 (2017): 129.

5. David Gilbert, "Cambridge Analytica's Tools Turned 'Kind' Duterte into a 'No-Nonsense' Strongman," *Vice News*, April 5, 2018, https://www.vice.com/en_us/article/xw7vyw/cambridge-analytica-duterte-strongman-2016. Apparently his "Dirty Harry" image as city mayor was originally a serious concern for Duterte's campaign team, and they wanted to cast him instead in more paternalistic terms. Data provided by Cambridge Analytica convinced them that his strongman political roots was the way to go.

I also point to a more humble, normed, and life-giving form of statecraft, one that I have found within the Reformed tradition.

This chapter, while brief, is meant to be written with the humble spirit of Moses, that first steward of the divine law. He declared, "The secret things belong to the LORD our God, but the things revealed belong to us and to our children forever, that we may follow all the words of this law" (Deut. 29:29). These words remind us of the danger of pompously ascribing God's will to any politician or political movement, over and against scriptural norms that limit state power and direct our citizenship. Here we cannot possibly outline the whole of normative politics, but we can begin to point a way forward. I encourage interested readers to dig deeper into the Reformed sources listed in the footnotes.

God's Anointed or God's Punishment?

The brutal killings began on Duterte's first day in office. The slums around Manila, a teeming metropolis of thirteen million citizens, were the first to be hit. Duterte purposefully compared his violent campaign against drug addicts to Hitler's infamous extermination campaigns. Like Hitler, Duterte would be "happy" to wipe the country clean of their existence.[6]

Sadly, neither Duterte's rhetoric nor his actions appear to bother the largely Christian nation of one hundred million. Now, four years into his term, he continues to enjoy unprecedented support from Catholic and Protestant clergy and laity alike.[7] Duterte can count on widespread Christian support from the megachurches of metropolitan Manila and even from the ramshackle congregations in the slums, where his systematic killings continue unabated. Four years in office, Duterte has publicly admitted that his violent antidrug campaign has failed, and yet his support among Christian leaders is still holding strong.[8]

Duterte's popularity among Christians is perplexing for a wide variety of reasons. He is a self-confessed womanizer. He is currently living with a

6. "Philippines: Duterte Threatens Human Rights Community," *Human Rights Watch Report*, August 17, 2017, https://www.hrw.org/news/2017/08/17/philippines-duterte-threatens-human-rights-community.

7. I use the term "evangelical" here to encompass a broad array of Protestant churches that self-identify as "born-again" believers, such as those under the umbrella of the Philippine Council of Evangelical Churches (PCEC), as well as independent churches that nevertheless make the same stress on personal conversion and are within the overarching framework of orthodox Protestantism.

8. Jeoffrey Maitem, "Philippine Drug War Deaths Pile Up as Duterte Admits Losing Control," *South China Morning Post*, June 19, 2019, https://www.scmp.com/news/asia/southeast-asia/article/3015255/philippine-drug-war-deaths-pile-duterte-admits-losing.

woman who is not his wife. Duterte has repeatedly admitted to having killed suspects while he was mayor.[9] He has publicly cursed God as "stupid" for creating heaven and hell.[10] Duterte has nonchalantly told police officers to "kill your [Catholic] bishops" when they criticize the government. He has thought nothing of making jokes about rape.[11] Inexplicably, none of these things appears to bother the evangelical leaders who support him. Instead, they make all sorts of excuses for his outrageous statements.

Filipino sociologists Jayeel Cornelio and Erron Media interviewed religious leaders in an attempt to understand this religious phenomenon. They spoke with one Baptist pastor, identified as "Pastor Julius." He leads a church in the district where Efren Morillo and his friends were attacked by the police. Pastor Julius reports that, no matter what Filipinos think of Duterte's character, God has clearly chosen and anointed him to lead the Philippines.[12] Moreover, if Filipinos really believe that God is in control, they need to accept Duterte's election (and his drug war) as a punishment for the nation's sins.[13] The pastor concluded that "God needed to appoint Duterte in order to get Filipinos to repent."[14] Reflecting on their conversation, the sociologists noted that, for Pastor Julius, "Duterte's election is God's way of testing the faith of Filipinos."[15] For many Filipino evangelicals, all of this dovetails with an ironclad reading of Romans 13 as a prooftext commanding Christian citizens to submit to and support government leaders—without question.

These evangelicals refer to Duterte as "*Tatay Digong*," a familial term of endearment and submission. The label frames the president as the beloved "father" of the nation. As *Digong*, he is the national patriarch, the embodiment of law and truth, the leader of the national family. To go against Tatay Digong is to go against the family of God—and God himself.[16]

9. "Philippines' Duterte Admits Personally Killing Suspects," *BBC News*, December 14, 2016, https://www.bbc.com/news/world-38311655.

10. Emily Schultheis, "Duterte vs. God," *Foreign Policy*, July 15, 2018, https://foreignpolicy.com/2018/07/15/duterte-versus-god-philippine-president-fights-catholic-church/.

11. Siobhán O'Grady, "Most of the Philippines Is Catholic—and Duterte Said Catholic Bishops Should Be Killed," *Washington Post*, December 7, 2018, https://www.washingtonpost.com/world/2018/12/06/most-philippines-is-catholic-duterte-said-catholic-bishops-should-be-killed/.

12. Paterno R. Esmaquel II, "Why Filipinos Believe Duterte Was 'Appointed by God,'" *Rappler*, June 27, 2019, https://www.rappler.com/newsbreak/in-depth/234115-why-filipinos-believe-duterte-appointed-by-god, quoted in Jayeel Cornelio and Erron Medina, "Christianity and Duterte's War on Drugs in the Philippines," *Journal of Politics, Religion, and Ideology* 20, no. 2 (2019): 159–61.

13. Esmaquel, "Why Filipinos Believe Duterte."

14. Esmaquel, "Why Filipinos Believe Duterte."

15. Esmaquel, "Why Filipinos Believe Duterte."

16. The authors of the study also explain this in Jayeel Cornelio and Erron Medina, "Duterte's Enduring Popularity Is Not Just a Political Choice—It Is Also Religious," *New*

Efren Morillo's testimony illustrates the power of the political cocktail of Tatay Digong fealty, populism, power politics, and a submissive Christian political theology. The government had executed Morillo's friends right in front of him. And yet—sitting there in the safe house—he still hesitated to blame Tatay Digong and his drug war for their murder. The father of the nation is either God's anointed or God's punishment. Either way, his power, his policies, and his executions all come from God. Despite a bullet hole in his chest, Morillo struggled to break free from this logic.

The Structure and Direction of Normative Statecraft[17]

How might thoughtful Christian citizens respond to claims that Duterte is either God's anointed or God's punishment? How might they respond to the claim that he is the father of the national family—the personification of Filipino law and truth?

Reformed theology begins with a simple confession that has far-reaching consequences for political life. "The earth is the LORD's, and everything in it, the world, and all who live in it" (Ps. 24:1). In the language of the Nicene Creed, God alone is the "Maker of heaven and earth." God alone wrote the normative law for creation and human community. Every area of society, including statecraft, rests under God's sovereign law and judgment.[18] In short, the infinite sovereignty of God's power and law relativizes the finite sovereignty of the state's power and law.

Although God's sovereignty will rightly humble human leaders and institutions, it will also raise them up. Social and political communities are never mere human constructs. They have God-given tasks and responsibilities. Politics, for example, is a holy calling, to be exercised according to a God-ordained *telos*.[19] The state is a public legal community: government is called by God to establish public justice. The state has a holy vocation, a responsibility to create a safe and just public space for human freedom and flourishing, commerce and communication.

According to the Reformed political imagination, there are God-ordained *structures*[20] for political life that should always be aimed in the God-ordained

Mandala, September 3, 2018, https://www.newmandala.org/dutertes-enduring-popularity-not-just-political-choice-also-religious/.

17. "Normative statecraft" is a term I borrow from James W. Skillen, *With or Against the World? America's Role among the Nations* (Lanham, MD: Rowman & Littlefield, 2005), 140.

18. Albert Wolters, *Creation Regained: Biblical Basics for a Reformational Worldview*, 2nd ed. (Grand Rapids: Eerdmans, 2005), 25.

19. Abraham Kuyper, "Sphere Sovereignty [1880]," in *Abraham Kuyper: A Centennial Reader*, ed. James D. Bratt (Grand Rapids: Eerdmans, 1998), 463–90.

20. Wolters, *Creation Regained*, 24–26, 26n18.

direction of public justice. Because of human sin, sadly, these political structures become distorted and directed away from public justice.[21] Moreover, because of human sin, political actors will not always be able to discern or agree on the proper structure and direction of political life. Human politics, conducted outside Eden, will always involve political disagreement. Our sinful blindness to God's perfect political will demands a healthy measure of political humility.

Johannes Althusius, a seventeenth-century German Calvinist, was one of the leading political theorists and jurists of his day.[22] Althusius may well be the first European political theorist to reject a universalist approach to the state in favor of an associational or pluralist approach. Up until Althusius, the European political imagination largely viewed diverse associations and social communities (families, tribes, churches, villages, artisanal guilds, etc.) as mere parts of the state's greater whole.[23] These communities were all members of the same body politic—the body of the king. The king and his kingdom enveloped all these diverse associations by divine right. What was good for the king was good for these associations. They were all one body, with the king as their head.[24]

While Althusius thought that local and provincial governments belonged to the body politic, he began to argue that "not every societal entity" was a "part of the state." This key insight came when Althusius realized and began to argue that there were different "structural principles governing distinct societal collectivities."[25] Families, artisan guilds, and churches, for example, each have their own distinct goods that they seek. These diverse goods are all unique, and they are not dictated to them by the state. They are gifts from God.

This associational insight had important implications for the future of Reformed statecraft. Suddenly proper laws (*leges propriae*) that governed the way in which these "particular associations are ruled" should be written and executed not by royal fiat but with careful attention to the community's distinct nature.[26] Under this principle, divine law and justice ultimately spring not from a king but from a careful form of political attention paid to God's people and the diverse communities that bind them together. Rulers of this world, including Duterte, are subject to God and to be measured against God's

---

21. Wolters, *Creation Regained*, 59–62.

22. John Witte Jr., *The Reformation of Rights: Law, Religion and Rights in Early Calvinism* (Cambridge: Cambridge University Press, 2007), 150–51.

23. D. F. M. Strauss, *Philosophy: Discipline of Disciplines* (Grand Rapids: Paideia, 2009), 532. See also Witte, *Reformation of Rights*, 181–84, 187–96.

24. See Ernst Kantorowicz, *The King's Two Bodies: A Study in Medieval Political Theology* (Princeton: Princeton University Press, 2016), 25.

25. Strauss, *Philosophy*, 533n23.

26. Strauss notes that this idea was explored further by the Dutch politician Guillaume Groen van Prinsterer and by his successor, Abraham Kuyper. See Strauss, *Philosophy*, 533n23.

complex and normative social order. God has given these diverse communities rights, freedoms, and laws—all of which the king must respect, honor, and observe.

Duterte has argued that he and he alone is empowered and competent to solve the drug crisis in the Philippines. He alone is the judge, jury, and executioner of the drug war. Duterte thus claims to be sovereign. His reach and competency have no limit. In this view, Duterte is the very person of the state.

An Althusian response would argue that Filipino families, hospitals, churches, nonprofits, schools, and local governments all have competency, responsibility, sovereignty, and roles to play in solving the country's drug crisis. Moreover, these communities do not exist to serve or empower Duterte. Nor should they blindly do his bidding. They have their proper ends that have nothing to do with him or the state.

An Althusian response to the Filipino drug crisis will not be simple. It will be as complex as the problem itself, and it will call on the complex associational resources of the country at large. It will not be embodied in *the* state or *the* leader alone. It will be made manifest in many diverse communities, vocations, and associations of the nation itself. An Althusian response will respect, honor, and call Filipinos of all walks of life to respond to the crisis. It will call on all Filipino families, doctors, churches, businesses, lawyers, and volunteer organizations to bring their diverse gifts and vocations to bear. Of course, it will involve policing, but this complex societal problem is not ultimately reducible to a mere question of criminality. Finally, the drug crisis is an *international* reality. Drug cartels are like multinational corporations. No single state and no single leader can solve this crisis alone. The Philippines therefore needs the cooperation of outside states and regional and international governmental organizations.

Johannes Althusius would rightly denounce Duterte's cavalier attitude toward the Filipino constitution and the rule of law. He would label it as tyranny.[27] The biblical call to obey divinely ordained rulers *presupposes* that these leaders are the legitimate representatives of God. However, Althusius argues, when leaders offend God and openly defy his law, they lose their political legitimacy, become private citizens, and are subject to the natural rights of self-defense.[28] At this point the people have the right to defend themselves against private citizens who attack them.[29]

27. Witte, *Reformation of Rights*, 200n23.
28. Witte, *Reformation of Rights*, 200n23.
29. Althusius is distinguished for his idea that a tyrant is a magistrate who has acted illegally and unnaturally (*contra legem et naturam*), in breach of the contractual and covenantal duties sworn before God and the people. For systemic violations, Althusius allowed for "sanctions,

If statecraft is a responsibility that is normed and limited by God, Christian citizens are to abhor and resist any politician who claims that they alone have the unfettered discretion to say who is a friend and who is an enemy; what is law and what is not; when there is a state of emergency and when there is a normal state of political affairs; or worse, who is human and who is not.[30] Duterte has broken every one of these basic political norms.

The "Public Interest" as a Blank Check

A key legal strategy adopted by Duterte's government is to claim, despite evidence to the contrary, that the brutal deaths in police operations are all acts of self-defense.[31] So framed, these deaths are labeled "deaths under investigation" as opposed to "extralegal killings." This legal framing allows police to claim that these killings exist outside public and legal accountability.[32]

Duterte couples this legal strategy with an equally abhorrent rhetorical strategy. In the media he and his government regularly argue that drug suspects are "not human." Instead, they imply that these subhumans are irredeemable and incorrigible. So labeled, they deserve to die.[33] So labeled, they are marked for liquidation.[34]

At the time of this writing, nearly six thousand people have officially been killed in Duterte's antidrug operations.[35] The government claims that every

restrictions, or removal of the offending magistrates, even revolutionary revamping of the government as a whole." Witte, *Reformation of Rights*, 200n22.

30. See a decisionist power politics theorized in Carl Schmitt, *Political Theology: Four Chapters on the Concept of Sovereignty*, ed. and trans. George Schwab (Chicago: University of Chicago Press, 2005), 5–6, 13.

31. "5,000 'Nanlaban' Killings, Zero Records? Rights Group Blasts Slays without Probes," *ABS-CBN News*, March 19, 2019, https://news.abs-cbn.com/news/03/19/19/5000-nanlaban -killings-zero-records-rights-group-blasts-slays-without-probes.

32. Emmanuel Tupas, "29,000 Deaths Probed since Drug War Launched," *Philippine Star*, March 6, 2019, https://www.philstar.com/nation/2019/03/06/1898959/29000-deaths-probed -drug-war-launched.

33. "Criminals Are Not Human: Philippine Justice Minister," *The Straits Times*, February 2, 2017, https://www.straitstimes.com/asia/se-asia/criminals-are-not-human-philippine-justice -minister.

34. In other words, the *homo sacer*'s "entire existence is reduced to a bare life stripped of every right by virtue of the fact that anyone can kill him without committing homicide." Giorgio Agamben, *Homo Sacer: Sovereign Power and Bare Life*, trans. Daniel Heller-Roazen (Stanford, CA: Stanford University Press, 1998), 103. Yet against Agamben, who ultimately vilifies the state as pure violence from the beginning, this present chapter echoes the Christian confession of the goodness and normativity of the state within the divine economy.

35. Romina Cabrera, "PNP: Official Death Toll from Drug War at 5,526," *Philippine Star*, July 19, 2019, https://www.philstar.com/headlines/2019/07/19/1936032/pnp-official-death-toll -drug-war-5526.

single one of them has been lawfully killed by police in an act of self-defense. But these are simply the official police numbers. Thousands more are missing and have been left uncounted. Human rights groups now estimate that Mr. Duterte's drug war has killed upward of thirty thousand people.[36]

Duterte's drug war is an abominable perversion of police power and a rejection of the creational and biblical norms governing his office. Yet, for Duterte and his supporters, these killings are necessary and even desirable, in the name of "the public interest."

The twentieth-century Reformed philosopher Herman Dooyeweerd was a professor of law and legal philosophy at the Vrije Universiteit Amsterdam. One aspect of his philosophical work explores how the language of "the public interest" is often bent by kings, emperors, dictators (and the philosophers who support them) to serve their own political whims.

Dooyeweerd argues that, in the name of public interest, Plato, Aristotle, and Johann Fichte each denied parental rights over children and supported state control over their care and education.[37] In the name of public interest, Plato sought to abolish private property. In the name of public interest, Rousseau spoke of diverse social institutions, communities, and free associations as a potential impediment to state power and the common good.[38] Dooyeweerd explains thus: "The slogan of the public interest was the instrument for the destruction of the most firmly established liberties because it lacked any juridical delimitation. The terrible threat of Leviathan is audible in this word [public interest] as long as it is used in a juridically unlimited sense. The universalistic political theories could conceive of the relation between the state and the nonpolitical societal structures only in the schema of the whole and its parts. This is why they could not delimit the idea of 'the public.'"[39] Without a clear understanding of the inherent normative limits of the state, politicians and citizens alike are in constant danger of enabling state overreach. Vague appeals to lofty political phrases like the public interest, the common good, human rights, equality, and national security can all be used to expand the state's ability to crush opposition. Evangelical support for Duterte rests in part on their tragic inability to rec-

36. Sheila Coronel, Mariel Padilla, David Mora, and the Stabile Center for Investigative Journalism, "The Unaccounted Dead of Duterte's Drug War," *The Atlantic*, August 19, 2019, https://www.theatlantic.com/international/archive/2019/08/philippines-dead-rodrigo-duterte -drug-war/595978/. The Duterte government questions this figure of 30,000 killed.

37. Herman Dooyeweerd, *The Structures of Individuality of Temporal Reality*, vol. 3 of *A New Critique of Theoretical Thought*, trans. David H. Freeman and H. De Jongste (Jordan Station, ON: Paideia, 1984; repr., Lewistown, NY: Mellon, 1997), 442–43.

38. Dooyeweerd, *Structures of Individuality*, 442–43.

39. Dooyeweerd, *Structures of Individuality*, 443.

ognize and defend the God-ordained limits and normative boundaries of the state.

Nationalism and International Law

Duterte's regime has consistently resisted international mechanisms of legal accountability. He withdrew Philippine membership in the International Criminal Court (ICC) after it announced a preliminary probe into the legality of his drug war.[40] He has marshaled the rhetoric of populism, patriotism, and national sovereignty against the ICC and international law.[41] Duterte has even threatened international human rights activists[42] and UN officials with all manner of harm for demanding legal accountability.[43]

Within a Reformed approach to statecraft, public justice in the international realm is the shared responsibility of all states governing under God's reign. God's call for law and justice is *international* in scope. It thus should be no surprise that, during the past century, Reformed scholars of international relations have been especially supportive of the development of an international legal system.[44] To be clear, Reformed calls for international law do not involve the establishment of a totalizing world government. Instead, they call for an international legal system to provide support when independent states encounter an utter failure in their responsibilities for normative statecraft.

When is international legal intervention necessary? What principles would guide this sort of intervention? These are critical and complex discussions

40. "Statement of the Prosecutor of the International Criminal Court, [Ms.] Fatou Bensouda, on Opening Preliminary Examinations into the Situations in the Philippines and in Venezuela," ICC Office of the Trial Prosecutor, February 8, 2018, https://www.icc-cpi.int/Pages/item .aspx?name=180208-otp-stat.

41. The Department of Foreign Affairs, "PH Officially Serves Notice to UN of Decision to Withdraw from the ICC," DFA Press Statement, March 16, 2018, https://dfa.gov.ph/dfa-news /dfa-releasesupdate/15975-ph-officially-serves-notice-to-un-of-decision-to-withdraw-from-icc.

42. "Philippines: Duterte Threatens Human Rights Community."

43. Aljazeera, "Duterte Attacks Rights Officials Callamard and Bensouda," *Aljazeera*, March 9, 2018, https://www.aljazeera.com/news/2018/03/duterte-attacks-rights-officials-callamard -bensouda-180309091927105.html.

44. A recent anthology of essays from the "Amsterdam school" attempts to mark out for the first time the metes and bounds of a Reformed approach to international relations marked by the Kuyperian-Dooyeweerdian tradition. See Govert J. Buijs and Simon Polinder, eds., *Christian Faith, Philosophy and International Relations: The Lamb and the Wolf* (Leiden: Brill, 2019). For an earlier anthology, also broadly animated by the tradition, see Jonathan Chaplin and Robert Joustra, eds., *God and Global Order: The Power of Religion in American Foreign Policy* (Waco: Baylor University Press, 2010). For an earlier book-length work on a particular issue, see Robert Joustra, *The Religious Problem with Religious Freedom: Why Foreign Policy Needs Political Theology* (New York: Routledge, 2018).

in Reformed political theory that can be traced all the way back to Abraham Kuyper and John Calvin.[45] In making his arguments for international law and intervention, Kuyper pointed to John Calvin himself, who supported a levy to pay German troops to enter France and help Protestants who were being persecuted by Catholic leaders.[46] Robert Joustra comments that Kuyper's own Reformed approach to "international law . . . was about recognizing the constraints under which power, even great global power, operates. The laws among nations, then, may be thought of as a kind of functional stewardship of deeper norms, most significantly the norms of Christ and his Kingdom."[47]

Nevertheless, Reformed conceptions of international law and intervention do not support the sort of crass militaristic or legal interventionism that has bedeviled much of contemporary international relations.[48] However, when states dramatically fail to discharge their task of normative statecraft, the international community needs to find effective, innovative, and nonviolent ways to execute international governance and legal accountability. These interventions should not weaken the states they seek to serve. Instead, they

45. See Abraham Kuyper, "Calvinism: Source and Stronghold of Our Constitutional Liberties [1874]," in Bratt, *Abraham Kuyper: A Centennial Reader*, 306.

46. Kuyper, "Calvinism," citing Jules Bonnet, *Lettres de Calvin*, 2 vols. (Paris: Meyreuis, 1854), 1:185; 2:182, 474.

47. Robert Joustra, "Globalization and the Kingdom of God: A Christian Perspective on International Relations," *Public Justice Review* 5 (2017), https://cpjustice.org/public/public _justice_review/article/56.

48. Indeed, humanitarian intervention is not a tidy matter requiring no reflection or justification. As Oliver O'Donovan writes, in the context of the long-standing Christian just-war tradition, "It is a discipline of deliberation, a way of focusing and posing questions of political responsibility to oneself and to others." He continues:

> There may well be dangers attached to the kind of humanitarian intervention which has been argued for; but they need to be overwhelmingly conspicuous if they are to provide support for a universal prohibition running counter to the humanitarian instincts of civilised peoples. To turn one's back while a neighbouring community is being slaughtered is not an easy thing to recommend; and international law should not demand it without reasons so strong as to seem, when pointed out, morally irresistible. Certainly, the maintenance of a "rather tidy legal regime" based on the sovereignty of the nation-state will not suffice. (*The Just War Revisited* [Cambridge: Cambridge University Press, 2003], 16, 29)

A present-day variation on just war as humanitarian intervention is the emerging doctrine in international law dubbed as the "Responsibility to Protect." The principle holds that the international community has the duty not only to intervene in situations of gross human rights violations but also to actually prevent them from happening. Esther D. Reed has flailed the uncritical Christian acceptance of this principle, warning that any doctrine of intervention founded on a universal high moral ground whose proponents are always from the Global North while those at the receiving end are always from the Global South "is not moral progress, it is geopolitical business as usual." *Theology for International Law* (London: Bloomsbury T&T Clark, 2013), 175–79, 214–15.

should seek to build up and strengthen both international and domestic legal capacities.[49]

Under the Reformed principle of "sphere sovereignty," the international legal order should ensure that faltering states are able to respond to the challenges of governance in a manner that nurtures the rights and responsibilities of diverse citizens, communities, and associations. In this Reformed approach, international law works in two ways. It limits and humbles proud and overbearing states; at the same time, it honors and strengthens states that are stumbling. Likewise, it elevates international laws and institutions while reminding them to respect the differentiated responsibilities of various domestic societal institutions, including the state.

Hope amid Horror

Although there are reasons for hope in the Philippines, Efren Morillo still bears the scars of his ordeal. His friends are still dead. The police and politicians responsible for their murder still walk the streets with impunity. The killings continue. Christian hope is not and cannot be deaf or blind to the people's cries for justice.

Yet there are small victories to celebrate. A writ of amparo (protection) was recently brought before the Philippine Supreme Court. It is the first challenge of its kind to Duterte's drug war. The act offered Efren Morillo and the slain men's families some relief from police harassment.[50] The legal proceeding served as a model for another landmark legal action, this time on behalf of an entire slum community in old Manila. Forty-five victims had been killed in this specific neighborhood. In the legal action, the Supreme Court required police to furnish the victims with all the records pertaining to those killed during Duterte's drug war.[51] These documents, once produced, will be invaluable to future legal actions.

God alone is the ultimate creator, sustainer, lawgiver, and judge of the Philippines. This basic Christian doctrine has political implications for the place of hope in Filipino politics. No amount of political tyranny can wipe

---

49. Skillen, *With or Against the World?*, 141n18.

50. The writ is a special procedure devised by the Supreme Court to address threats to the life, liberty, and property of anyone. See Edu Punay, "SC Issues Writ of Amparo on 'Tokhang,'" *Philippine Star*, February 1, 2017, https://www.philstar.com/headlines/2017/02/01/1667497/sc-issues-writ-amparo-tokhang.

51. Tetch Torres-Tupas, "Supreme Court Orders Release of All 'Tokhang' Police Reports," *Philippine Daily Inquirer*, April 2, 2019, https://newsinfo.inquirer.net/1102187/supreme-court-orders-release-of-all-tokhang-police-reports#ixzz6HjBTbr1N.

out God's normative demands and design for public justice in the Philippines. Being made in God's image, Filipino citizens bear God's law on their hearts. We can neither escape nor erase God's demands for law, justice, and equality. They haunt our public life. We can only ignore them at our own peril. God's norms for the political community to call citizens back to his designs for a kingdom of love, truth, and justice. Mortal tyrants come and go, but the immortal law of God, the immortal love of God, endures forever.

What shall we say about the Filipino church's submission to Rodrigo Roa Duterte? What rejoinder can we offer to the submissive political theology embodied in the nickname Tatay Digong? A Reformed approach to politics cuts down to size any political figure claiming a right to, or necessity for, unaccountable leadership. Our normative commitments to God must limit and direct our political behavior and goals. Power politics is unbiblical. Politics built around a personality cult is out of bounds. And, if the pogroms launched by all manner of revolutionary fervor throughout history have taught us anything, vox populi does not always reflect vox Dei.

We who place our hope in the providence of God know this: even when the state's powers are temporarily perverted by politicians, such distortions do not eliminate our political calling to normative order and justice. Political evil does not diminish the church's calling to shine a light on God's normative design for human flourishing. Despite our present suffering, we act in hope. We work in anticipation of that day when Christ's kingdom comes, when his justice and mercy will be seen in all the earth.

11

Reflections from a Reformed Activist

STEPHANIE SUMMERS

I have always been an activist. I stopped eating meat when I was twelve because of concerns about animal cruelty and the environment. While forming clubs in school, I wanted to change more than my local campus: my political vision and agenda functioned on a local, state, national, and even global level. In high school I organized and rallied for the release of jailed dissidents and journalists in foreign nations. I protested the proliferation of nuclear weapons. I read stacks of books and essays on a wide variety of political issues. Mentors encouraged me to use my young voice to speak out against injustice, and I did—with vigor.

As many young activists do, I viewed most issues along the binaries of good and evil, right and wrong. Those who disagreed with me were my opponents. For or against, I was wrestling to win. My opponents had to lose. I was shamefully proud of the power I could accrue through recruitment, organizing, and advocacy. Numbers mattered; gathering more constituents' voices was the path to pressure, and pressure was the path to change. I was constantly terrified of losing ground because, eventually, I needed to win.

At sixteen an encounter with Jesus upended everything. He revealed that my life of activism was filled with personal and political idols. Yearning to love God and my neighbors wholeheartedly in Christ alone, I saw political activism as a spiritually dangerous and potentially idolatrous temptation.

And yet, I was still haunted by this innate thirst for justice. Although I did not have the theological language for it, I had a vague sense that I had received this thirst for justice from God. Spurred on by this, I continued to protest, march, and organize, but I always did so with a torn and ambivalent heart. I remained an activist but always with the underlying anxiety that my activism was, at best, a spiritually dubious venture, something that God merely tolerated.

Was the world of political activism a good place for a Christian? Many of my friends and fellow activists wanted nothing to do with Christianity. Should I be marching shoulder to shoulder with them? The spiritual anxiety and ambivalence became unsustainable. Though I could not articulate it, I longed for a more coherent and sustainable approach to faithful activism.

An Activist Meets a Calvinist

I first learned about Reformed political thought from the Reformed philosopher Jim Skillen at a conference for college students. He was giving a lecture on the theme of justice throughout Scripture.[1] Christian citizens, he argued, are called to actively seek justice and cultivate just political communities. When they do so, they glorify God, who loves justice.[2] My activist heart was on fire.

After Skillen's lecture, I waited in line to talk with him and gushed about how encouraging it was to hear that citizenship and activism matter within the kingdom of God. My gushing word torrent ended with something like this: "I'm an activist, and you just said God wants us to be activists!" And I remember that Jim, patient and affirming, said, "But it seems to me that your activism has no root. Do you like to read?" And so began my journey of exploring the world of Reformed political theology.

Today I'm still a passionate activist, but a different sort. And it is that word *different* that I hope to explore in this chapter. I serve as the CEO of the Center for Public Justice in Washington, DC. We are a Christian think tank whose mission is rooted in the Reformed theological tradition.[3] We collaborate with

1. The themes of this talk are encapsulated in the five essays on justice in James W. Skillen's *Covenant to Keep: Meditations on the Biblical Theme of Justice* (Grand Rapids: CRC Publications, 2000).
2. "Guideline on Political Community," Center for Public Justice, https://cpjustice.org/index .php/public/page/content/political_community.
3. Placing myself and our work at the Center for Public Justice within "the Reformed tradition" does require some nuance. There are some aspects of the tradition that I do not embrace. It

scholars, churches, nonprofits, universities, advocacy groups, and foundations in a broad Christian effort to seek public justice in the United States.

My narrative of youthful activism is common. That same fiery passion for justice burns within many young citizens today. They long for racial and environmental justice. They march, advocate, and rally for women's rights, health care, education, economic opportunity, and more. Whether they believe in God or not, they yearn for God's justice and shalom to be realized. God's heart for justice burns in many of their hearts.

But, as Jim Skillen said to me years ago, all too often their activism lacks a root. They need a deeper well, one that can sustain and guide them wisely through a whole life of citizenship. They need a framework within which they can see their "opponents" as potential partners. They need ways to think, act, and collaborate institutionally. They need a framework for political rhetoric that is civil, inviting, and persuasive. Finally, they need to see politics as one of the fundamental ways in which they can love their neighbors and serve their God. For the remainder of this chapter, I will explore how Reformed theology might offer them some conceptual tools for doing exactly that.

Thinking Institutionally

As a young activist, I saw the electorate as a vast collection of autonomous individuals. These free citizens were like billiard balls, rolling freely and bouncing about in society. According to my political imagination, if the cause was true and the activist was persuasive, autonomous individuals could be gathered around any number of political causes.

In Reformed theology, I found a quite different political anthropology. The world is not filled with autonomous individuals who either consent to or reject a set of public policies. Instead, God created human beings to be communal. These communal creatures create a wide variety of diverse and purpose-filled institutions. Thus families, schools, churches, teams, artist collectives, churches, and nonprofits each contribute not only to individual flourishing but also to God's purposes in creation.[4] This complex web of

---

is not lost on me, for example, that the Reformed political theologian Abraham Kuyper would not have allowed me, a woman, to vote in his Netherlands. I am also quite aware that this theological tradition that I love was twisted to support the racist ideology of apartheid in South Africa. Yet I continue to claim this flawed human tradition as my own because, within its theology, I have found rich resources for faithful Christian citizenship that have transformed and sustained my activism in many profound ways.

4. As Richard Mouw explains, "God has ordained that these diverse spheres have their own places in the creation because they fulfill different creational purposes." *Abraham Kuyper: A Short and Personal Introduction* (Grand Rapids, Eerdmans, 2011), 24.

diverse communities and institutions is often referred to by social scientists as "civil society."

Reformed theology helped me to see the social and political importance of communities, institutions, and civil society. It helped me see that citizens require more than a just government: they also require a thriving network of purpose-filled communities. It is not enough for me to have individual rights, freedoms, and a safety net if I do not also have a rich set of communities and institutions within which I can enjoy them.

In the end the foundation of my more communal and institutional approach to politics and human flourishing was grounded in Abraham Kuyper's Reformed concept of "sphere sovereignty." Understanding that these diverse communities and institutions were created and beloved by God for distinct purposes means that these diverse spheres of life should respect and yield room for one another to flourish. For example, both the family and the business are important communities that matter to God. Their unique purposes, integrity, and freedom are important to God. If, at some point, economic communities and activities begin to overtake and endanger familial communities and activities, that is a problem. In such a case, according to sphere sovereignty, the state is responsible defend the institution of the family from the institution of the corporation.

God alone is completely sovereign. God's sovereignty limits the sovereignty of the state. The task of government is humble. It must ensure public respect for the diversity and freedom of communities and institutions in civil society. This means protecting them proactively or responsively in law. It also means that there is a limit to the state's authority to meddle in the internal affairs of free communities and that institutions must be carefully limited. The state must endeavor to make room for institutions other than itself to flourish.

Kuyper argues that the state must be limited because God has given other spheres of life important and diverse mandates that they need to fulfill.[5] Families, schools, businesses, and media each have their own unique and diverse social responsibilities. It is a key insight of Reformed political theology that government has a God-given purpose to ensure that diverse communities and institutions can fulfill their mandates in public justice and freedom.

---

5. Kuyper vividly illustrates the divinely ordered limits of the state's authority: "Neither the life of science nor of art, nor of agriculture, nor of industry, nor of commerce, nor of navigation, nor of the family, nor of human relationship may be coerced to suit itself to the grace of the government. The State may never become an octopus, which stifles the whole of life." *Lectures on Calvinism* (Grand Rapids: Eerdmans, 1931), 96–97. This remarkable statement is from a man who served as the head of government in the Netherlands (prime minister, 1901–5).

As a young activist, once I could see the importance of these diverse institutions in civil society, my approach to advocacy and public policy changed dramatically. This new political imagination forced me to begin with a new question: Which institutions are responsible for addressing this particular public issue, and how are they responsible?

As an example, during my time leading the Center for Public Justice, we have affirmed that governments must respect the sovereignty of the family as an institution created by God. The state, therefore, is not interfering with families when they are upholding their responsibilities. For over a decade the United States has had a debate about what to do with immigrants who were brought into the country illegally as children by their parents. These children obviously had no choice in the matter. The two dominant political voices argue for either amnesty or deportation. While opposing one another vehemently, both sides frame the issue individualistically.

At the Center for Public Justice, our Reformed understanding of institutions causes us to reframe the issue in terms of the family. We ask, "What public policy will best serve the rights, dignity, freedom, and flourishing of the family?" So framed, we argue that the government should not punish childhood arrivals for a crime committed by their parents. We also argue that the government should promote policies that keep these families together in the USA rather than breaking them apart. After all, the government has an obligation, under God, to safeguard the sacred, unique, and created institution of the family.

Reformed theology counsels that careful attention to the importance of diverse institutions should inform our political activism as Christians. Thinking institutionally impacts the way in which we approach issues like poverty, education, health care, criminal justice, and religious freedom. The freedom and flourishing of human beings cannot be secured by either a just state or a booming economy alone. Human beings require the diverse communities and institutions of civil society in order to flourish. Christian activists need a political imagination that can see, protect, and defend institutions and their diverse and God-given purposes.

Thinking institutionally also changes the way in which Christian activists respond to a perceived injustice. Before we march, organize, or advocate, we first need to stop and reflect institutionally. Regarding the perceived injustice, we need to determine which institutions and communities are responsible for attending to this perceived problem. Former US Congressperson Vernon Ehlers brought this idea home for me. The Center for Public Justice had hosted a political lecture at a Christian college. During the question-and-answer period, the audience began to express their deep frustration with

Congress and its perceived inaction on the subject. "Why won't Congress fix this?" Representative Ehlers got up from the audience, walked toward me onstage, and said, "Please," as he motioned me to give him the mic. He then lamented that, more often than not, Christian citizens show up in his office asking him to fix some problem that Congress has neither the authority nor responsibility to solve. He shared that he felt the same level of concern about the public issue as well. "However," he told the audience, "when you show up in the office of your representative, be sure that what you came to ask us to do is something Congress is actually responsible for. Otherwise, we can't actually help, no matter how much we share your concern."[6]

Thinking institutionally helps activists recognize the institutional complexity of public issues and public life in general. It also helps us identify what role the state must take within a broader societal response to that specific issue. Take the opioid crisis in America, for example. Federal, state, and local governments certainly have a role to play, and activists are right to hold them accountable. However, responsibility for addressing the opioid crisis is not limited to the state. All the pharmaceutical companies, medical schools, and medical associations share some responsibilities as well. In addition, families, schools, nonprofits, and churches also need to respond in their own unique and institutionally appropriate ways. Who is responsible for what? The Reformed principle of sphere sovereignty does not provide activists an exact answer for every public policy question, but it does provide us with a profoundly helpful public-theological framework for wrestling with the question.

Finally, Reformed public theology taught me that each institution bears ongoing responsibility for reforming their own unique internal practices to conform to the norm of justice. Take, for example, police violence against Black and Brown people in America. Merely enacting laws is not a sufficient way to solve this problem. Racial justice in policing will also require police unions, training academies, and departments to scrutinize and reform their own practices toward justice. Nongovernmental advocacy organizations for just policing need to be developed. Racism in policing is merely one aspect of a broader and more complex institutional culture of racism that needs to be addressed in families, schools, media, churches, and the marketplace.

6. Rep. Ehlers took the opportunity to educate constituents and encouraged his staff to explain the scope of work and role that Congress has within government more broadly. In meetings with constituents asking for solutions that are not the task of government, he also suggested that advocates had better determine what institution is normatively responsible for what beforehand. Additionally, CPJ has helped organize advocacy and has heard government officials thank us for asking them to do something that they actually are responsible for.

Thinking institutionally can help activists address the appropriate authority, be it a president or a mayor, a corporate CEO or a university dean, a news editor or a film director. Reformed theology makes plain the imperative that the state not supplant complex responsibilities of diverse institutions throughout society. The state's responsibility is to protect and enable the ability of these institutions to fulfill their own unique public responsibilities.[7]

Loving Our Neighbors through Politics

As a young activist, I always believed I was advocating for others. But my activism was all too often aimed at making myself look good and others look bad. I believed I was working *with* others, but—more often than not—I was using them to get what I wanted.

Reformed theology exposed my political selfishness. God's purpose for political community is that it be a space of holy Christian service both *with* and *for* our neighbors, not just for ourselves. Here we are called to love our neighbors *through political action*. No area of life is isolated from Christ's greatest command.

Christ-centered political love requires that we adopt the christological posture of a servant, one who places others first and the least of these before all else. The Reformed political philosopher Nicholas Wolterstorff puts it this way: "By listening to the cries of the oppressed and deprived we are enabled genuinely to hear the word of the prophets—and of him who did not count equality with God a thing to be grasped at, but took the form of a servant, walking the path of humble obedience to the point of accepting execution as a despised criminal: the Prince of Shalom."[8]

While Christ's love command is clear, nearly everything in the culture of American politics seems to work against being with and for our neighbors. Our culture prizes strong and antagonistic political statements for one's own identity, rights, and freedom over against those of others. We care about our own flourishing, our own community, and our own institutions before others.[9]

7. For five examples of this type of thinking in practice regarding public policy related to foster care, juvenile justice, college completion, just lending, and early childhood education, see Michael Gerson, Stephanie Summers, and Katie Thompson, *Unleashing Opportunity: Why Escaping Poverty Requires a Shared Vision of Justice* (Beaver Falls, PA: Falls City Press, 2015).

8. Nicholas Wolterstorff, *When Justice and Peace Embrace* (Grand Rapids: Eerdmans, 1981), 176.

9. Michigan's former state representative Steven V. Monsma straightforwardly details this problem, applies it to modern American political life, and makes recommendations in his *Pluralism and Freedom: Faith-Based Organizations in a Democratic Society* (Lanham, MD: Rowman & Littlefield, 2012).

Where does this political selfishness come from, and how does it continually recruit citizens? The Reformed philosopher James K. A. Smith offers the concept of a "cultural liturgy" as a way of indicating how a culture ritualizes and habituates a particular approach to public life.[10] The cultural liturgies of American politics train citizens to embody a self-centered consumer mentality toward the state. Trained to see themselves as consumers (rather than citizens), Americans feel that they have purchased a defective "product" when their candidate wins but fails to live up to expectations.

This consumerist liturgy shapes government officials as well. They come to view their role as providing customer service. Review almost any inaugural speech from the last decade at the state and local level, and you will find government officials pledging to run the best customer-service department in the nation.

Within the political liturgy, citizens and politicians do not see themselves as collaborators in upholding the norms of public justice for the political community.[11] Instead, they see themselves as service providers and service consumers. They are not governed by any specific norms other than the shifting whims of political consumption.

In contrast to these political liturgies of consumption, Reformed theology counsels that citizens are called by God to participate in God's complex symphony of public justice. We are called to love our neighbors through public action and political advocacy.[12] As citizens in God's political community, we are granted power by God to work for justice and the common good. We steward this divine political calling, not for ourselves, but for the flourishing of our neighbors and the glory of our God.

Common Grace, Civility, and Cobelligerency

As a young Christian activist, I can vividly remember feeling uneasy marching side by side with activists who were agnostic or even antagonistic toward the Christian faith. I did not know how to dialogue with them about the foundational reasons we felt passionate about justice and activism. As a young Christian, I did not know if it was okay to agree with non-Christians about

10. James K. A. Smith, *Awaiting the King: Reforming Public Theology* (Grand Rapids: Baker Academic, 2017).

11. For more on such collaborating, see David Koyzis, *We Answer to Another: Authority, Office, and the Image of God* (Eugene, OR: Wipf & Stock, 2014).

12. In numerous talks and discussions, James W. Skillen uses "symphonic justice" as a metaphor, first developed in his work *In Pursuit of Justice: Christian-Democratic Explorations* (Lanham, MD: Rowman & Littlefield, 2004), 36.

a particular public policy objective when we had different philosophical reasons for doing so.

The Reformed concepts of "common grace" and "convicted civility" taught me that it was *possible* to collaborate with, learn from, and even celebrate my fellow non-Christian activists. More than that, because of common grace, I learned that God was actively involved in their lives. I learned that God's purposes for public justice could be done by and through them just as much as they could be done through me. In short, I am not the only citizen through whom God can and will work. God can—and does—freely give diverse citizens of all faiths a passion for public justice.

By the grace of God, writes John Calvin, all humanity is served "by the work and ministry of the ungodly" in the sciences, arts, and society. Because of this, Christian citizens should not fail to thank God for the many political blessings they receive through non-Christian citizens and leaders. Calvin warns that such Christians must not "neglect God's gifts."[13] By the grace of God, non-Christians have the capacity to work toward promoting justice and the common good. This does not mean that they will necessarily do so; after all, Christians will not necessarily do so. Yet as Christians, we can trust our God to be faithful to work for justice, even through people who do not know God.

Working alongside those who do not share your faith is called cobelligerency. In Reformed political theology, I found a way to strategically practice cobelligerency with my non-Christian neighbors when our political goals found alignment.

In the tradition, however, I found that while cobelligerency is possible, ideological differences remain, and they do matter. In our difference, we need to listen to other people and groups carefully and take our differences seriously. Cobelligerency does not mean communion. We can cooperate, but we may not assimilate.

When expressing our own unique ideological convictions, we must do so with civility. The imperative for political civility is rooted in the theological understanding that every citizen is created in God's image. Richard Mouw describes political civility as a moral imperative containing three elements: (1) listen with care, (2) express your own convictions, and (3) do so with civility.[14] Even though we may deeply disagree, we must embody each of these three elements in our activism. Our political respect and civility toward our

13. John Calvin, *Institutes of the Christian Religion*, ed. John T. McNeill, trans. Ford Lewis Battles, 2 vols. (Philadelphia: Westminster, 1960), 2.2.16; cf. 1 Tim. 4:14.

14. Richard J. Mouw, *Uncommon Decency: Christian Civility in an Uncivil World* (Downers Grove, IL: InterVarsity, 1992).

interlocutors who bear the *imago Dei* is not in any way conditioned by our respect for their views or their actions. Nor is it conditioned in receiving respect from them in return. It is grounded in the holy image they bear.

The Center for Public Justice has long partnered with a diverse variety of groups who do not share our Christian values or perspectives. Working across deep differences, we rely on the Reformed understandings of common grace, civility, and cobelligerency on a daily basis. A recent example of this is our work in drafting and advancing H.R. 5331, "The Fairness for All Act." This piece of legislation is designed to *both* protect the civil rights of LGBTQ citizens *and* expand religious freedom protections for faith-based nonprofits who hold traditional views on human sexuality. Conflicts between these two groups have been growing during the past decade. These conflicts increasingly reach the court, where a hard winner and a hard loser must be declared. Fairness-for-all legislation works to expand and solidify public protections for both groups. Civil dialogue and cooperation across deep religious and moral differences was imperative in this effort for the Center for Public Justice. Our grounding in a Reformed theology of common grace, convicted civility, and cobelligerency was critical throughout.

Reformed Activism amid the Pandemic

In 2020 the COVID-19 pandemic launched a swift and massive economic crisis that impacted every sector of civil society. Early in this catastrophe, the Center was particularly concerned about the health and well-being of one vitally important sector of American public life: small faith-based nonprofits. Minority-led and focused nonprofits were especially vulnerable, and the impact of the pandemic on their financial health was particularly acute.

Working with federal legislators and administrators, the Center drafted language to make sure that organizations from a diverse range of faith backgrounds would receive equal treatment. In doing this, we ensured that these organizations would remain both relief-eligible and free from undue restrictions on their religious identity. We asked legislators to carefully allocate resources and assistance to smaller organizations, adding capacity to quickly apply for or successfully navigate the process established to access the relief.

Sadly, not everyone was supportive of these efforts. Some associations of larger nonprofits elected not to join our advocacy efforts for smaller organizations. Some of their Christian leaders privately shared with us that our work on behalf of smaller organizations "works against the interests of our members."[15] While I am sympathetic to those who would fight for their own justice, I long for Christian political engagement to be marked by fighting for *shared justice*.

A Lifelong Journey

I'm convinced that Jim Skillen was right. My youthful and passionate activism needed deeper roots. I needed a richer public theology to guide and sustain a life of faithful activism.

Every day I encounter activists in Washington who approach politics much as I did when I was young. They are well-trained in political tactics that exacerbate the deep chasms already yawning in the American body politic.[16] The holy vocation of activism is a fashioned weapon. Political tools (which God intends for the common good) are transformed into idols. Their political grasping might win the news cycle, but it is far from promoting the shared justice that God intends for the political community.

The Reformed tradition invites and equips Christian activists to love their neighbors through generous political action. It teaches them to value activism as a holy vocation that is pleasing to God.

Although this tradition has shown me how to enjoy and delight in my own work in politics, it has also taught me to enjoy and delight in the work of God even more. Through worship, prayer, reflection, and community, I am reminded that I serve a kingdom and a King whose reign extends beyond the present news cycle. Without a deep and lasting union with Christ, my early passion for activism would have quickly dissolved into bitterness and cynicism. Today I find strength and endurance for the day-to-day work of political activism not in the defeat of "enemies" but in the present and coming victory of Christ.

Finally, Reformed theology helped me to learn that the complex work of God in public life is much larger than me and my political activism. It is being unfolded over time. I am one part of a much larger body of believers, with many different gifts and callings in public life.[17] This helps me cease frenetic

15. These are their words, not mine.
16. Steve Monsma, former Michigan state representative, declares, "Great are the dangers of dishonoring our Lord and being used by political operatives more worldly wise and cynical than we are." Steven Monsma and Stephanie Summers, "Thinking as Christians in an Election Year [2010?]," *Q: Ideas for the Common Good*, http://208.106.253.109/blog/thinking-as-christians-in-an-election-year.aspx.
17. See James W. Skillen, *The Good of Politics: A Biblical, Historical, and Contemporary Introduction* (Grand Rapids: Baker Academic, 2014), 144–45.

political activities that would have destined me for burnout. I still get angry at injustice, and this righteous anger still drives me to public action. We all must do something, yet none of us can do everything. Like the biblical metaphor of the body, we do not all play the same part.[18] We must be people who cooperate with many others, working for the common good.

18. See Rom. 12:4–5; 1 Cor. 12:12; and elsewhere.

Part Four

Public Aesthetics

12

Japanese Aesthetics and Reformed Theology

Reflections on Rikyū, Kintsugi, and Endō

MAKOTO FUJIMURA

I am a Christian, a contemporary artist, and a Japanese-American. Navigating between these three worlds and the identities attached to them makes me a bit of a "border-stalker." These identities and spaces create unique cross pressures, resonances, and juxtapositions. My life and artistic work reflect the boundaries I inhabit and traverse. All three identities inform who I am, what I paint, and how I make sense of God and the world.

These three identities and their worlds produce central questions when it comes to art making. Moving from the world to God, we have the question regarding faith: How should I navigate my Christian faith within a "worldly" art space? Next, there is the question regarding culture: How should I understand my Japanese heritage within a "Western" space? Finally, there is the question regarding contemporary art: How should I understand my ancient art practice within a contemporary art world?

My thanks to Bob Covolo for serving as a theological and editorial partner in the refinement of this chapter.

First, how should an artist of faith inhabit and navigate so-called secular art spaces? This question struck me early in life as I transitioned from the gallery scene in Tokyo (where I began my career) to the Soho and Chelsea gallery scenes of New York. As a young artist I wanted to honor Christ through artistic excellence. I wanted to compete at the highest level of artistry, in New York City. Amid the skyscrapers of Manhattan, the Reformed preaching and teaching of Tim Keller at Redeemer Presbyterian Church was a turning point for me. Keller and Redeemer leadership training introduced me to a Reformed theology of culture and the theological work of Richard Mouw, in particular. In turn, both Keller and Mouw helped me to identify a faithful path forward in a secular space like New York. The exile metaphor found in Jeremiah 29 became an especially powerful image for me at the time. As a person of faith working in the secular art world, I was called to be a faithful exile who labored and prayed for "the peace and prosperity" of the arts in New York City (Jer. 29:7, 11). In essence, I was in search of a theological framework whereby I could *simultaneously* remain exclusively committed to my faith and also remain generously committed to the artistic flourishing of New York.

The second art-related question is with regard to the place of my Japanese heritage within a "Western" space. Part of my critical training was in the traditional Nihonga style of painting. The history and culture of Japan informs and influences everything that I do. In moving to New York, I was immediately thrown into the gap between the Eastern aesthetic tradition and the Western modern and postmodern visual diction. During the 1990s few artists were intentionally integrating Eastern and Western influences in New York.[1] As a young Japanese-American artist yearning to make art for the New York art scene, I had to cultivate my own method of bridging the East and West in a way that was authentic to my sense of calling and cultural identity. In this, I needed a theological framework for honoring the diverse cultural contexts of Japan and America, East and West.

Third and finally, how should my significant training in a centuries-old form of traditional painting inhabit the twenty-first-century world of contemporary art? In the fast-paced modern world that wants to quickly move on to the next new thing, I have always been drawn to sixteenth- and seventeenth-century traditions of Japanese painting and aesthetics. Traditional Nihonga painting is a "slow art" practice.[2] My work is guided by three traditional influences: a

1. Of course, modernist art, especially of the New York School and other twentieth-century movements, relies implicitly on an Eastern aesthetic—whether that be art by John Cage or by Mark Rothko.

2. I have chosen, even in New York City, to continue to use authentic seventeenth-century materials (a practice many modern Nihonga artists in Japan have abandoned).

Figure 12.1. Artist Makoto Fujimura, "Silence—Mysterion," 7´ x 33´ at Junct Museum, Gonzaga University

respect for a long history of craftsmanship, a willingness to move and work as slowly as necessary, and a desire to honor materiality and the raw material elements of the work. These historic and traditional values are largely absent in the contemporary art world. Modern art is defined by its emphasis on radical innovation, on breaking away from the past and the constraints of tradition. Rather than submit to materiality, moderns can often seek to transcend the boundaries of materiality through artistic practice. Navigating the world of contemporary art, I needed a theological aesthetic that valued three things: the raw materiality of God's creation, the beauty of slow craftsmanship, and the deep wisdom embedded in centuries of cultural history.

Should I try to resolve these tensions in my identity?[3] I could, for example, try to "fit in" with the worlds of Western culture, contemporary art, and secularism. In this way the tension could be resolved through an act of *cultural assimilation*. Or, if I liked, I could engage in an act of *cultural retreat*. I could run away from New York and flee to the guild of Japanese traditional arts or the world of "Christian art."

3. Culturally, I do not fit the homogenous cultural assumptions of either Japan or America. Artistically, I do not fit into the clear categories of "traditional" or "contemporary" art. Spiritually, I do not completely fit inside the religious boundaries of the church or the secular boundaries of the gallery. So I live and work on the boundaries.

But the truth is, neither cultural assimilation nor retreat is an option for me—artistically or theologically. As an artist, I do not like either/or choices. I want to play and make art in the transitional spheres that are sometimes filled with deep and generative tension. Not "fitting in" is what it means to be a faithful border-stalker. Moreover, by way of a Reformed theology, I now see that my border-stalking life is not a problem to be solved but a divine gift to be cherished.

Reformed Making on the Boundaries

The Reformed tradition has helped me not only navigate but also embrace these tensions in my identity and calling.[4] Here the seemingly disparate and competing parts of my work converge into a more fruitful and generative process of *making*. In this essay I intend to place Richard Mouw's Reformed theology of culture into a creative conversation with the traditional Japanese aesthetics found in Sen no Rikyū, Kintsugi, Kumohada, and Shūsaku Endō. In this unlikely conversation, I demonstrate how the Reformed tradition cultivates a "theology of making" that can flourish on the boundaries of life in our globalizing world.

One City, Many Nations

As a Japanese-American making art in Western spaces, I have often experienced a dissonance. Rather than run from it, I have learned to intentionally create into this divide. But the story is more complex.

Segments of American culture (and youth culture in particular) have moved in interesting ways toward Japanese culture. These segments, like Japanese culture itself, seek a deeper connection between culture and nature. As a result, the art of Takashi Murakami, the films of Hayao Miyazaki, and Japanese animation (broadly speaking) seems to hit the "sweet spot" of Americans hungering for a high visual aesthetic that is conversant with a pop-anime sensibility. This integrated view, whereby nature can serve as a birthplace of culture, has shaped a generation of environmentally conscious youth. But what are we to make of the "pagan" influence of Japanese culture on these segments of American culture?

Richard Mouw, in his book *When the Kings Come Marching In*, takes contemporary readers on a journey into the ancient world of Isaiah 60. Here

---

4. See Makoto Fujimura, *Culture Care: Reconnecting with Beauty for Our Common Life* (Downers Grove, IL: InterVarsity, 2017).

we find the new Jerusalem gathering in all the vast and diverse cultural treasures of "pagan" kings and nations before the Lord. Isaiah says of the city, "Nations shall come to your light, and kings to the brightness of your rising" (Isa. 60:3).[5] Isaiah's broad theological vision depicts diverse nations carrying their cultural riches and creations into the city of God.[6] The cultural gifts from pagan nations include cedars from Lebanon, commercial vessels, and "beautiful crafts." In chapter 2 Isaiah declares that all these nations and their cultural creations—including their ships—will be under divine judgment for their idolatrous uses. Even so, these cultural artifacts are somehow redeemed by God and rendered appropriate for use and glory within the new Jerusalem. Mouw offers the following conclusion: "My own impression is that the judgment that will visit the ships of Tarshish is of a purifying sort. We might think here of the 'breaking' of the ships of Tarshish as more like the breaking of a horse rather than the breaking of a vase. The judgment here is meant to tame, not destroy."[7]

If Mouw is right on this, the good gifts of God scattered through diverse nations can be redeemed for use within the eschatological city of God. In the light of Isaiah 60, a "non-Christian" culture like Japan, unaware of the Holy Spirit's work within it, contains cultural works that bear witness to the invisible work and wisdom of God. By the grace of God, the diverse cultural works of Japan bless the nations and glorify God.

Nihonga art, a form of painting that has enriched my life and work, emerged from a deeply Buddhist and Shinto worldview and culture. As a Christian informed by Isaiah 60, I am able to give thanks and praise for the richness and wisdom of God embedded in Nihonga practice. In this, the cultural wealth of so-called pagan Japan has blessed and informed my artistic career and my Christian faith in countless ways.

"Secular" Gifts Carried into the New Jerusalem

Christians often assume that they need to make explicitly "Christian" art. Isaiah 60 offers a rebuttal. Here "secular" crafts made outside the temple and Israel itself are welcomed into the new Jerusalem. The work's quality and excellence, its unique aesthetic ability to render glory to God, is what appears

5. All Scripture quotations in this chapter are from the ESV unless stated otherwise.

6. More than that, Isa. 60 directly implies that hidden with the diverse cultural riches, Israelites will find exegetical keys to better understand their own faith.

7. Richard J. Mouw, *When the Kings Come Marching In: Isaiah and the New Jerusalem*, rev. ed. (Grand Rapids: Eerdmans, 2002), 278.

to matter here. In the new Jerusalem the complex glory of God is reflected in the complex cultural artifacts of diverse nations.[8]

In this regard, Mouw's theological reflections on Isaiah 60 gives us a new model for cultural and artistic exegesis in a globalizing world. Stated simply, one's art, no matter its culture of origin, can constitute an offering fit for the new Jerusalem simply by virtue of its aesthetic excellence. Therefore, as an artist, I do not need to assimilate into the West or the world of "Christian art." Instead, I need to faithfully inhabit the art world as myself—full stop. My paintings do not need a Bible verse branded on them, nor do they need to follow Western aesthetic traditions. Their artistic excellence is, in and of itself, an offering to God's glory and his coming city.

In the case of my own artistic work, I have developed a visual language based on my reading of "secular" artists from the West (Mark Rothko and Archile Gorky) and the East (Tohaku Hasegawa and Sen no Rikyū). In the language of Isaiah 60, riding on my own "ship of Tarshish," my art explores the cultural riches of the nations. As a faithful Christian, my hope is to learn from, and faithfully create out of, the aesthetic wisdom of the East and West and appreciate their cultural glory just as God will in the new Jerusalem.

Undergirding all Mouw's reflections on Isaiah 60 is a Reformed theology of common grace.[9] This doctrine sees the Holy Spirit at work, culturally blessing all nations for the glory of God. According to common grace, the Holy Spirit has been moving in every culture, in every time, and in every place. This theological lens offers a way for Christians to listen to, learn from, and appreciate various cultural spaces with spiritual reverence. Moreover, common grace enables border-stalkers like myself to move through liminal spaces and across cultural boundary lines with a sense of excitement rather than dread. Finally, the language of common grace can have a bridging function amid the growing chasms in our tribalized late modern culture.[10] If the Holy Spirit is at work on both sides of various cultural and political divides, Christians are compelled to listen to and learn from those on the other side. In this sense, I see my artistic work as a series of small aesthetic efforts to mend cultural fractures. I build these bridges,

---

8. The Isa. 60 passage does not focus on what is ethically permitted and what is not, but rather focuses on the King's sovereign power over *all* created things and cultures, including what is known as "secular" cultural capitals.

9. Richard J. Mouw, *He Shines in All That's Fair: Culture and Common Grace* (Grand Rapids: Eerdmans, 2002).

10. Indeed, Richard Mouw has not only written about commonness but also given us a theology of civility. See his *Uncommon Decency: Christian Civility in an Uncivil World* (Downers Grove, IL: InterVarsity, 2010).

not through lectures on systematic theology, but through the practice of making art.[11]

Preserving the Old

In the light of Isaiah 60, Christians should protect, care for, and esteem the traditional cultural artifacts, riches, and traditions of the nations. A Japanese papermaker needs to be valued by Christians not because the papermaker is a Christian, but because the paper carries thousands of years of refinement. Again, in light of the new Jerusalem, Christians have a stewardship to preserve such refinement. According to Isaiah 60, artistic traditions and artifacts like these matter to God, and they will matter in the new Jerusalem. In the light of the new heaven and the new earth, Christians have a calling to steward and preserve ancient forms of craftsmanship. This is all the more important today as ancient crafts become endangered.[12] In the light of Isaiah 60, *followers of Christ preserve ancient cultural treasures and craftsmanship, not simply because they are beautiful to them; they do so, rather, because these traditions will one day be purified and welcomed into a continued use in the new Jerusalem.*[13]

Common Grace and Japanese Art: Rikyū and Kintsugi

The theological threads of common grace can be traced back to Augustine.[14] Yet it was Abraham Kuyper who drew the threads together into a firm strand.[15] Through the belief in common grace, Kuyper enables Christians to see how

11. New creation is the *telos* of salvation, and the artist's cultural labors count as one of the sources that God will use in the new creation. In light of Isa. 60, Mouw's theological reflection opens up the new creation to include cultural artifacts. Implicit in their inclusion is a central plank for a robust theology of making—namely, that a work of art can be done as a cogent theological reflection. In other words, works of art present cogent theological statements.

12. I use Kumohada paper, crafted in Imadate, Japan, in my own artwork. A decade ago the master papermaker passed away. Since his death, the quality of Kumohada paper has declined.

13. Moreover, the value of Kumohada papermaking to the new Jerusalem stands even if the spirituality of Shintoism played a pivotal role in the craft's conception. Traditional papermakers focused careful attention on the paper itself because of their animistic beliefs that gods were present in the paper fibers. Regardless of their spiritual intentions, God will be glorified forever by their aesthetic skill, patience, and care.

14. For example, see Augustine, *The City of God*, trans. Henry Bettenson (New York: Penguin, 2003), 1072.

15. Abraham Kuyper, *Wisdom and Wonder: Common Grace in Science and Art* (Grand Rapids: Christian's Library Press, 2011).

someone outside the church might glorify God and serve neighbors through cultural creativity and beauty.

For me, that someone is the renowned Japanese tea master Sen no Rikyū (1522–91). The aesthetics of Rikyū's tea ceremonies have impacted Japanese art and culture more than any single individual in Japanese history.[16] There is not one form of Japanese art, from the art of tea, to flower arranging, to Noh theater, that does not give a nod to this venerated master of tea. Rikyū and his followers (including Christians Furuta Oribe and Ukon Takayama, among others) gave birth to the Japanese aesthetic we know today. Even the popular notion of "wabi sabi suki" was Rikyū's aesthetic being passed down to the future generations.

In the light of God's common grace, I am personally convinced that Rikyū's tea ceremony will be one of Japan's cultural treasures that will be carried into the new Jerusalem. As an important aside, we remember that Japanese Christians, while under persecution, would use Rikyū's tea ceremony to celebrate communion together in secrecy. Rikyū is clearly an example of God's common grace, a divine cultural blessing to the people of Japan.

Rikyū's vast artistic and cultural contributions aside, I also mention Rikyū's interest in people and objects that society has deemed broken and therefore worthless. His aesthetic attention greatly influenced the refinement of a Japanese artistic practice known as Kintsugi. Through Kintsugi, broken bowls and vases are mended with gold. Rikyū's particular aesthetic imagination attends to and values the fissures and imperfections in both objects and people. Broken vessels are valued *because* of their potential for mending to make new, with the Kintsugi vessels being more valuable than the original. Families of tea masters are known to hand down broken fragments for generations until a ripe time when another master will recognize that the time has come to mend them. In a single artwork, Kintsugi speaks to humanity's experience of both a common curse and common grace. In Isaiah 60 we encounter a God who invites broken nations and cultures into his gates—mortal fractures, filled with immortal gold.

Thus, when God works in our lives, he does not simply repair us. He makes us anew in Christ (2 Cor. 5:17). Our brokenness is part of God's design in the whole project. And as with an artist, God is happy to display his masterpieces of grace for all eternity. This casts new light on our fissures of brokenness. To extend Mouw's thesis, even idols can be purified and brought into the new Jerusalem. After all, idols are (as my mentor Tim Keller is fond of saying)

---

16. For more on Sen no Rikyū, see Makoto Fujimura, *Silence and Beauty: Hidden Faith Born of Suffering* (Downers Grove, IL: InterVarsity, 2016), 132.

merely "good things that have become the One thing." Thus idolatry contains within it a remnant of our Edenic bliss, from the good gifts of a generous God. By paying careful attention to the good source of these gifts, we discover entry points where God's gold can be poured into the fissures of our lives.

Figure 12.2. Bowl

If common grace is the presence of God's sovereign blessings in all cultures, common curse identifies our shared bond of brokenness, suffering, and accursed reality. Just as the sun can cause plants to grow, the sun can also scorch and curse the land we all share. A rain can be a blessing, but it can equally cause massive flooding that destroys homes. If common grace helps us understand God as blessing those who may not share our faith, common curse helps us sympathize *with* and share *in* the suffering of those different from us. Such experiences of common brokenness lead us to compassion toward others, including our enemies. The gold of the new creation flowing into these fissures of our broken lives is the sacrificial offering of Christ's blood, a precious element found only in the broken body of Christ. Thus the art practice of Kintsugi reveals the dynamic of both common grace and common curse: both merge in a single artwork. God somehow invites us, just as he invites pagan kings coming on their ships of Tarshish, to be part of the *splendid gold that not only mends but also is part of the new Jerusalem by virtue of their broken fissures.*

Shūsaku Endō

Traumatic national experiences of war, persecution, and disaster loom large in Japanese aesthetics and culture.[17] As we consider the artistic "glory" that Japan has to offer to the nations, an intimation of the new Jerusalem, the aesthetics of trauma quickly come to mind. Upon reflection, it appears that the Holy Spirit has moved in and through Japan's artists throughout history as they have sought to artistically respond to the nation's trauma.

An excellent example of such an artist is the Roman Catholic novelist Shūsaku Endō (1923–96) and his acclaimed book *Silence and Beauty*. Recently

17. See Fujimura, *Silence and Beauty*.

adapted to film, Endō's novel is a profound exploration of faith and doubt amid human suffering and (perceived) divine silence.[18] Set in seventeenth-century Japan, *Silence* follows two Jesuit missionaries tasked with discovering the physical and spiritual fate of their mentor. He had been reported missing during the persecution of Christians in Japan. Reports had circulated that their mentor had, under pressure, renounced his faith and apostatized. Hoping to discover the truth, Fathers Rodrigues and Garrpe journey to Japan. To assist them, the missionaries purchase the services of a translator named Kichijiro, a dubious character who turns out to be an untrustworthy drunkard.

At the hands of cruel Japanese magistrates, the two priests are forced to endure a long series of ethical conundrums and forced reckonings with their faith. The interrogation and tortures the priests uncover are disturbing. One of the tortures foregoes physical pain for psychological torment. The "stepping picture," or Fumi-e, was a board featuring the revered images of Jesus or Mary. One by one, Japanese villagers are asked to step on or spit upon the images. Persecutors carefully watch the villagers' reactions, trying to smoke out and then persecute Christians.

One of the things that makes Endō's novel so profoundly disturbing is the way it exposes its readers. Entering the novel's world, readers are forced to consider their own reactions and responses to the sufferings and the ethical conundrums that ensue. At first readers cannot help but judge the traitorous Kichijiro—a figure who repeatedly betrays his master and his own conscience. Yet, by the end of the novel, readers are confronted with their own lives of betrayal. In the end, Christian or not, we all apostatize; we all step on our own Fumi-es.

With this novel set in the seventeenth century, Endō aimed to speak to his twentieth-century audience. We all have experienced faith and doubt, trauma and betrayal. Many in Japan had fervently believed in the nationalism of prewar Japan, others in the Marxism of the resistance. Father Rodrigues serves as an emblem for Japanese humiliation and the breakdown in Japan's faith in nationalism and Marxism. Fumi-e serves as a universal symbol—an emblem of the common curse flowing through the fissures of Japan's trauma.

In presenting his Japanese readers with questions rather than answers, Endō opens the door for non-Christians to engage in theological reflection. Through art rather than a sermon, Endō connects with his non-Christian neighbors and invites them to reflect on the meaning of their national trauma and betrayal. Here the "common curse" leads to the common longing for grace.

18. *Silence*, directed by Martin Scorsese (Los Angeles: Paramount Pictures, 2016). I had the honor of serving as a special adviser to Scorsese for *Silence*.

Endō has repeatedly stated that, spiritually speaking, he is a descendant of "failed faith." He is a spiritual heir of the abject character Kichijiro. After all, Endō insists, the faith of Jesus Christ in Japan managed to survive not only through the blood of the martyrs but also after the children of those who stepped on the Fumi-e.[19] The book, Endō notes, "is not about the silence of God . . . but [about] the voice of God speaking through silence and suffering."[20]

Missional Engagement

My work, life, and faith have all been greatly enriched and informed by these "foreign" or "pagan" artists, crafts, and cultural influences. The cultural riches of Japan are gifts to me. They are gifts from the Holy Spirit, who is alive and active in every culture and craft—not just now, but also from the beginning of time.

On a personal level, the Reformed doctrine of common grace has transformed my approach to my threefold identity as a Christian, a Japanese-American, and a contemporary artist. I do not see in these aspects of my life any tension that I need to resolve or a problem I need to fix. Instead, I welcome these aspects of my life as divine gifts that I need to cherish, callings I need to pursue.

This Reformed theological approach offers more than a way for Christians to value diverse and non-Christian cultures. It offers a way for art and culture to be missional as well. Reflecting on Mouw's theology and the aesthetic potency of Rikyū, Kintsugi, and Endō, we begin to see how the Holy Spirit's movement through art and culture works. Herein we can begin to identify missional points of contact and connection across diverse faiths, cultures, and artistic mediums.

A personal interaction I had with Richard Mouw illustrates the point. Upon hearing about a trip that I was planning to Japan, Mouw introduced me to a new church-planting effort in a hip and culturally vibrant neighborhood in Tokyo. Upon my arrival in the city, I sat down with the leaders. When they asked me how they should approach their efforts, I said to them, "Don't plant a church." Seeing that the church planters were somewhat taken aback, I clarified that anything Christians do to create and cultivate culture in the neighborhood will be a potential seed for church planting. "You are in a hip and artistic area of Tokyo," I said. "Here are many non-Christian families with young children who care about the arts." Instead of beginning

19. Yoichi Onaka, *The Voice of Silence* (Tokyo: President Publishing, 1992).
20. Fujimura, *Silence and Beauty*, 65.

with a church, I encouraged them to plant a Saturday art program for the children in the neighborhood. "Serve your neighbors first," I said, "before you think of 'planting' anything. The arts can be a form of cultural service and connection."

After a year or so, I returned to check on the leaders in Tokyo. It was a Saturday, and the space they had dedicated to this endeavor was filled with activity. Children were busily running, shouting, and making art. Two years later I visited again. Several parents had come to faith. As a New Yorker, I shared with them the pain and anguish we had experienced on 9/11. They shared with me their nation's tsunami trauma from March 11, 2011. The common curse of the trauma and the common grace of Christ connected us. The Tokyo church plant has now expanded to Hiroshima. Although not initially positioned as an official "church" (neighbors still view the community center as a cultural hub serving their families and neighborhood), the cultural initiative has become one of the most vibrant churches in the city.

Such is the enduring legacy of Richard Mouw's Reformed theology of commonness. Such theology extends beyond the borders of America and, by way of numerous "ships of Tarshish," brings with it the cultural and spiritual fruit of those hungering around the world.

13

Poetry and the Reformed Tradition

JAMES K. A. SMITH

Aesthetic life is as integral to being human as building sandcastles at the beach or giving your children names.

—Calvin Seerveld, *Rainbows for the Fallen World*

We will not detain ourselves with overwrought acrobatics in trying to "define" poetry. "What is poetry?" is the sort of question you ask when you prefer the abstract air of conceptual wrangling rather than the soul-grabbing incisiveness of poetry in its concreteness. In other words, asking "What is poetry?" is usually a way to avoid poetry.

But perhaps a working and "fuzzy" (as Ludwig Wittgenstein puts it) definition of poetry will at least help us know what we're *not* talking about. Poetry is a unique performance and deployment of language. Think of it as distillation of what words can do—an intensification of language's ability to play with meaning, to let significance dance by stripping language down and letting words shiver in their multivalence. Or you could say poetry is to language what a reduction is to cooking: poetry boils down the verbosity of speech to a more potent concoction of words that in themselves (diction) and in their interaction with one another (syntax) generate meaning that is more felt than processed.

You will notice we're not saying that poetry necessarily rhymes or follows rules of meter, though it can and often does both.[1] This is why poetry occupies a continuum of human language in the neighborhood of song. Some have suggested that the closest we can get to a defining characteristic of poetry is the line break—the unique way a poet decides where one line starts and another ends. We call this "enjambment."[2] The line break, like a breath, a pause, is one of the ways poets attune us to language anew, as a key feature of this distillation or reduction of meaning in language. The critic Terry Eagleton suggests that, if you need a "dreary-sounding definition, unpoetic to a fault," the best we might be able to do is: "A poem is a fictional, verbally inventive moral statement in which it is the author, rather than the printer or word processor, who decides where the lines should end."[3]

Reformed Aesthetics: Foundations for Approaching Poetry

For our purposes, let's assume that you know poetry when you see it and instead ask, How might the Reformed tradition uniquely affirm both the good and the significance of poetry? How might a Reformed sensibility encourage us to find delight in poetry?

A Reformed poetics would be grounded in a more fundamental Reformed aesthetics ("aesthetics" being a shorthand term for a philosophy of the arts, an account of what art does and why it matters). If we follow Calvin Seerveld's influential articulation of a Reformed aesthetic,[4] we note several baseline convictions.

First, the Reformed tradition affirms the significance of the aesthetic—the "artful," you might say—as its own good. The aesthetic is a fundamental aspect of creation and not merely a decorative or beautiful way to communicate or convey "messages" or theological truths. In other words, the

1. For a playful and somewhat satirical take on this, see Nicholson Baker's novel *The Anthologist*, in which the narrator is devoted to compiling an anthology of poetry organized around an outmoded idea: *Only Rhyme*.

2. For a helpful discussion, see James Longenbach, *The Art of the Poetic Line* (St. Paul: Graywolf, 2008).

3. Terry Eagleton, *How to Read a Poem* (Oxford: Blackwell, 2007), 25.

4. I cite Seerveld (see notes below) as an influential example of someone who has articulated a Reformed aesthetic, but I do not claim that he is the only embodiment of such. For a relevant discussion of John Calvin's aesthetics, see W. David O. Taylor, *The Theater of God's Glory: Calvin, Creation, and the Liturgical Arts* (Grand Rapids: Eerdmans, 2017). See also Abraham Kuyper, "Calvinism and Art," in *Lectures on Calvinism* (Grand Rapids: Eerdmans, 1931); and Nicholas Wolterstorff, *Art in Action: Toward a Christian Aesthetic* (Grand Rapids: Eerdmans, 1987).

arts are not justified because they are handmaids of theology or ministry. They have their own divine calling, their own creaturely expression within God's world.

The aesthetic is not optional. It plays a unique and irreplaceable role in human life. The aesthetic is not only the province of "artsy" people; rather, the aesthetic is a fundamental aspect of all creation and every human person. If the human person is like a guitar, the aesthetic is a string that is a part of all of us. The question is whether (or how) it gets played. The fullness of being human is a chord that plays our art strings.[5]

Second, just what aspects of my humanity are plucked by the aesthetic? The aesthetic activates our imaginations by means of what Seerveld terms "allusivity." Allusivity is characterized by a kind of play, an obliqueness that is playful, like Emily Dickinson's "certain slant of light."[6] Seerveld calls it "a disciplined suggestiveness."[7]

Rather than meeting us head-on, as it were, allusive words and images tickle and tug our imaginations, enlivening an aspect of us that wants to sing, even if that means sometimes singing the blues or lamentations. "Aesthetic life," says Seerveld, "is that zone of human existence in God's world where we are subject to the Lord's ordinance for being imaginative, for responding playfully to quirks and quarks, the wonderful nuances all around us, which are gifts of God, grist for shalom."[8]

Poetry, I suggest, is the most intense experience of allusivity in language. Poetry is a mode of language that brings the "nuancefulness"[9] and suggestiveness of words from the background to the foreground, helping us to see things in a way and from an angle that normally eludes us. From such poetic encounters with words, we return to our everyday use of language and our everyday immersion in the world with a new sense of creation's depths of possibility. One could say that such imaginative encounters expand our cosmos by bringing the depths in language to light, features that we might not have noticed before. For example, Ted Hughes's marvelous poem "The

5. Ironically, Seerveld's most famous picture for articulating this point is what he calls the "tin-can model of the human creature," which is a rather unalluring image. For an elucidation, see Calvin Seerveld, "Ordinary Aesthetic Life: Humor, Tastes, and 'Taking a Break,'" in *Normative Aesthetics*, ed. John H. Kok (Sioux Center, IA: Dordt College Press, 2014), 111–34.

6. This phrasing comes from Emily Dickinson's poem, "There's a Certain Slant of Light," available at https://poets.org/poem/theres-certain-slant-light-258.

7. Calvin Seerveld, *Rainbows for the Fallen World: Aesthetic Life and Artistic Task* (Toronto: Tuppence, 1980), 126.

8. Seerveld, *Rainbows for the Fallen World*, 125.

9. Calvin Seerveld, "Dooyeweerd's Legacy for Aesthetics: Modal Law Theory," in *Normative Aesthetics*, ed. John H. Kok (Sioux Center, IA: Dordt College Press, 2014), 79.

Thought-Fox," with its intertwining of metaphor and keen observation, will make you see not only nature but also your own consciousness as you never have before.

Third, as Reformed philosophers like Seerveld and Nicholas Wolterstorff emphasize, the aesthetic is not merely characteristic of *fine* art or professional artworks narrowly construed. While professional artists and artworks offer a particularly intense experience of the aesthetic,[10] there is an aesthetic element to all human life. Every sphere of life (the family, politics, business, sports, etc.) is enhanced by the aesthetic and the allusive.

Aesthetic and poetic blessings are sprinkled throughout our common life, bending it toward shalom. As Seerveld playfully puts it, "Nobody can get out of God's world or jump out of your human skin; so willy-nilly you are gifted with aesthetic life to live."[11] It is not just poetry, but also the poetic moment of every aspect of creaturely diversity. The lilt of a prayer, the playful craft of a syllabus, an email that fights the doldrums of corporate communication with a pithy verve, the singsong cadence of wedding vows, even the potent tropes of a couple's argument—all have an aesthetic aspect that can be enlivened by the poetic. Gratitude is the proper response to the pervasive, gratuitous, and divine gifts of the aesthetic.

Fourth, a Reformed aesthetic hallows the quotidian. It does not limit itself to the exotic, dramatic, or intensely spiritual aspects of life. Reformed aesthetics directly investigates (and plays with) the seemingly ordinary, mundane, and material aspects of human life.

The Protestant Reformers refused the late medieval dichotomy of so-called sacred and secular. They affirmed the "sanctification of the ordinary life" and the holiness of the domestic. The vocations of the farmer, the housekeeper, and the blacksmith were sacred. It is no accident, therefore, that artists in regions where the Reformation took hold turned their artistic attention from the narrowness of representing biblical narratives or mythic scenes to painting, and thereby hallowing, the landscapes they saw every day. Suddenly the common vocations of the peasants with whom they rubbed shoulders were worthy of artistic reflection. Rather than painting portraits of the nobility, painters like Vermeer and Rembrandt framed our attention on butchers and maidservants, shop clerks and dock workers—Abraham Kuyper's (and Richard Mouw's) beloved *kleine luyden* (little people). Rather than representing

---

10. To use Herman Dooyeweerd's framework, artworks are objects for which the aesthetic function is the "leading" or defining function: they are made to highlight or "front" the aesthetic. But *all* phenomena have an aesthetic aspect. For relevant discussion see Seerveld, "Dooyeweerd's Legacy for Aesthetics," 52–54.

11. Seerveld, "Ordinary Aesthetic Life," 118.

the great halls, they let us peer into the humble kitchens and thereby affirmed these spaces as worthy of investigation and celebration.

Fifth, aesthetics in the Reformed tradition resists any monolithic or myopic understanding of art. Art is not just one thing, nor does it exist to accomplish only one purpose. The arts, and intentions behind art making, are multiple.

Nicholas Wolterstorff has especially articulated a Reformed critique of the modern tendency to construe art as merely an occasion for contemplation. One of Wolterstorff's key contributions to aesthetics has been an emphasis on art as *action*—art as act, performance, intended to get something done. Art is not a gnostic retreat from action to a de-world-ed plane of contemplation but rather another way that we act in and on the world. "Art—so often thought of as a way of getting out of the world—is a man's way of acting *in* the world. *Artistically man acts.*"[12]

The same, then, is true of poetry. Poetry is not just an occasion for contemplative retreat; it is also the means of performing and enacting in a distinct way, a linguistic way of *doing* something. I am thinking of hip-hop, love letters, commercials, jokes, limericks. Indeed, what Wolterstorff suggests as a range of art's action can all be imagined as poetic performances: "Art plays and is meant to play an enormous diversity of roles in human life. Works of art are instruments by which we perform such diverse actions as praising our great men and expressing our grief, evoking emotion, and communicating knowledge. Works of art are objects of such actions as contemplation for the sake of delight. Works of art are accompaniments for such actions as hoeing cotton and rocking infants. Works of art are background for such actions as eating meals and walking through airports."[13] As an art form, poetry can do all these things and more; poetry can do them in ways that are distinctly meaningful, expressing and speaking to the imagination in a way that cultivates the fullness of being human. There are many ways to be poetic.

Case Study: Rod Jellema

If there are good Reformed reasons to affirm the significance and uniqueness of poetry as a way of being at play in the world, what does poetry in the Reformed tradition *feel* like, as it were?[14] What does a Reformed poetics

12. Wolterstorff, *Art in Action*, 4. Here Wolterstorff's gendered language reflects its time.
13. Wolterstorff, *Art in Action*, 4.
14. Of course, the Reformed affirmation of poetry does not at all entail only an affirmation of "Reformed poetry." In the spirit of (Mouw's beloved) common grace as well as catholicity, the Reformed affirmation of poetry can celebrate a wide range of poetry and poets. In the spirit

look like in practice? We could consider a range of examples—from William Cowper to Emily Dickinson. Indeed, Dickinson's famous poetic lines "Tell the truth but tell it slant— / Success in Circuit lies" capture the very heart of poetry.

I want to focus on a more recent poet in the Reformed tradition as just one example: Rod Jellema. A product of the Reformed tradition that includes his alma mater, Calvin College, Jellema was a longtime professor of literature at the University of Maryland, where he founded the Creative Writing program. He came to poetry somewhat late (at age forty), but his poetry embodies the aspects of a Reformed poetics I have described above. In *Incarnality*, a culminating collection of his poems from 1974 to 2010, Jellema remarked, "More and more my work has come to be celebratory. Good fertile darkness and lively physicality are often the subjects celebrated."[15] Here is the poetic equivalent of all those seventeenth-century Dutch landscape paintings or Vermeer's portraits of domestic life: an allusive, suggestive attending to what is right in front of us but we all too often miss.[16] Jellema's poetry pauses to notice, unfold, and hence invites us to pause and do the same. Such is celebration, even if it attends to heartbreak. Jellema's poetry is an extension of the Reformers' hallowing of the everyday, an attention to toil and the curse, a humanism that sees rather than looks past suffering.

"That's what Incarnality is about," Jellema continues. "It's about seeking and traveling until you get to a strange place called home and discover you belong there. Necessarily, of course, it also tries to catch the feel of a world

---

of the ancient Roman poet Terence, the Reformed Christian can happily say, "Nothing human is alien to me." And poets often bring aspects of humanity closer to me than prose.

15. Rod Jellema, *Incarnality: The Collected Poems* (Grand Rapids: Eerdmans, 2010), xv.

16. The poet Ted Hughes, whose poetry exhibits a similar celebration of the quotidian, articulates this beautifully:

> Because it is occasionally possible, just for brief moments, to find the words that will unlock the doors of all those many mansions inside the head and express something— perhaps not much, just something—of the crush of information that presses in on us from the way a crow flies over and the way a man walks and the look of a street and from what we did one day a dozen years ago. Words that will express something of the deep complexity that makes us precisely the way we are, from the momentary effect of the barometer to the force that created men distinct from trees. Something of the inaudible music that moves us along in our bodies from moment to moment like water in a river. Something of the duplicity and relativity and the merely fleeting quality of all this. Something of the almighty importance of it and something of the utter meaninglessness. And when words can manage something of this, and manage it in a moment of time, and in that same moment make out of it all the vital signature of the human being—not of an atom, or of a geometrical diagram, or of a heap of lenses—but a human being, we call it poetry. ("Words and Experience," in *Poetry in the Making* [London: Faber & Faber, 1969], 124)

in which that way seems missing and is sometimes longed for."[17] You can see this nuanceful attending in one of Jellema's later poems, "West Window," that ends with this stanza:

> I try to gather the flash and hum and dark of everything
> for a kind of hymn, a soft one, one that might rise daily
> over the hairy ice-age dune out front, floating over
> beachwear colors and staked boats on the beach to challenge
> at the shore the shipwrecking lovely lake to some antiphonal singing
> that I may almost have heard. Listen. It's closest in the still after
>   storms.[18]

Like Van Gogh's and Vermeer's art, Reformed poetry is populated with peasants, laborers, and others—like mothers and maids—working with their hands.[19] But because that work is also holy, the poet's attention to their labor can be a portal to the eternal, the divine glimpsed in fields and home fires.

Four-Square Gospel, by Rod Jellema

> Old Uncle Fred could squint along forty-foot beams
> And catch the gentlest wayward drift toward a curve
> That no one else saw. His calloused, pitch-stained hands
> Would tenderly stroke the flush seams of a perfect joint.
> We used to see him astride his unwavering rafters,
> Tall as the echoing blows of his worshiping arms,
> Looking with pride on the loving work of his mitred,
> Four-square world. He always looked sharply to see
> If some sinning board in somebody's house were off square.
> And longed to redeem it with the righteous tongue of his plane.
>
> And then he slumped into arches and curves of age,
> Propped up in a bed, looking out at the slanting east
> While unseen termites encircled his squared-off house.
> Puzzled, he eyed the long, sad arc of the geese,
> The easy bend of a tree-limb heavy with fruit,
> And then—we knew by the softening line of his mouth—
> Saw the curve of a neck swinging free from the beams of a cross.[20]

---

17. Jellema, *Incarnality*, xvi.

18. Jellema, *Incarnality*, 235. Reprinted by permission of the publisher.

19. Jellema has a remarkable sequence of poems that celebrates the life and work of Vincent van Gogh, whose work exhibits this same sensibility. Jellema, *Incarnality*, 153–57.

20. Jellema, *Incarnality*, 13. Reprinted by permission of the publisher.

But since the world we attend to, even celebrate, is a creation groaning, the poet who attends to the world must also show us the shadows. The Reformed poet will occasionally be called upon to investigate the cracks in the beams, to attend to the hunger, to give voice to the rage. Jellema lost a son in a car accident, and his poetry is often pierced with a sadness that is its own longing for resurrection and communion. And in such poems, the concreteness and specificity are precisely what make it possible for us to pick up the poem and find our own sorrows named, even if their sources and occasions are different. The last stanza of "Letter from Friesland to My Sons" captures something essential about this:

> So listen: old Frisians say what to do about mystery and loss,
>   about all the unspeakable beauty and grief:
> *if it can't be said*, a Dokkum proverb goes, *then you must sing it.*
>   I'm learning. Forgive me. I want to have words
> with you tonight, but the canal going back has no translation.[21]

Sometimes poetry is how we sing the ineffable.

Poetry is a way to take a break from the incessant chatter of our existence, where words of advertisers and politicians and even preachers wash over us in a stream of blah-blah-blah-ness in which words are just sonic atoms of noise. The poet grabs us by the collar, pushes us down in our chair, tries to still the air, and in the breath of that first silence invites us to hear words anew and grapple with our finitude afresh. Jellema does so in "Think Narrow," which concludes:

> Think narrow. Think the line of light
> that leapt under the bedroom door
> to save the frightened child who was you.
> Your thin escape from being someone else.
> The slender grace of a student thought
> that takes you past your self, walking
>
> the good gray heavy town,
> the bulge and muscle and long bone
> that enables a wisp of thought to walk
> these streets, themselves created by thought.
> Think how we stride the wide earth
> pressing down our weight and our love,
> exulting in the plump swell of growth,

21. Jellema, *Incarnality*, 70. Reprinted by permission of the publisher.

knowing the narrow gift of incarnality
is ours by the skin of our teeth.[22]

Common Grace and Poetry: On Reading Widely

It should be recognized, of course, that a Reformed affirmation and celebration of poetry does not reduce to a focus on Reformed poets. Indeed, a Reformed aesthetic sensibility should propel us to welcome the play of poetry from a wide array of voices. Although we still want to exercise aesthetic judgment (not all poetry is *good* poetry), we can celebrate the creaturely, deeply *human* expression of the *imago Dei* that is breathed to life in poetic language.

In fact, we should also be honest that the Reformed tradition has been a minor tributary in the river of poetry. (The Reformed tradition has yet to birth a Gerard Manley Hopkins, though we might claim George Herbert, the great Anglican poet, as at least a cousin.) While poets working from Reformational convictions will bring unique sensibilities to their creative task, the Reformed conviction concerning God's common grace means we can also expect the Spirit of beauty and meaning to be heard from surprising places. Richard Mouw succinctly encapsulates the intuition behind the doctrine of common grace: "If God is *glorified* by his non-human creation—which seems to be a fairly modest claim to endorse—then it seems reasonable to assume that God *takes delight* in those non-human created phenomena. And then it also seems to be quite plausible that God takes delight in various *human* states of affairs, even when they are displayed in the lives of non-elect human beings."[23] And if God takes delight in such artifacts of human creativity, so should his people.

Indeed, there is good reason to expect that Christian poetry may be prone to tropes and metaphors that could become predictable, a kind of rut of the imagination precisely because of their overfamiliarity.[24] One of the great temptations for all Christian art is to lapse into cliché, to parrot the familiar and keep reinventing the wheels with more and more layers of sentimentality.

22. Jellema, *Incarnality*, 118. Reprinted by permission of the publisher.
23. Richard J. Mouw, *He Shines in All That's Fair: Culture and Common Grace* (Grand Rapids: Eerdmans, 2001), 35.
24. This relates to what Charles Taylor calls the "fragility" of poetic language: "What reveals by resonation can cease to [do so]. The language may go dead, flat, become routinized, a handy tool of reference, a commonplace, like a dead metaphor, just unthinkingly invoked. We see this, of course, with traditional religious language." *A Secular Age* (Cambridge, MA: Harvard University Press, 2007), 758. This drives us to neologism, he continues, to find a new language that does justice to our reality and need for expression. Taylor points to the poetry of Gerard Manley Hopkins as a case in point (760–65). For further discussion of this point, see James K. A. Smith, *How (Not) to Be Secular: Reading Charles Taylor* (Grand Rapids: Eerdmans, 2014), 135–37.

Precisely for that reason, the Reformed conviction about common grace can propel us to dive into poetry whose subtle language can be an occasion to renew our own language. There will be aspects of creation, ourselves, and even God's character that can be illumined for us by poets of other faiths and even no faith at all. In this endeavor of cracking open the world and ourselves with the subtlety of speech, we find common cause with Muslim poets from Rumi to contemporary creators like Kaveh Akbar, Naomi Shihab Nye, and Saadi Youssef, to name just a few. Or one can hear a humility before mystery in the lyrics and poetry of Leonard Cohen, whose Jewish heritage continues to haunt and permeate his imagination, giving voice to broken hallelujahs. In an acceptance speech in Spain, Cohen once said, "Poetry comes from a place that no one commands and no one conquers. . . . If I knew where the good songs came from, I'd go there more often."[25] Here is a posture of humility that is also receptive to the winds of the Creator Spirit, wherever they may blow. And it is not only Christian poets with sails.

Indeed, there are many gifts to be received from so-called secular poets, those who wear their refusal and unbelief on their sleeve yet nonetheless grapple with the God they don't believe in and hence show us, sometimes, something of the confusions, obfuscations, and tired tropes we hide behind to protect ourselves from the ferocity of God's mercy and mystery. When Philip Larkin, in his poem "Church Going," comments on the quaint irrelevance of Christianity, there is something for us to attend to. The poet pauses to step inside "in awkward reverence," muses at the ceiling, signs the guest book, then reflects that "the place was not worth stopping for." And yet he did stop, something he confesses he does frequently, and departs wondering what he is meant to see that he does not see.

To approach poetry in the light of common grace is not to simply listen for poetry that confirms our prior biases. It requires of us a vulnerability, an openness, a kind of linguistic hospitality by which we ourselves are opened, decentered, and receptive to language that might rattle us, yet in so doing rattle us awake from the slumber of tired speech. Morgan Parker's collection *There Are More Beautiful Things than Beyoncé* has more than enough to scandalize readers who would prefer the staid predictability of Emily Dickinson or Mary Oliver. But precisely because of the eroticism of Parker's poetry, it is language on fire. There is a kind of surrealism to her stream-of-consciousness diction that nonetheless captures the peculiar confusion that is so often the voice inside our own heads. From "The Gospel of Jesus's Wife,"[26] for example:

---

25. In Leonard Cohen, *The Flame: Poems and Selections from Notebooks* (Toronto: McClelland & Stewart, 2018), 267.

26. Before being offended by the title, consider Scripture's description of the church.

Jesus loves me yes
Yes and my body
My steepled temple
O God your flesh is a word
My flesh by the grace of you
I believe in everything
Brown bodies in a salty river
Your praises in their swollen cheeks

The carnality of being human—and the specificity of Black womanhood—is invoked in ways that challenge us to question just how willing we are to affirm the goodness of creation, embodiment, and incarnation. Are we uncomfortable with the entendre, the play of language and bodies? Isn't our discomfort in fact a refusal of an erotic metaphor from which neither Solomon nor the apostle Paul shrinks? Later in the poem, Parker continues:

And Jesus said medium rare
And I bowed quietly eternally
Cleaned his cup on my apron
And poured him his blood
In this parable I am the goblet
Crater of birth and service[27]

Poetry is one of those means by which God's image bearers, these humans deputized to be makers, create allusive invitations to become craters of God's mercy, goblets filled with his grace, offering to our neighbors a drink that brings life.

---

27. Morgan Parker, *There Are More Beautiful Things than Beyoncé* (Portland, OR: Tin House Books, 2017). Copyright © 2017 by Morgan Parker. Reprinted by permission of ICM Partners.

14

Reformed Resources for Thinking about Fashion

ROBERT S. COVOLO

"Did you ever think there's more to life than being really, really, really, ridiculously good looking?" A fashion model poses this rhetorical question in the slapstick comedy movie *Zoolander*. The joke—and the entire film—capitalizes on the well-known foibles of the fashion world.

Joking aside, fashion poses several serious questions to all Christians who, let's face it, wear clothing of some sort. As Christians, what are we to make of fashion? Is it little more than a worthless obsession feeding a shallow existence? Should Christians dismiss fashion as mere frivolity and move on to more pressing issues? What about Christians who work in the industry? How should they understand their participation? Is it even possible to get dressed in the morning without participating in fashion's systems, structures, and patterns?

At the heart of these questions is a conundrum: What exactly is "fashion"? Where does it come from? And how does it work? Clearly, fashion involves change. After all, we often speak of things moving "in" and "out" of fashion. Indeed, it is not uncommon to hear of any number of things—cars, furnishings, and even ideas—as being "in fashion." Yet our interest here is with a more focused understanding of fashion: the rapid interplay of bodily adornment. Furthermore, this interplay, as numerous fashion theorists have argued, has a unique relationship to both the West and modernity.[1] Putting these ideas together, fashion can be understood as *the rapid interplay of dress that, although global in reach and evident in non-Western cultures, finds its historical eventuation primarily through developments in the modern West.* Having established how we are using the term, we turn to a second preliminary question: From whence does the Reformed theological tradition discuss fashion?

Reformed theology emerged in the early modern period in Western Europe. As such, the tradition's genesis is roughly concomitant with the rise of modern fashion.[2] The theological tradition's refusal to neatly seal off the church from the broader culture (something Richard Mouw calls "Holy Worldliness") makes the church's heritage uniquely positioned to theologize within the warp and woof of *this* life, within the fashioned clothing that adorns it.

Given the parallel provenances of the Reformation and early modern fashion and given the unique this-life impulse of Reformed theology, it should come as little surprise that the tradition gains unique traction when reflecting on the topic of fashion.[3] To evince this, we begin our survey with the most celebrated of all the forefathers of the Reformed tradition, John Calvin.

Gifts from a Good Father

Should Christians give thanks to God for clothing? For fashion? It may surprise modern readers to discover that John Calvin (1509–64) had quite a bit to say regarding the early modern fashions in his day.[4] Commenting on dress was unremarkable for theologians and pastors in the sixteenth century. Indeed, it was customary for ecclesiastical authorities to work with civil magistrates to detail and enforce laws regulating dress. Calvin was no different in this regard. As a result of Calvin performing this civic responsibility, many of Calvin's comments

1. Indeed, the word for fashion in French, *la mode*, is the root of the word "modernity." See Christopher Breward and Caroline Evans, eds., *Fashion and Modernity* (New York: Bloomsbury Academic, 2005); Elizabeth Wilson, *Adorned in Dreams: Fashion and Modernity*, 2nd ed. (London: Taurus, 2003), 16; Chris Breward, "Style and Modernity," in *The Culture of Fashion* (Manchester, UK: Manchester University Press, 2003), 159–68; Joan Entwistle, *The Fashioned Body: Fashion, Dress and Modern Social Theory*, 2nd ed. (Malden, MA: Polity, 2015), 44.

2. I say "roughly" since both fashion and the Reformation were birthed in early modernity: modern fashion can be traced back to the thirteenth or fourteenth century, and the Reformation began in the sixteenth century.

3. To suggest this proximity, I have listed the Reformed sources chronologically and labeled them in light of unique contributions they afford a theology of fashion.

4. Calvin's comments on dress are best found by examining his commentaries and sermons on key texts that speak of dress: Gen. 3:21; Deut. 22:5; 1 Tim. 2:9; etc.

focus on dress as it relates to its potential for public sin.[5] For example, when Calvin read the story of God supplying animal skins to the first couple (Gen. 3:19–22), he quickly associated it with the fall, pride, and humanity's temptation to construct an identity out of step with their true status. Thus, time and again, Calvin returns to the problematic nature of sumptuous clothing in the public square: such adornment was easily employed to deceive not only the self but also one's neighbor regarding one's true status before God.

In reading the numerous negative comments that Calvin offered about the sinful potential of dress, one might be tempted to dismiss Calvin as a prude, a curmudgeon, a sartorial killjoy. But on a number of counts, this would be a mistake. For starters, Calvin's corpus on dress reveals a desire to keep the focus on theological issues rather than offering detailed elaboration on which items of adornment were to be deemed appropriate. (Of course, even Calvin could not resist condemning the most offensive styles of his day, such as slashed sleeves.) Calvin's concerns were driven by more than the need to enforce sumptuary legislation, much less prudery or some kind of detestation of pleasure.[6] Rather, behind Calvin's call for sartorial restraint resided a desire to produce a self-disciplined and pious laity akin to the early monastics. Forgoing luxury enabled Christians to give generously lest, as Calvin warned, those wearing expensive clothing unwittingly cover themselves with "the blood of the poor."[7]

Although Calvin was cross-pressured by these concerns, he remained appreciative of beautiful things. (Calvin was, after all, French!) A humanist scholar trained to recognize human achievement and cultural innovation, Calvin reminds his readers that handsome clothing, like delicious food, should be celebrated as a gift for humanity from a good Father. A beautiful dress, a delightful shoe, and a well-fitting garment are all to be received with Christian gratitude and enjoyed with unblushing delight. After all, Calvin argues, sartorial beauty is sourced by a good God, who desires to add aesthetic delight, joy, and pleasure to our lives. Beautiful adornments are gifts from a creative and beautiful Father, who even cares about what flowers wear.

> Has the Lord clothed the flowers with the great beauty which greets our eyes, the sweetness of smell that is wafted upon our nostrils, and yet will it be unlawful for

5. In a moment of exuberance, Calvin once exhorted his parishioners, "If our Lord spat in our faces a hundred times, he could not better express how vile we are than when he clothed Adam and Eve with skins." See John Calvin, *Sermons on Genesis: Chapters 1–11*, trans. Rob Roy McGregor (Edinburgh: Banner of Truth Trust, 2009), 329.

6. John Calvin, *Institutes of the Christian Religion*, ed. John T. McNeill, trans. Ford Lewis Battles, 2 vols. (1960; repr., Louisville: Westminster John Knox, 2006), 3.10.1–3, on p. 720.

7. John Calvin, "On Luxury," in *Calvin's Ecclesiastical Advice*, trans. Mary Beaty and Benjamin W. Farley (Louisville: Westminster/John Knox, 1991), 86.

our eyes to be affected by that beauty, or our sense of smell to obey the sweetness of that odor? What? Did he not so distinguish colors as to make some more lovely than others? What? Did he not endow gold and silver, ivory and marble, with loveliness that renders them more precious than other metals or stones? Did he not, in short, render many things attractive to us, apart from their necessary use?[8]

Calvin gives us clues as to how a contemporary Christian should evaluate one's wardrobe. While dressing in the morning, one might pause to thank God for the gift of beautiful, well-fitting, well-made clothing. These are tangible reminders of a good Father, who provides beautiful things to his children. Or, while preparing the fall lineup, a Christian designer might be thinking of that work as an aesthetic offering to the neighbors. The sartorial gifts offered the community come from the giver of all good things (James 1:17).

The Market and the Zeitgeist

What are Christians to make of fashion as an industry? Moving from the sixteenth century to the twentieth, we encounter the Swiss theologian Karl Barth (1886–1968): as a young pastor, he cut his teeth by challenging unjust labor practices of the textile industry in Switzerland. Much later in life, Barth turned to the subject of fashion in his theological reflections on public life.[9] In doing so, Barth identified fashion with what the New Testament calls the "principalities and powers." Here Barth associated the industry with two things.

First, Barth associated fashion with rampant and unfaithful market forces. As Barth saw it, the consumptive forces of the market capture the imaginations of people while remaining under the radar as mere frivolity and fad.[10] For Barth, these forces were personified in the overlords of the garment industry (the "kings of fashion"). Barth despised these capitalist potentates for exploiting consumer's weaknesses, vanity, and fear of social stigma—all to line their own pockets.

Second, Barth associated fashion with the *Zeitgeist*, the spirit of the times.[11] Barth believed fashion played into the tacit social imagination of a culture, wherein an entire populace is scripted into capricious and consumptive rituals. His concern certainly makes sense, given his experience with the frenzied shift

8. Calvin, *Institutes* 3.10.2.
9. Karl Barth, *Church Dogmatics*, vol. IV/4, *The Christian Life: Lecture Fragments*, trans. Geoffrey W. Bromiley (Grand Rapids: Eerdmans, 1981), 228.
10. Barth, *Church Dogmatics* IV/4, 228.
11. Karl Barth, *Protestant Theology in the Nineteenth Century: Its Background and History*, trans. Brian Cozens and John Bowden, new ed. (Grand Rapids: Eerdmans, 2002), 405.

toward the zeitgeist of National Socialism. Akin to the way Hegel's historical dialectic conflated the *Geist* with a particular cultural-racial matrix, Barth saw global fashion trends assimilating diverse citizens into a uniform culture of machines.

Although these two critiques are strong, they did not lead Barth into a wholesale condemnation of fashion. Barth saw, hidden within society's craze for fashion, a collective consciousness where suppressed (theological) truth actually resides. For Barth, in spite of society's consumptive and capricious rituals, humanity's desire to adorn itself evinced an implicit "confession of faith": a fascination with a glorious and elusive humanity (*sensus humanitatis*) that corresponded with humanity's rightful claim to be robed with Christ.[12]

Informed by Barth, Christians are right to interrogate the economic and cultural forces behind the clothing they wear. Fashion is a global 2.5-trillion-dollar industry, employing hundreds of millions of people. Its demands for water and the use of toxic chemicals make it among the world's largest water polluters and carbon emitters. As Elizabeth Cline reminds us, cheap fashion for the consumer often comes at a high cost for the laborer and the environment.[13]

Furthermore, the inordinate desires behind "life-styling" in an economy driven by consumption is no laughing matter.[14] Although consumption is not wrong in itself, acquisition does not equal flourishing; in fact, it can actively undermine said flourishing (Matt. 16:26). Unable to make the distinction between consumption and flourishing, the social imagination of modern markets can produce fashion patterns and practices that are profoundly destructive. To combat this, Barth's assessment suggests that Christian producers and consumers of fashion must actively confront the destructive realities that plague the industry.

The Complexity of Fashion

It has been said that society is "founded upon cloth."[15] While this claim may be guilty of hyperbole, it is undeniable that modern fashion is a powerful, complex, and multifaceted force within modern life. Therefore, a Christian

---

12. Here Barth's view of fashion as holding an eschatological hope draws from the close relationship of clothing and *theōsis* in Scripture. See Dan Lé, *The Naked Christ: An Atonement Model for a Body-Obsessed Culture* (Eugene, OR: Pickwick Publications, 2012), 207–8.

13. See Elizabeth Cline, *Over-Dressed: The Shockingly High Cost of Cheap Fashion* (New York: Penguin, 2012); and her follow-up, *The Conscious Closet: The Revolutionary Guide to Looking Good While Doing Good* (New York: Penguin, 2019).

14. Daniel M. Bell Jr., *The Economy of Desire: Christianity and Capitalism in a Postmodern World* (Grand Rapids: Baker Academic, 2012).

15. Thomas Carlyle, *Sartor Resartus* (1836; repr., Oxford: Oxford University Press, 1987), 48.

approach to fashion must examine the complex and multilayered nature of its power. This leads us to the insights of the Reformed philosopher Herman Dooyeweerd (1894–1977).

Dooyeweerd's highly technical philosophical language can present challenges to new readers of his work. Thankfully, only two relatively straightforward aspects of his need to be understood to appreciate his views on fashion. The first is his claim that all reality is a complex creation of God and composed of irreducible aspects or modes of being (e.g., "physical," "biotic," "aesthetic," "social," "economic"). These diverse aspects of God's creation serve as unique lenses through which Christians can examine everything in creation and culture.

The second aspect important for understanding Dooyeweerd's view of fashion is his reading of cultural development and human history as a gift of God. According to Dooyeweerd, human beings are meant to explore, develop, and "open up" these diverse aspects of God's creation in human history and cultural development. Moreover, it is God's intention that human cultures should become more complex and multifaceted as they develop. As human beings grow and learn, they should develop from simple "tribes" to more multifaceted "societies" where the arts, sciences, industry, entertainment, religion, technology, and more can continue to develop in human freedom.

Combining these two features, Dooyeweerd offers a distinct Christian understanding of fashion as a unique seed that God planted in creation and humanity—a seed that human beings should explore, nurture, and develop with confidence and joy. For Dooyeweerd, fashion is a creational gift and, like all gifts, human beings need to open it up and explore its goodness in divine humility and joy.

For Dooyeweerd, fashion (as with everything in creation) is a complex and multifaceted phenomenon. Fashion, therefore, can (and should) be approached from a *variety* of angles. Fashion fulfills several complex functions in God's world. Dooyeweerd's nuanced understanding of fashion as maintaining an irreducibly multithreaded structure is echoed more recently by fashion theorist Elizabeth Wilson: "Dress in general seems then to fulfill a number of social, aesthetic, and psychological functions; indeed, it knits them together, and can express them all simultaneously."[16] Dooyeweerd's multiperspectival approach to fashion foreshadowed the various ways numerous disciplines in the modern university—from psychology to philosophy to political theory—have engaged the complex phenomenon we call "fashion."

16. Elizabeth Wilson, *Adorned in Dreams: Fashion in Modernity* (London: I. B. Tauris, 2010), 3.

Moreover, the aspects Dooyeweerd sees most dominant in fashion, the historical and social aspects, supply his most pronounced claims regarding its distinct capacity.[17] Specifically, Dooyeweerd believed fashion was a unique cultural catalyst in history that enabled cultures and relationships to progressively "open up" over time. In this way, modern fashion could help hierarchical societies transition from a class-stratified verticality to an interindividual horizontality. In contrast to Barth, Dooyeweed saw how fashion could actively push against the kind of groupthink and class-based rivalries of the zeitgeist that one might associate with both hierarchical society and, conversely, fascism.

Particularly important in the "opening process" for Dooyeweerd is the move from a "closed" and "primitive" to an "opened" and "differentiated" society. More specifically, Dooyeweerd tracks how, all things being equal, groups in history have tended to move from rigid walls of small tribes and insular populaces to more complex societies that require a divergent variety of social spaces. For Dooyeweerd, fashion can serve this historical process through its specific ability to both connect and differentiate diverse citizens across a variety of social spaces and communities.

Taking Dooyeweerd's insight in hand, Christians are reminded that fashion is not something to be narrowly analyzed, not purely in terms of consumerism, fads, and inordinate desires. Dooyeweerd's "multiperspectival" view of fashion gives Christians new eyes by which to assess the numerous ways the fashionable clothing they wear shapes the world. While fashion can certainly be deconstructed in terms of unjust labor and environmental disaster, there are many other angles to be considered—such as the critical way fashion trends have reinforced both individual liberties and communal solidarities within complex modern societies.

Playful Aesthetic Obedience

What are we to make of those for whom clothing is experienced primarily as a medium for aesthetic playfulness, joy, and delight? The Reformed philosopher Calvin Seerveld (1930–) has developed the aesthetic concepts of "allusivity" and "nuancefulness"—the human quality of creatively making allusions or of having nuances. When considering the creative playfulness of everyday fashion, Seerveld's concepts are quite helpful.[18] Seerveld argues

17. Herman Dooyeweerd, *New Critique of Theoretical Thought*, vol. 3 (Jordan Station, ON: Paideia, 1984), 588–693.

18. Calvin Seerveld, *Normative Aesthetics*, ed. John H. Kok (Sioux Center, IA: Dordt College Press, 2014), 88.

that our everyday creative "allusivity" and nuanced playfulness is built into us as created beings. Created and intended by God, Seerveld argues that such playful aesthetic delight and nuancefulness is normative for us.

Seerveld made strong use of his understanding of "allusivity" when taking up the subject of daily aesthetic tasks. In this regard, he paid particular attention to the implications of allusivity for daily dress. According to Seerveld, Christian dress can and should encourage an imaginative quality when it comes to capturing the nuance of various social occasions. And it should recognize the aesthetic depth of the human body.

But above and beyond these two actions, as Seerveld points out, *the way we dress* offers us a special opportunity to express joy. How so? Just as joy operates on a deeper register than happiness and thus heightens everyday life, so too a nuanced attention to our dress opens a deeper aesthetic register, thereby heightening every aspect of our daily routine. In other words, by thoughtfully working with the aesthetics of our body through attending to issues such as color and form, we don a handsome outfit or lovely dress; *in so doing* we display to the world the joyful enterprise of knowing Christ and being a beloved creature of God.

Here we must not confuse Seerveld's idea of "aesthetic obedience" with embracing fashion without remainder. Seerveld is leery of the power of fad and consumerism in fashion—forces he deems responsible for both thoughtless, sentimental, and kitschy dress and vain, slick, and gaudy outfits.[19] If fashion's aesthetics entail adherence to such, Seerveld strongly advises, "Christians . . . will rightly, normally, be out of fashion."[20] Even so, participation in the fashion system does not necessarily entail that one is driven by fad and consumerism. It can also involve the playful use of dress, such as for festive occasions. In this regard, Seerveld would find a place for a thoughtful Christian participation in the fashion system by way of aesthetic obedience.

If this is right, Christians can employ fashionable dress as one of the many ways they express their joy in having union with Christ. By giving nuanced attention to a style of dress, believers not only open a deeper aesthetic register inherent in creation; they also heighten every aspect of a daily routine. In other words, by thoughtfully working with the aesthetics of one's body and clothing (by attending to issues such as shape, color, and form), Christians can display to the world the joyful enterprise of knowing Christ; for we glorify God and enjoy him through a dress that proclaims the hope-filled joy found in a God who gives delights, the chief of which is himself.

19. Calvin Seerveld, *Rainbows for a Fallen World* (Toronto: Tuppence, 1980), 63–64.
20. Seerveld, *Normative Aesthetics*, 85.

Source for an Authentic Performance

Fashion exists at the intersection of individual and collective identity, conveying both personal expression and social performance. These two features have reason to give Christians pause. To the degree that fashion's personal focus feeds individualism and fashion's collective thrust propels duplicity, these dynamics most certainly stand in tension with the Christian faith. But is opposition indeed the case? This question leads us to our final Reformed thinker, Richard J. Mouw (1940–).

In his book *The God Who Commands*, Mouw seeks to understand the proper status of the individual in society. According to Mouw, it is only when we understand the individual before God that both overaccented and overdetracted understandings of individuality are avoided and an ethically informed understanding of individuality emerges.[21] For Mouw, in other words, not all individualistic schemes by which the "I" is accented are pernicious to human flourishing. Indeed, the celebration of the individualizing love of God actually serves to dislodge the individual from self-absorption.

This has immediate implications for fashion. For, as has been noted, fashion can easily play into the rampant self-expression*ism* (note the "ism": here we are talking about a philosophy of life) that has come to mark late modernity.[22] Fashion rightfully deserves critique to the degree it propagates what Mouw calls "the emotivist self" (the idea that there is no normative reality to which the self's preferences and expressions stand accountable). Even so, Mouw's defense of a *God-given* individuality suggests how fashion, though in danger of abuse, is not *necessarily* a conduit for individuals' "self-identifying" in ways that jettison God-given norms. Rather, it can serve as a legitimate display of individual distinction.

Additionally, Mouw's work offers a Reformed understanding of fashion as a series of social performances. As Mouw retraces the changes, the West has moved from a medieval social order, in which an individual's honor dictates hierarchical rules of social conduct toward others (premodern distributive justice), to one in which the individual performs emotively, often in disregard of one's neighbor (late-modern distributive chaos). Drawing from Calvin, Mouw offers a third way beyond the hierarchical roles of premodernity and the Wild West performances of the "emotive self." Accordingly, to be authentically

21. Richard J. Mouw, *The God Who Commands: A Study in Divine Command Theory* (Notre Dame, IN: University of Notre Dame Press, 1990), 43–54. Also see Richard J. Mouw, *Restless Faith: Holding Evangelical Beliefs in a World of Contested Labels* (Grand Rapids: Brazos, 2019), 159–61.

22. Charles Taylor, *A Secular Age* (Cambridge, MA: Harvard University Press, 2007), 481–83.

enlisted as a social performer involves performing one's fashion *toward* one's neighbor under the gaze of the Divine spectator (divine command distributive justice).[23] Said another way, one responds to one's neighbor not merely in light of inner realities or by way of cultural prescriptions, but in light of how the biblical narrative provides a script that suggests how one performs within any number of personal and cultural dynamics—be it a backyard barbeque with friends and neighbors, a holiday party with colleagues from work, or a gala event honoring a significant person in the community.[24]

Mouw's work offers Christians yet another lens from which to think about fashion. When Christians dress, they do so not *merely* as a form of self-expression, nor *merely* by way of adhering to cultural norms, but above all as a way of performing their identity as a people called to love and serve their neighbors *coram Deo*—"before the face of God." Believers take up everyday fashion as both actors (those wearing fashion) and directors (those producing fashion), so as to craft bold, imaginative, "fitting performances" within the divine theo-drama.[25] In so doing, Christians see others and are seen by them through the sight of the One for whom nothing is hidden (Heb. 4:13).

Reforming Fashion

Drawing on five Reformed thinkers, we have looked at fashion from five different vantage points: fashion as gift, fashion as market commodity, fashion as social force, fashion as aesthetic play, and fashion as social costume. While this list demonstrates the variety of ways Christians can understand and engage fashion, our survey is far from complete. Admittedly, such a survey is merely a teaser, meant to awaken awareness rather than offer the kind of satisfying details such connections suggest and deserve.[26]

Yet, as cursory as this brief chapter may be, it reveals an important insight. Far from the facile characterizations of fashion that comedic films like *Zoolander* (2001) portray, fashion is a subject worthy of serious intellectual and spiritual reflection. Indeed, the current multidisciplinary discourse on fashion taking place in universities around the world is doing just that.[27]

23. Mouw, *God Who Commands*, 72–73.
24. Kevin Vanhoozer, *The Drama of Doctrine: A Canonical-Linguistic Approach to Christian Theology* (Louisville: Westminster John Knox, 2005).
25. Vanhoozer, *Drama of Doctrine*, 22.
26. For a more fulfilling treatment see Robert S. Covolo, *Fashion Theology* (Waco: Baylor University Press, 2020).
27. Fashion has become a subject of serious theoretical inquiry in the modern academy, boasting not only degree programs, monographs, and academic journals dedicated to understanding

But this chapter also demonstrates another kind of breadth: we have unearthed the capacious nature of Reformed thought. Indeed, although fashion may seem to be a subject far removed from the Westminster Shorter Catechism or the Synod of Dort, Reformed scholars have long considered the world of fashion in all its diversity and complexity—created and redeemed by Jesus Christ—as fair game. This includes the current state of dress in our modern world. May the breadth of Christ's lordship invigorate us as we continue to explore the fascinating ways in which the *imago Dei* is adorned.

---

fashion, but also the attention of a host of academic disciplines, including anthropology, art history, classics, culture studies, economic history, film studies, gender studies, literary studies, marketing, theater studies, performance studies, psychology, philosophy, politics, semiotics, social history, sociology, and social psychology.

15

Streets of Shalom

Reformed Reflections on Urban Design

ERIC O. JACOBSEN

Does God care about sidewalks, freeways, and parks? Is there a biblical perspective on zoning laws? Does God have an opinion about strip malls, skyscrapers, and surface-level parking?

The world can be divided between the natural environment and the built environment. The natural environment refers to wilderness of all kinds, from deserts to rain forests. The built environment refers to terrain that has been intentionally altered by human intervention. This includes buildings and streets, bridges and culverts, benches and lampposts, and so on. Urban planning is the professional field most directly responsible for the shaping of the built environment.

From a Reformed theological perspective, a major aspect of humanity's collective vocation is not only to care for the natural environment but also to develop and arrange the natural environment in a way that serves our neighbor and glorifies our God. From a qualitative perspective, the built environment surrounds almost all our neighbors and occupies a significant amount of space. If this is the case, it stands to reason that the built environment and the vocation of urban planning are deserving of Reformed theological reflection.

The built environment deserves our theological attention not only because of its global ubiquity but also because of its tremendous impact on a wide range of things that God cares about—such as justice, beauty, family life, and the environment.[1] Although the impact of the built environment is profound, it is often easily overlooked in our day-to-day lives. Its subtlety is part of its power. The streets, sidewalks, and shopping spaces that make up our everyday lives shape our common life in thousands of untold ways. The power of urban design to either uplift or degrade people, to gather or scatter them, demands our theological reflection.

This chapter exposes and examines the forgotten but powerful realm of urban design, all too often ignored by theologians; it frames several key questions and provides some Reformed resources for reflection on such planning. Because of limited space and time, we focus our theological reflections on three major issues facing contemporary urban life: idolatry, aesthetics, and injustice. Further readings are suggested in the footnotes.

Urban Planners as Idolaters

Idolatry, simply put, attributes ultimate significance to something that is not God. Idols can involve the usual suspects like money, sex, and power. Or they can be somewhat surprising things like families, nations, and health. We do not normally think of the physical shape of cities and towns as a realm prone to idolatry—but it is. Those who shape the built environment certainly wield a tremendous amount of power. All too often, that power goes to their heads and to their hearts.

Left to their own devices, architects and urban planners are often in danger of using the city as their personal canvas—a space on which to express their own ideological, industrial, or aesthetic values and hubris. Through design, planners imprint their own ideas about the good life directly into the cityscape. Unfortunately, these worldviews, composed in steel and cement, can run at cross-purposes with common sense, creation, and the Creator.[2]

---

1. Timothy Gorringe, *A Theology of the Built Environment: Justice, Empowerment, Redemption* (Cambridge: Cambridge University Press, 2002); Eric O. Jacobsen, *Three Pieces of Glass: Why We Feel Lonely in a World Mediated by Screens* (Grand Rapids: Brazos, 2020); Jacobsen, *The Space Between: A Christian Engagement with the Built Environment* (Grand Rapids: Baker Academic, 2012); Jacobsen, *Sidewalks in the Kingdom: New Urbanism and the Christian Faith* (Grand Rapids: Brazos, 2003); and also Congress for the New Urbanism: Members' Christian Caucus, https://www.center4eleadership.org/cnu-members-christian-caucus.

2. Jan Gehl, *Cities for People* (Washington, DC: Island, 2010); Jane Jacobs, *The Death and Life of Great American Cities* (New York: Vintage, 1961).

Although it claims to be a "secular" profession, there is a profound religiosity to the field of urban design. Jan Gehl is a famous city planner from Denmark. In a lecture reflecting on the field of urban design during the twentieth century, he joked about the blind devotion he and his fellow students professed during their professional training. As we practiced urban design, he said, "Twice a day we bowed down and genuflected to a picture of Brasília."[3] Brasília is the capital city of Brazil, a well-known icon of a modernist approach to urban planning. Gehl's joke captures the over-the-top adulation that modernism commands in certain academic institutions. At the time, Brasília was widely praised because it expressed the core values of Western modernity: individualism, reason, power over nature, and a prioritization of modern abstraction.

Designed and built from scratch in 1956–60, Brasília represented a bold and godlike approach to modern planning. Rather than steering incremental and organic urban growth slowly from the ground up, Brasília's planners designed the entire city from the top down, to reflect their grand and unified modern vision. Like transcendent gods, the architects planned Brasília from the sky. From above, the city is laid out like a giant eagle. The parliament buildings form the head of the eagle, and the wings are where people live and work.

The design was extolled by modernists who peered down on the city from thirty thousand feet. Yet from the perspective of a six-foot-tall Brazilian walking its streets, "Brasília is sh—."[4] The expanses between the buildings are too wide. There is no protection from the wind. It is much too far to walk from one building to the next. The expansive cityscape makes human beings feel small, exhausted, exposed, and unwelcome. Brasília was not designed for humans. It was designed to serve the idols of modernity—speed, efficiency, political grandeur, and cold abstraction. Hence the epithet "sh—."

Up until the twentieth century, cities grew slowly and organically over centuries. Thousands of years of trial and error and accumulated wisdom were embedded into the streets, markets, and public buildings of historic cities.[5] In the twentieth century, modernist planners broke with this received wisdom and reoriented their cities to serve two new masters: the automobile[6] and the modern theorist.[7] While planners and architects did not physically bow

3. Jan Gehl, "Livable Cities for the 21st Century" (speech delivered at the Congress for the New Urbanism XXVI, Savannah, GA, May 18, 2018), https://www.gsd.harvard.edu/event/jan-gehl-livable-cities-for-the-21st-century/.

4. Gehl, "Livable Cities for the 21st Century."

5. Daniel Solomon, *Global City Blues* (Washington, DC: Island, 2003).

6. Jane Holtz Kay, *Asphalt Nation: How the Automobile Took Over America, and How We Can Take It Back* (Berkeley: University of California Press, 1998).

7. Robert Fishman, *Urban Utopias in the Twentieth Century: Ebenezer Howard, Frank Lloyd Wright, and Le Corbusier* (Cambridge, MA: MIT Press, 1982).

down before cars and theorists, they did offer these two icons nearly sacred and sovereign status.[8] The cityscapes designed during this period reflected their new gods.

The theological concept of idolatry can help us understand why some destructive trends in modern design proved to be so persistent, even after their ill effects were made manifest. Le Corbusier's plan for the reconstruction of central Paris offers an illuminating example of modernity's blind dogmatism. Le Corbusier was a Swiss architect and well-respected modernist in the early twentieth century. Plan Voisin was his scheme to bulldoze and redesign central Paris according to the same modern values as Brasília: power, rationality, individualism, expansive space, and cold abstraction. Le Corbusier's plan involved leveling every existing building in central Paris and replacing them with identical and symmetrical high-rise buildings, with ample space between them to allow for the free flow of air and sunshine. Although his idea looked rational and logical from a godlike position at thirty thousand feet, it was completely detached from the lives, culture, and history of Parisians on the ground. Plan Voisin completely ignored and sought to bulldoze the historic and lived reality of Paris.

While his plan was (thankfully) never adopted, Le Corbusier's modernist vision became the inspiration for a wide variety of disastrous urban designs in cities around the globe. The most famous failure was the Pruitt-Igoe project in St. Louis. When it was built, this low-income housing project won several prestigious design awards. Symmetrical and logical from the sky, Pruitt-Igoe was brutal, ugly, and inhumane on the ground. The buildings were too tall and far too spread out. Individuals, communities, commerce, and public spaces were too far detached from one another to interact in fruitful ways. Cut off from one another, they began to break down. Pruitt-Igoe did not provide any natural gathering places. The inhospitable stairwells and lawns quickly became settings for prostitution, drugs, and other illicit activity. Residents were so unhappy that the entire project was demolished only

8. Tom Wolfe, *From Bauhaus to Our House* (New York: Farrar, Straus & Giroux, 1981).

Figure 15.1. Plan Voisin

SiefkinDR, CC BY-SA / Wikimedia Commons / Public domain

twenty years after it was built. Designed in the sky, Pruitt-Igoe was a disaster on the ground.

Smashing Idols: The Reformed Iconoclastic Corrective

The critique of idolatry found in Scripture focuses on an idol's inability to deliver what it promises. False gods promise freedom and flourishing but leave their devotees downtrodden, displaced, and enslaved.

The Reformation's iconoclastic impulse can prove helpful in challenging the modern idols of urban design. Although the iconoclasm of the Reformed tradition was and is initially critical and even destructive, in the long term it can have a liberating and even constructive effect. When human creations and designs are idolized above God, people, and his creation, they lose their humility, creativity, and responsiveness to the world. On the other hand, when they are put "in their place" under God and alongside people and creation, human designs and creations are liberated to humbly serve, create, and innovate. When city planning ceases to be an idol,

Figure 15.2. Pruitt-Igoe

it can be reframed as a creative and servant-hearted instrument for the blessing of humanity and creation.

The training that Gehl had received was beholden to the idols of modernity. It taught him to ignore the human users of buildings and common spaces. It had taught him to float above creation and dominate it with his modern vision. He learned to rearrange creation and the *imago Dei* according to his modern, godlike reason.

It was Gehl's iconoclastic impulse that brought him back to earth. It called him back to the streets to humbly listen and learn. Convinced that he needed to learn to pay attention, he walked the sidewalks and plazas with a camera to observe how ordinary humans utilize the built environment. He sought to become the city's partner, not its god.

In looking at the city from the ground, Gehl began to notice small but crucially important things. He saw that people tended to gravitate toward the edges of large open spaces. He noticed that people feel more comfortable walking in cozily enclosed spaces rather than in wide-open expanses. He observed that a favorite activity in all cultures is people watching. By making basic and grounded observations like these, Gehl quickly emerged as a highly sought-after planning consultant for municipal leaders around the world. He helped cities become much more humane by paying attention to humans.[9] Rather than floating above, he came alongside.

To do their job well, urban planners need to learn to humbly pay attention to a city's local ecosystem, history, culture, and the ways in which the locals interact. Whether urban planners are believers or not, they do well when paying attention to and respecting the norms, limits, and patterns embedded in humanity and the natural world. God has created human beings with certain social, aesthetic, and spatial needs and limits; all planners, Christian or not, can pay attention to these embedded creational needs. Urban planners' humility and attentiveness to the surrounding world (or lack thereof) will have a tremendous impact on the city they help to design. Their designs may last and impact both people and creation long after they are gone.

Gehl is not a theologian, but he is an iconoclast. He noticed that planners were sacrificing human beings on the altars of their modernist visions and values. Planners had devalued the lived experience of human beings, and this led them to create inhuman cityscapes. While Gehl is not a theologian, he learned to notice and respect the norms and patterns embedded in God's creation. He demonstrates that good urban planners will learn to humbly come alongside an urban community that will, no doubt, outlast them.

Selfishness and the Suburbs

During the second half of the twentieth century, the United States undertook a radical social experiment known as "suburbia." American cities had always lacked the genteel grandeur of older cities in Europe. They had developed a reputation for being noisy, dirty, and dangerous. The suburbs began as an attempt to flee from the problems of the American city. They would do this

9. Some of Gehl's clients have included Copenhagen, New York City, and Moscow.

by creating domestic enclaves, suburban escapes from cities that were un-attractive living spaces.

The suburbs were developed through a new public policy tool known as zoning, which involved separating buildings of distinct use into geographically separate regions. Zoning began by simply separating residential and commercial buildings from one another. But over time the separation became much more fine-grained.[10]

Several modern American values directed these suburban zoning patterns. The first was a love for consumption. The postwar economy was booming. Families had the means to buy more things, and so they did. Naturally, they wanted larger houses to store all those things.[11] The suburban development pattern was able to deliver larger houses at affordable prices by building mass-produced homes on the edge of the city.

Another value that drove suburban design trends was an increased demand for private domestic space. Before World War II, houses were oriented toward the front of the house, with the most prominent feature being a front porch that connected the family to the larger neighborhood community. Suburban houses, on the other hand, are oriented toward the backyard. A two- or three-car garage is often a prominent, though not very welcoming, feature on the front of a suburban house.[12]

A third value directing suburban design was a desire to insulate the rich from the poor. Through strict zoning laws, different-sized lots with diverse density levels could no longer be placed near one another. In short, apartments could no longer be near single-family homes. This meant that families with different socioeconomic status no longer lived near each other or interacted.[13]

---

10. Housing was located in specific zones according to density (keeping large houses separated from small houses, which were separated from apartment buildings). Separate commercial zones were established for office parks, retail, and manufacturing. There were even zones for sports complexes.

11. In 1950 the average new single-family home was 983 square feet, and the average family size was 3.37 members. In 2017, the average house size had expanded to 2,599 square feet, while the average family size had shrunk to 2.54 members. "Residential Buildings Factsheet," University of Michigan Center for Sustainable Systems, 2018, http://css.umich.edu/factsheets/residential-buildings-factsheet.

12. The prioritization of privacy and private spaces was also signaled by the zoning prohibition of any commercial building in a residential area (including coffee shops) and by dedicating the best land for private development and letting public spaces utilize less desirable parcels.

13. This income separation was further helped by the cul-de-sac style of street design. With the traditional grid model of street design, one can use any street to get to any destination, which means that a poor person might walk through a wealthy area of town on the way to another destination. But in the cul-de-sac model, almost all the residential streets terminate in a dead end so that only people who live in a particular neighborhood have any reason to be there.

The strict zoning policies were soon challenged at the US Supreme Court as a violation of land-use rights. In articulating the majority decision, Justice George Southerland expressed concern that apartment buildings might monopolize "rays of the sun which would otherwise fall upon the smaller homes."[14] The court decided the health and protection of children in single-family homes demanded the enforcement of zoning. Questions of scientific validity notwithstanding, if this case was truly about the safety and health of children, it seems to be skewed toward children in the upper classes. As a critic quipped, "One wonders, given the omission, whether Justice Southerland knew [that] children were raised in apartment buildings."[15]

From a Reformed perspective, we can ask whether God cares about preferential zoning treatment for the rich. John Calvin believed that rich Christians had an obligation to seek justice and share their wealth with the poor. He argues, "God distributes unequally the frail goods of this world in order to investigate the goodwill of men."[16] Through our inequality, God "is examining man."[17]

Calvin was deeply critical of rich Christians who not only ignore the needs of the poor but also try to separate themselves from those of modest means as a way of disregarding their needs. "If they were able to do so," he argues, "such rich people . . . would have a sun all to themselves in order to say that the others have nothing in common with them."[18] Calvin would likely have had sharp words for Justice Southerland's efforts to prevent lower-class children from enjoying the "rays of sun" that the wealthier children "deserved."

Using zoning laws to geographically distance the rich from the poor would have been anathema to Calvin. Unfortunately, subdividing income levels is

14. "Very often the apartment house is a mere parasite, constructed in order to take advantage of the open spaces and attractive surroundings created by the residential character of the district. Moreover, the coming of one apartment house is followed by others, interfering by their height and bulk with the free circulation of air and monopolizing the rays of the sun which otherwise would fall upon the smaller homes." Village of Euclid, Ohio, et al. v. Ambler Realty Company, 272 U.S. 365 (1926).

15. Michael Kwartler, "Legislating Aesthetics: The Role of Zoning in Designing Cities," in *Zoning and the American Dream: Promises Still to Keep*, ed. Charles M. Haar and Jerold S. Kayden (Chicago: Planners Press, 1989), 205.

16. John Calvin, *Calvini Opera quae supersunt omnia: Ad fidem editionum principium et authenticarum ex parte*, ed. J. Guilielmus Baum, A. Eduardus Cunitz, and Eduardus W. E. Reuss, Corpus Reformatorum (Berlin: C. A. Scwetschke & Son, 1863–1900), 27:337–38, from Sermon XCV on Deut. 15:11–15, as quoted in W. Fred Graham, *The Constructive Revolutionary: John Calvin and His Socio-Economic Impact* (Richmond: John Knox, 1978), 67.

17. Calvin, *Opera*, quoted in Graham, *Constructive Revolutionary*, 67.

18. Calvin, *Opera*, quoted in Graham, *Constructive Revolutionary*, 68.

now a bedrock principle of American zoning law.[19] Calvin understood citizens, both rich and poor, to be a body politic who together played an essential role in supporting the common good and building society. It is essential for the rich to be geographically aware of the existence and the needs of the poor in their midst. According to Calvin, the physical proximity of the poor is one of the ways in which God tests and trains the well-to-do in gratitude, justice, and charity.

Beauty, Banality, and the Shaping of Urban Space

Postwar America was flush with land, cash, and cheap gasoline. Americans demanded more single-family homes, more things bigger, faster, and cheaper. This demand quickly led to standardized architecture for residential zones. Instead of building one home for one client, developers started mass-producing entire subdivisions, using a limited number of house designs repeated in an endless loop. Mass-produced neighborhoods were cheaper and quicker to establish; they were also boring and banal.

This might seem like an acceptable trade-off, a less personalized design in exchange for more affordable housing. However, almost one hundred years before this trend hit the housing market in the United States, the Reformed theologian Abraham Kuyper pointed out its critical flaw. Commenting on a new modern and mass-produced neighborhood in the Netherlands, Kuyper writes:

> Even the ash-colored plater that coats house after house in the new sections of our cities is virtually identical. There is not a gable to be seen which in any way violates the absolute symmetry to which door and window, cornice and roof window, have been fitted. Precisely those straight streets and rectangular corners, those utterly level gables and standardized houses[,] make the modern outgrowths of our cities fatally exhausting and boring. You have to number the streets and count them out so as not to get lost in so featureless a collection of houses.[20]

Though Kuyper made the comments a hundred years ago in Europe, they are prescient in the American suburbs today.

19. Even though the suburban pattern of development, with its strict segregation of people of differing socioeconomic statuses, is beginning to wane, the cultural habit of segregating housing in this way continues to have a strong pull on development patterns in the US. The term NIMBY (not in my backyard) captures a common sentiment among middle- and upper-class citizens who may support the *idea* of affordable housing but do not want to see the *reality* of poor people in their own neighborhoods.

20. Abraham Kuyper, "Uniformity the Curse of Modern Life [1869]," in *Abraham Kuyper: A Centennial Reader*, ed. James D. Bratt (Grand Rapids: Eerdmans, 1998), 26–27.

In contrast to the banality of mass production of the newer parts of the city, Kuyper praises the old Dutch cities and villages for their randomness: "You can immediately tell that no shoddy money-hungry developer threw up that line of houses, but that every dwelling is the fulfillment of a personal dream, the precious product of quiet thrift, based on personal plan and built slowly from the ground up."[21] Kuyper's architectural reflections were based on two theological convictions. First, that human beings are not built for living in nondescript boxes; they are creative and imaginative creatures made in the image of God. Second, the values of the family (and not the business) should be the primary driver of unique home design. Kuyper believed that in home design, families should be sovereign, not the marketplace or the state. The family should determine the look of "tufted, tiered, triangular, and shuttered gables" on the house.[22]

Of course, a counterargument could be asserted that by making houses more affordable, the developer is strengthening the family, allowing it to affordably procure a home. One might also argue that zoning laws and building codes enforced by the state do protect families. In this case, Abraham Kuyper's Reformed theology of architecture does not provide a simple answer to the question of standardized housing so much as to frame that question in a specific way. What is the role of the family, the marketplace, and the state in home design? How important are the aesthetic aspects of a home when considering its value to a family and its surrounding neighborhood?

We can ask similar aesthetic questions regarding the ways in which modern cities redesigned themselves to serve the automobile. Cars take up a lot of space.[23] They demand massive parking lots and wide roads, long driveways and loud freeways. Car-centric urban design creates noise and air pollution, marginalizes green spaces, and endangers and discourages pedestrians. A theology of beauty cannot tell us exactly how many lanes are proper to a specific road. It can, however, prompt a key question: How important is omnipresent parking and unlimited street access, compared to a safe, pleasing, and beautiful walk through town?

21. Kuyper, "Uniformity the Curse," 27.

22. The problem with standardized architecture, according to Kuyper, is that the sphere of commerce is exerting undue creative influence over the sphere of the family. The home should primarily reflect and honor the aesthetic values of the family, not the economic values of the marketplace. Kuyper understands the design of the home to be properly under the sphere of the family, not of commerce.

23. Parking requirements for new construction mandated that on-site parking be provided for every conceivable user of the building. This meant parking lots in front of a building or parking garages taking the basement and first floor of a building. To accommodate increased auto traffic in cities and suburbs, four-, six-, and even eight-lane arterials cut through areas of new development, as recommended by traffic engineers.

Figure 15.3. Fabric and monumental buildings

In traditional urban design, two kinds of buildings shape public space and direct the public eye. "Fabric" buildings provide an aesthetic framing and direct the public eye toward more important "monumental" buildings. Here the city itself directs a citizen's eyes toward buildings that represent the common, cultural, and civic goods of the city. With the advent of car-centric design, streets have no "end." They point the eye to nothing but increased mobility and speed.

According to the Reformed philosopher Nicholas Wolterstorff, an ugly city is an affront to creation and its God. Questions of beauty and aesthetics, he argues, should not be relegated to the artist and the museum. All human beings need beauty. The city itself should be concerned with aesthetics. Beautiful cities honor and uplift those bearing the *imago Dei*, who move through them day in and day out.

Wolterstorff argues that the aesthetic quality of a city can be found in the way in which it frames urban space:

A city consists of buildings, these buildings, along with trees and other objects shaping space—urban space we may call it. Think for a moment of a room, where the walls, ceiling, and floor shape space in a certain way, though indeed we usually allow the characteristics of the container to draw our conscious attention more than the character of the space contained. Even if the ceiling of a room, its "lid," were removed, space would nonetheless be shaped by the walk and the floor, though indeed less completely, for space would "leak out" the top. So too, then, the buildings and other objects of a city give definite characteristics to the space between them which we note and feel as we move about in that space.[24]

Expansive parking lots and endless streets make the framing of urban space impossible. This, according to Wolterstorff, is an aesthetic assault on the city and its residents. Those who care about beauty as an aspect of God's nature and an aspect of human flourishing cannot allow this assault to continue. Insofar as Reformed theology inspires us to care about human flourishing, we should care about the aesthetic quality of the built environments where bearers of the *imago Dei* spend their time.

Conclusion

Urban planning is an important topic for Christian reflection for two primary reasons. First, God has commanded human beings to cultivate, arrange, and fill the earth in ways that are responsible, faithful, and glorifying to him. Second, the wise and thoughtful design of cities is a critical ingredient in human flourishing. Designing good cities is a way to love our neighbor.

When urban planners ignore creational limits and human needs, when they idolize abstract ideas and serve shortsighted demands for profits and power, their designs become idolatrous—and destructive. Urban planning needs more iconoclasts, planners who will abandon their godlike visions for the city composed at thirty thousand feet. We need humble planners who will pay attention to the city, the people, and the very creation around them. Accordingly, we need planners who will listen, learn, and ultimately come alongside their city and humbly offer it more life-giving spaces for movement, commerce, and leisure.

When the zeitgeist pursues speed and efficiency, the values of beauty and charm can be easily overlooked. The suburban developments of the late twentieth century left a legacy of sterile and featureless subdivisions. Cities became inhospitable to pedestrians as they sought to serve the automobile. In response to this zeitgeist, we need urban planners who have the courage and creativity needed to tame the car and cultivate urban spaces that are more beautiful and humane.

When the poor are segregated from the wealthy, God's justice is perverted and both sides suffer. Isolated, the poor lose access to resources and

24. Nicholas Wolterstorff, *Art in Action* (Grand Rapids: Eerdmans, 1980), 17.

opportunities. They become stuck in geographically isolated cycles of poverty. When the rich are isolated, they lose touch with reality, and their consciences are no longer pricked by encounters with the poor. The rich miss out on opportunities for moral growth in charity, justice, and hospitality. In response to this economic injustice and segregation, we need urban planners who can creatively break down the walls that separate the classes.

Urban planning is important because the built environment is important. To revise the old saying, we shape urban spaces and—soon enough—urban spaces begin to shape us. Does the design of your city encourage you to interact with your neighbors? Does its shape and form encourage you to take a walk, to slow down and enjoy good food, nature, and art? Are the public buildings in your city beautiful and prominent? Do they encourage you to remember your city's rich history, its culture, the common good? Are your city's public spaces welcoming, uplifting, and inspiring? Good urban planning matters to people, and it matters to God. It contributes to everyday delight, beauty, and justice. It is, in other words, a critical aspect of what it means to seek the shalom of the city.

Part Five

Public Academy

16

Engaging the Pluralist Campus

Reformed Resources

BETHANY L. JENKINS

American college students are navigating an increasingly complex set of questions regarding identity, culture, morality, and spirituality. Like the society that surrounds them, their campuses are filled with meaningful differences—religious, ideological, racial, cultural, and more. These differences can create a rich and vibrant learning environment. Sadly, they can also produce deep division and pain.[1] Moreover, students are also facing an unprecedented mental

1. For example, Bari Weiss, "Jonathan Haidt on the Cultural Roots of Campus Rage: An Unorthodox Professor Explains the 'New Religion' That Drives the Intolerance and Violence at Places like Middlebury and Berkeley," *Wall Street Journal*, April 14, 2017, https://www.wsj.com /articles/jonathan-haidt-on-the-cultural-roots-of-campus-rage-1491000676; Brooke Sample, "Free Speech Is under Siege at U.S. Colleges," *Bloomberg*, September, 14, 2019, https://www .bloomberg.com/opinion/articles/2019-09-14/free-speech-under-siege-at-u-s-colleges-opinion; Thomas C. Williams, "Does Our Cultural Obsession with Safety Spell the Downfall of Democracy?," *New York Times*, April 27, 2018, https://www.nytimes.com/2018/08/27/books/review /splintering-william-egginton-coddling-greg-lukianoff-jonathan-haidt.html; Jillian Berman, "U.S. Colleges Spend Millions on Security to Host Controversial Speakers," *MarketWatch*, March 5, 2019, https://www.marketwatch.com/story/how-colleges-pay-for-free-speech-2018 -10-08.

health and loneliness crisis.[2] When they graduate, they enter a world of radical new possibilities—from virtual reality to artificial intelligence to gene editing.[3]

Students need a moral and spiritual framework to engage these emerging complexities. Unfortunately, questions of ultimate meaning or a guiding purpose are increasingly being exiled from campus discourse. Harry Lewis, the former dean of Harvard, laments that "anything resembling moral principles or suggestions of ultimate values has been isolated within the curriculum, if not removed from it entirely."[4] Anthony Kronman, the former dean of Yale Law School, agrees: "The question of what living is for—of what one should care about and why—is the most important question a person can ask. Yet our colleges and universities have expelled this question from their classrooms."[5] Martha Nussbaum, a professor at the University of Chicago, worries that if we continue turning away from the humanities and from questions that matter, we will produce "generations of useful machines" and experience a "generational suicide of the soul."[6]

Without a spiritual or moral framework for their research, students and scholars can cast about between unhealthy and unwise extremes: on the one side, becoming bitter and cynical about the world, the academy, and their own research; on the other side, putting too much faith and importance in the academy. Additionally, when the next generation of leaders lacks a coherent worldview that informs where to place moral guardrails, our entire society is at risk. It is worth remembering that Facebook, which now hosts (and makes controversial rules for) the largest online discussion platform in the world, was invented by a handful of college students at Harvard.

2. Steven Reinberg, "1 in 5 College Students So Stressed They Consider Suicide," *CBS News*, September 10, 2018, https://www.cbsnews.com/news/1-in-5-college-students-so-stressed-they -consider-suicide/; Varun Soni, "Op-Ed: There's a Loneliness Crisis on College Campuses," *Los Angeles Times*, July 14, 2019, https://www.latimes.com/opinion/op-ed/la-oe-soni-campus -student-loneliness-20190714-story.html; Saumya Joseph, "Depression, Anxiety Rising among U.S. College Students," *Reuters*, August 29, 2019, https://www.reuters.com/article/us-health -mental-undergrads/depression-anxiety-rising-among-us-college-students-idUSKCN1VJ25Z.

3. Rob Stein, "First U.S. Patients Treated with CRISPR as Human Gene-Editing Trials Get Underway," *NPR*, April 16, 2019, https://www.npr.org/sections/health-shots/2019/04/16 /712402435/first-u-s-patients-treated-with-crispr-as-gene-editing-human-trials-get-underway; Brian Merchant, "Gen Z Is Already Afraid Automation Will Eat Their Jobs," *Gizmodo*, September 6, 2019, https://gizmodo.com/gen-z-is-already-afraid-automation-will-eat-their-jobs -1837930958.

4. Harry R. Lewis, *Excellence without a Soul: Does Liberal Education Have a Future?* (New York: PublicAffairs, 2007), 71.

5. Anthony T. Kronman, *Education's End: Why Our Colleges and Universities Have Given Up on the Meaning of Life* (New Haven: Yale University Press, 2007).

6. Martha Nussbaum, *Not for Profit: Why Democracy Needs the Humanities* (Princeton: Princeton University Press, 2016).

A Reformed Offering

I work at a Christian organization called The Veritas Forum, a nonprofit that exists to address this serious gap. We work to elevate campus discussions on questions of ultimate meaning, identity, and purpose at universities around the world. More than simply raising questions, we seek to present Christianity as an intellectually credible participant in these discussions of ultimate meaning.

The Christian faith has not been an active, respected, or public participant in academic discourse on many of these campuses for years. While the academic marginalization of the Christian faith is certainly cause for concern, we also see reasons for hope. The vast majority of current college students report that they are on a "spiritual quest" and that their top goal in college is to discover a "coherent worldview."[7]

Two things are happening at once: college students are increasingly longing to explore questions of ultimate meaning and purpose, and college campuses are increasingly unwilling, unable, or unsure of how to cultivate those conversations in their classrooms. This disconnect presents an opportunity. Christian scholars of deep faith and academic rigor can constitute an unexpected gift to the university when they ask questions that matter. They can offer the Christian faith as a needed and credible contribution to a pluralistic conversation.

The challenges, however, are real. When it comes to elite academic institutions in the West, Christianity suffers from a profound intellectual credibility gap. Our research reveals that 72 percent of students say their courses do not treat faith traditions as sources of wisdom.[8] It shows that only 3 percent of faculty at elite universities—that is, the universities that educate the vast majority of faculty at universities across the United States[9]—identify as Christian. Some of these faculty are openly dismissive of the faith. Steven Pinker at Harvard, for example, says, "Few sophisticated people today profess a belief in heaven and hell, the literal truth of the Bible, or a God who flouts the laws of physics."[10]

---

7. An unpublished Veritas Labs research conducted in 2016 reports that 88 percent of college students say they are on a "spiritual quest." See also, however, "Atheism Doubles among Generation Z," Barna Group, January 24, 2018, https://www.barna.com/research/atheism-doubles-among-generation-z/.

8. Unpublished Veritas Labs research conducted in 2016.

9. Joel Warner and Aaron Clauset, "The Academy's Dirty Secret: An Astonishingly Small Number of Elite Universities Produce an Overwhelming Number of America's Professors," *Slate*, February 23, 2015, https://slate.com/human-interest/2015/02/university-hiring-if-you-didn-t-get-your-ph-d-at-an-elite-university-good-luck-finding-an-academic-job.html.

10. Steven Pinker, *Enlightenment Now: The Case for Reason, Science, Humanism, and Progress* (New York: Viking, 2018), 430. Here he defines "sophisticated people" as those who are "aware of the scientific realities of the last several centuries."

As a result, many students in the secular academy feel a sharp incongruence between the life of the mind and the life of faith. They gather that one can either be a person of faith or a person of reason, but not both. Given the binary choice, it is not surprising that 42 percent of students leave the Christian faith during their college years.[11]

What can be done? How can we close the credibility gap? How can the small minority of Christian students and faculty faithfully study, serve, and speak in these pluralistic academic spaces? In this chapter, I offer several theological concepts from the Reformed tradition that have been helpful to me in my work on college campuses around the country. Through these theological lenses, I demonstrate how students and scholars can serve as salt, light, and leaven in their academic disciplines and discourse.

The Life of the Mind Matters to God

> Take my intellect and use,
> Every pow'r as thou shalt choose.
> —Frances Ridley Havergal, "Take My Life and Let It Be"

Americans are more educated now than ever before. In 1940, only 24 percent of adults had completed high school, and only 4.6 percent had finished college. Today those numbers have skyrocketed: 90 percent have a high school degree, and 33 percent have a college degree or higher.[12]

At the same time, our interest in reading has dropped significantly, especially among young adults. In the 1970s, the vast majority of teens read a book or magazine every day; by 2015, only 16 percent did. In the early 1990s, some 70 percent of college students said they read a newspaper at least once a week; by 2015, that number had dropped to 10 percent.[13] In *The Death of Expertise*, professor Tom Nichols laments the ironic anti-intellectual strain in America: despite being more educated, we have lost interest in being informed. "These are dangerous times," he writes. "Never have so many people had so much access to so much knowledge yet have been so resistant to learning anything."[14]

---

11. Unpublished Veritas Labs research conducted in 2016.

12. United States Census Bureau, "Highest Educational Levels Reached by Adults in the U.S. since 1940," U.S. Census Bureau Release Number CB17-51, March 30, 2017, https://www.census.gov/newsroom/press-releases/2017/cb17-51.html.

13. See Jean Twenge, *iGen: Why Today's Super-Connected Kids Are Growing Up Less Rebellious, More Tolerant, Less Happy—and Completely Unprepared for Adulthood—and What That Means for the Rest of Us* (New York: Atria Books, 2017).

14. Tom Nichols, *The Death of Expertise: The Campaign against Established Knowledge and Why It Matters* (Oxford: Oxford University Press, 2017).

In the evangelical church, things might be even worse. Historian Mark Noll observes, "The scandal of the evangelical mind is that there is not much of an evangelical mind."[15] Philosopher Habib Malik goes so far as to say, "The greatest danger confronting American evangelical Christianity is the danger of anti-intellectualism."[16]

At the same time, the secular academy celebrates rigorous scholarship—and yet it pursues this knowledge apart from the wisdom or fear of the Lord. Paul warns against this type of intellectualism, saying that such "knowledge puffs up" (1 Cor. 8:1). Creational knowledge untethered from the Creator is dangerous. "It is sin that tempts man to disconnect [scholarship] from God, to steal it from God, and finally to turn it against God," writes the Reformed theologian Abraham Kuyper. "The plant of true [scholarship] has its roots, origin, motif, and point of departure in the fear of the Lord."[17]

The life of the mind matters to God. Research, critical thinking, exploration, and invention are ways for human creatures to honor their Creator and advance his purposes for creation. As the Reformed philosopher Richard Mouw writes, "We need to see critical thinking as one way in which we serve the Lord. Christian teaching and scholarship should aim at the ultimate goal of getting clearer in our hearts and minds about the basic issues of life in order more effectively to promote the cause of God's Kingdom."[18] Or, as Jesus put it, "Love the Lord your God with all your . . . mind" (Matt. 22:37).

Scholarship is a medium through which Christians might love and serve God, their neighbor, and all creation. Scholarship informed by Christian love is other-oriented. It is an act of giving, of service, of praise. It shares. It shows mercy. As Nicholas Wolterstorff writes, "Learning is a gift of God to humanity that we are to receive and practice with gratitude."[19]

The Doctrine of Creation

> For the beauty of the earth . . .
> —Folliott S. Pierpoint, "For the Beauty of the Earth"

15. Mark A. Noll, *The Scandal of the Evangelical Mind* (Grand Rapids: Eerdmans, 1995).

16. Charles Habib Malik, *A Christian Critique of the University* (Waterloo, ON: North Waterloo Academic Press, 1990).

17. Abraham Kuyper, "Common Grace in Science [1904]," in *Abraham Kuyper: A Centennial Reader*, ed. James D. Bratt (Grand Rapids: Eerdmans, 1998), 447.

18. Richard J. Mouw, *Called to the Life of the Mind: Some Advice for Evangelical Scholars* (Grand Rapids: Eerdmans, 2014).

19. Nicholas Wolterstorff, *Educating for Shalom: Essays on Christian Higher Education* (Grand Rapids: Eerdmans, 2004).

Meditating on the complexity, beauty, and wonder of God's creation is an essential practice for Christian academics. This foundational practice offers profound insights for cultivating a lifelong posture of academic gratitude and joy. A Reformed theology of creation offers two points of emphasis that may prove helpful for contemporary scholars and students on this point: creational joy and creational order.

Creational Joy

Creation is not a cold or bare necessity. It exists ultimately for delight. There is no biblical evidence that God needed creation. There is, however, evidence that God desires and delights in it. In the Genesis account, God repeatedly revels in creation. God declares that it is "good" and "very good" on multiple occasions (Gen. 1:4, 10, 12, 18, 21, 25, 31). The psalmist, too, invites the Lord to rejoice in what he has made (Ps. 104:31).

Extending these insights, Richard Mouw writes, "There is good reason to believe that the Lord is gratified by glowing sunsets and ocean waves breaking on a rocky coastline and a cherry tree in bloom and the speed of the leopard on the chase—and all of this without any necessary reference to elect and non-elect human beings."[20] God delights in stars we will never discover.

Late at night, alone in her lab, and after hours of trial and error, a graduate student finally makes a breakthrough. A shot of adrenaline pulses through her body. She is filled with delight. These experiences of academic delight felt in libraries, lecture halls, and art studios across campus are manifestations of the *imago Dei* built into every student. Regardless of their faith, when human beings experience delight in exploring and developing creation, they are reflecting the character of the One who gazed upon the complexity of creation and declared, "It is very good."

Creational Order

According to Reformed theology, God's creation is both ordered and complex, patterned and pluriform. Creation is a complex manifestation of God's will, beauty, and nature. These manifold works display God's manifold glory. For "the skies proclaim the work of his hands. Day after day they pour forth speech" (Ps. 19:1–2). To explore God's complex creation through scholarship is, in part, to examine the complex will, law, and nature of God.

20. Richard J. Mouw, *He Shines in All That's Fair: Culture and Common Grace* (Grand Rapids: Eerdmans, 2001), 35.

God's creation is not given to chaos or randomness; it is ordered. It is filled with patterns, laws, and a fundamental stability. Order and stability not only graciously allow for life but also allow for the cultural production of scholarship and technology. The laws of nature do not change from day to day. Because of this, scientists can depend on certain patterns, study them, explore them, and even build on and develop them.

Human beings are created for this order and cannot help but long for its lawful stability. Even the Harvard psychologist Steven Pinker cannot help but evince this longing in his seemingly atheistic statement: "Few sophisticated people today profess a belief in . . . a God who flouts *the laws of physics.*"[21]

This does not mean that there are no exceptions, aberrations, or miracles, but it does mean that when we engage in research or scholarship we are looking for patterns in creation—whether or not we acknowledge that God is their author. Human thinking strives to answer questions of origin, interconnection, and destiny: *How was the world formed? How is it sustained? What are its internal laws and norms, and what do they mean?*

This divine order is not limited to the natural sciences. The Reformed philosopher Al Wolters notes that orders and patterns begin to emerge in the social scientific investigation as well:

> We are all familiar with the laws of nature, the regular order in the realm of physical things, of plants and of animals. . . . We are not so familiar with, or feel less sure about, God's laws for culture and society, which we call norms. To be sure, we recognize norms for interpersonal relationships, but we are hesitant about any norms for societal institutions as such, or for something so mundane as agriculture. Yet both Scripture and experience teach us that God's will must be discerned here, too, that the Creator is sovereign over the state as much as he is over the animal kingdom, that he is Lord over agriculture as much as he is over energy exchanges. God's statutes and ordinances are over everything, certainly not excluding the wide domain of human affairs.[22]

The creation account hints that creation has patterns when it tells us that God brings forth from creation, from seeds to various kinds of animals, "each according to its kind" (Gen. 1:11, 12, 21, 24, 25). For example, lions are not trees, seeds are not elephants, copper is not aluminum. They have unique natures, expressions, and cultures.

21. Pinker, *Enlightenment Now*, 420, emphasis added.
22. Albert M. Wolters, *Creation Regained: Biblical Basics for a Reformational Worldview* (Grand Rapids: Eerdmans, 2005), 16.

In the same way every discipline, from anthropology to zoology, has its own unique God-given laws and norms, modes of inquiry, unique terminology, and eschatological trajectory. It is inappropriate, for example, to apply the scientific method to poetry; likewise, a psychological analysis of geometry would not quite work. To be sure, different disciplines can and should learn from one another, but we should also respect their unique modes of inquiry. They need to explore God's creation and develop according to their own kind. Both a chemist and a poet reveal something important and true about the world. They do so, however, in two fundamentally different ways. We need all the diverse disciplines to fully investigate and delight in God's complex creation. In summation, as Christians investigate the world—its patterns, rhythms, laws, and norms—they discover how these patterns display, in their own unique way, the kaleidoscopic order and beauty of God.

A Holistic View of Sin

> This world with devils filled . . .
> —Martin Luther, "A Mighty Fortress Is Our God"

Many Christians students arrive on campus with a narrow understanding of sin and evil. They imagine that these terms indicate a personal or spiritual rupture between themselves and God. Not surprisingly, their understanding of salvation and the gospel is also rather individualistic and myopic. Christ simply bridges the personal or spiritual gap between them and God. End of story. Accordingly, sin and salvation—being merely personal or spiritual— have little to do with their material and public life of study and scholarship.

At this point the Reformed tradition's more holistic and creation-wide understanding of sin and salvation has been profoundly helpful in my work with Christian students and faculty. In the Reformed tradition, sin is not simply a spiritual rupture in the recesses of my heart; instead, "sin introduces an entirely new dimension to the created order,"[23] a new dimension that affects every aspect of every academic discipline.

Genesis 3 discusses the origins of evil, and the rest of the Bible traces its pervasive spread.[24] Reformed theology describes our sinful condition as "total

---

23. Wolters, *Creation Regained*, 57.
24. Jeremiah tells us that our hearts are "deceitful above all things" (17:9). The psalmist says, "None is righteous, no, not one" (Pss. 14:3; 53:3; as cited in Rom. 3:10 ESV). Paul emphasizes that we are "dead" in our sin (Eph. 2:1, 5; Col. 2:13). And Jesus says our sin problem comes from within our hearts (Mark 7:15).

depravity." This does not mean that human beings are moral monsters through and through, lost in total corruption. The term, rather, is meant to indicate that sin is not an isolated spiritual rupture but a pervasive brokenness that has impacted every aspect of our lives and world.

Accordingly, there is no aspect of research, scholarship, or learning that is left untouched by sin. Education cannot save us, science cannot fix us, technology cannot solve our deepest problems, and the university is not a hermetically sealed place, safe from the ailments of the world. Our universal human will to dominate, to control, to bias, and to oppress is a part of every discipline. No academic field is neutral or immune from our brokenness. Indeed, Christian scholars are in no way immune to or above the effects of sin: all of us have fallen, and all of us are impacted.

Although sin has corrupted our ability to comprehend the fullness and coherence of creation, it has not completely destroyed our abilities of scientific perception, logic, and reason. As Al Wolters has said, "Muddled thinking is still thinking."[25]

In the light of our share in this pervasive fallen nature, Christians must embrace a posture of epistemic humility—that is, a posture of learning that recognizes that, while God has established truth, law, and order in the world, our ability to comprehend them is both finite and fallen. In practice, this means that Christian scholars should value questions and even critique from their colleagues. Having reckoned with our sin, we should assume that we stand in need of academic correction and challenge. In accepting such dialogue, the Christian student or scholar may be a rather strange creature within the, at times, competitive culture of academia. Yet they should stand out in their generous welcome of honest critique and diverse perspectives.

A Holistic View of Redemption

> Far as the curse is found . . .
>
> —Isaac Watts, "Joy to the World"

If our fall into sin is comprehensive, the redemption and healing we experience in Christ match and even exceed it. As the Reformed theologian Herman Bavinck writes, "Christ gives more than [what] sin stole."[26] Accordingly, Christ's redemption and transformation are not simply for the scholar's heart

25. Wolters, *Creation Regained*, 58.
26. Herman Bavinck, "Common Grace [1894, 1889]," trans. Raymond C. Van Leeuwen, *Calvin Theological Journal* 24, no. 1 (1989): 59.

or spiritual life; they also enact comprehensive transformation of a scholar's orientation toward the field under study, the colleagues, and the surrounding academic culture.

After his encounter with Jesus, Zacchaeus's heart was not the only thing that changed; his whole vocation in tax collecting—the way he ran his business and his home—was transformed for the good of himself, his neighbors, and his community. In the same way, the gospel transforms scholars and calls them to a new orientation toward their research, their students, and their school.

Abraham Kuyper argues that all creation is the variegated field of God's grace. He writes, "You cannot see grace in all its riches if you do not perceive how its tiny roots and fibers everywhere penetrate into the joints and cracks of the life of nature."[27] The sociologist explores better models for public education. The law professor takes care to build accountability into corporate governance. The history professor shines a light on hidden historical wounds. The theater professor accesses and harnesses the hidden dramatic talents of the students. All are participating in Christ's comprehensive work of making all things new.

The Doctrine of Common Grace

> He shines in all that's fair.
> —Maltbie Davenport Babcock, "This Is My Father's World"

What can I learn from an atheist professor? Can I be inspired by a Hindu poet? Will I allow myself to be convinced by a Muslim human rights activist?

Common grace refers to the grace of God that is common, given to all creation, believers and unbelievers alike. Despite human rebellion, unbelief, and perversion, God never lets go of creation. Common grace manifests itself in three ways. First, God providentially cares for his creation by sustaining the universe (John 1:1–4; Heb. 1:2–3) and giving natural gifts to all people (Matt. 5:45). Second, God graciously restrains sin by instituting civil authorities to administer justice (Rom. 13:1) and by limiting our sinful behavior (Gen. 20:6; 1 Sam. 25:26). Third, God empowers unbelievers to do good acts (Rom. 2:14–15). Unlike special or redeeming grace, which is only offered to the redeemed, these divine gifts of common grace are for all people.

Abraham Kuyper reflects on the implications of common grace in scholarship and admits that, although secular scholarship has led to "a worldview

27. Kuyper, "Common Grace," 173.

that runs directly contrary to the truth of God's Word," by the grace of God it has also produced "true and essential knowledge."[28] Common grace, he says, makes sense of this twofold truth: "That we may and must speak most positively of God's work in this regard is evident from the undeniable fact that in men like Plato and Aristotle, Kant and Darwin, shone stars of the first magnitude, geniuses of the highest degree, who uttered the most profound thoughts even when they were not confessing Christians. They had this genius not of themselves but received it from God who created them and endowed them for this kind of thinking."[29] Common grace is why Christians can lean on and learn from scholarship produced by non-Christian thinkers. It is why Christians can receive peer review from academics who do not share their faith.

The essential corollary to common grace is the Reformed concept of "the antithesis." In scholarship, context matters. Where you stand, who you are, the interpretive lenses you use—all impact the way in which you engage in academic inquiry. The Christian scholar studies creation from the context or position of being in Christ. The gospel is the lens through which they see the world. Studying fields from different starting points and using different lenses may, at times, produce opposing or "antithetical" results.

Thus two things are true at once. Because of common grace, Christian scholars might delight in, learn from, and even collaborate with their non-Christian colleagues. However, Christians scholars should also expect to en-counter academic opposition and deep differences because of the antithesis. Therefore, the Christian scholar who takes both common grace and the antithesis seriously can find common cause, beauty, and wisdom in Hindu poetry, Islamic art, or Chinese philosophy and, at the same time, is not surprised or scandalized by academic opposition.

In the end, the pluralistic academy will be blessed by Christian scholars and students who take both the antithesis and common grace seriously. Common grace can inspire a scholarly posture of collegial collaboration, appreciation, curiosity, and praise. Antithesis can inspire a scholarly courage, a willingness to oppose the academic zeitgeist, to speak an unpopular word, to challenge the norm. When Christian scholars and students gently resist and push back against assumed academic norms, and do so with deep humility and grace, they can contribute something vital to a vibrant and pluralistic academic discourse.

28. Abraham Kuyper, *Wisdom and Wonder: Common Grace in Science and Art* (Grand Rapids: Christian Library, 2011), 53.

29. Kuyper, "Common Grace in Science," 449. See also Mouw, *He Shines in All That's Fair.*

Conclusion

These theological resources (and many more) from the Reformed tradition enable Christian students and scholars to serve and bless pluralistic academies around the world. Reformed theology provides them with a coherent framework that not only offers deep meaning and purpose for academic pursuits but also a way for academics to navigate the increasing complexities and pluralities within higher education.

With that said, there are three ways in which Reformed thinking needs to advance so it can continue serving the university in the decades to come. First, Reformed scholars can sometimes limit their scholarship to answering questions that are pertinent only to their own Reformed subcultures. Yet there are discourses happening in pluralistic academies that these scholars need to engage, such as these: What is the future of personhood in a world of artificial intelligence? When it comes to climate change, have we sold our future? What is our responsibility? When Christian scholars thoughtfully engage the discourses within the larger pluralistic academy and from their perspectives, both sides stand to benefit.

Second, the Reformed tradition needs to broaden our understanding of pedagogy and intellectual growth and development. This thing we call "the academy" needs to extend beyond the formal lecture hall. Deep and transformative learning happens every year in study-abroad programs, internships, social clubs, and volunteer activities. Research shows that out-of-class experiences contribute to positive academic outcomes in at least five ways: cognitive complexity, knowledge acquisition and application, humanitarianism, interpersonal and intrapersonal competence, and practical competence. "Students who expend more effort in a variety of activities benefit the most intellectually and in the personal development domain," reads one report.[30] A Reformed theology of research and pedagogy needs to expand its imagination beyond the classroom.

Finally, it is one thing to offer Christian scholars a systematic theology to study; it is another thing to offer them a theological imagination for their scholarly vocation. Too often reduced to a cold "system" of theology, the Reformed tradition needs to emphasize the theological categories of exploration, creativity, innovation, and aesthetics. David Brooks makes this suggestion when he writes about how to bring the university back to its religious roots: "If a student spends four years in regular and concentrated contact with beauty—with poetry or music, extended time in a cathedral, serving a

---

30. George D. Kuh et al., *Student Learning outside the Classroom: Transcending Artificial Boundaries*, ASHE-ERIC Higher Education Report Series (San Francisco: Jossey-Bass, 1995), 2.

child with Down syndrome, waking up with loving friends on a mountain—there's a good chance something transcendent and imagination-altering will happen."[31] As people made in the image of God, we have the ability to embrace a big imagination about what is possible. So equipped, we can approach our studies with great joy, delight, and vision.

31. David Brooks "The Big University," *New York Times*, October 6, 2015, https://www.nytimes.com/2015/10/06/opinion/david-brooks-the-big-university.html.

17

A Reformed Understanding of Scholarship

NICHOLAS WOLTERSTORFF

My procedure in this chapter is to identify some themes characteristic of how members of the Reformed tradition have understood scholarship. Not everyone in the tradition embraces all these themes: there is no such thing as *the* Reformed tradition's understanding of scholarship. But I think there can be no doubt that the themes I identify are characteristic of the tradition.

First Theme: A Christian Worldview

John Calvin, in one of the best-known passages of his *Institutes of the Christian Religion*, compares Scripture to a set of spectacles through which one can behold both the creation and its Creator. The passage occurs in the *Institutes* 1.6. Calvin's topic in book 1 is "The Knowledge of God the Creator."

To understand the significance of his Scripture-as-spectacles image, we need to consider what Calvin says in the preceding chapter, "The Knowledge of God Shines Forth in the Fashioning of the Universe and the Continuing Government of It." "The universe," as Calvin understands it here, includes human beings. According to Calvin, all creation and its continued historical development reveal aspects of the glory, wisdom, power, and goodness of its Creator. Consider the following passages:

Wherever you cast your eyes, there is no spot in the universe wherein you cannot discern at least some sparks of [God's] glory. You cannot in one glance survey this most vast and beautiful system of the universe, in its wide expanse, without being completely overwhelmed by the boundless force of its brightness. . . .

There are innumerable evidences both in heaven and on earth that declare [God's] wonderful wisdom, not only those more recondite matters for the closer observation of which astronomy, medicine, and all natural sciences are intended, but also those which thrust themselves upon the sight of even the most untutored and ignorant persons, so that they cannot open their eyes without being compelled to witness them. Indeed, men who have either quaffed or even tasted the liberal arts penetrate with their aid far more deeply into the secrets of the divine wisdom.[1]

While Calvin insists that much knowledge of God can be gained by attending to God's creation, he also recognizes that human history is rife with widely divergent and thoroughly confused ideas about God:

Each man's mind is like a labyrinth, so that it is no wonder that individual nations were drawn aside into various falsehoods; and not only this, but individual men, almost, had their own gods. For as rashness and superficiality are joined to ignorance and darkness, scarcely a single person has ever been found who did not fashion for himself an idol or specter in place of God. Surely, just as waters boil up from a vast, full spring, so does an immense crowd of gods flow forth from the human mind.[2]

This is the context in which Calvin describes Scripture as a set of spectacles: "Just as old or bleary-eyed men and those with weak vision, if you thrust before them a most beautiful volume, even if they recognize it to be some sort of writing, yet can scarcely construe two words, but with the aid of spectacles will begin to read distinctly, so Scripture, gathering up the otherwise confused knowledge of God in our minds, having dispersed our dullness, clearly shows us the true God."[3]

Given that Calvin's overall concern in book 1 is knowledge of God the Creator, what he naturally emphasizes when he employs the image of Scripture as spectacles is the variety of ways in which Scripture enables us to rightly interpret the manifestations of God in creation. But not only are we human beings confused and conflicted in how we interpret the signs of God in creation; we are also confused and conflicted in how we understand creation

1. John Calvin, *Institutes of the Christian Religion*, ed. John T. McNeill, trans. Ford Lewis Battles, 2 vols. (1960; repr., Louisville: Westminster John Knox, 2006), 1.5.1, 1.5.2.

2. Calvin, *Institutes* 1.5.12.

3. Calvin, *Institutes* 1.6.1.

itself, especially in how we understand ourselves, our nature and destiny, our doings and makings. From his continued discussion it becomes clear that, in Calvin's view, Scripture also functions, at many points, as spectacles that enable us to rightly interpret the reality before us.

According to a common understanding of religion in general, and of the three "religions of the book" in particular—Judaism, Christianity, and Islam—religion is about the transcendent: God and the afterlife. Of course, religious people also have beliefs about the mundane; we all do. So the common thought is that religion is an add-on. To beliefs about the mundane, religious people add on beliefs about the supramundane; on the other hand, those who are not religious make do without that add-on.

Calvin's understanding of Christianity—and implicitly of Judaism and Islam as well—was decisively different. Christianity does not consist simply of beliefs about the transcendent added on to beliefs about the mundane. Christianity does, of course, make claims about the transcendent. In the same section of the *Institutes* in which he speaks of Scripture as spectacles, Calvin emphasizes that from Scripture we also learn of God as Redeemer. From Scripture we gain "two sorts of knowledge of God." But the point he is making with his Scripture-as-spectacles image is that Scripture presents to us an interpretation of significant aspects of *mundane* reality: of the basis of morality, of the role of forgiveness, of what it is that gives human beings dignity, of the priority of justice, of the task of government—on and on.

It is, of course, a *distinct* interpretation that Scripture presents—an interpretation different from views embraced by those who are not Christians. Implicit in Calvin's employment of the Scripture-as-spectacles image is his understanding that we human beings, one and all, are interpreters. Nobody just drinks in the facts. We are hermeneutic creatures, inescapably so. Not only do we interpret specific segments of reality. We also have more or less comprehensive interpretations, *worldviews*, such as naturalism, secular humanism, libertarianism, socialism, and so on.

The point Calvin makes in his Scripture-as-spectacles passage is a theme that has been as characteristic as any of the Reformed tradition's understanding of scholarship. Christianity is not an add-on. It does not consist of claims about the transcendent that can be added on, if one so wishes, to whatever one may believe about the mundane. Nor—to mention another view one sometimes hears—is it just an ethic that can be added on to whatever one believes about the "facts." Christianity incorporates a distinct interpretation of reality in general, both the transcendent and the mundane—a worldview.

A point of clarification that is important to make before we move on is that the worldview of a present-day Christian is not to be identified with the biblical worldview. Of course, strictly speaking, there is no such thing as *the* biblical worldview; one finds in Scripture a spectrum of worldviews. But no contemporary Christian embraces a worldview identical with any on that spectrum. The worldview of present-day Christians has been profoundly shaped by the worldviews of the biblical writers, but it has also been shaped by other factors as well: by natural scientific discoveries, by philosophical and theological reflections, by changes in our psychological views, and so on.

Second Theme: Diverse Worldviews

Might it be that scholarship offers the hope of an escape from the clash of worldviews and of disagreements grounded in our diverse worldviews? When human beings engage in scholarship, they do not cease to embrace their worldviews. But when we properly engage in the social practice of history, of sociology, of literary studies, and so on, can we put our conflicting worldviews in cold storage for the time being and employ nothing but our shared capacities of perception, introspection, and reason? This, as I interpret him, was the view of Immanuel Kant.

Late in *The Critique of Pure Reason*, Kant drew a distinction between what he called *revelational* theology (*theologia revelata*) and what he called *rational* theology (A631= B659). Rational theology, says Kant, is based "upon reason alone.[4]" Though Kant does not explain what it is for a theology to be based solely upon reason, I think one can make a reliable inference from his later identification and description of various forms of theology that he regards as based on reason, in contrast to those not so based. Theology is based solely upon reason and thus is rational only as it is based solely on premises and inferences that all cognitively competent adult human beings would accept if those premises and reasons were presented to them, if they understood them, if they had the relevant experience and possessed the relevant background information, and if they freely reflected on them at sufficient length. (What constitutes *sufficient* length is, of course, a nice question.) This reasoning is what I call *Kant-rationality*.[5]

It appears to me to me that a good many scholars have believed, intuitively and implicitly if not explicitly, that when engaged in the practice of

4. Immanuel Kant, *The Critique of Pure Reason*, trans. J. M. D. Meiklejohn (New York: Collier & Son, 1901), 469.

5. Though I have extracted the idea of Kant-rationality from the passage in the *Critique* in which Kant distinguishes various kinds of theology, it is obvious that the idea has application beyond theology to the academic disciplines in general. Scholarship possesses Kant-rationality as it fulfills these stated conditions.

scholarship, we can and should aim at Kant-rationality—or something very much like it. We must expect that we and our fellows will repeatedly fall short of the goal. We bring to our practice of scholarship biases, prejudices, jealousies, and the like that distort our employment of our shared capacities of perception, introspection, and reason. But when we notice such distortion in one of our colleagues, we point it out to them in the hope, if not always the expectation, that they will stand corrected. Aiming at Kant-rationality in one's practice of scholarship is not like banging one's head against a brick wall. Consensus is within reach.

A second theme characteristic of the Reformed tradition's understanding of scholarship is its rejection of the idea that scholars, in general, can and should aim at Kant-rationality, thereby eliminating any impact of their worldviews on their practice of scholarship. Aiming to use Kant-rationality, or something very much like it, is clearly appropriate in logic, mathematics, and most parts of natural science, but there is no hope whatsoever of achieving it in the social sciences and the humanities. When it comes to the disciplines that deal with ourselves, our societies, and our cultural artifacts, we find disagreements grounded in diverse worldviews among fully rational and competent scholars.

With typically flamboyant rhetoric, the Dutch Reformed theologian Abraham Kuyper (1837–1920) makes the point in this passage:

> The subjective character which is inseparable from all spiritual science [i.e., social sciences and humanities] in itself would have nothing objectionable in it if . . . the subjectivity of A would merely be a variation of the subjectivity of B. In virtue of the organic affinity between the two, their subjectivity would not be mutually antagonistic, and the sense of one would harmoniously support and confirm the sense of the other. . . . But alas, such is not the case in the domain of science [i.e., academic learning]. It is all too often evident, that in this domain the natural harmony of subjective expression is hopelessly broken. . . . By an investigation of self and of the cosmos you have obtained a well-founded scientific conviction, but when you state it, it meets with no response from those who, in their way, have investigated with equally painstaking efforts. . . . Of necessity we must accept this hard reality.[6]

Third Theme: Letting a Christian Worldview Shape Study

The claim that worldview-neutral scholarship is impossible implies a certain understanding of the calling of the Christian scholar: allow your Christian

---

6. Abraham Kuyper, *Principles of Sacred Theology*, trans. J. Hendrik de Vries (Grand Rapids: Eerdmans, 1954), 106–7.

worldview to shape how you engage in scholarship. When it speaks to what is important to study, let it shape your judgments of importance. When it offers an interpretation of the reality being studied, allow it to shape your interpretation. When it speaks to how you treat your fellow scholars, students, and the public, let it shape how you treat them. In general, when your faith speaks to how on you engage in your discipline, listen to what it says. In this way, engage in your discipline *as a Christian*, doing so in gratitude to God and as an act of service to your fellow human beings. Do not attempt or pretend to engage in scholarship as a generic human being. This is a third theme characteristic of the Reformed tradition's understanding of scholarship.

A qualification is required. Just as there is no such thing as *the* physicalist worldview but a range of physicalist views, so too there is no such thing as *the* contemporary Christian worldview but a range of such views. And some of those views are strange indeed, based on seriously flawed biblical interpretation, on suspicion of theologians, on a refusal to accept the well-established results of natural science, and so on. When speaking to persons engaging in such scholarship, one does not say, "Allow your Christian worldview to shape how you engage in scholarship" but "Get your house in order."

Fourth Theme: Cooperation amid Diverse Worldviews

I introduce a fourth theme by quoting another passage from Calvin, one deserving to be much better known than it seems to be. The passage counters the standard picture of Calvin as the dour Genevan. He writes that because

> the discovery or systematic transmission of the arts, or the inner and more excellent knowledge of them, . . . is bestowed indiscriminately upon pious and impious, it is rightly counted among [God's] natural gifts. Whenever we come upon these matters in secular writers, let that admirable light of truth shining in them teach us that the mind of man, though fallen and perverted from its wholeness, is nevertheless clothed and ornamented with God's excellent gifts. If we regard the Spirit of God as the sole fountain of truth, we shall neither reject the truth itself, nor despise it wherever it shall appear, unless we wish to dishonor the Spirit of God. For by holding the gifts of the Spirit in slight esteem, we contemn and reproach the Spirit himself.[7]

7. The passage continues:
   Shall we deny that the truth shone upon the ancient jurists who established civic order and discipline with such great equity? Shall we say that the philosophers were blind in their fine observation and artful description of nature? . . . What shall we say of all the mathematical sciences? Shall we consider them the ravings of madmen? No, we cannot

From Calvin's Scripture-as-spectacles passage we extrapolated that Scripture presents not only an understanding of God as manifested in creation but also an interpretation of mundane reality that is distinct from those of other religions and, by implication, also distinct from those of the various kinds of secularism on offer. What Calvin emphatically declares in the passage just quoted is that "secular" writers do not, however, get everything wrong. Far from it. "Though fallen and perverted from its wholeness," the human mind nevertheless remains "clothed and ornamented with God's excellent gifts," the result being a body of truly admirable discoveries by secular thinkers. To disdain the contributions they have made and continue to make our understanding of the world and ourselves is to be guilty of "ingratitude" to God. For it is the Spirit of God who is the "fountain of truth." Refusing to acknowledge anything praiseworthy in the writings of secular writers is "to dishonor the Spirit of God."

Calvin's brief comments here about the Spirit of God being the ultimate source of the intellectual gifts of the ancient secular writers were fleshed out by Abraham Kuyper in his expansive development of what he called the "doctrine of common grace." God bestows on human beings in general the grace of restraining the workings of sin so that academic learning may flourish, along with medicine, law, business, art, and so on. What Calvin called "God's natural gifts" (in the passage just quoted) is what Kuyper described as results of God's common grace.

The point made by Calvin and Kuyper in these passages is a fourth theme characteristic of the Reformed tradition's understanding of scholarship: the diverse life orientations of scholars, their diverse worldviews, do not prevent them from all together contributing to the fund of human knowledge. Nobody is entirely blind to reality. It behooves Christians to acknowledge and celebrate scholarly insight wherever it may be found, no matter how much they may disagree with the worldview of those whose insight it is. What someone says is not to be rejected just because one disagrees with the worldview held by the speaker.

There are many who think and act otherwise. They reject whatever liberal feminists say, resist conceding that at certain points they may be speaking a truth that must be heard, because they reject the liberal feminist worldview. They reject whatever a Marxist says just because they reject the Marxist world-

---

read the writings of the ancients on these subjects without great admiration. We marvel at them because we are compelled to recognize how preeminent they are. But shall we count anything praiseworthy or noble without recognizing at the same time that it comes from God? Let us be ashamed of such ingratitude. (Calvin, *Institutes* 2.1.14–15, with punctuation slightly altered)

view. If we take seriously the claim of Calvin and Kuyper that the Spirit of God enables human beings in general to discern some truth, then we need to accept being enlightened by our fellow scholars, whatever their worldview.

Fifth Theme: Dialogic Pluralism

As we saw earlier, the calling of the Christian scholar is to engage in scholarship *as a Christian* and not attempt or pretend to do so merely as a generic human being. A corollary of the point just made—that by virtue of God's common grace, human beings in general, whatever their worldview, are capable of discerning truth—is a fifth theme that is characteristic of the Reformed understanding of scholarship: Christians are not to go off in a corner somewhere to "do their own thing." They are to engage in the shared human practice of philosophy, of biology, of psychology or whatever while speaking, listening, teaching, learning, agreeing, disagreeing, correcting, being corrected, and in this way participate in the grand dialogue of one's discipline, doing so as a Christian. In some of my writings I have called this form of engagement *dialogic pluralism*; here the term "pluralism" alludes to the plurality of worldviews present in the academy.

The Christian scholar will be open to being corrected not just on matters of scholarly detail but also on elements of the Christian worldview held. This can seem alarming when stated baldly like this. But history provides us with examples that we all accept. For a thousand years and more, geocentricism was part of the worldview of Christians; it was assumed to be taught by Scripture. It was not any changes internal to Christianity but developments in astronomy that led Christians to embrace heliocentrism.

Even in the humanities and the social sciences, when Christian scholars engage fellow scholars in the manner that I have called "dialogic pluralism," they will always discover points of agreement between themselves and their colleagues. Given what Calvin and Kuyper taught about "common grace," that is to be expected. Christian scholars will try to expand the points of agreement for their position on some matter by devising arguments that others find persuasive and by listening for what seems right in others' arguments. They will not just "express" their views and walk off.

In his well-known address "How to Be a Christian Philosopher," my good friend and erstwhile colleague Alvin Plantinga argues that Christian philosophers should, in his words, "set their own agenda." He is right about that. But as his own practice makes clear, what must be added is that they should set their agenda in the light, among other things, of developments in philosophy generally. What holds for Christian philosophers holds for Christian scholars in general.

One might have expected that Calvin, whose scholarship was devoted almost entirely to theology and biblical commentary, would have ignored the ancient pagan writers and confined himself to reading fellow Christian theologians and biblical commentators. But not so. He read widely in the ancient philosophers, poets, jurists, and others. Not only did he read them, he also actively engaged them, disagreeing with them but also learning from them; in his writings he expressed not only his disagreement but also his agreement. He did not read them just to identify and highlight the error of their ways. It was especially Plato whom he engaged in this dialogic manner. Embedded within the many pages of the *Institutes* is a lengthy and detailed dialogue with Plato.

Summary

In this chapter I have briefly outlined five themes characteristic of the Reformed tradition's understanding of scholarship. Let me state them again:

1. Christian faith incorporates an interpretation of reality in general, mundane as well as supramundane: call it a "worldview."
2. Scholarship, especially in the humanities and the social sciences, does not offer an escape from disagreements grounded in our diverse worldviews.
3. The calling of the Christian scholar is to engage in one's discipline as a Christian.
4. The diverse worldviews of scholars do not prevent them from together contributing to the fund of human knowledge.
5. Christian scholars participate in the shared practice of academic learning, engaging with diverse scholars in a way that might be called "dialogic pluralism."

One could identify other themes characteristic of how the Reformed tradition understands scholarship. For example, it is characteristic of scholars in the Reformed tradition to regard the entire body of Christian thought as their religious heritage, not just the thought of Protestants. On this occasion, the five themes we have identified need to suffice.

There is a good deal of resistance to the project of Christian scholarship as I have described it. Religion, many insist, should be kept out of the academy. Some, including some Christians, base this view on a very different understanding of scholarship from that which I have presented; they think it can be and should be a consensus enterprise. Others hold this view on the basis of their understanding of religion. Some regard religion as inherently oppressive, benighted, and discriminatory; they insist that it should be kept out of the academy for that reason. A somewhat more common view, so it appears to me, is that religion should be kept out of the academy because it is inherently irrational. To be rational, the beliefs of religious people about the transcendent—God and the afterlife—need to be supported by good arguments. But they are not so founded, it is claimed. Religious people are said to hold their beliefs on faith and not on reason.

In my recently published work *Religion in the University*[8] I have addressed, in considerable detail, the charge that religion is inherently irrational and should, on that account, be kept out of the academy. I note that over the past three or four decades there has been an extraordinary resurgence of natural theology, with the traditional arguments reformulated with great sophistication and new ones developed. Over the same period, philosophers of religion have powerfully challenged the claim that religious beliefs, in general, must be based on arguments if they are to be rational. It is my judgment that, as a result of these developments, the charge that religion is inherently irrational cannot be made to stick. The philosopher Richard Rorty, who identified himself as an atheist, wrote the following in his book *Philosophy and Social Hope*: it is "hypocrisy" to say "that believers somehow have no right to base their political views on their religious faith, whereas we atheists have every right to base ours on Enlightenment philosophy. The claim that in doing so we are appealing to reason, whereas the religious are being irrational, is hokum."[9] It is clear from his discussion that what Rorty says about the political views of believers he would say about their views on many other matters as well.

Beyond the Academy: Public Scholarship

In this chapter I present Christian scholars as engaging their fellow scholars: speaking, listening, teaching, learning, agreeing, disagreeing, correcting, being corrected. But Christian scholars are not only members of the academy; they are also members of the church. As such, they have a responsibility to look beyond the guild of scholars and ask how they might contribute, as a body of scholars, to the flourishing of the church.

8. Nicholas Wolterstorff, *Religion in the University* (New Haven: Yale University Press, 2019).
9. Richard Rorty, *Philosophy and Social Hope* (London: Penguin, 1999), 172.

Likewise, Christian scholars are also members of the civic community. Recognizing that, they also have a responsibility to ask how they, as a body of scholars, might contribute to the justice and shalom of that wider community. They will do so because they have taken to heart the words of their Lord: "Love your neighbor as yourself" (Mark 12:31). Christian scholarship is, at bottom, an act of love.

18

Critical Race Theory, Campus Culture, and the Reformed Tradition

JEFF LIOU

No diploma and no graduation! That was the punishment. Five students had organized a large public protest on their university campus. A scholar who opposed the #blacklivesmatter movement had come to their school to deliver a public lecture. In response, the students formed a blockade in front of the venue, disrupting the speaker's event. Since it was a violation of school policy, the administration laid down the law and widened the gulf of mistrust between the students and the university. The student newspaper quickly published a series of critical editorials, and students railed against the administration on social media. One year later, prepared or not, I arrived on campus to serve as a student chaplain.

In today's tense cultural climate, universities are attempting to balance two important academic commitments as they serve and educate students. On the one hand, student affairs staff are working hard to welcome, retain, and help students of color so that the larger learning community can benefit from their presence and participation. These students possess valuable abilities and insights; they also offer diverse cultural wealth that enriches academic discourse. The wealth of their insight is often forged in the fires of marginalization and resistance to cultural and racial oppression.

On the other hand, some university leaders are committed to protecting a free dialogical space for open debate and disagreement. Such leaders work hard to welcome dissenting voices onto campus who do not accede to all the doctrines of Critical Race Theory (CRT). These dissenting voices may define key terms, like "racism," very differently. As the struggle to set the terms of the conversation goes on, the failure to agree on definitions and boundaries leads to accusations of libel and even injury. To be labeled a "racist" or a "snowflake" only deepens distrust and inhibits dialogue. University leaders who work to keep dialogical spaces open are condemned. From one side they are attacked for normalizing "political correctness" (another imprecisely utilized and weaponized term). From the other side they are dignifying a social imaginary circumscribed by racism. These dynamics play out at almost every kind of campus on which I have worked or spoken.

Navigating these campus conflicts as a Christian theologian and an East Asian American male is an ongoing challenge for me. I have served in university ministry for almost twenty years, and I have long been puzzled by the ubiquity of students who deny that racism *is*, in fact, the ordinary experience for many people of color.[1] The denial of this reality for Asian Americans *by* Asian Americans is all the more perplexing to me. That some university communities do not consider Asian Americans to be "people of color" both creates and reinforces this self-marginalization.[2] I have struggled with the Black-White nature of race dialogue in the United States, the way this binary positions Asian American Studies, and the havoc it creates for the formation of Asian American students.

Christians on campus today regularly encounter the complex language, presuppositions, and values of CRT. Christians who engage in CRT's critical questioning of power dynamics across race may learn to clearly assess inequities and unfairnesses that forestall meaningful relationships across race.

1. During the COVID-19 pandemic, the experience of anti-Asian racism prompted me and a group of Asian American Christian leaders to author a statement against racism and create a collaborative seeking to confront it. See www.asianamericanchristiancollaborative.com.

2. Scholars have asked why colleges and universities tout Asian American and Pacific Islander diversity statistics when, for example, their AAPI students experience lack of support and disproportionately negative mental health outcomes while on campus. Julie J. Park and Amy Liu, "Interest Convergence or Divergence? A Critical Race Analysis of Asian Americans, Meritocracy, and Critical Mass in the Affirmative Action Debate," *Journal of Higher Education* 85, no. 1 (January/February, 2014): 36–64, https://juliepark.files.wordpress.com/2009/03/park-liu-aff-action-jhe.pdf. See especially the illustrative discussion of "interest convergence" (a key tenet of CRT) in the article.

However, these Christians may—for that very reason—face greater challenges to building trusting relationships with those whom they critique as participating in and/or benefiting from inequitable systems. One who avers that "racism is ordinary" is saying that people of color have *not* been caught off guard or surprised when racist atrocities are reported. These reports of oppression are *not* a scandalizing aberration from the norms of polite society: they're ordinary. Yet this assertion—perhaps the most self-evident of the core tenets of CRT to college students—puts critical students at odds with those who behold American culture more adoringly.

Scholarship on Christianity and Critical Race Theory is beginning to pick up speed.[3] Some Christian individuals and institutions reject CRT out of hand while others embrace it without question. This essay seeks to resource those for whom a distinctively Christian vision of racial justice is desired: a vision that takes seriously the pain of oppressed communities, the Reformed confessions, and the rapidly evolving conversation on race.

Sketching Critical Race Theory

Although its enduring impact is undeniable, the civil rights movement in America has been criticized for not going far enough. The movement fundamentally lacked the critical tools necessary to fully understand and address the depth, breadth, and interconnected nature of racism, sexism, and classism within Western culture and its institutions. Critical Race Theory arose in the 1970s and 1980s to fill this gap when a group of scholar-activists independently arrived at this very conclusion.

Critical Race Theory began in legal studies, focusing on racial inequalities within the American justice system. Racial inequality, CRT argued, is embedded within the complex systems and interconnected structures of society. In

---

3. Here are a few examples: Duane Terrence Loynes Sr., "A God Worth Worshiping: Toward a Critical Race Theology" (PhD diss., Marquette University, 2017), https://epublications.marquette.edu/cgi/viewcontent.cgi?article=1749&context=dissertations_mu; Nathan Cartagena, "What Christians Get Wrong about Critical Race Theory," *Faithfully Magazine*, April 2020, https://faithfullymagazine.com/critical-race-theory-christians; Aida I. Ramos, Gerardo Martí, and Mark T. Mulder, "The Strategic Practice of 'Fiesta' in a Latino Protestant Church: Religious Racialization and the Performance of Ethnic Identity," *Journal for the Scientific Study of Religion* 59, no. 1 (March 2020): 161–79, https://onlinelibrary.wiley.com/doi/full/10.1111/jssr.12646; Brandon Paradise, "How Critical Race Theory Marginalizes the African American Christian Tradition," *Michigan Journal of Race and Law* 20, no. 1 (Fall 2014): 117–211, https://repository.law.umich.edu/cgi/viewcontent.cgi?article=1037&context=mjrl; Robert Chao-Romero, *Brown Church: Five Centuries of Latina/o Social Justice, Theology, and Identity* (Downers Grove, IL: InterVarsity, 2020).

other words, "racism" is deeper and more pervasive than isolated instances of racial strife between individuals. This inequality is reflected in and reinforced by the legal code itself; despite civil rights gains, the legal code was not so significantly altered as to prevent racial injustice from proliferating.

Since its genesis in the mid-1970s, the critical tools of CRT have been employed in a wide range of academic fields, including but not limited to educational, literary, historical, public policy, and now theological studies.[4] Foundational Western assumptions, canons, and methods in these fields, previously unquestioned, are now under tremendous critical scrutiny. The errors of racialized reasoning along with the disproportionate influence of whiteness are now a frequent target for academic critique.[5]

The demand for universities to expand their academic considerations beyond whiteness is already challenging. Critical Race Theory's philosophical reliance on the critical tools of the Marxist-influenced Frankfurt school causes even more discomfort. The Frankfurt Institute for Social Research provides CRT with the conceptual tools to understand the ways in which societal systems and structures can effectively reproduce patterns of inequality.

Let us take, for example, liberal individualism and its promise of a meritocratic society. For decades Wall Street and Hollywood Boulevard have projected the false promise that, if they work hard, people of color can succeed

4. As an example, CRT is applied in educational studies. Malcolm Knowles proposed traits of an "adult learner." According to Knowles, adult learners need to know why they are learning something, want to learn through experiences, learn by solving problems, and need to feel the relevance of what they are learning. See Malcolm S. Knowles, Elwood F. Holton, and Richard A. Swanson, *The Adult Learner: The Definitive Classic in Adult Education and Human Resource Development*, 7th ed. (New York: Routledge, 2012). According to Critical Race Theorists (who call themselves "crits"), Knowles's description of an adult learner overlooks learning dynamics related to race and ethnicity. He evinces cultural blindness to norms, customs, values, and ways of being in learners of color. His resulting theory of adult learning (what he calls "andragogy") is thus insufficient in educating for diversity. See Stephen D. Brookfield et al., *Teaching Race: How to Help Students Unmask and Challenge Racism* (San Francisco: Jossey-Bass, 2019).

5. "Whiteness" is here used in the sense that Willie Jennings has offered: "No one is born white. There is no white biology, but whiteness is real. Whiteness is a working, a forming toward a maturity that destroys. Whiteness is an invitation to a form of agency and a subjectivity that imagines life progressing toward what is in fact a diseased understanding of maturity, a maturity that invites us to evaluate the entire world by how far along it is toward this goal." Willie James Jennings, "Can White People Be Saved? Reflections on the Relationship of Missions and Whiteness," in *Can "White" People Be Saved? Triangulating Race, Theology, and Mission*, ed. Love L. Sechrest, Johnny Ramírez-Johnson, and Amos Yong (Downers Grove, IL: InterVarsity, 2018), 34. The editors of the volume with this essay helpfully add that whiteness is "an idolatrous way of being in the world at its core and thus activating a question that any reader needs to confront about the degree to which one's own praxis and worldview yearns for or participates in whiteness" (13).

economically, politically, and culturally in this purely meritocratic society. Through individual effort they can rise through the institutions of Western culture and self-actualize. Critical Race Theory seeks to dismantle the myth of meritocracy and expose the multiple ways in which formal and informal societal systems and patterns within the West raise some identities up and push other identities down.

Several tenets are especially foundational for CRT. Recognizing that the experience of racism is ordinary, systemic, and cultural (as opposed to isolated, individualistic, and intellectual) is both first and foundational to CRT. A second pillar is that of "interest convergence." Studying the limited successes of the civil rights movement, CRT scholars found that legislative victories for civil rights coincided "with the dictates of white self-interest. Little happens out of altruism alone."[6] Systems and structures of oppression only change when it is in their clear self-interest to do so. Third, CRT seeks to expose and deconstruct false claims of color-blindness and neutrality in scholarship, society, and politics. Critical Race Theory argues that abstract rationalistic claims of unbiased universality are an impracticable myth. Every scholar and every public leader bring to the table a complex set of cultural interests and biases. Hence, CRT seeks to root its theoretical work in the specific, concrete, daily, and lived experiences of peoples of color.

To make matters even more complex, CRT is self-aware that race is not the only arena of lived experience in which oppression occurs. In the early 1990s Kimberlé Crenshaw introduced the concept of "intersectionality" to describe more complex experiences of oppression.[7] A Black female living below the poverty line, for example, struggles at the intersection of racism, sexism, and classism. At one level, intersectionality is simply an attempt to accurately describe the threefold confluence of oppression that this particular woman is experiencing. That said, critics of CRT argue that, in CRT circles, intersectionality functions as more than simply a descriptive tool. Instead, critics describe intersectionality as a rhetorical race to the bottom, a race in which the most oppressed person is awarded the most sympathy.

Finally, scholar-activists working within CRT sometimes view themselves as standing within the "radical" tradition of well-known activists like César Chávez and Martin Luther King Jr., among many others in the abolitionist,

6. Richard Delgado and Jean Stefancic, *Critical Race Theory: An Introduction*, 2nd ed. (New York: New York University Press, 2012), 22.

7. Kimberlé Crenshaw, "Mapping the Margins: Intersectionality, Identity Politics, and Violence against Women of Color," *Stanford Law Review* 43, no. 6 (July 1991): 1241–99. When Crenshaw articulates the concept of intersectionality, she flags "liberals" as seeking to empty discourse of racial, gender, and other identity distinctives.

civil rights, Black power, and Chicano movements.[8] These scholar-activists view themselves as continuous with these figures because of their activist work to transform the relations between race and power. Here they contrast themselves with academics who do not regularly engage in activism. Concrete, praxis-oriented scholar-activism is, for critical race theorists, a matter of course.

Significant departures, however, should be observed. It has already been mentioned that CRT began when scholars concluded that the promises of the civil rights movement would not be realized. In what has become called "Civil Rights 2.0," it is not uncommon to hear CRT criticisms of Martin Luther King Jr. as a leader who was captive to the respect of whites and to the logic of the Constitution, which could never deliver on its promises. So while advocates of CRT may be continuous with these towering historical figures, they are boldly plotting their own ways forward.

Christianity and CRT

There have been a range of Christian responses to CRT. First, the more negative responses often tend to dismiss CRT wholesale because of its philosophical foundations within the Frankfurt school and what has been called "cultural Marxism."[9] These critics argue that CRT is overwrought in its concerns about systemic oppression and that this all comes from an uncritical acceptance of Marxist theory.[10] Their concerns typically fail (both optically and measurably) to take seriously the lived experiences of people who suffer. Evangelical critics may respond to suffering with acts of charity, but they are content to leave the systemic, structural, and reproductive mechanisms of inequality untouched. Their limited and narrowly individualistic conception of sin cannot (or will not) see the ways in which evil embeds itself in networks and institutions of oppression.

Second, while some Christians reject CRT wholesale, others appear to find nothing incommensurate between CRT and their Christian tradition. Many

8. Delgado and Stefancic, *Critical Race Theory*, 5. In the list of radical activists, César Chávez and Matin Luther King Jr. were selected mostly because of their explicitly Christian confession and spirituality.

9. See, e.g., Neil Shenvi and Pat Sawyer, "The Incompatibility of Critical Theory and Christianity," Gospel Coalition, May 15, 2019, https://www.thegospelcoalition.org/article/incompatibility-critical-theory-christianity/. See also its origins in William Lind, "The Roots of Political Correctness," American Conservative, November 19, 2009, https://www.theamericanconservative.com/the-roots-of-political-correctness/.

10. Whether such skeptics are right to be concerned falls outside the scope of this chapter. It seems important, nevertheless, to name this dynamic.

of them will narrate their own life experiences of racism primarily through the categories of CRT. Biblical and theological categories sometimes appear to be an afterthought. Their intellectual and societal responses to racism appear to be mostly directed by the categories and tactics of CRT.

Third, some Christians attempt to forge a moderate path of avoiding either a wholesale rejection or embrace of CRT. Some adopt what I call a "Christ and CRT in paradox" approach. Several Southern Baptists, for example, are open to listening to some aspects of CRT (because of general revelation, they explain) but ultimately see too much doctrinal incompatibility.[11]

For a variety of reasons, some of which I discuss below,[12] I find these three responses unsatisfying. In my own theological exploration of race and CRT, I have sought to develop a fourth option. In so doing, I have found unlikely and unexpected resources within the Reformed tradition.

CRT and Reformed Theology in Dialogue

Reformed theology affirms that the sovereignty, law, and justice of almighty God flow throughout the world's complex societal systems and structures.[13] The grace and mercy of Christ impact the academy, politics, marketplace, and every community and institution within society. The power of the Holy Spirit knows no institutional boundaries or limits. The work of God's justice is pervasive, cultural, and cosmic in scope. God's Word and power will not be limited to individual hearts, minds, or souls. All things are being reconciled to God through the cross of Christ, and in him all things will be made new (Acts 19:27; Eph. 6:12; Col. 1:20; Rev. 21:5).

Early in my pastoral and theological development, I came to the conclusion that the Reformed tradition's holistic theological vision of justice and culture had something important to offer to contemporary discussions of race that

11. Southern Baptist Convention, "On Critical Race Theory and Intersectionality," SBC 2019 Annual Meeting, June 1, 2019, http://www.sbc.net/resource-library/resolutions/on-critical-race-theory-and-intersectionality. Their expression "categories identified as sinful in Scripture" is cryptic. Some consider the very idea of race to be a sinful category. Since the initial draft of this chapter, six SBC seminary presidents have signed a statement declaring that CRT is incompatible with the SBC's Baptist faith and message. See G. Schroeder, "Seminary Presidents Reaffirm BFM, Declare CRT Incompatible," November 30, 2020, https://www.baptistpress.com/resource-library/news/seminary-presidents-reaffirm-bfm-declare-crt-incompatible/.

12. For a more in-depth theological reflection on these options, see Jeff Liou, "Much in Every Way: Employing the Concept of Race in Theological Anthropology and Christian Practice" (PhD diss., Fuller Theological Seminary, 2017).

13. Of course, none of these Reformed affirmations overlook the reality of sin and brokenness, which also flow throughout the world's systems and structures.

were increasingly structural and systemic. I sensed that Christians wrestling with CRT in both the academy and society could benefit from the resources found within the Reformed tradition.

One specific stream of Reformed theology that shares some fascinating resonances with CRT is that of neo-Calvinism. This stream is extremely critical of Western modernity and its oppressive claims of neutrality and universality. In contrast, neo-Calvinism emphasizes a sensitivity to the perspectival diversity and particularity of different human communities. It resists attempts to assimilate deep difference through societal systems of power (political, cultural, or institutional). Both CRT and neo-Calvinism argue for the liberation of diverse perspectives from under the oppressive universal claims and systems of Western modernity. Abraham Kuyper's neo-Calvinist lecture titled "Uniformity: The Curse of Modern Life" is an excellent case in point.[14]

The remainder of this chapter presents a brief attempt to explore what a critical and constructive dialogue between CRT and Reformed theology might look like. The two unlikely conversation partners, as we will soon see, share important resonances that cannot be ignored. In the pages that follow, we also explore how these two traditions would do well to learn from one another.

Mutual Critique of Modern Western Liberalism

The West has placed its faith in the modern liberal tradition and its promise to maximize the freedom of all individuals. According to the modern faith of liberalism, racial justice will be achieved when society fully accepts the ideals and language of liberalism: all persons are "created equal" (cf. the US Constitution). If we give liberalism enough time, if we allow it to rule, educate, and pervade our civil discourse, historical progress toward racial justice will be the natural result.[15] This is the modern Western faith in liberalism.

Critical Race Theory is no friend of liberalism. The promises and legislative protections of liberalism can be and have been manipulated to serve the powerful at the expense of the vulnerable. Derrick Bell argues that Black Americans must reject liberal optimism and assume a "racial realism" about

14. Abraham Kuyper, "Uniformity: The Curse of Modern Life [1869]," in *Abraham Kuyper: A Centennial Reader*, ed. James D. Bratt (Grand Rapids: Eerdmans, 1998), 20–44.

15. From 2016 to 2020, the number of times "progress" in race relations was mentioned in the seminary course I teach on Martin Luther King Jr. has dropped to zero. This, however, is not to neglect the important economic analyses that focus on the correlations between neoliberal economics and the alleviation of global poverty. The paragraph connected with this footnote focuses instead on constitutionalism more generally.

the ways in which liberalism ignores and even perpetuates racial inequality. Bell asserts "that the whole liberal worldview of private rights and public sovereignty mediated by the rule of law needed to be exploded." Its worldview "is an attractive mirage that masks the reality of economic and political power."[16] According to CRT, the forces of racism and liberalism actually combine to twist our institutions, our imaginations, our economies, and our social relations.

Reformed theologians describe the pervasive effects of sin while using comprehensive terms strikingly similar to CRT. Consider, for example, Abraham Kuyper's remarks on the connection between sin and systems, evil and social structures. Here he is speaking specifically about how human sin took on institutional form in the structures of modern Western politics and economics:

> In time, both error and sin joined forces to enthrone false principles that violated human nature. Out of these false principles systems were built that varnished over injustice and stamped as normal that which actually stood opposed to the requirements for life. . . . The stronger, almost without exception, have always known how to bend every custom and magisterial ordinance so that the profit is theirs and the loss belongs to the weaker. Men did not literally eat each other like cannibals, but the more powerful exploited the weaker by means of a weapon against which there was no defense.[17]

The neo-Calvinist doctrine of sin displayed here is profoundly structural and systemic in its scope. Evil is understood, not simply as an individual action or disposition of the heart, but as an institutional and cultural virus that is pervasive. From sin, Kuyper argues, "systems were built that varnished over injustice." On this point the resonance between Kuyper and Bell is striking. Additionally, on this point, Kuyper appears to be a breath away from structural formulations of evil that can commonly be found in twenty-first-century Black and Latinx liberation theologies.

Mutual Affirmation of Cultural Wealth

Historically speaking, the modern West has looked down on communities of color and the "developing world." Consciously or unconsciously, it has largely accepted the dogma of Western superiority and, in so doing, has framed the

---

16. Derrick Bell, "Racial Realism," *Connecticut Law Review* 24, no. 2 (Winter 1992): 363–79, https://www.yumpu.com/en/document/read/5890538/connecticut-law-review-iu-school-of-liberal-arts.

17. Abraham Kuyper, *The Problem of Poverty*, trans. James W. Skillen (Sioux Center, IA: Dordt College Press, 2011), 31–32.

global Other in terms of perceived cultural deficits. So framed, the modern West is always the rescuer, and the global Other is always the rescued.

This kind of deficit thinking was challenged by the education scholar Tara Yosso in 2005.[18] Deficit thinking is a blind spot in scholarship, which causes educators to characterize pedagogical work as supplying what students lack. The educational experiences of students from communities of color diverge from the presumed norms that inform, for example, educational policy. Yosso's critical lens is aimed at those norms. Over and against deficit thinking, she defines community cultural wealth as "an array of knowledge, skills, abilities and contacts possessed and utilized by Communities of Color to survive and resist macro- and micro-forms of oppression."[19] This cultural wealth includes the following: resiliency in aspiration, lingua-cultural skills, the sense of belonging from robust family systems, a sense of history, and ethical formation engaging inequality. Educators, she argues, should recognize these forms of cultural wealth.

Sadly, more often than not, the Western church has not only accepted modern deficit thinking; it has also actively *strengthened* it in theology and public life. The history of global missions is marked by a back-and-forth about deficits and wealth in global cultural contexts.[20] Informed by deficit thinking, Christian giving can frequently be little more than charity. Similarly, Christian action can fail to dismantle the structural machinery that propagates global inequality. Deficit thinking in the church shuts out the possibility of meaningful cross-cultural dialogue, partnership, and mutual exchange between Christian communities. Always looking to fill the perceived deficits of others, Western and white Christians fail to see their own need for the cultural assets and wealth that communities of color possess. As we will soon see, Reformed Christians are not innocent bystanders here. They have often accepted deficit thinking uncritically and, more than that, have perpetuated cultural ideas, doctrines, and political systems that actively harm communities of color.

Deficit thinking is theologically problematic; it is also biblically puzzling. Scripture repeatedly uses the phrase "wealth of nations" and related ideas (Ps. 105:44; Isa. 60:11; 61:6; 66:12, 20; Hag. 2:7; Zech. 14:14; Rom. 15:16; Rev.

18. Tara J. Yosso, "Whose Culture Has Capital? A Critical Race Theory Discussion of Community Cultural Wealth," *Journal of Race, Ethnicity, and Education* 8, no. 1 (August 2006): 69–91.

19. Yosso, "Whose Culture Has Capital?," 69.

20. See, e.g., Henry Morton Stanley, *In Darkest Africa: Or the Quest, Rescue, and Retreat of Emin, Governor of Equatoria*, 2 vols. (London: S. Low, Marston, Searle, & Rivington, 1890). See also the rebuttal in the same year by William Booth, *In Darkest England: And the Way Out* (New York: Funk & Wagnalls, 1890).

21:26). The usages refer to material *and* cultural wealth of distinct cultures and nations beyond Israel. In Scripture, their diverse cultural productions and offerings are made pleasing to God. The Reformed eschatology of Richard Mouw, in particular, highlights the theological, cultural, and public implications of this biblical truth.[21] If the cultural wealth of Ghana, Guatemala, the Emirates, and the Philippines will all be welcomed into the new Jerusalem, how might this challenge the deficit thinking that is so pervasive in white and Western Christianity today?

Reformed Theology from the Underside

In this section I explore how a conversation with CRT might bear fruit within the Reformed tradition. Yosso has argued that oppressed communities develop a unique moral clarity and insight about the nature of injustice. Survivors of the Holocaust joined the struggle for civil rights. Survivors of (US's) Japanese interment and Chinese exclusion decried the mistreatment of migrants at the US southern border. Their experiences of oppression and the moral insight it produces are profound cultural and intellectual assets that leap off the protest sign and take up residence in a nation's memory and imagination. Reformed Christianity needs this.

Allan Boesak is a Reformed theologian and a Black South African who was deeply invested in the anti-apartheid movement. Black South Africans who, like Boesak, struggled during apartheid have produced profound works of political, prophetic, and theological clarity. Boesak's theology and his life demonstrate the power of asset thinking and are—in and of themselves—profound theological assets. Boesak's life and work are gifts of cultural and theological wealth for the global Reformed community.

Consider the following words from Boesak. He offers a harsh prophetic critique, not simply of apartheid, but also of Reformed Christianity's systemic complicity in its structural evils. Reformed readers could receive these words as a stinging rebuke (as they should), but they should also receive Boesak's rebuke as a gift of cultural wealth from a brother who possesses moral insight and theological wisdom to offer:

> It is Reformed Christians who have spent years working out the details of apartheid, as a church policy and as a political policy. It is Reformed Christians who have presented this policy to the Afrikaner as the only possible solution,

21. See Richard J. Mouw, *When the Kings Come Marching In: Isaiah and the New Jerusalem*, rev. ed. (Grand Rapids: Eerdmans, 2002).

as an expression of the will of God for South Africa, and as being in accord with the gospel and the Reformed Tradition. It is Reformed Christians who have created Afrikaner nationalism, equating the Reformed tradition and Afrikaner ideals with the ideals of the kingdom of God. It is they who have devised the theology of apartheid, deliberately distorting the gospel to suit their racist aspirations. They present this policy as a pseudo-gospel that can be the salvation of all South Africans.[22]

How should Reformed Christians respond to Boesak's prophetic critique? He prescribes prophetic action. "Reformed Christians are called on not to accept the sinful realities of the world. Rather we are called to challenge, to shape, to subvert, and to humanize history until it conforms to the norm of the kingdom of God."[23]

Forged in suffering, Boesak's calls for an active form of fidelity to the Reformed confessions that are *practical and public*, rather than merely *intellectual or personal*. What do sixteenth-century Reformed confessions have to do with twenty-first-century racism? Boesak reflects on the first question and answer of the Heidelberg Catechism and applies it directly to the dehumanizing experience of Black South Africans. He keys in on the catechism's insistence that our bodies and souls belong to Jesus Christ alone. Boesak's writing crescendos in moving detail as he describes the suffering of black bodies and souls under systems of racism and oppression.[24] Persons who assert that they belong to Christ directly contest and subvert the institutional control and violence of apartheid. Here Boesak's method situates the Reformed confessions within the context of real, lived experiences of racial injustice.

By contrast, during the civil rights era some white Reformed churches in the American Midwest limited discussions of racism to "a matter of the heart."[25] Many Reformed Christians continue this line of thinking today. Boesak's lived struggle on the underside of power produced profound moral and

22. Allan Boesak, *Black and Reformed: Apartheid, Liberation, and the Calvinist Tradition* (New York: Orbis Books, 1984), 88. Do not think that the World Alliance of Reformed Churches' official anti-apartheid declaration settled the matter in 1982. Its North American rebranding in the form of "Kinism" (a white nationalist interpretation of Christianity) was declared a heresy by the Christian Reformed Church of North America in 2019. Kinism attributes its segregationist theology to Calvin, Kuyper, and Berkhof. Students of these Reformed figures should be prepared to produce a road map that actively leads away from racial injustice, not toward it. Without such preparedness, what guarantee can there be that the vulnerabilities will not be exploited again?

23. Boesak, *Black and Reformed*, 90.

24. Boesak, *Black and Reformed*, 97.

25. Eugene P. Heideman, *The Practice of Piety: The Theology of the Midwestern Reformed Church in America, 1866–1966*, Historical Series of the Reformed Church in America (Grand Rapids: Eerdmans, 2009), 251.

theological insights on the public calling of a Christ-follower amid systems of racism. The theological wisdom of Boesak's insights are freely available to the children of white Reformed churches who are looking for resources to navigate contemporary conflicts over race and CRT. The cultural wealth is there if they will take it.

Conclusion

As I write this chapter, North American Christians are processing and responding to the high-profile deaths of three Black Americans at the hands of police: Ahmaud Arbery, Breonna Taylor, and George Floyd. Their deaths have been met with what I consider to be a novel and uncharacteristic outpouring of support by white Christians. The use of #blacklivesmatter is now more fashionable than ever before. As long as the hashtag and the rhetoric of CRT are little more than a sentiment, it will require nothing of the students who use them. Sadly, universities can train students to employ liberative rhetorics without preparing them for the long and hard work for liberation off campus. A comfortable safety can be found in rhetorical wordplay and theoretical abstraction.

Like CRT, Reformed theology can fall prey to the dangers of abstraction, inaction, and self-centered comfort that hyperdoctrinarism produces. Students of Reformed theology can easily be tempted to sit back in self-satisfied intellectual analysis of racism and CRT. They can comfortably affirm aspects of CRT by using the theological doctrines of general revelation and common grace. Or they can comfortably dismiss CRT by asserting a clean antithesis between the gospel of Jesus and the gospel of Marx.

If Reformed Christians are going to deeply engage racist systems and structures with their minds and their hearts, their ideas and their institutions, they are going to need to go beyond abstract theological or sociological reflection. They need to actively listen to and learn from the embodied struggles of their brothers and sisters on the underside of these systems of power. They must do more than casually read the prophetic witnesses of Boesak and the Belhar and Accra Confessions. They are going to need to actively engage in Reformed action themselves. After all, the best Reformed theology has always been done in the streets, whether in Geneva or in Cape Town.

Part Six

Public Worship

19

A Migrant at the Lord's Table

A Reformed Theology of Home

ALBERTO LA ROSA ROJAS

I was ten years old when my family and I left Peru. It was 2001. Economic instability coupled with a long series of political scandals, terrorism, and corruption all played a role in our decision to emigrate. We settled in the suburbs of Chicago and stayed in my uncle's home. He had offered to sponsor my father's application for US residency. Sadly, our family was unable to gain legal status because of a series of unforeseen and unfortunate circumstances.[1] As a result, I lived as an unauthorized immigrant in the United States for fourteen long years. It was not until 2018 that I finally received full citizenship in the United States.[2] For the majority of my young life I was "an illegal immigrant," according to the derisive label of some in the United States.

---

1. One of the unforeseen events which most impacted my family's capacity to gain legal residency status in the US was the attack on the Twin Towers in New York City on September 11, 2001. The terrorist attacks on 9/11 led to a massive overhaul of US immigration policies, with the effect that immigrants, particularly from the Global South, were increasingly perceived as possible threats to US national security. In the years that followed, many laws that had previously opened up pathways toward legal status for immigrants were either eliminated, or the criteria for an applicant's eligibility were made much more narrow and specific, leaving out many.

2. I am grateful for the many privileges of being a US citizen; yet the questions about home, which I began to have after we left Peru and which intensified during my time as an unauthorized

Once I finally achieved official status as a US resident, one of the first things I did was to return to my homeland of Peru with my wife, Anna. Stepping out of the Jorge Chávez International Airport, I was immediately surprised by the powerful smell of the Pacific Ocean as it filled my nostrils. My senses quickly became overloaded and my mind whirled as I struggled to absorb every detail of a place that had lived in my memory and my imagination for fourteen years. The next morning I ran to the rooftop of my childhood home to take in the view of my hometown of Callao. I felt like the glittering Pacific to my left and the Andean foothills on my right were extending a warm embrace to me—a prodigal son who had finally come home.

However, that feeling of home, its sacred mystery, was snatched from me as quickly as it had come. It happened first as I descended from the rooftop and encountered *mi tía* (my aunt) Nelly. When I was a young boy in Peru, she had been like a second mother to me. But now, fourteen years later, she spoke to me with a subtle but distant reserve, almost as if she were speaking with a friendly stranger. I encountered the same feeling of tempered familiarity in so many of my interactions during my time in Peru. Although I had envisioned this trip as a triumphant homecoming, I felt more and more like a guest—native and yet a foreigner, recognized and yet unknown. The haunting question could not be ignored: If Peru was no longer my home, where *was* my home?

Despite having spent most of my life in the United States, growing up as an unauthorized immigrant made it incredibly challenging to feel fully "at home." As an unauthorized immigrant, I could not legally apply for a job, a driver's license, or financial aid for college. I could not leave the country with my youth group or soccer team. I lived in constant fear of being deported and separated from my family. Growing older, I came to understand and accept this permanent state of contingency and liminality. I recognized that a very thin thread connected me to the people and places that surrounded me. I always knew that thread could be severed at any time. Even after becoming a US citizen, I still feel a sense of ambiguity about where and what home is. Many Hispanics in the US refer to this ambiguity as being *ni de aqui, ni de alla* (neither from here nor there), or simply from no place. As I theologize about the crisis of immigration, I am at a visceral level talking about the longing for home and the crisis of home loss.

---

immigrant, continue to be at the core of my theological reflection. I also hope, through this chapter, to provide a voice to the over ten million unauthorized immigrants in the US who live in the shadows and who remain silent in fear of deportation and of losing their homes again. Having said that, I recognize that my story is but one among many and by no means can represent the diversity of hopes, fears, and realities faced by my immigrant brothers and sisters.

My own biography highlights a few of the ways in which many immigrants around the world are wrestling with questions of home and homelessness.[3] That said, those who see themselves as "natives," "hosts," or "citizens" also struggle with questions of home and homelessness. Some of them ask questions such as these: Are immigrants a threat to the safety and order of our homeland? How can we preserve our cultural traditions and sense of home in an increasingly globalized world? Is the experience of a stable home only possible for those with money and power?

In the twenty-first century, dominant cultures are increasingly being disrupted by the forces of globalization and mass migration. These global forces have led some citizens into relentless and fear-driven attempts to secure their "homes" by rendering others homeless.[4] Global questions about immigration and pluralism, the ecological crisis, and the resurgence of vicious forms of populism and nationalism all point toward widespread questions regarding how humans envision, experience, and perform ways of being at home in this world.

As signs of the times, these realities beckon the global church into deeper theological reflection about the meaning of home in light of the self-revelation of God.[5] As an immigrant, theologizing about the meaning of home is not an abstract activity or a form of sentimentalism, but a pressing existential demand and an urgent political task. This is partly because immigrants, regardless of their status, are increasingly being blamed for this growing global sense of homelessness.

In view of this increased sense of homelessness felt by migrants and citizens, a clash of desires emerges: the migrant's desire to make a home for themselves in their new land and the citizen's desire to protect and preserve their own sense of

3. Throughout the rest of the chapter, I will use the term "homelessness" to refer to the experience of those who live with the constant burden of finding, establishing, or preserving a sense of home in the world, even while perhaps inhabiting a stable physical house or shelter. For a sociological lens on the interconnectedness of home and the experience of migrants, see Paolo Boccagni, *Migration and the Search for Home: Mapping Domestic Space in Migrants' Everyday Lives*, Mobility and Politics (New York: Palgrave Macmillan, 2017).

4. In an essay Latinx theologian Jacqueline Hidalgo observes that, throughout history, "dominant populations continually struggle to build home on the backs of others." Jacqueline Hidalgo, "La Lucha for Home and La Lucha as Home: Latinx/a/o Theologies and Ecologies," *Journal of Hispanic/Latino Theology* 21, no. 1 (May 2019): 10, https://repository.usfca.edu /jhlt/vol13/iss1/1.

5. For recent works reflecting theologically on "home," see Steven Bouma-Prediger and Brian J. Walsh, *Beyond Homelessness: Christian Faith in a Culture of Displacement* (Grand Rapids: Eerdmans, 2008); Natalia Marandiuc, *The Goodness of Home: Human and Divine Love and the Making of the Self*, AAR Academy Series (New York: Oxford University Press, 2018); Miroslav Volf, "The World as God's Home," three of the Edward Cadbury Lectures, University of Birmingham, UK, May 2019, recorded, https://www.birmingham.ac.uk/schools /ptr/departments/theologyandreligion/events/cadburylectures/2019/index.aspx.

home amid an undulating ocean of change.[6] The questions emerging from these conflicting desires are the impetus for the theological reflections that follow.

Home at the Lord's Table

Throughout this chapter I demonstrate how a Reformed theology of home, embodied in the practice of the Lord's Supper, can help us reform our desires for home and point toward ways of escaping the present and destructive tension. At the Lord's Supper, immigrants and citizens alike are invited to bring their longings for home and ultimately find their true home in Jesus Christ. Yet, paradoxically, the Lord's Supper also invites us into a divine drama in which the eternal Word assumes flesh and makes a home in creation.[7] I begin with a reflection on the universal human desire for home as a desire for God, drawing on the work of John Calvin. From there, the relationship between being at home in God and being at home in the world is explored, as shown in the Reformed theology of Brian Walsh and Steven Bouma-Prediger. Finally, through the work of Karl Barth, I argue that Christian migrants and citizens are called to journey home by following Christ on the way to Golgotha. It is there, in Christ's exile, that humanity finds its homecoming in God. Throughout the essay I draw attention to the Lord's Supper as a formative practice, in which believers are invited to enact, embody, and bear witness to this triune and Christocentric drama of home.[8] Called to Christ's table, the immigrant and the citizen can be oriented toward the biblical narrative of God's homecoming in creation and their true home in Christ.

God as Our Home

Where and what is home? For centuries, Christians have often answered this question by affirming that heaven is our one true home. Often cited, Hebrews

---

6. Throughout the chapter, I am deploying the terms "immigrant" and "citizen" as a heuristic device to signal the difference between those who live in their country of birth and feel a relatively strong sense of being at home there and those who do not live in their country of birth and therefore whose experience in their place of residence is that of being foreigners. However, in legal usage, the terms are more fluid than that. Immigrants can and do become naturalized citizens, as is the case with me.

7. See John 1:14. Scripture quotations in this chapter are taken from the NRSV.

8. My aim in this chapter is not to offer "the solution" to the migration crisis, nor to offer a concrete theory for how to practice being at home in the world, but rather to offer some key theological foundations upon which to construct a holistic Reformed theology of home that seeks the mutual flourishing of migrants and citizens.

11:13–16 appears to make exactly this point. It describes Israel's patriarchs as strangers and aliens faithfully awaiting their entrance into the heavenly country.[9]

In his commentary on Hebrews, John Calvin observes that Israel's patriarchs saw heaven "from a distance," but for Christians, the heavenly home has been made intimately manifest in the person of Jesus Christ.[10] In light of this, Calvin warns Christians who yearn to find their home in this world with these words: "If the land of Canaan did not engross [the patriarch's] attention, how much more weaned from things below ought we to be, who have no promised habitation in this world?"[11]

A Reformed theology of home begins with this foundational affirmation: our life in this world is a pilgrimage toward the triune God, in whom we encounter our ultimate home.[12] To "be home" is to dwell in the presence of the One who alone is our refuge, who alone offers true rest.[13]

According to Calvin, this perfect fellowship, this complete at-home-ness in God, is precisely what is missing from a world cast under the spell of sin. In this present age, we "have no promised habitation"; home remains an eschatological hope. For Calvin, home is thus not simply a place but a time. Home is not now; it is not yet. Home will occur when the Spirit gathers us into the resurrected Christ and into the new Jerusalem, the Holy City of God, in the age to come.

Nevertheless, to human beings aware of their present homelessness, the Lord's Supper offers an eschatological taste of their future homecoming. In the bread and the wine, those who presently feel far off are—through the

9. "All of these [patriarchs] died in faith without having received the promises, but from a distance they saw and greeted them. They confessed that they were strangers and foreigners on the earth, for people who speak in this way make it clear that they are seeking a homeland. If they had been thinking of the land that they had left behind, they would have had the opportunity to return. But as it is, they desire a better country, that is, a heavenly one. Therefore God is not ashamed to be called their God; indeed, he has prepared a city for them" (Heb. 11:13–16).

10. "But if [the patriarchs] in spirit amid dark clouds, took a flight into the celestial country, what ought we to do at this day? For Christ stretches forth his hand to us, as it were openly, from heaven, to raise us up to himself." John Calvin, *Commentaries on the Epistle of Paul the Apostle to the Hebrews*, trans. John Owen (1539; Grand Rapids: Christian Classics Ethereal Library, 1853), on Heb. 11:13, http://www.ccel.org.

11. Calvin, *Hebrews*, on 11:13.

12. Alluding to this same passage eleven centuries before Calvin, Augustine wrote, "Still less then, should the name of Christian be reproached with the captivity of its servants, who, awaiting a heavenly fatherland with true faith, know that they are pilgrims even in their own habitations." *Augustine: The City of God against the Pagans*, ed. and trans. R. W. Dyson, Cambridge Texts in the History of Political Thought (Cambridge: Cambridge University Press, 1998), 1.15.

13. John Calvin, *Institutes of the Christian Religion*, ed. John T. McNeill, trans. Ford Lewis Battles, 2 vols. (Philadelphia: Westminster, 1960), 3.25.10.

power of the Holy Spirit—offered a seat alongside the resurrected Christ, the table's host.[14] It is in and through table fellowship with Christ that believers are made recipients of the table's fruits: the forgiveness of sins, eternal life, and ultimately, an eschatological homecoming. Our temporal and spatial longings for home converge at the Lord's Table.

Having practiced table fellowship, the immigrant and the citizen have their understanding of and desire for home challenged and reordered toward our eschatological home with God. At the Lord's Table, we hear, see, and taste the good news that God is our one true home. Our earthly patterns of homemaking are not set aside by the supper, but they are transfigured and redirected toward God and his gracious will. Having experienced the hospitality of Christ at the communion table, believers can now see their earthly homes in a new light. Earthly "homes," be they nations, neighborhoods, or actual houses, become witnesses to our eternal home in God. This eucharistic reframing of "home" means that we no longer treat our earthly homes as ends in and of themselves. Instead, they become aids for us in anticipating the coming city, the new Jerusalem, where all God's creatures share in perfect fellowship with each other and with God.

A Reformed theology of home will recognize and affirm our earthly desires for home as a good and natural inclination created in us by God. It will, however, also urge us not to look to a groaning creation to meet our eschatological longing for home. No nation, neighborhood, people group, or family could meet the yearning for belonging. This challenge is for the immigrant and the citizen alike. Only Christ's table can offer the sojourner, the migrant, and the refugee the ultimate rest and homecoming they long for. The same holds true for those who identify themselves as "natives," "citizens," and "hosts"; the table challenges their relentless drive to preserve their sense of home from the perceived threats of outsiders. Once again, the table of Christ reminds us that no earthly home is ultimate, that no earthly home will fully satisfy our yearning to belong. In this sense, the table calls its participants to live as pilgrims who have tasted the feast that will come. The table provides these pilgrims with the welcome, the nourishment, and the redirection they need on their eschatological journey home.

God's Homecoming

If our one true home is in God, should we reject any sense of belonging on earth? One of the challenges of confessing God as our one true home is that

---

14. For a Reformed account of the Lord's Supper as "delighting in Christ," see J. Todd Billings, *Remembrance, Communion, and Hope: Rediscovering the Gospel at the Lord's Table* (Grand Rapids: Eerdmans, 2018), 30–56.

it can be interpreted as a call to forsake any sense of belonging, rootedness, or responsibility to specific places and peoples here on earth. This type of gnostic spirituality sees the material world as something that needs to be transcended or escaped in order to truly be at home in God.

In their book *Beyond Homelessness*, Reformed theologians Steven Bouma-Prediger and Brian Walsh diagnose the gnostic impulse as one of the underlying causes of what they call the global crisis of homelessness.[15] In response to this gnostic tendency, the authors invite Christians to consider that the biblical narrative is not primarily about humans and their longing for home, but rather about a God who elects, creates, and arranges creation as a fitting place for habitation—not only for creatures but for the Creator as well.[16] In the beginning, God intends to dwell within creation and, as the story proceeds, the fall does not extinguish that intention. The story begins with God's act of homemaking in Genesis, and it ends with God's final act of homecoming in the book of Revelation.[17] These themes of divine homemaking and divine homecoming show up again and again within Israel's covenantal story with God. "My dwelling place shall be with them; and I will be their God, and they shall be my people. Then the nations shall know that I the LORD sanctify Israel, when my sanctuary is among them forevermore" (Ezek. 37:27–28 NRSV).[18]

For Christians, this covenantal story of God's desire to dwell with Israel and make a home for them reaches its climax and fulfillment in the incarnation of Jesus Christ. Herein the Word of God "[took on] flesh and dwelt among us" (John 1:14). There is a redemptive purpose to God's homecoming in Jesus Christ. By making a dwelling among us, the Word assumes our creaturely modes of dwelling. In Christ, the omnipresent Creator

15. Walsh and Bouma-Prediger describe homelessness not only as socioeconomic homelessness (those who have no physical shelter in the world) but also as ecological homelessness due to the systematic destruction of ecosystems, and as the existential homelessness of the postmodern nomad who experiences rootlessness or a profound lack of a sense of a place in the world despite enjoying the privilege of a physical house and of a stable national home. Bouma-Prediger and Walsh, *Beyond Homelessness*, 41–46.

16. According to these authors, the Scriptures teach us that "at the heart of the Christian gospel is the message that we are all homeless, but that there is a home in which our yearning hearts can and will find rest. That home is creation redeemed and transfigured, a place of grace that is inhabited by an indwelling God of unfathomable love." Bouma-Prediger and Walsh, *Beyond Homelessness*, 320.

17. Bouma-Prediger and Walsh, *Beyond Homelessness*, 15–28.

18. Throughout the Old Testament, God's desire to be at home in creation is mediated through the people of Israel and especially through the temple in Jerusalem. For another example see Ps. 132:13–14: "For the LORD has chosen Zion; he has desired it for his habitation: This is my resting place forever; here I will reside, for I have desired it."

assumes a small village and a childhood home, a human family, a culture, and a nation. Indeed, the infinite God of the universe enters into the finite human experience of love, memory, and longing for home.[19] Moreover, it is because God assumes our earthly homes, villages, and nations—our modes of dwelling—that we are enabled to come home to God. In Christ, our earthly modes of dwelling and homemaking are taken into the triune life of God.

In light of this, a Reformed theology of home will not destroy or demean the migrant or the citizen's desires for home. The gnostic mistake is out of bounds. The biblical vision of home is not and cannot be one of spiritual escape from creation. Instead, Reformed theology will reframe their longing for home within this larger story of God's homecoming and homemaking within creation, Israel, the church, and the new creation. As John of Patmos declares in Revelation, heaven will descend to the earth in a holy marriage, whereby God and creatures share a single dwelling place for eternity.[20] In the new creation we will find our home in God's holy city.

God's redemptive homecoming grants dignity to our earthly homes and forces us to look at our present modes of homemaking as all at once fallen and being redeemed in Christ. God in Christ saw fit to make his home with a particular people at a particular time and place—Israel. So too, Christians are called to make and maintain specific homes with concrete peoples and places that matter to God as well. Healing our global crisis of homelessness will not come from denying or downplaying our rootedness and our embeddedness in our creational homes. It will come by witnessing to God's redemptive work of homemaking in our nations, neighborhoods, families, and churches through the power of the Holy Spirit.

The Lord's Supper invites believers to participate in the redemptive triune drama of homecoming. Here, table fellowship functions somewhat like an icon through which participants are drawn by the Spirit into the eschatological

19. In his rejection of the Apollinarians, Gregory of Nazianzus writes, "For that which He [Christ] has not assumed He has not healed; but that which is united to His Godhead is also saved." I'm applying Gregory's teaching here to suggest that in assuming an earthly home in Christ, God also redeems our humble earthly dwelling places as well as our modes of dwelling. Gregory of Nazianzus, *To Cledonius the Priest against Apollinarius*, New Advent, https://www.newadvent.org/fathers/3103a.htm.

20. This vision of God's redemptive homecoming in creation is best captured by the eschatological vision of Rev. 21. "Then I saw a new heaven and a new earth. . . . And I heard a loud voice from the throne saying, 'See, the home of God is among mortals. He will dwell with them as their God; they will be his peoples, and God himself will be with them'" (vv. 1, 3–4 NRSV). This is not a Gnostic account whereby earth is replaced by heaven as our dwelling place, but rather an incarnational account whereby God dwells with human creatures in a creaturely way while these creatures are exalted to dwell with God and thereby to partake in the divine.

feast of the Lamb.[21] According to the book of Revelation, this holy banquet takes place when God's home has finally been established in the new creation and among the faithful (Rev. 21:3).

Turning our eyes to the current global crises of homelessness, participation in the Lord's Supper has deep and profound public implications. Two principal benefits merit a mention at this point. For all those who feel homeless, for all those who wander, table practices are an experience of welcome, an adoption into God's household. On the other hand, for all those who fearfully grasp to secure and sustain their earthly homes, table practices offer an experience of both disruption and liberation. Security and a sense of home are not something mortals can fully secure with money, status, political power, or even by birthright. In a world of contingency and displacement, the table reminds us that "home" is a gift of God that is coming: it is not yet fulfilled. Prior to Christ's return, citizens will never feel fully at home, regardless of how high they build their walls.

Golgotha: The Way Home

It is good and right to love our creational homes, neighborhoods, cultures, and nations. In a sinful world, however, this love for home can often become twisted, exclusionary, and even violent. In this final section, I demonstrate that the experience of the marginalized, the displaced, and the homeless is a critically important lens through which Christians can begin to witness and participate in the redemption of their present modes of homemaking.

Living in a safe neighborhood with community gardens next to neighbors who think and vote alike can give one the impression that home is possible right here and now. However, the global migration crisis, the ongoing destruction of ecosystems, and the unseen homeless in our cities—all these are signs that the world is far from being God's home. Witnessing to the redemption of our homes must therefore begin with the crisis of homelessness experienced by those on the margins.

This dynamic becomes apparent when we consider the life, and specifically the death, of Jesus as the concrete means by which God redeems our earthly homes. Christ himself was sent outside the city, Christ himself was exiled, and Christ himself suffered marginalization and death. In birth, there was no room for him in the inn. In death, there was only exclusion and expulsion. And yet the upside-down beauty of the life of Christ lies in the fact that, in Christ's rejection at Golgotha, humanity is welcomed home.

21. For the notion of the Lord's Supper acting as an icon and drawing believers into the triune drama witnessed in Scripture, see J. Todd Billings, *Remembrance, Communion, and Hope*, 7–29.

According to the Swiss Reformed theologian Karl Barth, the parable of the prodigal son, when read through a christological lens, reveals to us two journeys that take place simultaneously in the person of Jesus Christ.[22] The first journey, which the parable describes as the journey of a son away from his father's house and into a strange land, is the journey of the Son of God from the heavenly country of the Father and into the world of finite and fallen humanity. This is the journey of the incarnation.[23] In assuming flesh, the eternal Son of God makes a home with the people of Israel who, though living in their homeland, remain in a type of exile under Roman imperial occupation. Dwelling amid a particular people, land, and history, the Son of God partakes not only in humanity's exile from Eden because of sin but also in the concrete lived experience of exile. He lives with those under imperial rule—displaced, homeless, and marginalized. The Son of God experiences Rome's vicious homemaking power intimately.

Simultaneously, in Christ's life, death, and resurrection we witness God taking on the responsibility for giving humanity its way back home.[24] Barth alludes to this as the second journey taking place in the person of Christ. What the parable describes as the homecoming of a repentant prodigal son, Barth reads christologically as the journey of exaltation of Christ, the Son of Man, to the right hand of the Father. For Barth, these two journeys constitute the shape and nature of the reconciling work of Jesus Christ.[25] In sum, for Barth, every instance of the life of Jesus Christ is simultaneously a revelation of humanity's homelessness and of humanity's homecoming to God.[26]

22. See "The Way of the Son of God into the Far Country" (*CD* IV/1:157–210) and "The Homecoming of the Son of Man" (*CD* IV/2:20–153), both in Karl Barth, *Church Dogmatics*, ed. Thomas F. Torrance and Geoffrey W. Bromiley (Peabody, MA: Hendrickson, 2010).

23. In this sense, the far country is always east of Eden, that place of human exile from God the Father and therefore of sinful existence; to use Barth's own words, the far country is "the evil society of the being which is not God and against God." Barth, *CD* IV/1:158.

24. The far country is thus also the place of repentance because it is there that the prodigal son recognizes his mistake and turns back home to his father's house. This is why, for Barth, it is necessary that the Son of God make this journey to the far country, for by binding himself to humanity in exile, the Son makes himself responsible for guiding humanity back home to the Father.

25. "Herein, the Son of Man returned home to where he belonged, to His place as true man, to fellowship with God, to relationship with His fellows, to the ordering of His inward and outward existence, to the fullness of His time for which He was made, to the presence and enjoyment of the salvation for which He was destined." Barth, *CD* IV/2:20.

26. The homecoming and exilic motifs become, for Barth, a kind of dialectic that parallels the dialectic of the cross and resurrection. Just as the resurrected one is always already the crucified one, so the homecoming one is always of the exiled one. Just as we cannot gaze upon the resurrected Christ without seeing the wounds on his hands and feet, so we cannot look at the Son of Man, who is at home with the Father, without seeing in him the marks of exile and rejection. The homecoming God is the God revealed in exile. As such, the exile of the Son

Barth's christological reading of the parable reveals that God's homecoming in a broken and violent world does not correspond very well with our tranquil visions of "home." God's homecoming looks like a baby sleeping in a trough outside of an overbooked inn. It looks like a family fleeing home and seeking refuge in a foreign land. It looks like a homeless teacher with no place to rest his head. It looks like a dead messianic failure hanging on a cross outside of the city gates.[27]

To confess that *this* Jesus is our homecoming is to be faced with an uncomfortable truth. Our comfortable, safe, and secure notions of home need to be radically destabilized. Barth invites us to recognize that the only way home to the Father is revealed on the way of Golgotha. The path home runs through exile; it goes by way of the cross.

This means that disciples looking for the redemption of their homes cannot afford to be tempted by visions of stability, comfort, and rest. They must instead look for the homecoming of God among the marginalized, the poor, the displaced. Such an understanding entails a rejection of any form of homemaking that renders one's neighbor homeless.

This theological understanding of home also amounts to what the Peruvian liberation theologian Gustavo Gutiérrez called a "preferential option for the poor." In this case, the poor can be substituted for the displaced. This entails an epistemological shift for the way citizens view migrants. The displaced are not guests whom we need to host; they are those through whom God is making a home in the world. In Christ, migrants and citizens *share* a common journey home. Both must journey through Christ's cross and resurrection. It is in participating in Christ's exile and homecoming, through the power of the Holy Spirit, that both the migrant and the citizen can find their way home.

When I was an unauthorized immigrant, the Lord's Supper represented a profound practice of homecoming. At the table, I was assured that I belonged in *this* place with *these* people. I belonged, not because of my desire to belong, or my parent's decision to migrate, or even because of the status the

---

of God is always an indictment on human ways of making home in the world insofar as they are built on rendering others homeless. However, it is an indictment that ultimately points to the Yes of God, for in gazing at the cross we also recognize that God has dwelt with us in our homelessness and thus that God has taken on responsibility for our exile, setting us on our way back home to the Father. In sum, Christ is God's Yea and Amen to the words of the psalmist: "Where can I go from your spirit? Or where can I flee from your presence? If I ascend to heaven, you are there; if I make my bed in Sheol, you are there" (Ps. 139:7–8 NRSV).

27. In fact, for Barth, this is what distinguishes the God of Israel as the only true God, for "God shows Himself to be the great and true God in the fact that He can and will let His grace bear this cost, that He is capable and willing and ready for this condescension, this act of extravagance, this far journey." Barth, *CD* IV/1:159.

government granted me. I belonged by the grace and the power of the Spirit. In uniting me to Christ, the Spirit united me to everyone else around that table. Despite the walls of division that we put up on the basis of ethnicity, gender, language, or even migratory status, Christ and his Table drew us together.

In the supper the church declares that all those gathered around the table are members of a single family and of a single household. Through one cup and one loaf, they are bound together, not by political power, but by the body and blood of the Lamb. The table makes a home. It is a homemaking practice. In light of this, the meal functions as a disruptive act of resistance to the forces of exclusion, marginalization, and homelessness that we experience in the world and—sadly—in the church.

Conclusion

My aim in this chapter is to show how a Reformed account of home sees the Christian life as entailing two movements. First, we move toward God, who is our one true home. Second, we move to dwell more deeply in our creational homes in ways that bear witness to God's homecoming in the incarnation and in the eschaton. These two theological truths are embodied, practiced, and habituated at the Lord's Table. At the table two things happen at once. Not only are our sinful desires, beliefs, and practices around homemaking in this present age exposed, we are also offered an opportunity to remember, practice, and anticipate our final homecoming in God.

The Lord's Supper does not offer any easy or simple answers to the political crisis of homelessness for either migrants or citizens. We each, in our own geographical, cultural, and communal contexts, are called to creatively bear witness to God's eschatological homecoming in creation. This chapter offers a theological foundation for this much-needed and contextual work. Nevertheless, as we go about this work of homemaking, we must be mindful and attentive to the experiences and voices of the homeless, the displaced, and the marginalized. If we wish to participate in the Spirit's work of transforming all creation, heaven and earth, into the eternal home of God, we need to share a table with these suffering fellow humans.

20

Public Trauma and Public Prayer

Reformed Reflections on Intercession

JOHN D. WITVLIET

The Perceived Public Silence of the Church

We live in a world full of public trauma and tragedy. Most mornings, we wake up to discover newsfeeds and social media accounts churning with fear, anger, guilt, and shame stoked by global public health epidemics, racism, human trafficking, systemic poverty and hunger, climate change, refugee displacement, political corruption, religious persecution, moral injury, gun violence, mass incarceration, abortion, sexual violence, fraud, predatory lending, warfare, malicious bullying, pornography, false imprisonment, domestic violence, clergy misconduct, anti-Semitism, and environmental degradation. In this age of ubiquitous information, our heads and hearts are quickly flooded by the rising waters of public trauma and tragedy.

Painfully, in the worship of far too many churches, there is barely even a mention of the world's horrors. Far too many churches in the United States never prayed out loud for the cities of Ferguson, Charleston, or Charlottesville in the wake of racist acts of violence that struck at their very hearts. Far too many worshiping communities have never directly spoken about injustice to indigenous peoples, do not practice lament as a regular dimension of life together, and only rarely—if ever—pray for the plight of persecuted peoples or refugees, or about and for sexual predators, racists, predatory lenders, and other enemies of flourishing humanity.

As we survey the broad spectrum of Christian worship practices through our work at the Calvin Institute of Christian Worship, we see churches working hard to provide uplifting sermons, uplifting music, uplifting fellowship opportunities, and uplifting children's programs. Although "uplifting" is not a bad thing—indeed, in worship we "lift up our hearts to the Lord"—the operational definition of "uplifting" at work in many contexts is essentially sentimental. Instead of lamenting, confessing, and interceding about public horrors with specificity and honesty, these churches tend to avoid, deny, or minimize the public trauma that is all around them. The understandable desire for a respite from trauma ends up perpetuating a pattern of disengagement.

In the parable of the good Samaritan, a priest and a Levite, leaders of the people's liturgy, dismiss and walk past the wounded man on the roadside. The parable offers an implicit critique of liturgical disengagement with the world's travail. While the parable impresses on us the need for public Christian action in the world, it also implicates our gathered liturgies and liturgical leaders as well. How tragic it is when our liturgies ignore and avoid the wounded man sitting on the street outside, when our public worship becomes a prime site for public disengagement from the world's pain!

A decade ago I began to record every time I heard the statement "The church is so silent about X." My anecdotal list is now very long. That phrase has been used repeatedly to introduce discussions about sexual abuse and harassment, racism, creation care and environmental justice, religious persecution, and more.

To be sure, there are lots of Christians talking about these things—in denominational reports and statements, in academic books and blogs, and within seminary and continuing education classes. And yet, these complaints about the complicit silence of the church almost always ring true simply because most Christians do not participate in these academic, denominational, parachurch, or social media ecologies.

What matters for most believers is that a congregation is willing to name and engage these public issues *in public worship*. It is *the sanctuary's* silence on these public horrors that is particularly deafening. It is possible, and in some places highly likely, to participate in worship every week for a year and not hear a single reference to the world's horrors.

There are many interrelated reasons for this liturgical silence. First, some churches operate with a thin, individualistic view of the gospel, focusing nearly all their liturgical attention on individual conversion and comfort. Second, some churches are conflict avoidant, eager to do anything to stay away from public controversy during worship.[1] In this chapter, my focus will be on a third reason for liturgical silence: the atrophy of intercessory prayer. I argue that congregations need to revive a weekly practice of public intercession that is deeply conversant with the world outsides the walls of the sanctuary.

Intercessory Prayer and Public Life

The church needs more than a public theological response to public traumas; it needs a public *liturgical* response to them as well, with liturgies and spiritual practices that promote a posture of awareness and engagement with the world's needs.

In many worship contexts today, intercessory prayer has fallen on hard times. It is stunning to me how often my students report that while their churches have robust practices of congregational singing and preaching, they include almost no prayer at all in public worship. Students routinely report that their churches will pray about the physical health needs of members but never mention any larger societal concerns. My teaching colleagues across the ecumenical spectrum of Christianity repeatedly confirm this emerging pattern. As Constance Cherry memorably discovered in one sample study of some Protestant traditions, songs and sermons are getting longer while prayers are getting shorter.[2]

Yet it remains realistic to hope for a better future. At the 2020 Calvin Symposium on Worship, conference leader David Bailey offered the prayers of the people. David prayed generally for shalom in the world and then added a specific prayer for God to restrain the horrors of human trafficking at the Super Bowl (a game being played the next day). That single sentence placed a profound concern on the hearts of a thousand conference participants. After the conference an illuminating series of informal comments by conferees point to what is needed:

- "We never would hear a prayer like that in our church; this is unacceptable."

1. Addressing these two concerns has been a specialty for Richard Mouw. Praise God for his vigorous defense of a large vision of the gospel—a gospel that encompasses special grace and common grace, individual repentance and cultural transformation, the promise of future glory and the importance of advocacy for justice in the present tense. Praise God for his lifelong concern for civility, for his call to engage deeply divisive issues with conviction, clarity, and charity.

2. Constance Cherry, "My House Shall Be Called a House of . . . Announcements," *Church Music Workshop* (Nashville: Abingdon, 2005), https://static1.squarespace.com/static/50412884e4b0b97fe5a5411a/t/5328b2c6e4b0e8b344d4a498/1395176134878/My_House_Shall_be.pdf.

- "Leaders of public prayer should actively seek to name what we all are afraid to name, and to do it in a profoundly pastoral way."
- "More thoughtful intercessions would not add a dime to our church's budget and yet could make such a difference in our congregation."

I heartily concur. Expanding the range of concern in our public prayer to match the public scope of God's redemptive activity offers a number of benefits to the congregation: it aligns our prayers with the breadth of divine concern, it forms us to become people of priestly concern for the world God loves, and it responds directly to clear biblical commands to pray in and about all circumstances.

Historic Models for Public Intercessions

In the early centuries of the church, public worship services routinely featured intercessory prayers for public needs, issues, and leaders. These prayers were grounded in a vision of the church as the gathering of a "royal priesthood" (1 Pet. 2:9),[3] responding to God's call to be a people bringing the needs of the world to God. These prayers were shaped by New Testament commands that emphasize the comprehensiveness of prayer: "Pray in the Spirit at *all* times in *every* prayer and supplication. To that end keep alert and always persevere in supplication for *all* the saints" (Eph. 6:18); and "in *everything* by prayer and supplication with thanksgiving let your requests be made known to God" (Phil. 4:6). Although liturgical prayers were offered for the church and its ministries (cf. Matt. 9:38), prayers also explicitly focused on the needs and callings of those outside the church, following Paul's injunction: "I urge, then, first of all, that petitions, prayers, intercession and thanksgiving be made for all people—for kings and all those in authority, that we may live peaceful and quiet lives in all godliness and holiness" (1 Tim. 2:1–2 NIV).

Documents describing worship in the early church routinely include wide-ranging litanies and other prayer forms that bring before God the travails of the world. These early prayers ask for God's mercy and reinforce a sense that human agency alone is insufficient to heal the pain of the world's trauma.[4]

3. Scripture in this chapter is from NRSV unless otherwise indicated; emphasis has been added to some quotes.
4. John D. Witvliet, "Embodying the Wisdom of Ancient Liturgical Practices: Some Old-Fashioned Rudimentary Euchology for the Contemporary Church," in *Ancient Faith for the Church's Future*, ed. Mark Husbands and Jeff Greenman (Downers Grove, IL: IVP Academic, 2008), 189–215.

These early patterns of priestly intercession have been refined in diverse ways across Christian traditions through the centuries and across cultures.

In the Reformed tradition, John Calvin's 1542 *Form of Church Prayers*, subtitled *After the Use of the Ancient Church*, sets the pace. It calls for an extended fifteen-hundred-word intercessory prayer each week after the Sunday sermon. There, Calvin fuses two liturgical traditions into a single prayer, opening with an extended paraphrase of the Lord's Prayer and concluding with an set of petitions covering a wide range of personal, ecclesial, and civic topics.[5] Both sections are notable for their comprehensive vision of what Christians can and should pray for in light of God's pluriform work in the world. Calvin's comprehensive approach to public intercessions on Sunday was complemented by an additional prayer service held during the week. This service also included a similarly robust approach to intercessory prayers for public life.[6]

All told, the prayers and songs of the early Reformers were meant to spill out of the sanctuary and into the public lives of the people. Reformed Christians were encouraged to turn the melodies they learned at church into the soundtrack by which they lived their lives, whistling them at work, singing them at school, repeating them at domestic mealtimes—in contrast to medieval Roman Catholic practices, which restricted the singing of sacred, liturgical songs to the sanctuary.

For Calvin, prayer and action were intertwined with his theological understanding of the priesthood of all believers. Calvin describes prayer as an opportunity to "testify, by our request, that we do hate and lament all that we see to be opposed to the will of God."[7] He urges believers to pray for a breadth of public concerns, declaring, "It is by the benefit of prayer that we have an entrance into the riches which we have in God. . . . God does not tell us anything which we are to hope from Him, without likewise commanding us to ask for it by prayer." Cherishing how all our prayers are gathered up into the intercessions of Christ who "intercedes for us at God's right hand" (cf. Rom. 8:34; 1 John 2:1; 1 Tim. 2:5), Calvin advocates intercession: "God not only allows each individual to pray for himself, but allows all to intercede mutually for each other."[8] Calvin urges, "If, at any time, we are cold in prayer

---

5. For a broader history, see C. F. Miller, "Intercessory Prayer: History, Method, Subjects, and Theology," *Studia Liturgica* 3, no. 1 (1964): 20–29.

6. Elsie Anne McKee, *The Pastoral Ministry and Worship in Calvin's Geneva* (Geneva: Librairie Droz S.A., 2016), 310–48. Also see McKee, "Calvin and Praying for 'All People Who Dwell on Earth,'" *Interpretation* 63, no. 2 (April 2009):130–40.

7. John Calvin, *A Harmony of the Gospels*, vol. 1 (Grand Rapids: Eerdmans, 1960), 208–9. This is his commentary on "Thy kingdom come" (Matt. 6:10).

8. John Calvin, *Institutes of the Christian Religion*, trans. Henry Beveridge (Edinburgh: Calvin Translation Society, 1846), 3.20.19.

or more negligent than we ought to be, . . . let us instantly reflect on how many are worn out by varied and heavy afflictions. . . . If we are not roused from our lethargy, we must have hearts of stone."[9] Calvin scholar Elsie McKee has explained that while Calvin's earliest writings stress the importance of these intercessions in private or personal prayer, later texts insist that a comprehensive concern for the world's needs should also be reflected in the public prayers of the church.[10]

What Calvin and his contemporaries bequeathed to the Reformed tradition of prayer was, then, *both* a public theological vision of praying for the needs of the world *and* a set of liturgical practices to embody that public theology. A generation after Calvin, the 1563 Palatinate Order of Worship featured a "Prayer for All Needs and Concerns of Christendom," which was emulated in the "Prayer for the General Needs of Christendom" in Dutch Reformed service books of the 1580s and beyond. Both of these are counterparts to Thomas Cranmer's "Prayer for the Whole State of Christ's Church Militant,"[11] a notable text in the *Book of Common Prayer*.

Two centuries later, the 1772 *Liturgy of the French Protestant Church* featured a weekly prayer that conveyed petitions (1) for all people, (2) for all ministers, (3) for all in political authority, (4) for all who suffer from various afflictions, (5) for the country, and finally (6) for "the duties and business of our several callings."[12] Still later, the 1906 *Presbyterian Book of Common Worship* called for a weekly prayer, featuring "Supplications: for the supply of all our needs temporal and spiritual, and for the aid and comfort of the Holy Ghost in all our duties and trials," as well as a robust list of public intercessions

for the whole world of mankind; remembering especially our country and all who are invested with civil authority; the Church Universal and that with which we are particularly connected; all missionaries and ministers of the Gospel; and

9. John Calvin, *Calvin's Commentaries: The Epistles of Paul the Apostle to the Galatians, Ephesians, Philippians, and Colossians*, trans. T. H. L. Parker (Grand Rapids, Eerdmans, 1965), 222.

10. Elsie Anne McKee, "Calvin Never Changed His Mind—Or Did He? Evidence from the Young Reformer's Teaching on Prayer," in *John Calvin, Myth and Reality: Images and Impact of Geneva's Reformer*, ed. Amy Nelson Burnett (Eugene, OR: Cascade Books, 2011), 18–36.

11. For more on this complex history, see Daniel James Meeter, *Bless the Lord, O My Soul: The New-York Liturgy of the Dutch Reformed Church, 1767* (Lanham, MD: Scarecrow, 1998), 193–202.

12. Charleston (S.C.) French Protestant Church, *The liturgy, or forms of divine service, of the French Protestant Church, of Charleston, S.C., translated from the liturgy of the churches of Neufchatel and Vallangin: Editions of 1737 and 1772, with some additional prayers, carefully selected; The whole adapted to public worship in the United States of America*, 3rd ed. (New York: A. D. F. Randolph, 1853), 29–31.

all others who are seeking to do good on earth; all poor and sick and sorrowful people (especially those for whom our prayers are asked); all little children and the youth assembled in schools and colleges; those who are in the midst of great danger or temptation; and all who are bound to us by ties of kinship or affection.[13]

These prayers and liturgical texts have been complemented throughout history by any number of pastoral theologians who both assumed and defended the importance of comprehensive public prayers. Princeton's Samuel Miller speaks of the "comprehensive character" that "belongs to the exercise of [public prayer]."[14] Regarding his vision for Christian engagement in anti-racism efforts, Francis Grimké cautions that "we should make our troubles more a subject of prayer than we do."[15]

At its best, this tradition of public intercession was a part of a larger set of Reformed connections between worship and public life. This included public preaching that addressed the people's daily habits and concerns. It also included hymns and songs intentionally composed for the laity's use, not simply in the sanctuary, but also in the workplace and in homes.[16] These public liturgies were the result of a public theology that had a comprehensive soteriological and eschatological vision of God's redemptive activity.

Indeed, one of the most reliable guides to what a Christian actually believes God's intentions are for the world can be found in what they pray for. Put another way, our public prayers reveal our public theology. In the things they mention (and fail to mention), these prayers demonstrate precisely which elements of public life we believe God truly cares about.

To be sure, these comprehensive prayers of intercession have an uneven history in the Reformed tradition. They have been ignored, shortened, and contested. Yet, in spite of all the vagaries and complexities, one constant is an aspirational desire for public prayers that convey comprehensive civic and public concern and actively resist escapism and sentimentality. The 360-degree vision of Reformed prayers of intercession confront contemporary worship

13. Presbyterian Church in the U.S.A. Special Committee on Forms and Services, *Book of Common Worship* (Philadelphia: Presbyterian Board of Publication and Sabbath-School Work, 1906), 6.

14. Samuel Miller, *Thoughts on Public Prayer* (Philadelphia: Presbyterian Board of Publication, 1849), 183.

15. Francis J. Grimké, "Signs of a Brighter Future," in *The Works of Francis J. Grimké*, vol. 1, *Addresses Mainly Personal and Racial*, ed. Carter G. Woodson (Washington, DC: Associated Publishers, 1942), 280.

16. John D. Witvliet, "The Spirituality of the Psalter: Metrical Psalms in Liturgy and Life in Calvin's Geneva," *Calvin Theological Journal* 32 (1997): 273–97.

leaders and challenge us to do better, to pray in a way that is consistent with the breadth and depth of the gospel we preach.

Improvising Intercession

It goes without saying that public intercessions from Calvin's Geneva or John Knox's Edinburgh should not be woodenly repeated by twenty-first-century congregations in Jakarta, Seoul, New York, and Rio de Janeiro. That said, their intercessions can challenge us to develop faithful and culturally appropriate approaches to comprehensive prayers in our unique contexts. Indeed, their value can perhaps best be conveyed in the form of a proverb or beatitude: "Blessed is the Christian community whose public prayer is comprehensive in concern, with requests for divine action that match the full range of divine activity narrated in Scripture."

That proverb, in turn, sets in motion any number of promising liturgical strategies, including some quite different from Calvin's. Once I visited a non-denominational church-planting ministry in which a wise pastor had paused early in the church's life to establish a robust practice of public intercessory prayer. Every week the church paused to pray about a specific public topic or concern beyond its own ministry context. Before the prayer, the pastor conducted a brief interview with someone outside the congregation who was at work addressing that concern; then the church prayed for them and the situation they were seeking to improve. By the end of each year, because of this simple weekly pattern, that congregation has prayed for fifty-two quite concrete matters of public concern. Although each week's public prayer is narrowly limited to one specific topic, over time that congregation prays for a remarkably diverse set of concerns.

In another congregation, a group of four people gathers every Saturday morning at a local coffee shop to choose which newspaper headlines will be used to call the congregation to prayer. Each week they choose three headlines of national and international concern, three headlines related to the local community, and three headlines from the church's newsletter about local ministry. On Sunday, these nine headlines are projected on a large screen, and a worship leader offers a one-sentence prayer on each of them, such as this one: "Lord God, have mercy on our local public schools, and equip each teacher and staff member who serves there to create a loving, just, patient, and transformative culture for every student." These nine single-sentence prayers, structurally similar to several ancient litanies, influence worshipers to go into public life and continue praying (and looking) for God's redemptive agency in all spheres of life.

In our work at Calvin Institute of Christian Worship, we notice how diverse contexts and cultures produce diverse practices of public prayer. For example, in a culture with a circular, relationship-oriented view of time, a comprehensive public prayer might unfold over an hour or longer; in a culture with a linear, task-oriented view of time, a prayer leader will labor over shaping a specific and pithy comprehensive prayer of no more than five hundred words. Likewise, in a culture with a more hierarchal understanding of power, it is essential that topics of great concern be named by a senior pastor. In a more egalitarian culture, it will be more important that a variety of voices be represented among the prayer leaders. In a culture that prizes direct communication, it will be essential to resist spiritual euphemisms in describing the world's horrors; in a setting that prizes indirect communication, it would be offensive to use overly direct speech for sensitive topics.[17]

These contemporary practices of intercession take Calvin's comprehensive approach to public prayer and creatively add to it a concern for public specificity. Adding this pastoral wisdom to our earlier beatitude, we might say, "Blessed is the Christian community whose public prayer is comprehensive in concern (with requests for divine action that stretch toward the full range of divine activity narrated in Scripture), and also specific in focus (calling to mind particular places, people, needs)." Any of these approaches would create space for naming each of the specific horrors I listed at the outset of this chapter with enough regularity to convince even occasional worshipers that the church is truly concerned about public evils.

Improvising Intercessions: Fragmentary and Eschatological

I have noticed one more attribute in the many pastorally and publicly sensitive prayer leaders: their intuition to deepen the stark contrast between public lament and public hope, even within the very same prayer. Their prayers about public life are both profoundly dark and bright. At one and the same time, their words of intercession tell the harsh truths about public evil and suffering and the blindingly good news about a God who will one day wipe away every public tear.

On the one hand, this involves more stammering in public prayer, greater willingness to publicly admit our utter inadequacy and speechlessness in the

---

17. These themes are developed in burgeoning literature on cultural intelligence, including David A. Livermore, *Cultural Intelligence: Improving Your CQ to Engage Our Multicultural World* (Grand Rapids: Baker Academic, 2009) and Livermore, *Expand Your Borders: Discover 10 Cultural Clusters*, CQ Insights Series (East Lansing, MI: Cultural Intelligence Center, 2013).

face of horror. If we honestly face and name the world's evils, one of the first things we must say to God is "We do not know what to say. We don't know how to pray." How does a person pray after the Holocaust? After a gunman walks into a synagogue and murders people at prayer? After the death of Breonna Taylor or George Floyd, especially in a congregation that did not pray in public about the tragedies of Charleston and Ferguson?

One of the most significant gifts that churches can give to Christians is the permission to pray in a halting, fragmentary way. It is gift to our children when poised pastoral leaders say, "God of grace, we are at a loss for words. . . . We do not know how to pray as we ought. How we need the Spirit, who 'intercedes with sighs too deep for words'" (cf. Rom. 8:26–27). How fitting to give voice to those in our communities who are, at any time, "simply undone" by the tragedies all around us.[18]

On the other hand, this practice involves greater intentionality in naming our ultimate eschatological hope alongside our stammering lament. It is remarkable that the most vivid passage in the New Testament about our stammering prayers comes only a few verses after Paul's stunning claim, "I consider that the sufferings of this present time are not worth comparing with the glory about to be revealed to us" (Rom. 8:18). For Paul, it seemed perfectly possible to declare that and also to say, "We groan inwardly as we wait" (v. 23) and "We do not know how to pray as we ought" (v. 26). This is much like Job's aching lament, "Have pity on me, . . . for the hand of God has struck me" could somehow lead right into "I know that my redeemer lives, . . . and after my skin has been . . . destroyed, yet in my flesh shall I see God" (Job 19:21, 25–26; cf. NIV).

To further refine our proverb once more: "Wise is the community that prays for concerns as far-reaching as the scope of divine redemption, that names specific human horrors and traumas, and that practices both its fragmentary aching laments and God's ultimate eschatological promises."

Connecting Public Prayers to Public Life

If we are going to engage the world's horrors, as surely we must, we need habits and patterns of prayer that routinely acknowledge and speak the world's horrors out loud. This public act, in turn, sets the tone and models an approach to prayer that can echo all week long in the lives of individual believers.

---

18. See, e.g., the poignant reflections on liturgical lament in Deanna A. Thompson, *Glimpsing Resurrection: Cancer, Trauma, and Ministry* (Louisville: Westminster John Knox, 2018), 124–26.

A single public prayer about human trafficking can prompt echoes in our hearts all week long. At its best, public intercession is a hyperconcentrated expression of a congregation's engaged stance toward the world. It articulates a congregation's priestly relationship with creation: the holy priesthood presents the groaning of creation before God. Such intercessions pack a potent centrifugal power that radiates outward far beyond Sunday morning.

How, exactly, might this relatively small and forgotten practice become a compressed expression of our public ministries of care, ethics, and missions? This process must assuredly begin by honestly facing and then naming areas of public pain and trauma each week in prayer, thus actively resisting the temptations to an escapist and sentimentalized faith.

To be sure, changing our public prayers is entirely insufficient if it is not also paired with public action. Prayer only becomes compelling and formative within a community when it is matched with redemptive ways of life. But it is not always clear which comes first. At times, a community begins to feed the hungry—and later becomes convicted to pray about the causes of systemic poverty and the tragedies of payday lenders. At other times, a pastor may lead a congregation in prayer about the vexing tenacity of structural poverty, and that—in turn—might prompt an informal discussion about gaps in local support services, gaps the church might fill. Regardless of the route toward sanctification, there stands a call to significantly change the trajectory of public prayer. Either path calls for God's people to intercede before God on behalf of the world.

Through the weekly practice of public prayer, diverse congregations carry diverse public traumas before God and pursue their priestly calling in the ministry of intercession. In so doing, they embody and enact their priesthood in Christ, a public priesthood that is commanded and empowered to cross the road and help a neighbor in need.

21

Sexism, Racism, and the Practice of Baptism in South Africa

A Reformed and Transformative Perspective

NICO KOOPMAN

I was born and raised in South Africa under apartheid. At the time, the law of the land delineated and recognized four distinct racial groups: white, Black, Indian, and colored.[1] According to the law, I was "colored," a person of mixed race.

From childhood and onward, this comprehensive system of racial classification determined every aspect of my life. It determined where I could play, with whom I could study, how I could receive health care, with whom I could fall in love, where I could work, and in what neighborhood I could raise my

---

1. Apartheid law made provision for four racial or color groups: (1) white people or Europeans; (2) Indians, i.e., people from India and broader Eastern origins; (3) the majority of the population groups, those described as Blacks or Africans; and (4) coloreds, the so-called mixed or hybrid peoples, with some ancestry among the indigenous Khoi and San first (or native) people, indigenous Black people, European persons, and also people from various Eastern countries like India, Indonesia, and Malaysia.

children. Even in death, apartheid would determine where my body would be buried. Differently colored bodies would remain separate, in life and in death.

During the 1980s I served as a pastor just outside Cape Town. Our local white and colored congregations decided to bring our young people together for an evening of fellowship. Afterward, a young man from my congregation confessed to me that he had touched the hand of a white person for the first time that night.

But apartheid did more than separate us from white people. It portrayed and treated us as inferior. Nonwhites were systematically made to doubt their full humanity and, in this, their equal status alongside white people as children of God. Colored citizens, like me, faced an additional stigma. Being "mixed," we were not considered a "pure race"; therefore, we were the most inferior race of all. Some Christians even misused the Bible and Christian theology to support and advance this discrimination against those of "hybrid" or "mixed" race.

As if racism were not enough, women in apartheid South Africa had to cope with the powers of sexism in law, culture, and religion. Women faced a wide variety of intersecting racial and sexual pressures in their homes, churches, schools, the marketplace, and the public square. Parents, teachers, politicians, and preachers supported sexist policies and patterns that suppressed women and denied their full humanity. In apartheid South Africa, about the only thing that knew no boundary was the push and pull of racism and sexism in our lives.

Although the reforms of post-apartheid South Africa have largely dismantled the racist and sexist legal structures, the cultural patterns of division and hierarchy remain. During our first twenty-five years of South African democracy, a lot of progress has been made in our laws and institutional cultures, but there is still so much work to be done.[2] The virus of racism and sexism continues to contaminate every sphere of our lives together.

2. For a recent set of essays on the challenges of racism in scientific research in South Africa, see Jonathan Jansen and Cyrill Walters, eds., *Fault Lines: A Primer on Race, Science, and Society* (Stellenbosch: African Sun Media, 2020). For a helpful collection of essays by mostly Reformed scholars on the challenges of sexist prejudices and practices on the continent of Africa, see Elna Mouton et al., eds., *Living with Dignity: African Perspectives on Gender Equality* (Stellenbosch: African Sun Media, 2015). The South African Reformed feminist theologian L. Juliana M. Claassens analyzes the challenge of discrimination, violence, and rape of women in her book *Claiming Her Dignity: Female Resistance in the Old Testament* (Collegeville, MN: Liturgical Press, 2016). For a reflection on the inadequate attention of Black Liberation Theology to sexual injustice and inequality, see a recent book by the stalwart South African Reformed theologian Allan Aubrey Boesak, *Children of the Waters of Meribah: Black Liberation Theology, the Miriamic Tradition, and the Challenges of Twenty-First-Century Empire* (Eugene, OR: Wipf & Stock, 2019).

Sadly, the Reformed Churches in South Africa still reflect many of these same divisions and inequalities. All too often Reformed Christians play an active role in perpetuating the patterns and practices of division and hierarchy. In Scripture, members of the church of Jesus Christ are clearly called to love their neighbors, to do justice, and to unite diverse members together in the body of Christ. Although the biblical call for action is clear, the church draws back in fear, division, and animosity.

This chapter declares that the Reformed practice of baptism should inform and initiate our public response to the forces of racism and sexism in society. I argue that baptism is not merely a private or personal ritual that is bound within the four walls of the church. *Baptism is a profoundly public act, with far-reaching implications for our cultural and political lives in the world.*

Throughout my life and the struggles with racism and sexism, I have always found comfort, encouragement, and direction in the practice of baptism. In a world that questions and undermines my dignity and identity, the sacrament reminds me of my status, position, and worth within the person of Jesus Christ. As a child growing up under apartheid, I was promised a life of constant exclusion from cradle to grave. In the church's baptism I was offered a life of infinite inclusion. The waters of baptism were a living witness to me, a public proclamation, sign, symbol, affirmation, celebration, and anticipation of my place in the Lord's baptismal embrace. Those waters would spill out of the font into my public life; they impacted how I responded to sexist and racist laws, institutions, and cultural patterns. The primary and inclusive identity that I found in baptism informed my response to all the secondary identities that I encountered in myself and those around me.

Baptismal Politics

During the 1970s, racial tensions in the United States were particularly heated. Many white Reformed churches wanted to avoid the discussion of race and politics altogether. The church, they believed, should be spiritual, not political.

Rather than shouting, "You're wrong!" Richard Mouw, a Reformed philosopher and ethicist, pointed these Christians to their own practice of baptism. He asked them to reflect on what baptism actually means in the Reformed tradition. What does it accomplish? What does it signify? And finally, what are its consequences for their public lives?

Mouw built his case not through a moral lecture but through a story. He recalls a moment in the life of his white church when a Black child named

Darryl was brought forward to be baptized. The Reformed ritual called for white bodies to stand. It called for white voices to affirm that this black body was now joined to their bodies. As one body, the ritual demanded that they vow to defend, nurture, instruct, and love this Black child as he grows into the life and witness of Christ and his church.

Mouw invites his readers to reflect on the impact this liturgical practice *should* have on a white congregation who stands with Darryl as he is baptized:

> To love Darryl will require that we try to look at the world from his point of view, to make his hopes and fears our very own. To assume an obligation for his Christian instruction and nurture is to commit ourselves to attempting to understand what the gospel means for him, with his tradition and history. It means that from here on in we will have to keep Darryl in mind when we plan our sermons, write our liturgies, plot out our educational programs. All of this will involve us in change, in patterns of "contextualization" that are different from those which have characterized our lives in the past. We are also going to have to pay close attention to what others are saying to and about Darryl. If American society tries to treat him like a second-class citizen, we will have to protest on his behalf, since he is our brother in a holy nation of kings and priests. If he is ever the object of a cruel joke or a vicious slur, we will have to consider this to be an affront to the very Body of Christ. If someone ever complains that he is not "one of our own kind," we will have to respond with the insistence that, through the blood of Jesus, we are Darryl's "kind."[3]

Mouw does not offer an abstract lecture on racial justice. The story, the practice of baptism, does much of the work for him. Amid a culture of white supremacy and racist exclusion, Darryl's baptism can and must be understood as a profoundly public and subversive act. Darryl's baptism has consequences for the public life of every person who stood up for him that Sunday.

Building on Mouw's witness, this chapter briefly explores the pervasive psychological, structural, and social power of racism and sexism.[4] It then examines how these destructive cultural forces intersect with Reformed theological insights on baptism. In all, the chapter is meant to construct a "baptismal lens" through which Christians might see their public calling to seek the justice, equality, and unity of Christ—*in and through baptism.*

3. Richard J. Mouw, "Baptismal Politics," *Reformed Journal* 28, no. 7 (July 1978): 2–3.
4. This analysis of racism, sexism, and the meaning of baptism draws heavily from Mouw's decades-long work on these themes. It is, of course, revisited, expanded, contextualized, and freshly applied.

A Threefold Understanding of Racism and Sexism

I have long found Hans Opschoor and Theo Witvliet's multileveled framing of racism profoundly useful. Together they define racism as "the specific ideology that organises and regulates the exploitation and dependence of a specific 'race' on the basis of the assumed cultural and or logical inferiority of that 'race.' In this way actual differences in power are maintained and intensified."[5] Herein racism consists of three elements: first, the conscious and mainly subconscious racist picture that we have of other races; second, the embodiment of this picture in social and political structures; third, a religious or philosophical rationale for this picture and its corresponding structures.[6]

In South Africa racial prejudices and their corresponding structures were continuously justified by religion. Apartheid theology provided an ideological support for the culture and politics of apartheid. This religious dimension enhanced, deepened, and internalized racism to subconscious levels and further justified the racist structures that were built on these mostly subconscious prejudices.

Swimming in the waters of apartheid, both oppressor and oppressed internalized these racist beliefs, patterns, and structures. Some of those on the underside of racism came to believe that they were inferior and therefore accepted the oppressive structures that corresponded with those beliefs. They, too, needed liberation from deeply embedded racial prejudice.[7] Thus, on the level of racial prejudice, all people are racist. That said, the model also makes clear that, on the level of structural racism, the truly racist are only those who have the political and economic power to structurally embody and enforce their racial prejudices.

Finally, this threefold understanding of racism as subconscious, structural, and religious can help us understand many other forms of discrimination, including

5. Hans Opschoor and Theo Witvliet, "De Onderschatting van het Racisme," *Wending* 38, no. 9 (1983): 554–65, my trans. from Dutch.

6. This picture of the other races entails categorization in terms of inferiority and superiority. In a 1998 article, I refer to the categorization of various race groups by some anthropologists into Caucasians, i.e., the white races who are closest to the so-called ideal human form, the Greeks. The other races are increasingly further from this ideal and closest to the ape tribes. These races are the Mongoloids, Australoids, and Negroids. In that article I also express my reservations about the continued use of the term "race." See Nico Koopman, "Racism in the Post-Apartheid South Africa," in *Questions about Life and Morality: Christian Ethics in South Africa Today,* ed. Louise Kretzschmar and Len Hulley (Pretoria: Van Schaik, 1998), 153–68. The famous Black social theorist Cornel West traces the development of modern racism back to the classical revival in the Early Renaissance (1300–1500) and to the scientific revolution of the seventeenth century. Both the revival of classical aesthetics and cultural ideals and the positivistic scientific investigation have fed the exploitation and violence that racism is. See Cornel West, *Prophesy Deliverance! An Afro-American Revolutionary Christianity* (Philadelphia: Westminster, 1982), 50–59.

7. This point is argued strongly by Frantz Fanon, *Black Skin, White Masks* (London: Pluto, 1952).

sexism.[8] Like racism, sexism involves a threefold (subconscious, structural, and religious) system of inequality and injustice. The sinful human desire to dominate, divide, and dismiss is not limited to race. Women of all colors experience its power as they live and move through sexist spaces. Here I commend the work of the American feminist and Reformed theologian Serene Jones, among others.[9]

Within the psychosocial world of sexism, women are linguistically and structurally construed as inferior to men in their physical, psychological, intellectual, moral, spiritual, and leadership abilities (among others). Gendered hierarchies and structures reflect, solidify, and—in turn—inform these beliefs in male superiority.

Gender essentialism can be a critical tool in the hands of sexists. Thus persons of a particular gender are said to have essential qualities that make up their core identity. It is assumed that these gendered characteristics do not vary over time, are immune to historical forces, and cannot be attributed to culture or convention. Within this form of essentialism, features of women and men are framed in oppositional terms: women are relational and dependent, men are autonomous and independent. Such lists are often framed in complementary terms: women are emotional and men rational, women are receptive and men assertive. Such lists of gender essentials often reflect and reinforce gender hierarchies: men are physically superior and women are emotionally superior. In a sexist society, gender essentialism is weaponized for the purposes of gender dominance.

In the end, psychological, structural, and theological sins of racism and sexism embed themselves in our minds and hearts, our culture and politics, and even—sadly—our worship. Where does one even begin to respond to these deep and pervasive forms of division and domination? In the next section we begin to explore the liberating and unifying power of God's baptismal flood.

Waters of Justice, Dignity, and Belonging

The South African Reformed theologian Adrio König[10] gives a helpful fourfold description of the inclusive work of baptism.[11] First, baptism confirms

---

8. It is not difficult to explain how these three dimensions of racism are also constituent elements of classism, sexism, ageism, ableism, and speciesism.

9. See Amy Plantinga Pauw and Serene Jones, eds., *Feminist and Womanist Essays in Reformed Dogmatics* (Louisville: Westminster John Knox, 2006); and Serene Jones, *Feminist Theory and Christian Theology: Cartographies of Grace* (Minneapolis: Augsburg Fortress, 2000).

10. Adrio König, *Die doop as kinderdoop èn grootdoop* (Pretoria: NGK Boekhandel, 1986), 18–59.

11. Besides these four inclusive meanings of baptism, König also states that baptism confirms our forgiveness, cleansing from sin, rebirth into new spiritual, moral, and material life, and receiving the gift of the Holy Spirit. König, *Die doop as kinderdoop èn grootdoop*, 46–53.

and celebrates that our baptized bodies and souls belong to God. Baptism is a public declaration that we are God's prized property. Through his blood on the cross, he has purchased us. Like a king or a queen in the Old Testament who has just conquered a city and placed their own name on it (2 Sam. 5:9), we are baptized in the triune name of God. This naming implies both victory and ownership. The public implications of this divine purchase are clear: if baptized bodies belong to God, no one else can own or ultimately control them. An attack on a baptized body is an attack on God's property.

Second, according to König,[12] baptism also means that we are grafted into God's covenant promise (Acts 2:38–39; Gal. 3–4; Col. 2:11–12). The Old Testament covenantal formula is now applicable to us: I shall be your God, and you shall be my people (Jer. 7:23).[13] Through the baptismal waters the people of God are initiated into a *covenantal* mode of relating to God, neighbor, and all creation. The animals, plants and all the rest of creation are included in God's covenantal promises. Our care for the environment and our joyous relationship with it are a central theme in both the Old Testament and New Testament covenantal theology (cf. creation narratives, Sabbath and Jubilee laws, prophetic and eschatological visions). Baptism is therefore meant to initiate a public life that reflects the covenantal promises and work of God in the church, the society, and all creation.

Third, baptism solidifies our union with the life and work of Jesus Christ in history.[14] In its waters we are bound to Christ's historical patterns of love, justice, reconciliation, sacrifice, death, and resurrection. Baptism draws our story and our life into Christ's. The public implication of this is clear. In baptism I am called to participate in Christ's ministry of racial and sexual reconciliation in history. I have been recruited. We become participants in his cruciform life (Rom. 6:1–14; Gal. 2:19–20; Eph 2:1–10; Col. 2:12–13). The so-called Negro spiritual powerfully points to this participation when it hauntingly asks, "Were you there when they crucified my Lord?"

---

12. König, *Die doop as kinderdoop èn grootdoop*, 33–46.

13. The South African Reformed theologian Steve de Gruchy even argues that it is in and through this covenantal relationship with God that we enjoy the status of *imago Dei*. He affirms the traditional Christian conviction that to be human is to be created in God's image. In the framework of the covenantal relationship with God and fellow humans and even with the rest of creation, however, this status of being created in God's image comes to full fruition. See Steve de Gruchy, "Human Being in Christ: Resources for an Inclusive Anthropology," in *Aliens in the Household of God: Homosexuality and Christian Faith in South Africa*, ed. Paul Germond and Steve de Gruchy (Cape Town: David Philip, 1997), 247–48.

14. König, *Die doop as kinderdoop èn grootdoop*, 21–31.

Fourth and finally, baptism celebrates our incorporation into the church as the body of Christ.[15] We are not alone in the public work and witness of reconciliation. We are bound to brothers and sisters around the world. We are connected to a great cloud of witnesses that extends thousands of years into both the past and the future (1 Cor. 12; Eph. 4).

Here it is important to note that *the christological belonging found in baptism does not cut us off from those who have not been baptized.* In fact, baptism in Christ should inspire a deeper sense of connectedness, solidarity, and responsibility with our neighbors who exist outside the church. They are, after all, still a part of Christ's world. Through baptism we see whom they belong to.

This was precisely the argument made by Hendrikus Berhof, a Reformed theologian in the Netherlands.[16] He argues that, because of the grace experienced in baptism, Christ's grace needs to be publicly extended to those outside the walls of the church. Baptism, in this way, begins a public life and pattern of inclusion. Christ's grace, experienced in baptism, must be extended to those on the sociopolitical margins of society: the poor, the oppressed, the disabled, the foreigner, children, and others.

The American Reformed theologian Allen Verhey echoes the view that baptism restores a life of inclusion, equality, and mutual service:

> Baptism was also, of course, an act of the church, an act in memory of Jesus and in hope for God's good future, an act of faith, an act of receiving the grace of God and the promise of God by welcoming those who were different into a community of mutuality and equality. . . . A new identity was owned in baptism, and a new world was envisioned—an identity and a world in which sexual hierarchies (along with ethnic and class hierarchies) were radically subordinated to community and equality in Christ. . . . "No longer male and female" was an eschatological reality, but it made its power felt already in the mutuality and equality of members of the community and in a sexual ethic that honored singleness and chastity.[17]

Africa's most prized Reformed document is the Confession of Belhar.[18] This confession was formulated during the years of the high point of

---

15. König, *Die doop as kinderdoop èn grootdoop*, 31–33.

16. Hendrikus Berkhof, *Christelijk Geloof* (Leiden: Callenbach, 1979), 369–70.

17. Allen Verhey, *Remembering Jesus: Christian Community, Scripture, and the Moral Life* (Grand Rapids: Eerdmans, 2002), 194–95.

18. See Nederduitse Gereformeerde Sendingkerk in Suid-Afrika, *Die Belydenis van Belhar, 1986* [*The Confession of Belhar, 1986*] (Belhar, South Africa: LUS, 1986); https://www.research gate.net/publication/281585902_The_Belhar_Confession_-_English.

apartheid. It was drafted in 1982 and finally adopted in 1986. Since then, it has been adopted by many Reformed churches around the world, including in the United States. In an unforgettable manner this African confession articulates the public implications of Christ's one baptism for cultures struggling with systems of oppression and discrimination. Belhar confesses that the church is called to a public life of unity (art. 1), reconciliation (art. 2), and justice (art. 3). "We believe," the document declares, that the church's

> unity must become visible so that the world may believe; that separation, enmity and hatred between people and groups is sin which Christ has already conquered, and accordingly that anything which threatens this unity may have no place in the church and must be resisted. . . .
>
> We share one faith, have one calling, are of one soul and one mind; have one God and Father, are filled with one Spirit, are baptised with one baptism, eat of one bread and drink of one cup, confess one Name, are obedient to one Lord, work for one cause, and share one hope. . . . We [therefore] need one another and upbuild one another, admonishing and comforting one another; that we suffer with one another for the sake of righteousness; pray together; together serve God in this world; and together fight against everything that may threaten or hinder this unity. . . .
>
> This unity can take form only in freedom and not under constraint; that the variety of spiritual gifts, opportunities, backgrounds, convictions, as well as the diversity of languages and cultures, are by virtue of the reconciliation in Christ, opportunities for mutual service and enrichment within the one visible people of God.

Before we conclude this cursory exploration of the public implications of Reformed baptism, we should consider an important challenge from the Reformed feminist theologian Leanne Van Dyk. Like others before her, Van Dyk argues that sacraments like baptism have public and political implications. Van Dyk adds, however, that these public implications need to be made *explicit* to the people of God in worship.[19] The baptism of a women, for example, should be clearly communicated as a public declaration of her value, dignity, and full personhood in Christ.

Here Van Dyk draws on Calvin's sacramental theology, which sees God's grace moving powerfully in and through the sacrament of baptism. Baptism is not merely a symbolic act of memory for Calvin or for Van Dyk. Nor is

19. Leanne Van Dyk, "The Gifts of God for the People of God: Christian Feminism and Sacramental Theology," in Pauw and Jones, *Feminist and Womanist Essays in Reformed Dogmatics*, 204–20.

it merely a "spiritual" ritual of private devotion. Baptism is a public action that involves the presence and power of the living God, a power that has undermined and overcome the principalities and powers of this world. For Van Dyk, these powers include sexism, misogyny, and patriarchy. This sacramental approach to baptism implies both power and action when it comes to public life.

Van Dyk's emphasis of this action-oriented nature of baptism is very important. It aligns with the so-called *ex opera operato* nature of the sacraments.[20] This means there is action in and through baptism. Calvin viewed baptism indeed as a sign and symbol of God's invitational, inclusive, dignifying, and humanizing love and grace. In the washing of water, Van Dyk calls the people of God to recognize and respond to the presence and power of God and the divine call to publicly advocate for the dignity and equality of women in the sanctuary and the public square. For Calvin and Van Dyk, sacraments are promises, anticipations, and expectations of this new life. Through the work of the Holy Spirit, the sacraments are actively affecting, working, and bringing into being a whole new life. Calvin writes remarkably about this effectuating character of baptism:

> By these words, [Paul] not only exhorts us to imitation of Christ, as if he had said, that we are admonished by baptism, in like manner as Christ died, to die to our lusts, and as he rose, to rise to righteousness; but he traces the matter much higher, that Christ by baptism has made us partakers of his death, ingrafting us into it. And as the twig derives substance and nourishment from the root to which it is attached, so those who receive baptism with true faith truly feel the efficacy of Christ's death in the mortification of their flesh, and the efficacy of his resurrection in the quickening of the Spirit.[21]

According to Calvin, baptism *does something*. Through the washing of water, the Holy Spirit buries the old and lifts up the new. The power and presence of the Holy Spirit in baptism is good news for people hungering to overcome evils like racism and sexism. The Holy Spirit is alive and active in the waters of baptism, working to free us from racism and sexism for a new life of inclusive community. And, as Van Dyk argues, the congregation must *explicitly* hear this good news when the sacraments are celebrated in worship.

---

20. The Reformed theologian Daniel Migliore emphasizes the active, dynamic, and efficacious meaning of the sacraments. See Daniel L. Migliore, *Faith Seeking Understanding: An Introduction to Christian Theology*, 3rd ed. (Grand Rapids: Eerdmans, 2014), 291–99.

21. John Calvin, *Institutes of the Christian Religion*, trans. Henry Beveridge (Edinburgh: Calvin Translation Society, 1845; via Bible Library, 2010), 4.5.130.

Baptismal Action

Black and white, male and female alike—all are challenged through Christ's covenantal waters to join him in his historical work of racial and gender justice today. For those who wish to publicly honor their baptisms through tangible public action, I encourage them to consider three public avenues for baptismal engagement: raising awareness, reforming institutions, and mobilizing for action.

Here "raising awareness" has multiple meanings. It means that we must raise awareness of the substantial and subtle forms of racism and sexism all around us. It also means that we must raise awareness of the rich resources, the deep theological and spiritual wells that we Christians can drink from as we struggle against racism and sexism. The baptized need to understand that, when they emerge from the baptismal waters, they are entering into Christ's life of hospitality, justice, equality, and embrace. Finally, awareness means that we must persuade one another that the struggle against discrimination is not simply a "political" struggle. It is also a spiritual contest. The struggle for equality demands our best spirituality, theology, ministry, and worship. Baptism matters in the struggle for spiritual and political wholeness.

A second way in which we can publicly honor our baptism is through the reformation of our institutions—our Christian churches, families, and schools. Richard Mouw, in his words cited under the heading "Baptismal Politics" (above), calls for liturgical organizing. He argues that the presence of a new Black baptized member in the congregation should impact the congregation's planning and organizing, its sermons and its songs. The institution itself needs to change. It needs to be reformed in such a way as to remember and honor the baptism of Darryl. The church is not the only institution that may need to be reformed. How might our family systems need to change in order to honor the fact that our wives and daughters have been baptized into the power and dignity of Christ? I lead within a university, a notoriously difficult institution to reform. How might I honor my own baptism through the reformation of structures and practices within my own institution that still advance racist and sexist prejudices? How do I plan and work for a life of inclusion and equality with people from other religious and secular backgrounds? How do I ensure that the so-called thicker meaning of baptism does impact appropriately on the development of institutional policies, plans, procedures, processes, and especially practices that advance inclusion and equality?

Third and finally, baptismal visions of justice and equality need to be embodied and enacted through the people of God mobilized for public action.

Intentions need to be actualized, aspirations need to be operationalized. Our new baptized life in Christ needs to be made visible and tangible.

And yet, in all this action, we must realize the baptismal truth. We do not mobilize or empower ourselves. The Spirit of God, in and through Christ's baptism, mobilizes, directs, and empowers us. The Spirit enables us to both will (*thelein*) and do (*energein*) what is good (Phil. 2:13). The principalities and powers of racism and sexism cannot stand against the raging river of the baptismal font.

CONFESSION

22

Confession

Practice for Civil Public Discourse

KYLE DAVID BENNETT

On Valentine's Day 2020, the journalist Charles Pierce wrote in the magazine *Esquire* that American President Donald Trump "confessed" to the Ukraine charges. Pierce was referring to an interview in which Trump responded that he was not sorry he had sent his personal lawyer Rudy Giuliani to Ukraine. As indicated in the headline, "So Trump Basically Confessed to the Ukraine Charges," Pierce apparently took Trump's response as a confession. The URL link to the article, however, uses the word "admit," and Pierce begins by remarking that Trump "copped to it."[1] What's going on here? Did Trump confess? Or did he admit he was wrong? Or did he disclose that he did something wrong by denying it was wrong?

From the direction of Pierce's article, confession, admitting a wrong, and copping to it are evidently not the same. Pierce longs for Trump to *own up* to his wrongdoing and *acknowledge* the damage that has been done. Such acknowledgment would be more than accepting the claim that one did wrong

1. Charles P. Pierce, "So Trump Basically Confessed to the Ukraine Charges," *Esquire*, February 14, 2020, https://www.esquire.com/news-politics/politics/a30927792/trump-admit-rudy-giuliani-ukraine-impeachment/.

or admitting the wrong one did. Pierce's piece captures the spirit of the times. In the present day we not only want a truth that is told or disclosed; we also want a truth that is manifested by a person owning up to one's own wrongdoing and acknowledging the damage that has been done. In a culture of casual manipulation of power for personal interest and ubiquitous deceit across party and institutional lines, we not only want truth-telling, we also want confession. We long for restored relationships. And we know that restoration can only be secured through confession.

In this chapter I claim that the regular practice of confession is a profoundly public, social, and even political act. Christian practices, particularly those engaged in liturgical worship and beyond (e.g., spiritual disciplines), concretely and practically shape our everyday lives outside the institutional church. They are designed to shape our dispositions, comportment, and overall way of being in the world. Confession is no different. Rather than being a private practice of disclosing sin between us and God, confession patterns and organizes our overall manner of relating to others and communicating with them. The result of its practice cultivates society with others beyond the four walls of the sanctuary. To that end, I believe it behooves us as Christians to practice it. If confession is healthy for us and for society, then we should practice it for the health of society.

After discussing several manifestations of confession, I draw on a few insights from the Reformed tradition to help us understand more fully and richly the public nature of this practice and its end game. Our practice of confession is tied to how we as Christians should be engaging in discourse with our neighbor. Our confessing lives and our conversing lives should be consistent. There is a horizontal dimension to this practice that positively shapes our everyday interactive habits with our neighbor.

Confession: A Guide for the Perplexed

What *is* confession? What do we do when we confess? Common answers land somewhere in the terrain of saying we are sorry or admitting wrongdoing. But biblically, theologically, and philosophically, it is so much more than this. In the New Testament, the word *confession* [*exomologeō*/ἐξομολογέω] (e.g., Matt. 3:6; Mark 1:5; Acts 19:18; James 5:16) primarily means confession of sin. Those who confess their sins each say aloud, "I have been living out of sync with [*ek*] what we together [*homou*] say [*legō*] is right and ought to be done." It foremost signals that the confessor has not resembled something fully and is acknowledging it. In other words, "I am not like or similar to something I should be and I know it"; or, conversely, "I want to be like or similar to something." All confession has to do with how one lives and making others aware of our pursuit of a certain way of life and our shortcomings on the way. And there will always be shortcomings.

Using this as a guide, I make explicit and unpack several expressions of confession that many believers voice on a weekly basis. One might take the following as a sort of phenomenology of confession that unearths a typology of confession, a description of confession and the different ways we encounter and practice it. Confession is something: it is a phenomenon, and we recognize it when we see, hear, or do it. Here are a few forms it takes.

There is more than one way we as Christians refer to and practice confession. When we take stock of all these expressions, I think we better understand the force of this practice and the full scope of its influence. There are five forms: (1) confession of particular sins to God in private prayer; (2) confession of general sins to God in corporate worship; (3) confession of particular sins to a pastor, priest, or other fellow in the body of Christ; the final two are not focused on naming sins but on naming beliefs: (4) confession of beliefs or faith in public with or to the body of Christ; (5) beliefs codified in the noncanonical written word as corporately affirmed statements (e.g., the Westminster Confession of Faith). Our focus in this chapter will be on the first four, with most ink being spilled on the fourth expression.

Confession of sins in private prayer is most likely what comes to mind when we think of confession. When I enter my closet or kneel in the dark at the edge of my bed, I intentionally hide from the gaze of others and their earshot. I begin to pray with a greeting and almost immediately slide into "I'm sorry for . . . Please forgive me." In this particular expression of confession, we call to mind—that is, face up to and own—the subtlest and the significant wrongdoings that we are willing to identify and acknowledge, even the smallest demons. This is done exclusively before God; we privately and quietly apologize to him for committing them. When I name these misses of the mark, there is a sense in which I know that I am always *coram Deo*—that is, always present before the face of God. Like a baptized owl of Minerva, I show up late to what has already been seen and only now am mustering up the courage or strangling my pride to own up to what occurred.[2] The unique features of this expression of confession are that it (1) is done in private and (2) names my own specific wrongdoings.

---

2. Confession is tied to repentance but is slightly different. When I repent, I deny myself and my pursuit of myself as self-grounding. It is a revolution of my entire orientation. When I confess, however, I reject specific acts or deeds I have done that were wittingly or unwittingly pursued in a movement to ground myself in myself. The former is broader in scope and universal; the latter is specific and particular. For an enlightening discussion of the movement of

The second expression of confession is a corporate liturgical statement to God of our general sinful nature. "Please stand," I hear before I make this movement. My eyes then pass over words on a screen or a firm glossy paper I have in my hands. These are not my words, but I join in the rhythm of others, and my voice unites with theirs. "We have not loved you with our whole heart; we have not loved our neighbors as ourselves. We are truly sorry, and we humbly repent." This form of confession brings awareness to our condition or state as sinners. It does not have so much to do with the individual sins I have committed, though those do come to mind. Out of all the expressions of confession, this one can easily become routine, a formality. I can slyly hide behind the human race when I collectively utter admission of my general fallenness and proclivity toward sin. But that is part of the point: I need to confess, and I am not the only sinner. I am in the same condition as everyone else. Distinguishing features of this expression are that (1) it is done in corporate worship, (2) it is done in unison, and (3) it focuses on our condition as fallen creatures, not particular wrongdoings.

Confession of specific sins to a pastor, a priest, or representative (James 5:16) is another form of confession. For Christians who are not Catholic or Orthodox, this is not a typical understanding or experience of confession. But, on an experiential level, I wonder if it is. Don't I, as a Protestant, confess to a "priest" when I call my spiritual director or friend to confess my sin? Intention tells me that I hope and anticipate that after this conversation I will be "absolved" of my wrongdoing. As a Protestant I might claim that there is no mediator besides Christ, but in my everyday living I certainly behave as though I have "everyday priests" who, through pastoral encouragement and friendly challenging, help absolve me of my sins. I see them as authorities, and I receive their words as affirmations of grace that I should accept.[3] Unique features of this form of confession are that it is (1) disclosed to an individual and (2) done in private (apart from the congregation).

These first three forms of confession could be categorized as *penitential*.[4] That is, they display an acknowledgment of wrongdoing. The fourth expression

---

repentance, see Anthony J. Steinbock, *Moral Emotions: Reclaiming the Evidence of the Heart* (Evanston, IL: Northwestern University Press, 2014), 137–59.

3. Dietrich Bonhoeffer captures this insight: "A confession of sin in the presence of all the members of the congregation is not required to restore one to fellowship with the whole congregation. I meet the whole congregation in the one brother to whom I confess my sins and who forgives my sins." *Life Together*, trans. John W. Doberstein (New York: Harper Collins, 1954), 113.

4. Thomas Aquinas identified three acts or parts to penance: contrition, confession, and satisfaction. In contrition, I feel sorry for my sins and decide not to sin again; in confession, I call to mind my sins and confess them to a priest or religious authority; in satisfaction, I am

could be categorized as *creedal*. This confession is focused on stating our beliefs as we are surrounded by the believing community. In Reformed communities we sometimes refer to this as a public *profession* of faith. Generally speaking, there are two kinds of confessions we profess: (1) written documents key in identifying Christian orthodoxy in response to heresy (e.g., the Nicene Creed or the Athanasian Creed), and (2) written documents summarizing our particular tradition of Christian faith and practice (e.g., the Belgic Confession, Westminster Confession of Faith, Belhar Confession). When reciting or stating these, I am reminded that I come from a long line of believers. "My" faith is not something I created from scratch; it is something that is handed down to me.

As we can see in the context of several of these expressions, confession is not merely an *act*; it is also a *practice*. Christians are meant to habituate themselves to prayer in a variety of ways. This may be in the silence and solitude of the bedroom or participating in the liturgy with the congregation. Confession is practiced in its various forms on a daily and weekly basis.

But what is its goal? Why do it with such regularity? I propose that the end of confession is not merely to acknowledge wrongdoings or to make us aware of our sins. The purpose of confession is really about establishing and practicing "right relating"—between us, our triune God, our neighbors, and God's creation. The goal of confession is to live rightly with all creation and the Creator, who designed it. Confession reminds and thrusts its practitioner into that eschatological vision. In what follows, we will explore how confession, even in its most private form, is a social, public, and even political act.

Flipping Confession on Its Side: A Reformed Push

The practice of confession stretches beyond the four walls of the church. It spills into bedrooms at home, bathrooms at school, and cubicles at work. It lingers and latches on to everyday activities. Confession has what we might call a public or "horizontal dimension," a way in which it benefits wider society.[5] That is, confession is a way of loving our neighbor even when we do not intend it so.

This has been a key practice in the Reformed tradition since John Calvin. Calvin notes the importance of confession in cultivating humility and building

---

absolved by the priest and practice fasting, prayer, and almsgiving. See Thomas Aquinas, *God's Greatest Gifts: Commentaries on the Commandments and the Sacraments* (Manchester, NH: Sophia Institute Press, 1992), 95–96.

5. On the meaning of "horizontal dimension" and its relation to spiritual disciplines, see my book: Kyle David Bennett, *Practices of Love: Spiritual Disciplines for the Life of the World* (Grand Rapids: Brazos, 2017), particularly 9–15.

community: "Besides the fact that ordinary confession has been commended by the Lord's mouth, no one of sound mind, who weighs its usefulness, can dare disapprove it."[6] For, Calvin writes, "if you consider how great is our complacency, our drowsiness, or our sluggishness, you will agree with me that it would be a salutary regulation if the Christian people were to practice humbling themselves through some public rite of confession."[7] There is a sort of practical bent here. Calvin sees confession as a practice not simply commanded by God but also as a profoundly *useful* and *public* practice—a practical tool for awakening hard and forgetful hearts and drawing them together. Confession is a practice that disciples may use to construct community and cultivate right relations.

The Dutch Calvinist Abraham Kuyper (1837–1920) was clued in to the usefulness of public confession. In his treatise titled *The Implications of Public Confession*, he connects the practice of confession to a believer's public membership in society.[8] Here Kuyper's focus is on a young person's *public* profession of faith.[9] He argues for the need to catechize children in the tenets of the faith and prepare them for eventual public articulation of those tenets. Parents must teach their children to "sing [their] Savior's praise" so that they might publicly rise to their "Lord's defense at every occasion."[10] In other words, *profession of faith within the church is a training ground for profession of faith in public.*

Throughout the essay, Kuyper's prescriptions show the rigorous process by which public confession incrementally settles into our interactive habits and practices. Kuyper understood that one's ability to confess and defend the faith in the public square does not happen overnight. Confession must be practiced. For the content of the faith to settle in and the benefit to be seen, one must practice confession for a lifetime. This practice, Kuyper believed, should begin early in one's development.

What Kuyper's essay reveals is that our profession of faith within the sanctuary has concrete bearing on how we interact with our neighbor in the public

6. John Calvin, *Institutes of the Christian Religion*, ed. John T. McNeill, trans. Ford Lewis Battles, 2 vols. (Philadelphia: Westminster, 1960), 3.18.

7. Calvin, *Institutes* 3.18.

8. Abraham Kuyper, *The Implications of Public Confession*, trans. Henry Zylstra (Grand Rapids: Zondervan, 1934). These devotions, published in a newspaper Kuyper founded, were part of a series of reflections on the sacraments, baptism, public confession, and the Lord's Supper. Of the forty-four devotions written, twelve were on public confession. He makes a strong link between confession and the other practices.

9. For a discussion of Kuyper's view of public discourse in his dialogue with a contemporary American pragmatist, see Kyle David Bennett and Jeppe Bach Nikolajsen, "The Practice of Pluralism: Jeffrey Stout and Abraham Kuyper on Religion and Civil Solidarity," *International Journal of Public Theology* 8, no. 1 (February 2014): 67–84.

10. Kuyper, *Implications of Public Confession*, 24.

square. Insofar as public confession helps us remember the content of our faith and build up the courage to state it in front of others, there is an apologetic strand to confession. It eventually assists us in defending the faith.[11] According to Kuyper, we are God's viceroys on earth, here to represent and defend him. Practicing confession is a form of honoring God and serving Christ. It is "suitable armor" for battle, and the practice of confession trains and qualifies us for battle.[12]

Here Kuyper is clearly shining light on a deep social imaginary within the Reformed tradition. The practice of confession, whether done in public or private, shapes how we concretely interact with our neighbors in the world. Seemingly private practices like confession actually have significant public import. They shape us, and in turn we shape others and thus society. Acknowledging my sins and faith before God is a vertical practice, but there is a horizontal dimension to it. Similarly, this horizontal practice of professing my faith to the body of Christ has an inverted horizontal dimension to it that shapes and benefits the public square. It shapes a citizen's interactions with those outside the body of Christ.

Whether our confession is penitential or creedal, we are publicly naming and witnessing to ultimate goods and a vision of the good life. We are doing this not simply for ourselves, but also for our neighbors. In each confession we are, directly or indirectly, explicitly or implicitly, stating the nature of the world and declaring how human society ought to be patterned. Every time we confess a word like "creation," we are telling others that all materiality was designed and is good; every time we ask for "forgiveness," we are pointing to an alternative way of relating; every time we say "Lord," we mark our political allegiance. Hidden in the vocabulary, posture, attitude, and desires of confession is a vision of the good life. Confession is political through and through. In confession, we are remembering, anticipating, and creating a politic—a way of living together.

In his essay, Abraham Kuyper focuses primarily on the confessions of young people. Youth pastors have much to champion here. But the principles and understanding of confession are relevant for all of us, regardless of our age. Confession is a way of rehearsing the grammar of our faith.[13] Through it, we learn how to speak and to name reality. Through it, we remind ourselves how to live in this reality.

11. Kuyper, *Implications of Public Confession*, 24, 27.
12. Kuyper, *Implications of Public Confession*, 23; cf. 71. For insight into the metaphor of combat and battle in the public square in Kuyper, see Henry R. Van Til, *The Calvinistic Concept of Culture* (Grand Rapids: Baker Academic, 2001), 131.
13. James K. A. Smith, *Letters to a Young Calvinist: An Invitation to the Reformed Tradition* (Grand Rapids: Brazos, 2010), 52.

Finally, as Kuyper rightly notes, confession instructs us in how to publicly interact with those who disagree with us. Stating where we stand (creedal) or where we have failed to stand (penitential) is a public witness to our neighbor. By what we say, we are introducing them to an alternative vision and understanding of the world, which they may not have ever heard or thought about. By what we do, we are revealing to them how to embody this vision and live within this understanding of the world, which might cause them to reflect on their own personal and political habits and practices.[14] In any of its forms, confession has as much to do with the world as it does with God and with the church.

Confessing for the Health of Society

What does it mean to be human? How do humans glorify God? The Reformed theologian Zacharius Ursinus (1534–83) put forward six responses in his commentary on the Heidelberg Catechism.[15] The last two declare that human beings were made (1) to preserve human society and (2) to give others what is due to them: "duties, kindness, and benefit." Human beings were made to cultivate, protect, and build up human society. They were made to offer justice and fairness, to "give others what is due."

The reason we all yearn for some form of society is precisely because we were made in God's relational image. We were made by a God who rightly relates within his intertrinitarian self and to his creation. This relational Creator calls his creatures to pursue the way of right relations. We were made to rightly relate to everyone (even enemies) and everything (even the land) in justice and fairness. *We publicly confess because we want to be right with our God and his creation.* Inherent within the Reformed catechesis of the Heidelberg Catechism is a certain vision of relating that the confessor enacts through the practice of confession.

Confession massages our hardened hearts, closed minds, and self-directed tongues and slowly trains them to interact with others, especially those who

14. If we want other residents in our homes, neighborhoods, and cities to practice confession, we must do so ourselves. What the seventh-century monk John Climacus stated regarding confession in the monastery can stand in our context as well: "Because there are others in the brotherhood who have unconfessed sins, I want to induce them to confess too." *The Ladder of Divine Ascent* (Boston: Holy Transfiguration Monastery, 2012), 72.

15. Zacharaias Ursinus, *The Commentary of Zacharaias Ursinus on the Heidelberg Catechism* [1616, Latin], trans. G. W. Williard, ed. E. D. Bristley, 2nd American ed. (Columbus: Scott & Bascom, 1852), 80–82, http://www.rcus.org/wp-content/uploads/2013/09/UrsinusZ_HC-Commentary-17-NEW-HC.pdf; Heidelberg Catechism, Lord's Day 3, Question 6, https://www.crcna.org/welcome/beliefs/confessions/heidelberg-catechism.

are very unlike us. The formative practices being habituated in confession will impact what comes to mind and what is blurted out when one is publicly accused of being wrong. In confession, our hearts are being reminded of our faults and our need for both God and neighbor. Our emotions are being invited to acknowledge where we have broken union with others. Our mouths are being trained to speak hard truths out loud. Our hands are learning to uplift others. Our feet are learning to rise in reverence and stand up for what is right and just. Over time, these movements of body and soul become like deposits in our bones. They come to find public expression, slowly and clumsily, in everyday interaction with our neighbors.

Our neighbor longs for this way of relating, just as we do. Who does not like humility, honesty, and forthrightness? Intellectual virtues like these can be traced back to similar movements in the practice of confession.[16] Confession cultivates salubrious characteristics in our lives that are beneficial for building up society with others. It invites society and contributes to its welfare. It builds up families and schools, businesses and teams, organizations and governments. Confession cultivates healthy cultures. Like every other liturgical practice or spiritual discipline, confession works on individuals and the institutions they form.

Society wants and needs confession. Charles Pierce yearns to see it in Donald Trump. Whether they know it or not, our neighbors are longing for public postures of humility, attitudes of self-examination and critique, and a desire for reconciliation and peace. We look for such characteristics and long for them in others. These are desirable features that attract interlocutors. They invite conversations and make space for substantive disagreement. Thereby

---

16. Calvin, *Institutes* 3.18. Calvin also writes:

Besides the fact that ordinary confession has been commended by the Lord's mouth, no one of sound mind, who weighs its usefulness, can dare disapprove it. For since in every sacred assembly we stand before the sight of God and the angels, what other beginning of our action will there be than the recognition of our own unworthiness? But that, you say, is done through every prayer; for whenever we pray for pardon, we confess our sin. Granted. But if you consider how great is our complacency, our drowsiness, or our sluggishness, you will agree with me that it would be a salutary regulation if the Christian people were to practice humbling themselves through some public rite of confession. For even though the ceremony that the Lord laid down for the Israelites was a part of the tutelage of the law, still the reality underlying it in some manner pertains also to us. And indeed, we see this custom observed with good results in well-regulated churches: that every Lord's Day the minister frames the formula of confession in his own and the people's name, and by it he accuses all of wickedness and implores pardon from the Lord. In short, with this key a gate to prayer is opened both to individuals in private and to all in public. (*Institutes* 3.4.11)

Note, in particular, Calvin's remarks on the usefulness of confession as it pertains to humility.

they draw others into fellowship and friendship,[17] promoting what the Reformed philosopher Richard Mouw calls "societal health."[18]

As followers of Jesus, our public interactions should always aim for communion and building up society *with* our neighbor. It should "keep the conversation going," not cut it off.[19] The practice of confession can set us on this path. We become confessors who are habituated in confessing hard truths and seeking justice and reconciliation. Thus we become practiced interlocutors who witness to another way of engaging in discourse. Our confession can be recognized as an act of civility. If civility leads us to genuinely care about others while being committed to truth, then there is much in the practice of confession that pushes us in that direction.[20]

Confession is a kind of "organizational therapy" that brings healing, not only to the community of faith but also to the various communities of this world.[21] Confession reveals patterns of communal interaction that are healthy and contribute to harmonious living with others. But it does not just *witness* to these patterns. It also *heals* existing patterns in our everyday living. Our familial, social, economic, and political patterns of interaction can all bear the salubrious marks of confession.

When we practice confession, we do not simply point to alternative ways of interacting; we also actually heal the broken ways in which we already interact with our neighbors. As we are shaped by confession, we are formed as citizens of political society.[22] When we carry the posture of confession into our everyday dealings in the world, it revitalizes, comforts, and pleases those

17. Cf. Charles Cummings, OCSO, *Monastic Practices*, rev. ed. (Collegeville, MN: Liturgical Press, 2015), 148–59. Communication (cf. the Latin *communicare*, "to share"), from a Christian standpoint, is ultimately about communing with others. It is existential: sharing space with others and living harmoniously with them. In all our dealings, to some degree, we should be communicating with the hope of fitting securely, efficiently, comfortably, and peacefully with others in our world.

18. Richard J. Mouw, *He Shines in All That's Fair: Culture and Common Grace* (Grand Rapids: Eerdmans, 2002), 76.

19. Richard J. Mouw, *Uncommon Decency: Christian Civility in an Uncivil World* (Downers Grove, IL: InterVarsity, 2010), 144.

20. Mouw, *Uncommon Decency*, 14.

21. Mouw, *Uncommon Decency*, 14; also see 48: "I wish the Christian churches could offer some guidance for this kind of organizational therapy. After all, we are supposed to be a model community in which other people can see how God intends diverse individuals and groups to get along."

22. Like Abraham Kuyper, Nicholas Wolterstorff draws a parallel between the knitting together of a congregation through practices and how a nation is bound by shared practices, such as the pledge of allegiance, education in history, and development of language: "A nation is bound together by shared practices—a common lifestyle which enables the members of the nation to work together and to communicate with one another on a broad spectrum of issues. Usually a common language is an important part of these shared practices." *Until Justice and*

who are on the receiving end of it. As Kuyper rightly argued, the practice of confession is never a private affair. It makes ripples far beyond the immediate, the individual, and the institutional church.

The posture, attitude, and embodied acts of confession are those we will one day fully inhabit. Our future is one in which it will become natural for us to say, "I'm sorry; I was wrong," and "This is what I believe; this is who I am." It can become natural for our neighbor to do the same. In confession we anticipate a new kingdom interaction with our God, our neighbor, and all creation. Here we anticipate communication that leads to communion, interaction that brings integration. We long for this day, and so does our neighbor.

Our ability to confess, reconcile, and communicate with our neighbor is not automatic. It is actually a spiritual exercise that all citizens must practice, as the philosopher Pierre Hadot (1922–2010) reminded us.[23] In order to dialogue well, a citizen must be spiritually formed. For us as Christians, this is further charged: to interact like Christ, we need to be formed by the Spirit (Gal. 5:22–23). This involves being sensitive to the wounds of others. We must genuinely care about the conversation. As an act of hospitality, we need to make space, for us and for our neighbor, to be wrong. We need to get behind confession's goal of redemption and healing. We must examine our conscience and be willing to acknowledge our obstinacy when it gets in the way.

Though it seems minor, changing the way we interact is good news to the broken and ostracized. Changing how the city interacts is, in and of itself, an act of seeking the welfare of the city (Jer. 29:4–7). We bring the healing of Christ to neighbors when we practice confession. And we serve neighbors when we bring those movements and habits of confession into our conversation with them. Thus we witness to an alternative politic, a present and coming kingdom, one we are destined for and one for which we all long.

Peace Embrace (Grand Rapids: Eerdmans, 1987), 100–101. The practice of confession knits together a society as much as it builds up a congregation.

23. Pierre Hadot, *Philosophy as a Way of Life: Spiritual Exercises from Socrates to Foucault* (Oxford: Blackwell, 1995), 89–93; especially see 93: "Dialogue is only possible if the interlocutor has a real desire to dialogue; that is, if [the other] truly wants to discover the truth, desires the Good from the depths of [the] soul, and agrees to submit to the rational demands of the Logos."

23

Piety and Public Life

The Public Imitation of Christ

JESSICA JOUSTRA

How we spend our days is, of course, how we spend our lives.
—Annie Dillard, *The Writing Life*

I witnessed a profound testament to Annie Dillard's observation during a recent memorial service. John, a much beloved citizen in my community, had passed away.[1] On the day of his memorial service, hundreds of cars from all over town filled the parking lot of our local church.

Inside the sanctuary, Dillard's insight took on flesh as the community testified to the power of John's life by recalling mundane but beautiful anecdotes from his day-to-day work and service. A community-driven volunteer, John devoted much of his time to various organizations and community institutions as a committed supporter and board member. A front-runner in computer technology, John was a sought-after business leader and consultant. He was known for his unique blend of generosity, humility, and skill in the

---

1. John is not his actual name.

marketplace. A family man, John was devoted to his wife of fifty-plus years. He was an attentive and supportive father, grandfather, and great-grandfather. And, most importantly, John was a faithful disciple of Jesus Christ.

The stories that friends, family, and coworkers shared about John's life were beautiful. As I listened to them, however, I began to notice an uncomfortable pattern. "John did wonderful work in the community," friends recalled, "*but* when he got sick, none of that mattered anymore. All that mattered was his love for Jesus." "We were grateful for John's technical acumen and business savvy, *but* what was really significant were the Bible studies he started in the business community."

That little word "but" haunted many of the stories told about his day-to-day life. John was indeed a picture of Christian piety, and I am grateful the community could recognize, give thanks for, and find comfort in that aspect of his life. *But* what about his public life? What about his work, his volunteering, his board service? What about the jobs he created? The community problems he solved? The organizations and institutions he helped to build? Is it really true that John's "spiritual" life was the only thing that truly mattered?

Piety and Public Life: A Destructive Dichotomy

The stories told at John's funeral are hardly unique. Emphasizing the importance of personal spirituality above, or even in opposition to, public action is a common refrain in North American evangelicalism. Rather than attest to the ways in which piety and action are interwoven, evangelicalism has all too often pulled the two apart with a synthetic (and destructive) dichotomy. According to David Miller, a theologian and a businessman, the church in North America "all too frequently sends the signal that work in the church matters but work in the world does not."[2]

Within this synthetic dichotomy, so-called spiritual elements like prayer and piety, missions and evangelism are what truly matter. While material and mundane tasks, like jobs, errands, committee meetings, email, and so on—the things that, for most of us, make up much of "how we spend our days"—are at

2. David W. Miller, *God at Work: The History and Promise of the Faith at Work Movement* (Oxford: Oxford University Press, 2006), 10. Pastors, too, have reflected on the pervasive nature of this dichotomy. One pastor reported, "In sermon after sermon I had called [my congregation] to give more time, more money, more energy to the work of the church. Little did I understand or affirm their callings in the world. I had inadvertently created a secular/sacred divide in which the 'sacred' calling of the church was pitted against their 'secular' callings in the world." Skye Jethani, "Uncommon Callings," *Christianity Today*, January 14, 2013, http://www.christianity today.com/le/2013/winter/uncommon-callings.html.

best indifferent to the gospel. At worst, these material things are antagonistic to gospel work, distracting us from our *true* service in God's kingdom. These material things will waste away; the only thing that will truly last is the spiritual.

Piety and Public Action in Reformed Theology

John's life, shown by his day-to-day action, refused to accept this evangelical dichotomy between piety and public action. John's work and worship were one: whether he was solving a technological issue or studying the Scriptures, he was living his day-to-day life *coram Deo*, before the face of God. Though it is too late to ask him, I am confident that John's more integrated life of piety and public action was deeply informed by the Reformed community that raised him.

John's integrated life bears the fingerprints of the holistic theology of Herman Bavinck (1854–1921). Raised within the conservative Calvinistic pietism of the Netherlands, Herman Bavinck knew and cherished a rich spiritual tradition of worship and prayer.[3] But, as Bavinck's theology developed, he came to argue that knowing and following Jesus did not mean disengaging with the world, but quite the opposite. For Bavinck, a spiritual and personal union *in Christ* should drive the Christian toward material and public action *in the world*.

As a young man, Bavinck took a decisive step toward world engagement in his choice of schooling. Opting against the confessional university of his denomination, Bavinck attended the "aggressively modernist theological faculty" at Leiden University.[4] For some in Bavinck's community, his choice signaled a departure from the pietistic theology of his youth toward the more world-engaging (even worldly!) modern theology.[5] But Bavinck did not see it that way. He refused to capitulate to this "duality of faith and culture."[6] As he matured, Bavinck went on to develop and publicly model a form of Christian spirituality that was deeply committed to public life. To use Richard Mouw's terminology, Bavinck sought to develop a holy form of worldliness.[7]

---

3. James Eglinton, *Trinity and Organism: Towards a New Reading of Herman Bavinck's Organic Motif* (London: Bloomsbury T&T Clark, 2012), 5.

4. Eglinton, *Trinity and Organism*, 4.

5. James Eglinton, *Bavinck: A Critical Biography* (Grand Rapids: Baker Academic, 2020), 71–72, 87–89.

6. George Harinck, "'Something That Must Remain, If the Truth Is to Be Sweet and Precious to Us': The Reformed Spirituality of Herman Bavinck," *Calvin Theological Journal* 38 (2003): 252.

7. Richard J. Mouw, *Called to Holy Worldliness* (Philadelphia: Fortress, 1980).

Two theological themes ground and direct Bavinck's approach to a spirituality of cultural engagement. First, he works with the dual metaphors of "pearl" and "leaven" in his description of the gospel. These metaphors, mixed as they may initially seem, undergird his creative fusion of piety and public action. The second is how Bavinck understood the imitation of Christ in the world. This public and pious vision for discipleship was, for Bavinck, the "heart of the spiritual life."[8] In this brief chapter, I offer these two concepts as theological resources for Christians wrestling with the relationship between their spiritual and material lives in the world.

Pearl and Leaven

"The kingdom of heaven," Jesus declares, "is like leaven that a woman took and hid in three measures of flour, till it was all leavened" (Matt. 13:33). To this, Jesus adds, "The kingdom of heaven is like a merchant in search of fine pearls, who, on finding one pearl of great value, went and sold all that he had and bought it" (13:45–46).[9]

For Bavinck, these two images describe not only *what* the gospel proclaims but also *how* that proclamation is manifested in the world. First and foremost, Bavinck asserts, the gospel is a pearl. It is a unique and irreplaceable treasure, an object of great cost and affection. In order to obtain it, we "sell everything" we have.[10] And why would we forfeit everything for this pearl? Because it is the "'power of salvation to everyone who believes' (Rom. 1:16)."[11]

However, as precious as it is, the pearl of the gospel cannot be hidden away, out of sight. Instead, like a *leaven*, the gospel goes out into the world and transforms, restores, and lifts it up.[12] The gospel is not simply precious; it

---

8. Dirk van Keulen, "Herman Bavinck's Reformed Ethics: Some Remarks about Unpublished Manuscripts in the Libraries of Amsterdam and Kampen," *The Bavinck Review* 1 (2010): 38.

9. All Scripture quotations in this chapter are from ESV unless otherwise indicated.

10. Herman Bavinck, "The Catholicity of Christianity and the Church," trans. John Bolt, *Calvin Theological Journal* 27 (1992): 224.

11. Herman Bavinck, *Reformed Dogmatics*, vol. 4, *Holy Spirit, Church, and New Creation*, ed. John Bolt, trans. John Vriend (Grand Rapids: Baker Academic, 2008), 396.

12. As Bavinck writes,

> Sin has corrupted much; in fact, everything. The guilt of human sin is immeasurable; the pollution that always accompanies it penetrates every structure of humanity and the world. Nonetheless sin does not dominate and corrupt without God's abundant grace in Christ triumphing even more (Rom. 5:15–20). The blood of Christ cleanses us from all sin[;] it is able to restore everything. We need not, indeed we must not, despair of anyone or anything. The Gospel is a joyful tiding, not only for the individual person but also for humanity, for the family, for society, for the state, for art and science, for the entire cosmos, for the whole groaning creation. ("Catholicity of Christianity," 244)

also is powerful and public. In the words of Bavinck, it is an "invisible change agent" moving in and through the world.[13] God's kingdom does not sit apart from or above this world; it permeates it.[14] The church, therefore—in spite of its flaws and failures—has made and will continue to make a real and tangible difference in society. It succeeds in this not by its own power and perfection but by the grace and power of the Holy Spirit.

Though Bavinck's thesis might look good on the page, holding both the precious and the pervasive nature of the gospel together in one life is difficult, to say the least. Some Christians today have a keen understanding of the gospel's precious, unique, and pearl-like qualities. They readily perceive how the Christian faith demands deep and costly piety, spiritual discipline, and an unbreakable and exclusive relationship with Jesus Christ. With their eyes fixed on heavenly reward, they hear Jesus's words clearly: "My kingdom is not of this world" (John 18:36) and "Great is your reward in heaven" (Matt. 5:12 NIV). But an exclusive or one-sided emphasis *only* on the pearl-like nature of the gospel will quickly privatize a gospel that is meant to be public.[15]

Other Christians have an acute sense of the leavening power of the gospel for public life and public action. They emphasize the way Jesus's words and actions are meant to change things *here* and *now*. Christianity brings with it a public and ethical program, not just for an individual's life, but also for the whole of society. Attentive to the public "reforming and renewing" power of the gospel for *this* world,[16] they proclaim the words of the prophets and of Jesus Christ: "Let justice roll down like the waters"; "do justice, . . . love kindness"; "I was a stranger and you invited me in, I needed clothes and you clothed me, I was sick and you looked after me, I was in prison and you came to visit me. . . . Whatever you did for . . . the least of these brothers and sisters of mine, you did for me" (Amos 5:24; Mic. 6:8; Matt. 25:35–36, 40 NIV). But with an exclusive emphasis on the leavening power of the gospel, Christians

13. Dirk van Keulen, "Herman Bavinck on the Imitation of Christ," *Scottish Bulletin of Evangelical Theology* 29, no. 1 (Spring 2011): 86. The gospel, Bavinck writes, "preached a principle so deep and rich and extraordinarily powerful that it was bound to exert a reforming influence on all earthly circumstances." "Christian Principles and Social Relationships," in *Essays on Religion, Science, and Society*, ed. John Bolt, trans. Harry Boonstra and Gerrit Sheeres (Grand Rapids: Baker Academic, 2008), 140.

14. Bavinck, "Christian Principles," 141. With this claim, Bavinck rejects any conception of Christianity that posits a dualistic relationship between grace and nature. Rather, grace *restores* nature. Grace, then, is not opposed to *nature*; it is opposed only to sin.

15. "The Gospel only changes the inward man, the conscience, the heart; the remainder stays the same until the final judgment." Bavinck, "Catholicity of Christianity," 237.

16. Bavinck, "Catholicity of Christianity," 237.

are in danger of conceding the distinctive driver and source of their power. Without a rootedness in the pearl-like nature of the gospel, the church could become like any other community organization seeking social and political change for its own ends.

In contemporary life, we hear these tensions echoed when evangelicals debate the relative importance of evangelism versus social justice, prayer versus policy, faith versus work. Bavinck refuses the dichotomy: the gospel is not *either* a pearl *or* a leaven. The gospel is *both* a pearl *and* a leaven.[17] Bavinck both connects the pearl and leaven and distinguishes them in a very particular, precise, and purposeful way. Exactly how Bavinck accomplishes this feat is important: it has real consequences for the church and its mission in the world.

The Pearl Precedes the Leaven

According to Bavinck, the gospel as a pearl must always precede its leavening power. This order and distinction is critically important. The gospel is, first and foremost, a pearl. Even if "Christianity had resulted in nothing more than this spiritual and holy community, even if it had not brought about any modification in earthly relationships, . . . it would still be and remain something of everlasting worth."[18]

With or without successful social change, the gospel of Jesus Christ is and always will be a pearl of great price. The meaning and worth of the gospel are not dependent on the social or political change it makes in the world. In the gospel, we receive the "good news of reconciliation and redemption from sin through the blood of the cross."[19] To miss the pearl-like qualities of the gospel, then, is to miss the crux of the story.

Although the pearl comes first, Bavinck is quick to declare that the gospel *does* affect change in the world. The pearl is, and must be, the impetus for leavening action in public life. Thus, while Bavinck's priority is undoubtedly on the gospel as pearl, he refuses to create a dichotomy between the pearl and the leaven. Instead, he establishes an order of causality—and this is critical. If the pearl does not come first, the gospel loses its distinctive claim. With no attention to its unique and precious power, the gospel becomes a rootless social movement, suddenly one more political ideology among many. The gospel is therefore *first* the "proclamation of the kingdom

17. Bavinck, "Catholicity of Christianity," 236.
18. Bavinck, "Christian Principles," 141.
19. Bavinck, "Christian Principles," 142.

of heaven and [God's] righteousness." This, Bavinck argues, "is the gospel that must remain, first in church and missions, but also beyond it, everywhere. It may not be robbed of its contents or dissolved into a political or social program."[20]

However, if the pearl is not accompanied by the leaven, Bavinck warns, Christians lose the rest of the gospel story and fail to grasp its transformative power for their public lives, their bodies, their vocations, their communities, and their world. "From this center" in the pearl, Bavinck writes, the leaven goes out and "influences all earthly relationships in a reforming and renewing way."[21] When the gospel, as a pearl, exerts extraordinary power in the world; it is a leaven. Rather than being in opposition to or indifferent toward public action, here piety drives and directs our action in the world.[22]

Therefore, for Bavinck, the pearl-like and leaven-like qualities of the gospel cannot and ought not be separated. They must, however, be distinguished. In short, Bavinck's scheme enables Christians to make a helpful distinction between the pearl and leaven without making a separation between the two that would truly prove fatal. Bavinck's model clarifies where the gospel's leavening power originates. It upholds the distinctive, precious, and unique salvific claims of the gospel as well as its public power and consequences. Though the pearl and the leaven remain distinct, Bavinck refuses to tear these two aspects of the gospel apart.

Rather than placing the material and spiritual in eschatological opposition, Bavinck argues that the two will one day experience a deep eschatological unity. For him, it is not simply the pearl-like qualities of the gospel that have eschatological import; the earthy, leavening work of the gospel with this present age will somehow both matter and endure in the next. Scripture, he argues, "consistently maintains the intimate connectedness of the spiritual and the natural," which will be "harmoniously united" when Christ returns in the new heaven and the new earth.[23] These words contain an astounding claim: not only is our present action deeply—though mysteriously—connected to God's coming kingdom, our vision of life in the Holy City (Rev. 21:2) must

20. Bavinck, "Christian Principles," 142.
21. Bavinck, "Christian Principles," 142.
22. Thus, for Bavinck, the gospel does not simply remain set apart, transcending the world; it also exercises a leavening power that permeates the whole. As Bavinck writes in another essay, "The Christian faith is not a quantitative reality that spreads itself in a transcendent fashion over the natural but a religious and ethical power that enters the natural in an immanent fashion and eliminates only that which is unholy. The kingdom of heaven may be a treasure and a pearl of great price, but it is also a mustard seed and a leaven." "Catholicity of Christianity," 236.
23. Bavinck, Reformed Dogmatics, 4:720.

also be filled with action. The Holy City is not merely spiritual, for "what we have sown [on earth] is harvested in eternity."[24]

The Imitation of Christ: Personal and Public

Distinguished, but never separated, the metaphors of pearl and leaven clarify the integral relationship between Christian piety and public action. But we are still left with an important question: How exactly does our piety undergird our public life? For Bavinck, part of the answer can be found in his nuanced understanding of the imitation of Christ. For him, knowing and following Jesus is *simultaneously* an act of personal piety and public action.

In the fifteenth century, the Roman Catholic monk Thomas à Kempis wrote a widely influential devotional titled *The Imitation of Christ*. In his opening chapter, reflecting on what it means to follow Jesus, Thomas à Kempis urges readers to "shift your affections from the things that you can see to the things you cannot see."[25] His understanding of imitation, saturated in a rich and Christocentric piety, emphasized self-denial, humility, cross-bearing, and detachment from the world. For Thomas à Kempis, and the thousands who read his devotionals, imitating Christ was profoundly *other*worldly.

Reacting against this otherworldliness, a more recent exemplar of christological imitation pledged to literally emulate the actions of Jesus as directly as possible in day-to-day life.[26] Charles Sheldon, an early proponent of this literalistic approach, articulated imitation in this way: "Our aim will be to act just as [Jesus] would if He was in our places."[27] Sheldon's work, "a classic of turn-of-the-[twentieth]-century popular Protestantism,"[28] drew strongly on the person of Jesus, who would transform the lives of those who follow him. His understanding of imitation is less attentive to Christ as *savior*, instead

24. Bavinck, *Reformed Dogmatics*, 4:727.

25. Thomas à Kempis, *The Imitation of Christ*, trans. William C. Creasy (Notre Dame, IN: Ave Maria, 1989), 31.

26. In his writing on imitation, Bavinck elaborates four dominant traditions of interpreting the imitation of Christ: the martyr, the monk, the mystic, and the modernist. See Herman Bavinck, *Reformed Ethics*, vol. 1, *Created, Fallen, and Converted Humanity*, ed. John Bolt (Grand Rapids: Baker Academic, 2019), 326–38.

27. Charles Sheldon, *In His Steps* (1896; repr., Old Tappan, NJ: Spire Books, 1975), 16. As many have noted, Sheldon's novel became quite popular during the social gospel movement. Later, Sheldon's work directly inspired the "What Would Jesus Do?" trend in North American evangelicalism in the 1990s. For part of the story about the popularity of the "WWJD" trend among young evangelicals, see "What Would Jesus Do? The Rise of a Slogan," *BBC World News*, December 8, 2011, http://www.bbc.com/news/magazine-16068178; and "What Would Jesus Do?," *World Magazine*, January 10, 1998, https://world.wng.org/1998/01/what_would_jesus_do?

28. John Howard Yoder, *The Politics of Jesus*, 2nd ed. (Grand Rapids: Eerdmans, 1994), 4.

focusing on Christ as the "moral ideal *par excellence*."[29] Such an understanding of imitation focuses our attention on Jesus primarily as an *ethical* example who guides our actions in this world.[30] For many who read Sheldon's work, imitating Christ was an activity that was profoundly *this*-worldly focused.[31]

Rather than alleviate the problematic dichotomy between piety and action, these two conceptions of imitation actually exacerbate the divide. Either we must imitate Christ in a distinctly *other*worldly manner, or we must look to Christ *as an* example while we focus on what is truly important: this-worldly action.

Bavinck's Reformed approach to imitation refuses to capitulate to such a dichotomy. He argues that, properly understood, the imitation of Christ has two distinct and yet necessarily connected aspects. The imitation of Christ is, first and foremost, an intimate and spiritual *union* with Christ. Second, as a consequence of that union, imitation "consists in shaping our lives in accord with Christ."[32] Our primary, spiritual fellowship with Christ must lead us toward active and public imitation of his "words and deeds."[33] In both the content and ordering of Bavinck's vision for imitation, we can hear resonances with his conception of the gospel as a pearl and a leaven.

29. James Gustafson, *Christ and the Moral Life* (Chicago: University of Chicago Press, 1968), 156. Gustafson elaborates on the tradition out of which Sheldon comes. In it, ethics "is basically the study of the *summum bonum*. The personal ethical question becomes, 'What is your ideal of life?'" Given this, as John Howard Yoder sharply contends, "the values" found in Sheldon's book that constitute imitating Christ "are not *materially* related to Jesus. 'Do what Jesus would do' means for Sheldon simply, 'Do the right thing at all costs'; but *what* is the right thing to do is knowable for Sheldon apart from Jesus." *Politics of Jesus*, 4–5.

30. Bavinck, *Reformed Ethics*, 1:336; Herman Bavinck, "The Imitation of Christ II (1918)," in *A Theological Analysis of Herman Bavinck's Two Essays on the* Imitatio Christi, trans. John Bolt (Lewiston, NY: Edwin Mellen, 2013), 402–40, here 407–8. In his essays on the imitation of Christ, Bavinck consistently raises these critiques of "modern" understandings of the imitation of Christ, as do more recent scholars, including Alister McGrath and James Gustafson. See James M. Gustafson, *Christ and the Moral Life* (Chicago: University of Chicago Press, 1979), 155–56; Alister McGrath, "In What Way Can Jesus Be a Moral Example for Christians?," *Journal of the Evangelical Theological Society* 34, no. 3 (September 1991): 290. With these emphases, Christianity can simply be reduced to the moral teachings of Jesus. Clement Attlee, though not a theologian, highlighted the trajectory this emphasis can take in a conversation with his biographer, Kenneth Harris. When asked if he believed in Christianity, he replied, "Believe in the ethics of Christianity. Can't believe the mumbo-jumbo." Kenneth Harris, *Attlee* (London: Weidenfeld & Nicolson, 1995), 564.

31. As E. J. Tinsley argues, there is a "marked *anti*mystical outlook of old Liberal theologians." "The Way of the Son of Man: The 'Imitation of Christ' in the Gospel Tradition," *Interpretation* 7 (1953): 418, emphasis added.

32. Bavinck, *Reformed Ethics*, 1:340.

33. Herman Bavinck, "The Imitation of Christ I [1885–86]," in Bolt, *Bavinck's Two Essays on the* Imitatio Christi, 372–401, here 400. Bavinck expands his definition of the *second* aspect of imitation with these words, in the same essay: we imitate the "virtues and obligations which conform to God's law that Christ in his words and deeds leaves as an example for us."

For Bavinck, Jesus Christ is both the redeemer of our souls and the moral director of our public lives. These two aspects should be distinguished but never separated. Christ is not *merely* an example of moral or public action. Moral action is not a first step leading to spiritual union with Christ. If this were the case, Christian discipleship would be an exercise in fear and futility, for who could, on their own, earn union with Christ or live up to his demands for public justice and righteousness?[34] If Christ is our moral model and nothing more, "then he comes to judge us and not to save us."[35] Facing such an unattainable goal on our own, we would quickly—and rightly—become discouraged. All imitation and public moral action must therefore begin with the spiritual union and redemption that is found in Jesus Christ. Once we know Christ as our savior, Bavinck argues, only then can we dare look to him as our moral example.[36]

Although imitation begins with spiritual union in Christ, it must end with public action that emerges from said union.[37] The lives of those who have been saved by grace through the work of Christ on the cross are called to take on the very form and shape of Christ's life in their own lives. Followers can only do this because Christ has first been united to them, through the work of the Holy Spirit.[38]

Molding one's public life to a christological pattern that is *external* feels awkward at best; at worst it feels either impossible or even coercive. Therefore, this first aspect of public discipleship must always be a deep *internal* union with Christ as forged by the Holy Spirit. Our moral pattern cannot remain outside of us, as an imposed, foreign, or unachievable moral ideal.

And therein lies the confounding, remarkable claim of the gospel: the one to whom we must be conformed, Jesus Christ, has already united himself to us through the power of his Spirit![39] Thus the public pattern we are called to follow is no longer external to us: it is living and active within us through our union in Christ. Time and again, Bavinck stresses the importance of this

---

34. Bavinck, *Reformed Ethics*, 1:336.
35. Bavinck, "Imitation of Christ I," 394.
36. Bavinck, "Imitation of Christ I," 394.
37. Bavinck, *Reformed Ethics*, 1:337.
38. As Bavinck says, "Our lives can be directed to Christ only when they proceed from him and abide in him." *Reformed Ethics*, 1:339.
39. Christians, then, are called to follow Christ, our pattern, as he follows the law, in perfect obedience. For Bavinck, this has an important *creational* focus, for these laws are the laws that God has set down for his people in creation. Christ's life, while directing us eschatologically, also points us protologically back to God's created intent. For more on the relationship between the moral law and the imitation of Christ, see Bavinck, "Imitation of Christ I," 400; Bavinck, *Reformed Ethics*, 1:377–78; John Bolt, "Christ and the Law in the Ethics of Herman Bavinck," *Calvin Theological Journal* 28 (1993): 73.

spiritual union for public discipleship. The imitation of Christ, he writes, is first and foremost a *"spiritual life-relationship with Jesus."*[40] The "heart of imitation" is a *"spiritual, believing communion with Christ."*[41] Without that, any public or material attempt to imitate Jesus is futile.

Law-Patterned Public Spirituality

When we think about Christian spirituality, the law, judgments, and commandments of God are not typically the first things that come to mind. In fact, elements like these are often placed in opposition to Christian love, grace, and spirituality. The Old Testament gives us a law, it is said, while the New Testament gives us a person with whom we can have a spiritual relationship of grace and mercy.

Once again, Bavinck refuses to follow these dichotomies. For him, Christ is not in tension with the law: Christ's life reveals, fulfills, and embodies God's law. Bavinck argues that Jesus is the "living law"[42] and thus a concrete pattern for life in the world.[43] In thought, word, and deed, and in life and death, Jesus has "completely fulfill[ed] the moral law."[44] His life demonstrates the "virtues and obligations which conform to God's law."[45] Christians, then, are called to imitate Jesus *in* his following of God's law. This is nothing less than a call to law-patterned imitation of the virtues of Jesus in our personal and communal life.

Bavinck's emphasis on the *law-patterned* nature of public discipleship flows from the Reformed tradition's emphasis on God's laws as a "positive guide" for both public life and spirituality.[46] As a pattern for life, the law teaches God's

40. Bavinck, *Reformed Ethics*, 1:321, emphasis original.

41. Bavinck, *Reformed Ethics*, 1:322, emphasis original.

42. Bavinck, *Reformed Ethics*, 1:341.

43. Importantly, argues Bavinck, Jesus is a *concrete* pattern, not a *literal* pattern. Jesus concretely shows us how one can perfectly apply the demands of the law; his life is a "concrete example" (Bavinck, "Imitation of Christ II," 413). We then must contextualize Christ's application of the law and the virtues that Christ embodies in our own time and place (Bavinck, "Imitation of Christ II," 418, 426, 438).

44. Bavinck, "Imitation of Christ I," 396.

45. Bavinck, "Imitation of Christ I," 400. Here Bavinck is careful to note that not everything in Jesus's life is to be imitated (we cannot, e.g., imitate Christ's salvific work), nor is everything in Jesus's life to be literally emulated. Rather, Christ is an example of the "most important virtues which the law requires of us." *Those virtues* in accordance with the law are what we ought to imitate in our own daily lives and contexts, not only in personal piety but also in every part of our lives (Bavinck, "Imitation of Christ II," 426).

46. John Calvin, *Institutes of the Christian Religion*, ed. John T. McNeill, trans. Ford Lewis Battles, 2 vols. (Philadelphia: Westminster, 1960), 2.7.12. The commandments, then, have three uses: they have a punitive use, acting as a mirror to "show God's righteousness" and, in turn, to show our unrighteousness. Thus the law "warns, informs, convicts, and lastly condemns"

people two very important things: the first table teaches proper worship and piety for God; and the second table teaches proper love in public action affecting the neighbor. Given this twofold understanding, it should come as no surprise that theologians like John Calvin turned to the law of God for questions that included *both* the ordering of worship *and* the ordering of public life.[47]

Bavinck argues that this spirituality of law-patterned public obedience does not take our eyes off Jesus's saving work, nor does it focus our attention away from the things of this world. Instead, it focuses the disciple's attention on both, and does so in the proper order. Imitating Jesus is only possible on account of a primary "spiritual-life relationship with Christ."[48] To be a public example of a lawful life, Christ must first redeem us *for* lawful living. But from Christ's redemptive work "proceeds reforming, recreating, renewing power,"[49] enabling Christians to actively pattern their lives on his example and law.

Christ's Spirit sends us out *to follow him* in our "various walks of life,"[50] including the "state, society, art, science, agriculture, industry, [and] commerce."[51] Rather than following Jesus out of the world, Christ's Spirit drives us into the world, toward a law-patterned and culturally engaged form of holy worldliness. Christians can and must, therefore, imitate Christ not only in prayer and piety but also in the public square.

Conclusion: Turning Our Eyes upon Jesus and the World

> Turn your eyes upon Jesus,
> Look full, in his wonderful face,
> And the things of earth will grow strangely dim,
> In the light of his glory and grace.[52]

---

humanity. Second, the law has a restraining function: it is a "deterrent to those not yet regenerate." The law also has a "third and principal use," its primary use: revealing God's intent; thus the law offers a positive guide for the lives of Christians (Calvin, *Institutes* 2.7.6–12).

47. In Calvin's sermons on the Decalogue, among many other themes he preaches against superstition and idolatry (see his sermons on Deut. 5:4–7 and Deut. 5:8–10) and preaches on how we live alongside our neighbors, honoring them with our words and thoughts (see his sermon on Deut. 5:17), keeping in mind civil legislation. John Calvin, *John Calvin's Sermons on the Ten Commandments*, ed. and trans. Benjamin W. Farley (Grand Rapids: Baker Books, 1980).

48. Bavinck, *Reformed Ethics*, 1:321.

49. Bavinck, "Imitation of Christ I," 400.

50. Bavinck, "Christian Principles," 142.

51. Bavinck, "Imitation of Christ II," 429. In his work on the imitation of Christ, Bavinck elaborates further on the contents of this imitation.

52. Helen Howarth Lemmel, "Turn Your Eyes upon Jesus," 1922; this refrain is now sung by popular evangelical singers and songwriters, including Lauren Daigle and Hillsong Worship.

I once heard a well-known Reformed theologian comment on this song, which wonderfully encapsulates the evangelical dichotomy between piety and public action. He remarked that only one word needed to be altered in that beloved old hymn to rightly capture the relationship between the two. Instead of "dim," he asked us to sing the hymn again with the word "clear." And so we did.

With that single alternation, our song leader fixed our eyes upon a vision of a savior who commissions us to go out into the world, embracing the leavening power of the gospel for all of life. In the arts, politics, business, and sciences, we are called to follow the one by whom "all things were created," the one in whom "all things hold together," and the one through whom God will "reconcile to himself all things" (Col. 1:16–20).

Those of us in contemporary evangelical circles often hear echoes of this hymn's mistaken dichotomy, just as I did that afternoon at John's memorial service. Faith is of the utmost importance, we are told, while the other aspects of our day-to-day lives in the public square are relegated to footnote status with that one little word, *but.*

And yet, as that Reformed theologian remarked, we should not simply get rid of the hymn and its important focus on commitment to, and steadfast assurance in, Jesus Christ. However, we would do well to tweak its lyrics, just a bit, to take away the "but" I heard so often at John's memorial service and to notice the way in which the things of this world grow strangely *clear* in the light of God's glory and grace.

Piety is primary to the Christian life but is not its end. Piety ought to drive us toward kingdom-oriented action in the public square—as we anticipate the new heaven and the new earth. This is good news for those of us who "spend our days"[53] in the material and mundane matters of the "state, society, art, science, agriculture, industry, commerce."[54] To that list we might add the work of neighborhood associations and school boards, cooking dinner and childcare, playing basketball and plucking weeds, and a host of other "this-worldly," seemingly ordinary, and unimportant tasks. These things, too, have eternal significance *in and through Christ*, whose gospel is for us, as both pearl *and* leaven.

---

53. Annie Dillard, *The Writing Life* (New York: Harper & Row, 1989), 32.
54. Bavinck, "Imitation of Christ II," 429.

Contributors

Katherine Leary Alsdorf (MBA, The Darden School, University of Virginia) is senior adviser to the Global Faith & Work Initiative at Redeemer City to City, in New York City. From 2002–12 she served as the founding director for Redeemer's Center for Faith and Work. In collaboration with Tim Keller, she wrote *Every Good Endeavor: Connecting Your Work to God's Work* (Dutton, 2012). Before entering the world of theology and work, Katherine held chief executive roles at three different technology companies specializing in distance learning.

Bruce Riley Ashford (PhD, Southeastern Baptist Theological Seminary) is professor of theology and culture at Southeastern Baptist Theological Seminary. He is the author of eight books, including *The Doctrine of Creation: A Constructive Kuyperian Approach* (InterVarsity Academic, 2020), coauthored with Craig Bartholomew; and *The Gospel of Our King* (Baker Academic, 2019). A Reformed public theologian, he has served as research fellow at the Kirby Laing Institute for Ethics (Cambridge, UK) and with the Ethics and Religious Liberty Commission (Nashville).

Romel Regalado Bagares (MA, Vrije Universiteit) has a law degree from the University of the Philippines and is visiting professor of Christianity, politics, and society at the Asian Theological Seminary (Manila). As the executive director of the Center for International Law, he helped litigate, among many public interest cases, the first legal challenge to President Duterte's drug war. His doctoral project is on the relevance of Herman Dooyeweerd's *Encyclopedia of the Science of Law* to international law.

Kyle David Bennett (PhD, Fuller Theological Seminary) is the author of *Practices of Love: Spiritual Disciplines for the Life of the World* (Brazos, 2017). Kyle has taught at Azusa Pacific University, Providence Christian College, King's College, and most recently was associate professor of philosophy at Caldwell University.

Agnes Chiu (PhD, Fuller Theological Seminary) is an attorney and adjunct professor of Christian ethics and systematic theology at China Evangelical Seminary in California. She received her law degree from the University of California, Los Angeles. A native of Hong Kong, her work on Chinese labor policy emerges from her own Chinese upbringing and her extensive legal background in employment law. Chiu's next book will focus on Abraham Kuyper's public theology in the Chinese context.

Robert S. Covolo (PhD, Vrije Universiteit and Fuller Theological Seminary) has served as a scholar at the Visual Faith Institute of Art and Architecture, on faculty at the Torrey Honors Institute, and currently as director of the Center for Pastoral Residents, Christ Church Sierra Madre. A cultural theologian in the Reformed tradition, he has authored numerous publications. His most recent, *Fashion Theology* (Baylor University Press, 2020), takes up the dynamic relationship between fashion and the Christian faith.

James Eglinton (PhD, University of Edinburgh) is Meldrum Senior Lecturer in Reformed Theology at the University of Edinburgh in Scotland. He is the author of *Bavinck: A Critical Biography* (Baker Academic, 2020) and has written extensively on the history and ideas of the neo-Calvinist movement. A passionate advocate of linguistic diversity and the importance of minority languages in theology, his work—writing, preaching, broadcasting, and lecturing—is communicated in English, Scottish Gaelic, Dutch, and French.

Lucas G. Freire (PhD, University of Exeter) is assistant professor at Mackenzie Presbyterian University in São Paulo and serves as a research fellow at the Mackenzie Center for Economic Freedom. He is the winner of Acton Institute's 2018 Michael Novak Award and has authored articles in *Philosophia Reformata*, the *Journal of Church and State*, and the *Journal of Markets & Morality*. Freire is currently helping to develop the Associação Reformada de Cultura e Ação Política, a new Reformed think tank focused on Brazilian politics and culture.

Makoto Fujimura (MFA, Tokyo University of Fine Arts and Music) is a leading contemporary artist whose paintings fuse traditional Nihonga painting with contemporary art. Fujimura is the founder of IAMCultureCare and Fujimura Institute. His recent books—including *Culture Care* (InterVarsity, 2017), *Silence and Beauty* (InterVarsity, 2016), and *Art and Faith: A Theology of Making* (Yale University Press, 2021)—explore the intersection between art, culture, and theology.

Dennis Greeson is associate director of the BibleMesh Institute and adjunct instructor in the School of Theology and Missions at Union University in Jackson, Tennessee, and at Southeastern Baptist Theological Seminary in Wake Forest, North Carolina. He is a PhD candidate in systematic theology at Southeastern Baptist Theological Seminary. His research explores the relationship between the doctrine of divine providence and Kuyperian social ethics, political theology, and the church's cultural mission.

Eric O. Jacobsen (PhD, Fuller Theological Seminary) is the senior pastor of the First Presbyterian Church in Tacoma, Washington. His research and writing focus on the intersection between faith, community, and the built environment. His books include *Sidewalks in the Kingdom: New Urbanism and the Christian Faith* (Brazos, 2003) and *The Space Between: A Christian Engagement with the Built Environment* (Baker Academic, 2012).

Bethany L. Jenkins is vice president of media at the Veritas Forum, where she spends her time connecting theology, media, higher education, and the felt needs and interests of today's college students. She received her MA from George Washington University and JD from Columbia Law School. She has also worked in Congress, at the State Department, on Wall Street, and in Big Law. Bethany spent fifteen years in New York City, where she was a member of Redeemer Presbyterian Church. She now lives in Pensacola, Florida.

Jessica Joustra (PhD, Fuller Theological Seminary and Vrije Universiteit) is assistant professor of religion and theology at Redeemer University (Hamilton, ON). She also serves as an associate researcher at the Neo-Calvinism Research Institute (Theologische Universiteit Kampen). She is an editor and translator (with John Bolt et al.) of Herman Bavinck's *Reformed Ethics* (3 vols., Baker Academic, 2019–) and co-editor of *Calvinism for a Secular Age: A Twenty-First Century Reading of Abraham Kuyper's Stone Lectures* (InterVarsity Academic, 2021). In addition, she serves as an associate editor of the *Bavinck Review*.

Matthew Kaemingk (PhD, Vrije Universiteit and Fuller Theological Seminary) is assistant professor of Christian ethics at Fuller Theological Seminary and associate dean for Fuller Texas in Houston. Matthew serves as a research fellow at the Center for Public Justice in Washington, DC. He is the author of two books on public theology: *Christian Hospitality and Muslim Immigration* (Eerdmans, 2018) and *Work and Worship: Reconnecting our Labor and Liturgy* (Baker Academic, 2020), coauthored with Cory Willson.

Nico Koopman (DTh, University of the Western Cape) is vice rector for social impact, transformation, and personnel, as well as professor of systematic theology and ethics at Stellenbosch University in South Africa. He was the first chairperson of the Global Network for Public Theology and is a fellow of the Center of Theological Inquiry in Princeton, New Jersey. His most recent monograph, *Reading Bonhoeffer in South Africa after the Transition to Democracy* (Peter Lang, 2020), was coauthored with Robert Vosloo.

Alberto La Rosa Rojas is a ThD candidate in Duke University Divinity School. Alberto's experience as an immigrant from Peru informs and fuels his research, which engages the ethical and theological dimensions of migration and the human longing for home. His work weaves together insights from the Reformed theological tradition as well as Latinx theology. He is a graduate of Western Theological Seminary (Holland, MI) and a member of the Reformed Church in America.

Jeff Liou (PhD, Fuller Theological Seminary) is national director of theological formation for InterVarsity Christian Fellowship and adjunct assistant professor of Christian Ethics at Fuller Theological Seminary. He has contributed to two volumes: *Intersecting Realities: Race, Identity, and Culture in the Spiritual-Moral Life of Young Asian Americans* (Cascade, 2018) and *Discerning Ethics: Diverse Christian Responses to Divisive Moral Issues* (InterVarsity Academic, 2020). Jeff is an office-bearer in the Christian Reformed Church of North America.

Rubén Rosario Rodríguez (PhD, Princeton Theological Seminary) is professor of systematic theology at Saint Louis University. Recent publications include *Dogmatics after Babel: Beyond the Theologies of Word and Culture* (Westminster John Knox, 2018) and the *T&T Clark Handbook of Political Theology* (Bloomsbury/T&T Clark, 2019). Rosario engages global migration and social justice issues as director of the Mev Puleo Program in Latin American

Theology, Politics, and Culture at Saint Louis University and through advocacy work with Missouri Immigrant and Refugee Advocates.

James K. A. Smith (PhD, Villanova University) is professor of philosophy at Calvin University, where he holds the Gary and Henrietta Byker Chair in Applied Reformed Theology and Worldview. He also serves as editor in chief of *Image*, a quarterly journal of fiction, poetry, and visual art at the intersection of faith and mystery. His books include *You Are What You Love* (Brazos, 2016) and *On the Road with Saint Augustine* (Brazos, 2019).

Stephanie Summers (MS, Eastern University) is the CEO of the Center for Public Justice, an independent Christian think tank rooted in the Reformed tradition. Based in Washington, DC, Summers empowers citizen-activists to address issues of public justice through her public speaking, writing, and leadership. Her most recent book, coauthored with Michael J. Gerson and Katie Thompson, is *Unleashing Opportunity: Why Escaping Poverty Requires a Shared Vision of Justice* (Falls City Press, 2015).

N. Gray Sutanto (PhD, University of Edinburgh) is assistant professor of systematic theology at Reformed Theological Seminary, Washington, DC. Sutanto grew up in Jakarta, Indonesia, and in Singapore. He recently served as a teaching elder at Covenant City Church in Jakarta. He is the author of *God and Knowledge: Herman Bavinck's Theological Epistemology* (Bloomsbury T&T Clark, 2020) and one of the editors and translators of Bavinck's *Christian Worldview* (Crossway, 2019). Sutanto is also ordained within the International Presbyterian Church.

Cornelis van der Kooi (PhD, Vrije Universiteit) is professor emeritus of systematic theology at the Vrije Universiteit Amsterdam and distinguished lecturer at Erasmus University Rotterdam. Among his many publications are his 2014 Warfield Lectures *This Incredibly Benevolent Force: The Holy Spirit in Reformed Theology and Spirituality* (Eerdmans, 2018) and *Christian Dogmatics: An Introduction* (Eerdmans, 2017).

Margriet van der Kooi (MA, Vrije Universiteit) is a chaplain in the Netherlands at the Daan Theeuwes Centrum, a rehabilitation center for young people with brain and spinal cord injuries. She is an ordained pastor and has served as a chaplain for forty years. She is a prolific author in the Netherlands on the pastorate and end-of-life questions. Her chapter "Spirit, Chaplaincy, and

Theology: Why Should a Chaplain Read Dogmatics?" was recently published in *The Spirit Is Moving* (Brill, 2019).

Nico Vorster (ThD, Potchefstroom University) is professor of systematic theology at the North-West University in South Africa. His studies focus on theological anthropology and topics related to human rights, social justice, and dignity in South Africa. He recently published *The Brightest Mirror of God's Works: John Calvin's Theological Anthropology* (Pickwick Publications, 2019).

John D. Witvliet (PhD, University of Notre Dame) is professor of worship and congregational and ministry studies at Calvin University and Calvin Theological Seminary. He serves as director of the Calvin Institute of Christian Worship and its programs of grantmaking, conferences, and publications. He is the author of *The Biblical Psalms in Christian Worship* (Eerdmans, 2007) and *Worship Seeking Understanding* (Baker Academic, 2003), and he is coeditor of *The Worship Sourcebook* (Faith Alive/Baker, 2013) and several collections of congregational songs.

Nicholas Wolterstorff (PhD, Harvard University) is Noah Porter Professor Emeritus of Philosophical Theology at Yale University and senior research fellow in the Institute for Advanced Studies in Culture at the University of Virginia. He is now retired, after teaching philosophy for thirty years at Calvin College and for fifteen years at Yale University. He has published extensively on liturgy, justice, art, and education. His essays on higher education have been collected in *Educating for Shalom: Essays on Christian Higher Education* (Eerdmans, 2004).

Index

DATE DUE

The Library Store   #47-0103